Fast 'n Easy
Phrase Book

by Carolyn M. Heard

FRENCH
GERMAN
ITALIAN
SPANISH

A FROMMER BOOK
Published by
Simon & Schuster, Inc. • New York

Published by Frommer/Pasmantier Publishers
A Division of Simon & Schuster, Inc.
1230 Avenue of the Americas
New York, New York 10020

ISBN 0-671-466739

Library of Congress Cataloging in Publication Data

Heard, Carolyn M.
  Fast 'n' easy phrase book.

  1. Languages, Modern—Conversation and phrase books.
I. Title.   II. Title: Fast and easy phrase book.
PB73.H42   1983   413   83-14198
ISBN 0-671-46673-9

Manufactured in the United States of America

Contents

Preface
HOW TO USE THIS BOOK

The *Fast 'n' Easy Phrase Guide* provides you with all the words and sentences you'll need for travel and everyday life in France, French-speaking Belgium, Luxembourg, Switzerland, Germany, Austria, Italy, and Spain. I have chosen those phrases that my own travels have shown to be particularly useful and grouped them according to the situations you'll encounter—beginning with your arrival and entry into the country, and continuing with accommodations, restaurants, transportation, sightseeing, shopping, entertainment, and public services. You'll also find phrases that the native speaker will use in speaking with you; these are identified by a vertical line to the left of the phrase and the absence of any phonetic translation.

The sentences illustrate the basic patterns of everyday conversation. By following these patterns, and with the help of the dictionary at the end of each section, you'll soon be able to form sentences of your own by substituting the appropriate words.

Grammar is an essential element of each language. If you can read the grammar section before starting to use the phrases and sentences, you'll get a basic grasp of the rules of the language that will greatly improve your communicative skill.

Every word and phrase in this book is presented in English, in the foreign language, and in an easy-to-read phonetic transcription that shows you correct pronunciation. For best results, look at the pronunciation guide at the beginning of each section. Listen attentively to the spoken language and try to imitate the sounds of the native speakers. Depending on the degree of your interest, ingenuity, and flair for language, you may be able to develop your conversational skills to an extent that will surprise you.

Acknowledgments

I wish to express my appreciation to the following people who helped me in the preparation of this phrase guide: Luigi Ballerini and Daniela Noé (Italian); Stéphane Taboulet and Ourida Mostefai (French); Peter Reichenbach and Marga Behner (German); Tomàs Fabregas (Spanish); and a special thank you to Milton Diaz for his contribution to the Spanish section.

Carolyn M. Heard

FRENCH

FRENCH

PRONUNCIATION GUIDE

	Phonetic Symbol	Approximate Pronunciation	French Example	Phonetic Transcription	Meaning
Vowels					
a	a	as in cat	bal	bal	dance, ball
a	ah	as in father	classe	klahs	class
a ̲ i	ee	as in feet	Paris	Paree	Paris
e	uh	as in father	le	luh	the
			venir	vuhneer	to come
é	ay	as in hate	café	katay	coffee, café
è	eh	as in there	père	pehr	father
o	u	as in but	poste	pust	post office
ô	oh	as in note	rôle	rohl	role
eau			chapeau	shapoh	hat
ou	oo	as in boot	touriste	tooreest	tourist
oi	wa	like "wa" in water	soir	swar	evening
u	ü	round lips as if to form "oo" but say "ee"; no English equivalent	publique	pübleek	public
eu	eu	like u in urge	docteur	dukteur	doctor
Consonants					
c (before consonants or **a, o, u**)	k	like k in kite	cadeau	kadoh	gift
c (before **e** or **i**)	s	like s in see	difficile	deefeeseel	difficult

8

ç	s	like s in see	façade	fasad	front
ch	sh	like sh in short	château	shatoh	castle
g (before consonants or a, o, u)	g	like g in get	gare	gar	station
g (before e or i)	zh	like s in measure	rouge, garage	roozh, garazh	red, garage
gn	ny	like ny in canyon	espagnol	ehspanyul	Spanish
h	|	almost always silent	hôtel	ohtehl	hotel
j =	zh	like s in measure	je	zhuh	I
y	y	like y in yes	griller	greeyay	to grill
qu	k	like k in kite	qui, quel	kee, kehl	who, which
r	r	is rolled	—	—	—
w	v	like v in velvet	wistaria	veestarya	wisteria

Nasal Sounds

These sounds, which do not exist in English, are nonetheless easy to make. Say the English word *taunt* without touching the tongue to the roof of the mouth to articulate the *nt* at the end of the word. You have just said either the French *temps* or *tant*—note that since the *m* or *n* is not actually pronounced, there is no difference in the sound. In the phonetic spellings in this book, a stroke through the *m* or *n* indicates that the preceding vowel is nasalized.

français	frahn̄seh
station	stasyon̄
faim	fehm̄
un	eun̄

FRENCH

GRAMMAR

Nouns and Articles

There are two genders in French, masculine and feminine. The plural is generally formed by adding s to the singular form of the noun. Articles agree in number and gender with the nouns they modify.

The Definite Article (the)

				plural
masculine	le (l' before a vowel or silent *h*)			
feminine	la (l' before a vowel or silent *h*)			les

le livre	the book	l'homme	the man	les livres	les hommes
la maison	the house	l'orange	the orange	les maisons	les oranges

The Indefinite Article (a, an, one)

				plural
masculine	un	un crayon	a pencil	
feminine	une	une chaise	a chair	des

The Partitive (some, any)

			plural
masculine	du	before a consonant	
	de l'	before a vowel or silent *h*	des
feminine	de la	before a consonant	**plural**
	de l'	before a vowel or silent *h*	des

du sucre	some sugar	de la glace	some ice cream
de l'encre	some ink	de l'eau	some water

Adjectives

The adjective agrees in gender and number with the noun it modifies and usually follows the noun. The feminine is most often formed by adding an *e* at the end, the plural by adding *s*.

			plural
masculine	le chien noir	the black dog	les chiens noirs
feminine	la valise lourde	the heavy suitcase	les valises lourdes

FRENCH

Demonstrative Adjectives (this, that, these, those)

Demonstrative adjectives precede the noun they modify.

			plural
masculine	ce	before a consonant	ces
	cet	before a vowel or silent *h*	
feminine	cette		

Possessive Adjectives

Possessive adjectives agree with the noun they modify, not with the possessor, as in English. Hence, *sa maison* can mean his house or her house.

	masculine	feminine	plural (m. and f.)
my	mon	ma	mes
you (familiar)*	ton	ta	tes
his, her, its	son	sa	ses
our	notre	notre	nos
your (plural and/ or formal)	votre	votre	vos
their	leur	leur	leurs

Personal Pronouns

	subject	indirect object	direct object	disjunctive (after preposition)
I, me	je	me	me	moi
you (familiar)*	tu	te	te	toi
he/it	il	lui	le	lui
she/it	elle	lui	la	lui
we	nous	nous	nous	nous
you (plural)	vous	vous	vous	vous
they (m.)	ils	leur	les	eux
they (f.)	elles	leur	les	elles

*The *tu* (familiar) form is used with children, relatives, young people, and good friends. The *vous* form is used with people you don't know well or wish to remain on rather formal terms with.

Interrogative Pronouns

qui	who, whom
qu'est-ce que	what
que	what
lequel, laquelle	which

Interrogative Adjectives

quel	what, which
combien	how much/many

Relative Pronouns

subject

qui	who, which
ce qui	what
tout ce qui	all that which

object

que	whom, which
ce que	what
tout ce que	all that which

after a preposition

lequel, laquelle, etc.	whom, which
quoi	what
qui	whom

dont is used in place of *de* + a relative pronoun, meaning whose, of which, of whom.

où is the equivalent of *à* or *dans* + the relative pronoun, and means in which, at which, where.

The comparative is formed by placing the word *plus* (more) in front of the adjective: *plus important* (more important). The superlative is formed by placing the article before the adjective: *le plus important* (the most important). As in English, the adjectives *bon* and *mauvais* have special forms to denote better–best and worse–worst: *bon–mieux–le mieux; mauvais–pire–le pire.*

Verbs

The two most important auxiliary verbs are *être* (to be) and *avoir* (to have).

être (to be)		*avoir* (to have)	
je suis	I am	j'ai	I have
tu es	you are	tu as	you have
il, elle est	he, she is	il, elle a	he, she has
nous sommes	we are	nous avons	we have
vous êtes	you are	vous avez	you have
ils, elles sont	they are	ils ont	they have

FRENCH

Regular verbs are conjugated in one of four ways, according to their endings:

	I	II	III	IV
	parler	finir	recevoir	vendre
	to speak	to finish	to receive	to sell
je	parle	finis	reçois	vends
tu	parles	finis	reçois	vends
il, elle	parle	finit	reçoit	vend
nous	parlons	finissons	recevons	vendons
vous	parlez	finissez	recevez	vendez
ils, elles	parlent	finissent	reçoivent	vendent

Some of the most common verbs are irregular:

	aller	faire	comprendre	voir	pouvoir	savoir
	to go	to do	to understand	to see	to be able	to know
je	vais	fais	comprends	vois	peux	sais
tu	vas	fais	comprends	vois	peux	sais
il, elle	va	fait	comprend	voit	peut	sait
nous	allons	faisons	comprenons	voyons	pouvons	savons
vous	allez	faites	comprenez	voyez	pouvez	savez
ils, elles	vont	font	comprennent	voient	peuvent	savent

Negatives

Negatives are most often formed by placing *ne* (or *n'* if a vowel follows) before the verb and *pas* after it.

Je parle français.	Je ne parle pas français.	I speak (don't speak) French.
Il va à l'ecole.	Il ne va pas à l'école.	He goes (doesn't go) to school.

Questions

Questions are formed either by inverting the subject and the verb, or by using the expression *est-ce que* (literally, is it that) followed by the affirmative word order:

Parlez-vous français?	Do you speak French?
Est-ce que vous parlez français?	
Va-t-il à l'école?	Does he go to school?
Est-ce qu'il va à l'école?	

Past Tense

One form of the past tense combines the proper form of the auxiliary verb *avoir* or *être* (*être* being used with verbs of motion, state of being, and reflexive verbs) with the past participle. The past participle is formed by adding one of three endings to the stem of the verb: *é* for *-er* verbs; *i* for *-ir* verbs, and *u* for *-oir* and *-re* verbs. Like the adjective, it agrees in number and gender with the noun modified.

parler:	j'ai parlé	I spoke, I have spoken
finir:	j'ai fini	I finished, I have finished
vendre:	j'ai vendu	I sold, I have sold
voir:	j'ai vu	I saw, I have seen
rester:	je suis resté/restée	I stayed, I have stayed
partir:	je suis parti/partie	I left, I have left

Prepositions

Two prepositions (*à* and *de*) contract with the definite article.

à (to, at)	de (of, from)
à + le = au	de + le = du
à + les = aux	de + les = des

Here are some other useful prepositions:

for	pour
after	après
before	avant
in front of	devant
in back of	derrière
with	avec
without	sans
toward	vers
through	à travers
during	pendant
until	jusqu'à
inside	dedans
outside	dehors
up/upstairs	en haut
down/downstairs	en bas
against	contre
in	dans

FRENCH

EXPRESSIONS FOR EVERYDAY USE

Basic

Yes.
Oui.
wee

No.
Non.
noñ

Please.
S'il vous plaît.
seel voo pleh

Thank you.
Merci.
mehrsee

Yes, thank you.
Oui, merci.
wee, mehrsee

No, thank you.
Non, merci.
noñ, mehrsee

Thank you very much.
Merci beaucoup.
mehrsee bohkoo

You're welcome.
De rien.
duh ryehñ

Excuse me.
Excusez-moi. Pardon.
ehksküzay mwa. pardoñ

Just a moment.
Un moment.
euñ mumañ

Of course.
Bien sûr.
byehñ sür

How much?
Combien?
koñbyehñ?

Where is the restroom?
Où sont les toilettes?
oo soñ lay twaleht?

I don't understand.
Je ne comprends pas.
zhuh nuh koñprahñ pah

What did you say?
Comment?
kumahñ?

I beg your pardon.
Je vous demande pardon.
zhuh voo duhmañd pardoñ

That's quite all right.
Il n'y a pas de quoi.
eel nee a pah duh kwah

Greetings

Good morning. Hello.
Bonjour.
boñzhoor

Good evening.
Bonsoir.
boñswar

Good night.
Bonne nuit.
bun nwee

Goodbye.
Au revoir.
oh ruhvwar
Salut. (informal)
salü

FRENCH

See you soon.
À tout à l'heure.
a toot a leur

See you this evening.
À ce soir.
a suh swar

See you tomorrow.
À demain.
a duhmehn

How are you?
Comment allez-vous?
kumahn alay voo?
Comment vas-tu? (informal)
kumahn va tü?

How are things?
Comment ça va?
kumahn sa va?

Everything's fine.
Ça va bien.
sa va byehn

Good.
Bon.
bon

Communication Problems

Do you speak English?
Parlez-vous anglais?
parlay vooz ahnglay?

**Do you speak French/
German/Spanish?**
Parlez-vous français/
allemand/espagnol?
*parlay voo frahnsay/alman/
ehspanyul?*

I don't speak French.
Je ne parle pas français.
zhuh nuh parl pah frahnsay

I don't understand you.
Je ne vous comprends pas.
zhuh nuh voo kornprahn pah

Could you speak more slowly?
Pourriez-vous parler plus lentement?
pooryay voo parlay plü lahntmahn?

Could you repeat that, please?
Pourriez-vous répéter, s'il vous plaît?
pooryay voo raypaytay, seel voo pleh?

Could you write that down, please?
Pourriez-vous écrire cela,
s'il vous plaît?
*pooryay vooz aycreer suhla,
seel voo pleh?*

**Could you translate this for me,
please?**
Pourriez-vous me traduire ceci,
s'il vous plaît?
*pooryay voo muh tradweer suhsee,
seel voo pleh?*

I understand.
Je comprends.
zhuh kornprahn

Do you understand?
Comprenez-vous?
kornpruhnay voo?

**Just a moment. I'll see if I can find
it in this book.**
Un moment. Je vais voir si je
le trouve dans ce livre.
*eun mumahn. zhuh vay vwar see zhuh
luh troov dahn suh leevr*

**Please point to your answer
in this book.**
Indiquez la réponse dans ce livre,
s'il vous plaît.
*ehndeekay la raypons dahn suh leevr
see voo play*

**Is there someone here who speaks
English?**
Y a-t-il quelqu'un ici qui parle anglais?
*ee ateel kehlkeun eesee kee parl
ahnglay?*

What does that mean?
Que veut dire cela?
kuh veu deer suhla?

How do you say that in French?
Comment dit-on cela en français?
kumahṅ deet-oṅ suhla ahṅ frahṅsay?

Questions

Where?
Où?
oo?

Where is/are ... ?
Où est/sont ... ?
oo eh/soṅ ... ?

What?
Quoi?
kwah?

Why?
Pourquoi?
poorkwa?

How?
Comment?
kumahṅ?

When?
Quand?
kahṅ?

How much/many?
Combien?
koṅbyehṅ?

What time is it?
Quelle heure est-il?
kehl eur ehteel?

Is there/Are there ... ?
Y a-t-il ... ?
ee ateel ... ?

Could you tell me ... ?
Pourriez-vous me dire ... ?
pooryay voo muh deer ... ?

Could you show me ... ?
Pourriez-vous me montrer ... ?
pooryay voo muh moṅtray ... ?

Could you tell me how to get to ... ?
Pourriez-vous me dire comment je
puis aller à ... ?
*pooryay voo muh deer kumahṅ zhuh
pweez alay a ... ?*

It Is/Isn't

It is ...
C'est ...
seh

It isn't ...
Ce n'est pas ...
suh neh pah

Isn't it ... ?
N'est-il pas ... ?
nehteel pah ... ?

There is/are ...
Il y a ...
eel ee a ...

There isn't/aren't ...
Il n'y a pas ...
eel nee a pah ...

..., isn't it?
..., n'est-ce pas?
..., nehs pah?

Here it is/they are.
Le/La/Les voici.
luh/la/lay vwasee

FRENCH

Common Adjectives and Adverbs and Their Opposites

beautiful/ugly	beau/laid	boh/leh
before/after	avant/après	avani/apreh
better/worse	mieux/pire	myeu/peer
big/small	grand/petit	grani/puhtee
cheap/expensive	pas cher/cher	pah shehr/shehr
clean/dirty	propre/sale	pruhpr/sal
cold/hot	froid/chaud	frwa/shoh
cool/warm	frais/chaud	freh/shoh
early/late	tôt/tard	toh/tar
easy/difficult	facile/difficile	faseel/deefeeseel
empty/full	vide/plein	veed/plehn
first/last	premier/dernier	pruhmyay/dehrnyay
good/bad	bon/mauvais	boni/mohvay
heavy/light	lourd/léger	loor/layzhay
here/there	ici/là-bas	eesee/labah
high/low	haut/bas	oh/bah
ill/well	malade/en bonne santé	malad/ahni bun sahnitay
inside/outside	dedans/dehors	duhdahni/duh-ur
long/short	long/court	loni/koor
more/less	plus/moins	plü/mwehni
at most/at least	au plus/au moins	oh plü/oh mwehni
much/little	beaucoup/peu	bohkoo/peu
narrow/wide	étroit/large	aytrwa/larzh
near/far	près/loin	preh/lwehni
now/later	maintenant/plus tard	mehnitnahni/plü tar
often/rarely	souvent/rarement	soovahni/rarmahni
old/new	vieux/nouveau	vyeu/noovoh
	vieux/neuf	vyeu/neuf
old/young	vieux/jeune	vyeu/zheun
open/closed	ouvert/fermé	oovehr/fehrmay
pleasant/unpleasant	agréable/désagréable	agrayabl/dayzagrayabl
quick/slow	rapide/lent	rapeed/lahni
quiet/noisy	tranquille/bruyant	trahnikeel/brüyahni
right/left	droite/gauche	drwat/gohsh
right/wrong	correct/incorrect	kurehkt/ehnikurehkt
still/not yet	encore/pas encore	ahnikur/pahz ahnikur
thick/thin	épais/mince	aypay/mehnis
under/over	en-dessous/au-dessus	ahni duhsoo/oh duhsü
vacant/occupied	libre/occupé	leebr/uküpay
well/badly	bien/mal	byehni/mal

FRENCH

More Useful Words

also	aussi	ohsee
and	et	ay
enough	assez	asay
not	ne . . . pas	nuh . . . pah
nothing	rien	ryehṅ
or	ou	oo
perhaps	peut-être	peutehtr
soon	bientôt	byehṅtoh
very	très	treh

To Help You Further in Conversation

according to	selon	suhloṅ
as you wish	comme vous voulez	kum voo voolay
best wishes	meilleurs voeux	mehyeur veu
certainly	certainement	sehrtehnmahṅ
entirely	entièrement	ahṅtyehrmahṅ
everyone	tout le monde	too luh moṅd
I don't know	je ne sais pas	zhuh nuh say pah
I have forgotten	j'ai oublié	zhay oobleeay
indeed?	c'est vrai?/ah bon?	seh vreh?/ah boṅ?
in any way	de n'importe quelle façon	duh nehṅpurt kehl fasoṅ
in what way	de quelle façon	duh kehl fasoṅ
it's not important	ça n'a pas d'importance	sa na pah dehrṅpurtahṅs
never mind	peu importe	peu ehrṅpurt
no one	personne	pehrsun
on the contrary	au contraire	oh koṅtrehr
precisely	précisément	prayseezaymahṅ
same to you	à vous aussi	a vooz ohsee
sometimes	de temps en temps	duh tahṅz ahṅ tahṅ
that is to say	c'est-à-dire	sehtadeer
that's all	c'est tout	seh too
that's correct	c'est correct	seh kurehkt
that's impossible	c'est impossible	seht ehṅpuseebl
that's incredible	c'est incroyable	seht ehṅkrwahyabl
that's it	c'est ça	seh sa
that's not right	ce n'est pas juste	suh neh pah zhüst
that's too bad	c'est dommage	seh duhmazh
with pleasure	avec plaisir	avehk plehzeer
Where are we going?	Où allons-nous?	oo aloṅ noo?

Asking for Something

Could you help me, please?	Pourriez-vous m'aider, s'il vous plaît?	*pooryay voo mehday, seel voo pleh?*
Could I have . . . ?	Pourrais-je avoir . . . ?	*poorayzhuh avwar . . . ?*
Could you give me . . . ?	Pourriez-vous me donner . . . ?	*pooryay voo muh dunay . . . ?*
Could I have one?	Pourrais-je en avoir un?	*poorayzhuh ahn avwar eun?*
I would like . . .	Je voudrais . . .	*zhuh voodray . . .*
I'm looking for . . .	Je cherche . . .	*zhuh shehrsh . . .*
I need . . .	J'ai besoin de . . .	*zhay buhzwehn duh . . .*

ARRIVAL
Passport and Customs

Your passport, please.
Votre passeport, s'il vous plaît.

Here it is.
Le voici.
luh vwasee

Where will you be staying?
Quelle sera votre résidence?

What is the purpose of your visit?
Quel est le but de votre visite?

How long will you stay here?
Combien de temps restez-vous en France?

I'll be staying . . .
Je resterai . . .
zhuh rehstray . . .

a few days quelques jours *kehlkuh zhoor*	**a month** un mois *eun mwa*
a week une semaine *ün suhmehn*	**a few months** quelques mois *kehlkuh mwa*
a fortnight quinze jours *kehnz zhoor*	

I'm just passing through.
Je suis juste de passage.
zhuh swee zhüst duh pasazh

I'm on my way to . . .
Je vais à . . .
zhuh vayz a . . .

I'm visiting relatives/friends.
Je rends visite à des parents/des amis.
zhuh rahn veezeet a day parahn/ dayz amee

I'm here on vacation.
Je suis en vacances.
zhuh swee zahn vakahns

I'm here on business.
Je suis en voyage d'affaires.
zhuh sweez ahn vwayazh dafehr

I'm here to study.
Je suis étudiant.
zhuh sweez aytüdyahn

This is my address.
Voici mon adresse.
vwasee mon adrehs

How much money do you have?
Combien d'argent avez-vous?

Do you have any food or plants?
Avez-vous de la nourriture ou des
plantes?

Do you have anything to declare?
Avez-vous quelque chose à déclarer?

**No, nothing. I have only personal
belongings.**
Non, rien. J'ai seulement des effets
personnels.
*noň, ryehň. zhay seulmahň dayz ehfeh
pehrsunehl*

I have . . .
J'ai . . .
zhay . . .

cigarettes	**wine**
des cigarettes	du vin
day seegareht	*dü vehň*
liquor	**some gifts**
de l'alcool	des cadeaux
duh lalkul	*day kadoh*
perfume	
du parfum	
dü parfeurh	

It's for my personal use.
C'est pour mon usage personnel.
seh poor moň üsazh pehrsunehl

Open your bag, please.
Ouvrez votre sac, s'il vous plaît.

You'll have to pay duty on this.
Vous devrez payer des droits
de douane sur cet article.

How much do I have to pay?
Combien dois-je payer?
korhbyehň dwahzhuh pehyay?

I can't (afford it).
Je ne peux pas.
zhuh nuh peu pah

May I go through?
Puis-je passer?
pweezhuh pasay?

Porter/Luggage

Where can I find a luggage cart?
Où puis-je trouver un chariot
à bagages?
*oo pweezhuh troovay euň sharyoh
a bagazh?*

Are you using this cart?
Il est à vous, ce chariot?
eel eht a voo, suh sharyoh?

Porter!
Porteur, s'il vous plaît!
purteur, seel voo pleh

Please take this luggage . . .
Portez ces bagages, s'il vous plaît . . .
purtay say bagazh, seel voo pleh . . .

    to the bus/train/taxi/checkroom
    à l'arrêt du bus/au train/jusqu'au
      taxi/à la consigne
    *a lareh du büs/oh trehň/zhüskoh
      taxee/a la koňseenyuh*

Follow me, please.
Suivez-moi, s'il vous plaît.
sweevay mwa, seel voo pleh

How much do I owe you?
Combien vous dois-je?
korhbyehň voo dwahzhuh?

Changing Money

Can you change these traveler's checks?
Pouvez-vous changer ces chèques de voyage?
poovay voo shahńzhay say shehk duh vwayazh?

I would like to change dollars/ pounds.
Je voudrais changer des dollars/ des livres.
zhuh voodray shahńzhay day dular/ day leevr

What is the exchange rate?
Quel est le cours du change?
kehl eh luh coor dü shańzh?

Here is my passport.
Voici mon passeport.
vwasee mon paspur

Could you please give me . . .
Pouvez-vous me donner . . .
poovay voo muh dunay . . .

Belgian/French/Swiss francs
des francs belges/français/suisses
day frahń behlzh/frahńsay/swees

    large bills
    en grosses coupures
    ahń grohs coopür

    small bills
    en petites coupures
    ahń puhteet coopür

Could you change this bill?
Pouvez-vous me changer ce billet?
poovay voo muh shańzhay suh beeyay?

GETTING INTO TOWN

Taxi

Where can I find a taxi?
Où puis-je trouver un taxi?
oo pweezhuh troovay euń taxee?

Please call a taxi for me.
Appelez-moi un taxi, s'il vous plaît.
aplay mwa euń taxee, seel voo pleh

Please take me to . . .
Conduisez-moi à . . . s'il vous plaît.
końdweezay mwa a . . . seel voo pleh

How much will the fare be?
Quel sera le tarif?
kehl suhra luh tareef?

How far is it?
À quelle distance se trouve-t-il?
a kehl deestahńz suh troove-teel?

Turn the meter on.
Mettez le compteur, s'il vous plaît.
mehttay luh końteur, seel voo pleh

Turn right/left . . .
Tournez à droite/à gauche . . .
toornay a drwat/a gohsh . . .

    at the next corner
    au prochain coin de rue
    oh prushehń kwehń duh rü

    at the stoplight
    au feu rouge
    oh feu roozh

Go straight ahead.
Allez tout droit.
alay too drwa

Are you sure we're going the right way?
Êtes-vous sûr qu'on est sur le bon chemin?
eht voo sür kon eh sür luh bon shuhmehn?

Please don't drive so fast.
Ne conduisez pas si vite, s'il vous plaît.
nuh kondweesay pah see veet, seel voo pleh

I'm rather in a hurry.
Je suis pressé.
zhuh swee prehsay

Let me out, please.
Je vais descendre ici.
zhuh vay dehsahndr eesee

Stop here, please.
Arrêtez-vous ici, s'il vous plaît.
arehtay vooz eesee, seel voo pleh

Could you wait for me here?
Pouvez-vous m'attendre ici?
poovay voo matahndr eesee?

How much do I owe you?
Combien vous dois-je?
konbyehn voo dwahzhuh?

Bus/Train

Where can I get a bus/train to . . . ?
Où puis-je trouver un bus/
train pour . . . ?
*oo pweezhuh troovay eun büs/
trehn poor . . . ?*

Which bus/train do I take for . . . ?
Quel bus/train dois-je
prendre pour . . . ?
*kehl büs/trehn dwahzhuh
prahndr poor . . . ?*

When is the next bus/train for . . . ?
Quand part le prochain bus/
train pour . . . ?
*kahn par luh prushehn büs/
trehn poor . . . ?*

Do I have to change buses/trains?
Faut-il changer de bus/train?
fohteel shanzhay duh büs/trehn?

Where do I buy the ticket?
Où puis-je prendre le billet?
oo pweezhuh prahndr luh beeyay?

**Could you tell me when
we reach . . . ?**
Pourriez-vous me dire quand nous
arrivons à . . . ?
*pooryay voo muh deer kahn nooz
areevonz a . . . ?*

Please let me off!
La porte, s'il vous plaît!
la purt, seel voo pleh

Car Rental

I have a reservation for a car.
J'ai fait réserver une voiture.
zhay fay rayzehrvay ün vwatür

I'd like to rent a small/large car . . .
Je voudrais louer une petite/grande
voiture . . .
*zhuh voodray looay ün puhteet/grahnd
vwatür . . .*

    with an automatic shift
    avec changement de vitesse
      automatique
    *avehk shanzhmahn duh veetehs
     ohtumateek*

I need it for . . .
J'en ai besoin pour . . .
zhahn ay buhzwehn poor . . .

a day/two days
un jour/deux jours
eun zhoor/deu zhoor

a week/two weeks
une semaine/deux semaines
ün suhmehn/deu suhmehn

How much is it per . . . ?
Quel est le tarif par . . . ?
kehl eh luh tareef par . . . ?

hour	week
heure	semaine
eur	*suhmehn*

day	kilometer
jour	kilomètre
zhoor	*keelumehtr*

Is gas included?
Est-ce que l'essence est comprise?
ehskuh lehsahns eh kornpreez?

Is insurance included?
L'assurance est-elle comprise?
lasürahns ehtehl kornpreez?

I would like comprehensive insurance.
Je voudrais une assurance tous risques.
zhuh voodrayz ün asürahns too reesk

Do I have unlimited mileage?
Le kilométrage est-il compris?
luh keelumehtrazh ehteel kornpree?

Can I pay by credit card?
Puis-je payer avec une carte de crédit?
pweezhuh pehyay avehk ün kart duh kraydee?

Here is my driver's license.
Voici mon permis de conduire.
vwasee mon pehrmee du kondweer

What's the deposit?
À combien s'élève la caution?
a kornbyehn saylehv la kohsyon?

May I look at the car first, please?
Pourrais-je regarder la voiture d'abord, s'il vous plaît?
poorayzhuh ruhgarday la vwatür dabur, seel voo pleh?

I'm not familiar with this kind of car. Could you show me . . . ?
Je ne connais pas ce type de voiture. Pouvez-vous me montrer . . . ?
zhuh nuh kunay pah suh teep duh vwatür. Poovvay voo muh montray . . . ?

the headlights	the ignition
les phares	le contact
lay far	*luh kontakt*

the directional signals
les clignotants
lay kleenyutahn

the hood release
comment on ouvre le capot
kumahnt on oovr luh kapoh

the gas cap
le bouchon du réservoir
luh booshon dü rayzehrvwar

What kind of gas must I use, regular or super?
Faut-il que je mette du normal ou bien du super?
fohteel kuh zhuh meht dü nurmal oo byehn dü süpehr?

Must I return it to this office?
Faut-il la rendre à ce bureau?
fohteel la rahndr a suh büroh?

May I return it in another city?
Est-ce possible de la rendre à une autre ville?
ehs puseebl duh la rahndr a ün ohtr veel?

Is there an extra charge for that?
Y a-t-il un supplément à payer pour cela?
ee ateel eun süplaymahn a pehyay poor suhla?

Have you got a branch in . . . ?
Avez-vous un bureau à . . . ?
avay vooz eun büroh a . . . ?

What do I do if I have car trouble?
Que dois-je faire en cas de panne?
kuh dwahzhuh fehr ahn ka duh pan?

ACCOMMODATIONS

Hotel/Pension

I'm looking for . . .
Je cherche . . .
zhuh shehrsh . . .

    a good hotel
    un bon hôtel
    eun bon ohtehl

    a pension
    une pension
    ün pahnsyon

    an inexpensive hotel
    un hôtel pas trop cher
    eun ohtehl pah troh shehr

    a youth hostel
    une auberge de jeunesse
    ün ohbehrzh duh zheunehs

I have a reservation.
J'ai fait réserver.
zhay fay rayzehrvay

My name is . . .
Je m'appelle . . .
zhuh mapehl . . .

Do you have a room for tonight?
Avez-vous une chambre pour ce soir?
avay vooz ün shahnbr poor suh swar?

I would like . . .
Je voudrais . . .
zhuh voodrayz . . .

    a single room
    une chambre pour une personne
    ün shamnbr poor ün pehrsun

    a double room
    une chambre pour deux
    ün shahnbr poor deu

    a room with a double bed
    une chambre avec un grand lit
    ün shahnbr avehk eun grahn lee

I want a room with . . .
Je voudrais une chambre avec . . .
zhuh voodrayz ün shahnbr avehk . . .

    a bath/shower
    salle de bain/douche
    sal duh behn/doosh

    running water
    l'eau courante
    loh koorahnt

    a balcony
    balcon
    balkon

    hot water
    l'eau chaude
    loh shohd

    a view of the sea
    vue sur la mer
    vü sür la mehr

How much is the room per day/ per week?
Combien coûte la chambre par nuit/ par semaine?
konbyehn koot la shahnbr par nwee/ par suhmehn?

That's too expensive. Do you have anything cheaper?
C'est trop cher. N'avez-vous rien de meilleur marché?
seh troh shehr. navay voo ryehn duh mehyeur marshay?

How much is the room . . . ?
Quel est le prix . . . ?
kehl eh luh pree . . . ?

    without meals
    sans les repas
    sahn lay ruhpah

    with breakfast only
    avec petit déjeuner seulement
    avehk puhtee dayzheunay seulmahn

with half board
en demi-pension
ahṅ duhmee pahṅsyoṅ

with full board
en pension complète
ahṅ pahṅsyoṅ koṅpleht

Is there a reduction for children/ a longer stay?
Est-ce qu'il y a une réduction pour les enfants/pour un séjour plus long?
ehs keel ee a ün raydüksyoṅ poor layz ahṅfahṅ/poor ün sayzhoor plü loṅ?

May I see the room?
Puis-je voir la chambre?
pweezhuh vwar la shahṅbr?

Yes, this room will do.
Oui, celle-ci ira bien.
wee, sehl see eera byehṅ

No, this room won't do.
Non, celle-ci ne va pas.
noṅ, sehl see nuh va pah

Do you have any bigger/better rooms?
Avez-vous des chambres plus grandes/ meilleures?
avay voo day shahṅbr plü grahṅd/ mehyeur?

This is the only room vacant right now.
Celle-ci est la seule qui soit disponible en ce moment.

We'll have another room tomorrow.
Nous en aurons une autre demain.

How long will you be staying?
Combien de temps resterez-vous?

I will be staying . . .
Je resterai . . .
zhuh rehstray . . .

tonight only
cette nuit seulement
seht nwee seulmahṅ

two or three days
deux ou trois jours
deu oo trwah zhoor

a week
une semaine
ün suhmehn

I haven't decided yet.
Je n'ai pas encore décidé.
zhuh nay paz ahṅkur dayseeday

Here is my passport.
Voici mon passeport.
vwasee moṅ paspur

When may I have it back?
Quand est-ce que je pourrai le ravoir?
kahṅt ehskuh zhuh pooray luh ravwar?

May I go to the room now?
Puis-je aller à la chambre maintenant?
pweezhuh alay a la shahṅbr mehṅtnahṅ?

May I have the key?
Puis-je avoir la clef?
pweezhuh avwar la clay?

Shall I take the key with me when I go out or leave it with you?
Devrais-je prendre la clef quand je sors, ou bien voulez-vous que je vous la laisse?
duvrayzhuh prahṅdr la clay kahṅ zhuh sur, oo byehṅ voolay voo kuh zhuh voo la lehs?

At what time do you lock the front door at night?
À quelle heure fermez-vous la porte le soir?
a kehl eur fehrmay voo la purt luh swar?

How do I get in if I come later?
Comment puis-je entrer si je rentre plus tard?
kumahṅ pweezhuh ahṅtray see zhuh rahṅtr plü tar?

When is check-out time?
À quelle heure faut-il quitter la chambre?
a kehl eur fohteel keetay la shahṅbr?

Could I please have . . . ?
Pourrais-je avoir, s'il vous plaît . . . ?
poorayzh avwar, seel voo pleh . . . ?

another pillow	un autre oreiller	*eu*ñ *ohtr urehyay*
an extra blanket	une couverture supplé- mentaire	*ün koovehrtür süplay- mah*ñ*tehr*
some towels	des serviettes de bain	*day sehrvyeht de beh*ñ
some soap	du savon	*dü savo*ñ
a glass	un verre	*eu*ñ *vehr*
some toilet paper	du papier hygiénique	*dü papyay eezhyayneek*
some hangers	des cintres	*day seh*ñ*tr*
writing paper	du papier à lettres	*dü papyay a lehtr*
a bottle of mineral water	une bouteille d'eau minérale	*ün bootehyuh doh meenayral*
an ashtray	un cendrier	*eu*ñ *sah*ñ*dreeay*
a light bulb	une ampoule	*ün ah*ñ*pool*

The . . . doesn't work.
. . . ne fonctionne pas.
*. . . nuh fo*ñ*ksyun pah*

air conditioning	la climatisation	*la kleemateezasyo*ñ
heating	le chauffage	*luh shohfazh*
hot water	l'eau chaude	*loh shohd*
light	la lumière	*la lümyehr*
lock	la serrure	*la sehrür*
radio	la radio	*la radyoh*
shower	la douche	*la doosh*
tap	le robinet	*luh rubeeneh*
toilet	les toilettes	*lay twaleht*

Can the heat/air conditioning be turned up/down?
Est-ce possible d'augmenter/de baisser le chauffage/la climatisation?
*ehs puseebl dohgmah*ñ*tay/duh behsay luh shohfazh/la kleemateezasyo*ñ*?*

The mattress is too soft. May I have a firmer one?
Le matelas est trop mou. Puis-je en avoir un plus dur?
*luh matehla eh troh moo. pweezhuh ah*ñ *avwar eu*ñ *plü dür?*

Could you wake me up tomorrow morning at . . . ?
Pouvez-vous me réveiller demain matin à . . . heures?
*poovay voo muh rayvehyay duhmeh*ñ *mateh*ñ *a . . . eur?*

May we have breakfast in our room?
Pouvons-nous prendre le petit déjeuner dans la chambre?
*poovo*ñ *noo prah*ñ*dr luh puhtee dayzheunay dah*ñ *la shah*ñ*br?*

Until what time do you serve breakfast?
Jusqu'à quelle heure servez-vous le petit déjeuner?
zhüska kehl eur sehrvay voo luh puhtee dayzheunay?

What time is lunch/dinner?
À quelle heure le déjeuner/le dîner
   est-il servi?
*a kehl eur luh dayzheunay/luh deenay
   ehteel sehrvee?*

**Could you please have the linen
   changed today?**
Pouvez-vous changer les draps
   aujourd'hui, s'il vous plaît?
*poovay voo shahñzhay lay dra
   ohzhoordwee, seel voo pleh?*

Are there any letters for me?
Y a-t-il du courier pour moi?
ee ateel dü kooreeay poor mwa?

I would like to call this number . . .
Je voudrais téléphoner à
   ce numéro . . .
*zhuh voodray taylayfunay a
   suh nümayroh . . .*

Checking Out

We'll be leaving tomorrow.
Nous partirons demain.
noo parteeroñ duhmehñ

May I have the bill, please?
Pourrais-je avoir la note, s'il vous plaît?
*poorayzhuh avwar la nut, seel
   voo pleh?*

Could you give me a receipt, please?
Pouvez-vous me donner un reçu,
   s'il vous plaît?
*poovay voo muh dunay euñ raysü,
   seel voo pleh?*

Could you explain this item, please?
S'il vous plaît, à quoi faites-vous
   référence ici?
*seel voo pleh, a kwah feht voo
   rayfayrahñs eesee?*

Thank you for a most enjoyable stay.
Je vous remercie pour un séjour très
   agréable.
*zhuh voo rehmehrsee poor euñ
   sayzhoor trehyz agrayabl*

**I hope we'll be able to return
   some day.**
J'espère que nous pourrons revenir
   un jour.
*zhehspehr kuh noo pooroñ rehvneer
   euñ zhoor*

Youth Hostel

Do you have room for . . . people?
Avez-vous de la place pour . . .
   personnes?
*avay voo duh la plas poor . . .
   pehrsun?*

Is there a curfew?
Y a-t-il une heure de fermeture?
ee ateel ün eur duh fehrmuhtür?

Do I have to do chores?
Dois-je remplir une tâche?
dwahzhuh rahñpleer ün tash?

**Is there a limit on the number of
   days we can stay?**
Y a-t-il une limite à la longueur
   du séjour?
*ee ateel ün leemeet a la loñgueur
   dü sayzhoor?*

Camping

Is there a camp site nearby?
Y a-t-il un terrain de camping près d'ici?
ee ateel euñ tehrehñ duh kahrñpeeng preh deesee?

May we camp here?
Pouvons-nous camper ici?
poovoñ noo kahrñpay eesee?

What's the charge?
C'est combien?
seh korhbyehñ?

Are there . . . ?
Y a-t-il . . . ?
ee ateel . . . ?

baths	**toilets**
des bains	des toilettes
day behñ	*day twaleht*
showers	
des douches	
day doosh	

Where can I find . . . .?
Où puis-je trouver . . . ?
oo pweezhuh troovay . . . ?

Are there cooking/washing facilities?
Y a-t-il des cuisines/salles d'eau?
ee ateel day kweezeen/sal doh?

Is it possible to rent a tent/bungalow?
Peut-on louer une tente/un bungalow?
peutoñ looay ün tahñt/euñ beuñguhloh?

May we light a fire?
Peut-on faire du feu?
peutoñ fehr dü feu?

Where can we find drinking water?
Où peut-on trouver de l'eau potable?
oo peutoñ troovay duh loh putabl?

a camping equipment store	un magasin de camping	*euñ magazehñ duh kahrñpeeng*
a laundry	une blanchisserie	*ün blahñsheesehree*
a restaurant	un restaurant	*euñ rehsturahñ*
shops	des magasins	*day magazehñ*
telephones	des téléphones	*day taylayfun*
electric hook-ups	des prises électriques	*day preez zaylektreek*

Signs

NO CAMPING	INTERDICTION DE CAMPER
NO TRAILERS	INTERDIT AUX CARAVANES
NO TRESPASSING	DÉFENSE D'ENTRER
PRIVATE PROPERTY	PROPRIÉTÉ PRIVÉE

FRENCH

TRAVELING

Signs

ARRIVALS	ARRIVÉE
DEPARTURES	DÉPART
ENTRANCE	ENTRÉE
EXIT	SORTIE
TICKETS	BILLETS
INFORMATION	RENSEIGNEMENTS
BAGGAGE CHECK	CONSIGNE
CHANGE	CHANGE
TO THE PLATFORMS	ACCÈS AUX QUAIS
CUSTOMS	DOUANE
NO SMOKING	DÉFENSE DE FUMER
WAITING ROOM	SALLE D'ATTENTE
TOILETS	TOILETTES

Traveling by Air

Is there a bus/train to/from the airport?
Y a-t-il un bus/train à l'aéroport/
de l'aéroport?
*ee ateel eun büs/trehn a la-ayrupur/
duh la-ayrupur?*

Where?
Où?
oo?

When?
Quand?
kahn?

Is there a flight to . . . ?
Y a-t-il un vol pour . . . ?
ee ateel eun vul poor . . . ?

What time?
À quelle heure?
a kehl eur?

Is there an earlier/later flight?
Est-ce qu'il y a un vol qui part plus tôt/
plus tard?
*ehs keel ee a eun vul kee par plü toh/
plü tar?*

When is check-in time?
À quelle heure dois-je enregistrer
mes bagages?
*a kehl eur dwahzhuh ahnruhzheestray
may bagazh?*

When does it arrive?
À quelle heure le vol arrive-t-il?
a kehl eur luh vul areevteel?

How much is the fare to . . . ?
Quel est le tarif pour . . . ?
kehl eh luh tareef poor . . . ?

What's the flight number?
Quel est le numéro du vol?
kehl eh luh nümayroh dü vul?

**I'd like to book a seat on the next
flight to . . .**
Je voudrais réserver une place sur
le prochain vol pour . . .
*zhuh voodray rayzehrvay ün plas sür
luh prushehn vul poor . . .*

one way	**round trip**
un aller simple	un aller-retour
eun alay sehrnpl	*eun alay ruhtoor*

FRENCH

I'd like a seat . . .
Je voudrais une place . . .
zhuh voodrayz ün plas . . .

  in the aisle
  près de l'allée
  preh duh lalay

  at the window
  près de la fenêtre
  preh duh la fuhnehtr

  in the front
  à l'avant
  a lavaṅ

  in the back
  à l'arrière
  a laryehr

  in the smoking section
  dans la section fumeurs
  dahṅ la sehksyoṅ fümeur

  in the non-smoking section
  dans la section non-fumeurs
  dahṅ la sehksyoṅ noṅ-fümeur

Is it a non-stop flight?
Est-ce un vol direct?
ehs euṅ vul deerehkt?

Will it be necessary to change planes?
Faudra-t-il changer d'avion?
fohdrateel shahṅzhay davyoṅ?

How many bags am I allowed?
À combien de bagages ai-je droit?
a korṅbyehṅ duh bagazh ayzh drwa?

How much is charged for excess weight?
Faut-il payer un supplément pour l'excès de bagage?
fohteel pehyay euṅ süplaymahṅ poor lehkseh duh bagazh?

How long is the flight delayed?
Combien de retard a l'avion?
korṅbyehṅ duh ruhtar a lavyoṅ?

Traveling by Train

When is the next train to . . . ?
Quand part le prochain train pour . . . ?
kahṅ par luh prushehṅ trehṅ poor . . . ?

I would like to buy/reserve a one way/round trip ticket to . . . in first/second class.
Je voudrais acheter/faire réserver un aller/aller retour pour . . . en première/deuxième classe.
zhuh voodrayz ashtay/fehr rayzehrvay euṅ alay/alay ruhtoor poor . . . ahṅ pruhmyehr/deuzyehm klahs

What is the fare to . . . ?
Quel est le tarif pour . . . ?
kehl eh luh tareef poor . . . ?

How much is it for a child of . . . years?
C'est combien pour un enfant de . . . ans?
seh korṅbyehṅ poor euṅ ahṅfahṅ duh . . . ahṅ?

What time does the train leave?
À quelle heure le train part-il?
a kehl eur luh trehṅ parteel?

When does it arrive?
À quelle heure arrive-t-il?
a kehl eur areevteel?

At what platform?
Sur quel quai?
sür kehl kay?

Do I have to change trains? Where?
Faut-il changer de train? Où?
fohteel shahṅzhay duh trehṅ? oo?

When will there be a connection to . . . ?
Quand y aura-t-il une correspondance pour . . . ?
kahṅt ee ohrateel ün kurehspoṅdahṅs poor . . . ?

Is there a sleeping car?
Est-ce qu'il y a un wagon-lit?
ehs keel ee a euñ vagoñ lee?

Are there couchettes?
Y a-t-il des couchettes?
ee ateel day koosheht?

Is this train going to . . . ?
Est-ce que ce train va à . . . ?
ehskuh suh trehñ va a . . . ?

Which car for . . . ?
C'est quel wagon pour . . . ?
seh kehl vagoñ poor . . . ?

Could you tell me where car number . . . is?
Pouvez-vous me dire où se trouve le wagon numéro . . . ?
poovay voo muh deer oo suh troov luh vagoñ nümayroh . . . ?

I have a reservation.
J'ai fait réserver.
zhay fay rayzehrvay

Where is my couchette?
Où est ma couchette?
oo eh ma koosheht?

Is this seat taken?
Cette place est-elle occupée?
seht plas ehtehl uküpay?

Excuse me. I think this is my seat.
Excusez-moi. Je crois que c'est ma place.
ehksküzay mwa. zhuh krwah kuh seh ma plas

May I get by?
Puis-je passer?
pweezhuh pasay?

Where is the dining car?
Où est le wagon-restaurant?
oo eh luh vagoñ rehsturahñ?

May I open/close the window/the curtains?
Puis-je ouvrir la fenêtre/les rideaux?
pweezhuh oovreer la fuhnehtr/lay reedoh?

Can the heating be turned down/ off/higher?
Peut-on baisser/éteindre/augmenter le chauffage?
peutoñ behsay/aytehñdr/ogmahñtay luh shohfazh?

Could you refrain from smoking, please?
Pourriez-vous vous abstenir de fumer, s'il vous plaît?
pooryay voo vooz abstuhneer duh fümay, seel voo pleh?

This is a non-smoking compartment.
Ceci est un compartiment non-fumeurs.
suhsee eht euñ korñparteemahñ noñ-fümeur

What station is this?
À quelle gare sommes-nous?
a kehl gar sum noo?

Is this where I change for a train to . . . ?
C'est ici que je dois changer pour . . . ?
seht eesee kuh zhuh dwah shahñzhay poor . . . ?

Traveling by Boat

Is there a boat to . . . ?
Est-ce qu'il y a un bateau pour . . . ?
ehs keel ee a eun batoh poor . . . ?

When does the next boat leave?
À quelle heure part le prochain bateau?
a kehl eur par luh prushehn batoh?

I would like to buy a one-way/round-trip ticket in first/second class.
Je voudrais acheter un aller/aller-retour
en première/deuxième.
*zhuh voodrayz ashtay eun alay/alay
ruhtoor ahn pruhmyehr/deuzyehm*

When does it arrive?
À quelle heure arrive-t-il?
a kehl eur areevteel?

When does it return?
À quelle heure est-ce qu'il revient?
a kehl eur ehs keel ruhvyehn?

When must I go on board?
À quelle heure est l'embarquement?
a kehl eur eh lahrnbarkuhmahn?

Where can I find pills for seasickness?
Où puis-je trouver des cachets
contre le mal de mer?
*oo pweezhuh troovay day kashay
kontr luh mal duh mehr?*

Traveling by Bus/Streetcar/Subway

Where is the bus station?
Où est la station d'autobus?
oo eh la stasyon dohtubüs?

Where is the nearest bus stop/streetcar stop?
Où se trouve l'arrêt du bus/tramway le
plus proche?
*oo suh troov lareh dü büs/tramvay luh
plü prush?*

Where is the nearest subway station?
Où se trouve la station de métro la
plus proche?
*oo suh troov la stasyon duh maytroh la
plü prush?*

Where can I get a bus/train to . . . ?
Où puis-je prendre un bus/métro
pour . . . ?
*oo pweezhuh prahndr eun büs/maytroh
poor . . . ?*

How long does it take?
Combien de temps faut-il compter?
konbyehn duh tahm fohteel korhtay?

Does this bus/train go to . . . ?
Ce bus/train va-t-il jusqu'à . . . ?
seh büs/trehn vateel zhüska . . . ?

Which line do I take for . . . ?
Quelle ligne faut-il prendre pour
aller à . . . ?
*kehl leenyuh fohteel prahndr poor
alay a . . . ?*

Where do I buy a ticket?
Où est le guichet?
oo eh luh geeshay?

What is the fare to . . . ?
Quel est le tarif pour . . . ?
kehl eh luh tareef poor . . . ?

Do I get off here for . . . ?
Dois-je descendre ici pour . . . ?
*dwahzhuh dehsahndr eesee
poor . . . ?*

Could you tell me when we reach . . . ?
Pouvez-vous m'avertir quand nous arriverons à. . . ?
poovay voo mavehrteer kahπ nooz areevehroπz a . . . ?

Let me off, please.
La porte, s'il vous plaît!
la purt, seel voo pleh

Traveling by Car

Where can I find a gas station/garage?
Où puis-je trouver une station-service/un garage?
oo pweezhuh troovay ün stasyoπ sehrvees/euπ garazh?

How much is gas per liter?
Combien l'essence coûte-t-elle par litre?
koπbyehπ lehsahπs kootehl par leetr?

Could you . . .
Voulez-vous . . .
voolay voo . . .

fill her up
faire le plein
fehr luh plehπ

give me . . . liters of standard/ premium
me donner . . . litres d'essence/ de super
muh dunay . . . leetr dehsahπs/ duh süpehr

give me a liter of oil
me donner un litre d'huile
muh dunay euπ leetr dweel

check the oil/water/battery/tires/ brake fluid
verifier l'huile/l'eau/la batterie/les pneus/l'huile des freins
vehreefyay lweel/loh/la batree/lay pneu/lweel day frehπ

clean the windshield
nettoyer le parebrise
nehtwayay luh parbreez

adjust the brakes
régler les freins
rayglay lay frehπ

. . . please?
. . . s'il vous plaît?
. . . seel voo pleh?

In Case of a Breakdown

Excuse me. My car has broken down.
Excusez-moi. Ma voiture est en panne.
ehksüzay mwa. ma vwatür eht ahπ pan

May I use your phone?
Puis-je me servir de votre téléphone?
pweezhuh muh sehrveer duh vutr taylayfun?

I've had a breakdown at . . .
Je suis tombé en panne à . . .
zhuh swee toπbay ahπ pan a . . .

Can you send a mechanic/ tow truck?
Pouvez-vous envoyer un mécanicien/ une dépanneuse?
poovay vooz ahπvwa-yay euπ maykaneesyehπ/ün daypaneuz?

How long will you be?
Combien de temps faut-il compter?
koπbyehπ duh tahπ fohteel koπtay?

Thank you for stopping. Could you help me?
Vous êtes bien aimable de vous être arrêté. Pourriez-vous m'aider?
vooz eht byehñ ehmabl duh vooz ehtr arehtay. pooryay voo mehday?

I have a flat tire.
J'ai un pneu crevé.
zhay euñ pneu krehvay

The battery is dead.
La batterie est à plat.
la batree eht a plah

Do you have a jack/jumper cables?
Avez-vous un cric/des câbles de connection?
avay vooz euñ kreek/day kahbl duh kunehksyoñ?

There's something wrong with the . . .
. . . ne marche/marchent pas.
. . . nuh marsh pah

accelerator	l'accélérateur	*laksaylayrateur*
brakes	les freins	*lay frehñ*
carburetor	le carburateur	*luh karburateur*
clutch	l'embrayage	*lahñbrehyazh*
engine	le moteur	*luh moteur*
fan	le ventilateur	*luh vahñteelateur*
gears	les vitesses	*lay veetehs*
hand brake	le frein à main	*luh frehñ a mehñ*
headlights	les phares	*lay far*
horn	l'avertisseur	*lavehrteeseur*
ignition	le contact	*luh koñtakt*
spark plugs	les bougies	*lay boozhee*
directional signals	les clignotants	*lay kleenyutahñ*

I don't know what's wrong with it.
Je ne sais pas ce qui ne va pas.
zhuh nuh say pah suh kee nuh va pah

A light went on on the dashboard.
Un voyant est allumé sur le tableau de bord.
euñ vwayahnt eht alümay sür luh tabloh duh bur

I've run out of gas.
Je n'ai plus d'essence.
zhuh nay plü dehsahñs

Could you please notify the next garage?
Pourriez-vous avertir le prochain garage?
pooryay vooz avehrteer luh prushehñ garazh?

Could you have a look at my car?
Pouvez-vous jeter un coup d'oeil à ma voiture?
poovay voo zhuhtay euñ koo deuyuh a ma vwatür?

Will spare parts be needed? Do you have them?
Est-ce qu'il faudra des pièces de rechange? Les avez-vous?
ehs keel fohdra day pyehs duh ruhshahñzh? layz avay voo?

How long will it take to repair?
Combien de temps vous faudra-t-il pour la réparer?
korñbyehñ duh tahm voo fohdrateel poor la rayparay?

How much will it cost?
Combien cela va-t-il coûter?
korhbyehm suhla vateel kootay?

When will the car be ready?
Quand est-ce que la voiture sera prête?
kaht ehskuh la vwatür suhra preht?

Where's the nearest garage that can fix it?
Où se trouve le garage le plus proche qui puisse la réparer?
oo suh troov luh garazh luh plü prush kee pwees la rayparay?

Is the car repaired?
La voiture est-elle reparée?
la vwatür ehtehl rayparay?

How much do I owe you?
Combien vous dois-je?
korhbyehm voo dwahzhuh?

Could you give me an itemized bill, please?
Pourriez-vous me détailler le contenu de la facture, s'il vous plaît?
pooray voo muh dayta-yay luh komtuhnü duh la faktür, seel voo pleh?

Trouble with the Police

I don't speak French very well.
Je ne parle pas bien français.
zhuh nuh parl pah byehm frahmsay

Do you speak English?
Parlez-vous anglais?
parlay vooz ahmglay?

I'm sorry, I don't understand.
Je suis désolé, mais je ne comprends pas.
zhuh swee dayzulay, meh zhuh nuh komprahm pah

Here's my driver's license.
Voici mon permis de conduire.
vwasee mom pehrmee duh komdweer.

Was I driving too fast?
Est-ce que je conduisais trop vite?
ehskuh zhuh komdweezay troh veet?

What did I do wrong?
Qu'est-ce que j'ai fait?
kehskuh zhay fay?

Must I pay a fine?
Dois-je payer une amende?
dwahzhuh pehyay ün amahmd?

How much is it?
À combien s'élève-t-elle?
a korhbyehm saylehvtehl?

Traveling by Bicycle/Moped

Where can I rent a bicycle/moped?
Où puis-je louer une bicyclette/un vélomoteur?
oo pweezhuh loooay ün beeseekleht/eum vaylumuteur?

I'd like to rent a moped.
Je voudrais louer un vélomoteur.
zhuh voodray looay eum vaylumuteur

How much is it per hour/day?
Quel est le tarif par heure/jour?
kehl eh luh tareef par eur/zhoor?

At what time must I return it?
À quelle heure faut-il la rendre?
a kehl eur fohteel la rahmdr?

This bicycle is too big/small.
Cette bicyclette est trop grande/petite.
seht beeseekleht eh troh grahmd/puhteet

FRENCH

This tire needs air.
Ce pneu doit être gonflé.
suh pneu dwat ehtr gonflay

The motor keeps stalling.
Le moteur cale sans cesse.
luh muteur cal sahn sehs

**Something's wrong with the brake/
   headlight.**
Le frein/Le phare ne va pas.
luh frehn/luh far nuh va pah

Hitchhiking

**Could you please give me a lift
   to . . . ?**
Pourriez-vous m'amener jusqu'à . . . ?
pooryay voo mamnay zhüska . . . ?

I'm only going as far as . . .
Je vais juste jusqu'à . . .

I can take you as far as . . .
Je peux vous amener jusqu'à . . .

Asking the Way

Excuse me. Could you tell me . . . ?
Excusez-moi. Pouvez-vous me
   dire . . . ?
*ehksküzay mwa. poovay voo muh
   deer . . . ?*

   how to get to . . .
   comment je puis aller à . . .
   kumahn zhuh pweez alay a . . .

   how far is it to . . .
   à quelle distance se trouve . . .
   a kehl deestahns suh troov . . .

   am I on the right road for . . .
   suis-je sur la bonne route pour . . .
   sweezhuh sür la bun root poor . . .

   which road do I take for . . .
   quelle route dois-je prendre pour . . .
   *kehl root dwahzhuh prahndr
      poor . . .*

   what is the name of this town
   quel est le nom de cette ville
   kehl eh luh nom duh seht veel

Could you direct me to . . .
Pouvez-vous m'indiquer la route
   pour . . . ?
*poovay voo mehndeekay la root
   poor . . . ?*

**Could you show me where we are
   on this map?**
Pouvez-vous me montrer où nous
   sommes sur la carte?
*poovay voo muh montray oo noo
   sum sür la kart?*

It's not far from here.
Ce n'est pas loin d'ici.

It's a fair distance from here.
C'est assez loin d'ici.

Go straight ahead.
Allez tout droit.

Turn left/right . . .
Tournez à gauche/à droite . . .

   at the first/second traffic light
   au premier/deuxième feu rouge

   at the next intersection
   au prochain carrefour

   at the next corner
   au prochain coin de rue

   at the traffic circle
   à la rocade

   follow the signs for . . .
   suivez les instructions sur les
      panneaux pour . . .

Highway Signs

EXIT	SORTIE	*surtee*
ENTRANCE	ENTRÉE	*ahntray*
ONE WAY	SENS UNIQUE	*sahns üneek*
NO ENTRY	DÉFENSE D' ENTRER	*dayfahns dahntray*
NO PARKING	DÉFENSE DE STATIONNNER	*dayfahns duh stasyunay*
DETOUR	DÉVIATION	*dayvyasyon*
DANGER	DANGER	*dahnzhay*
MEN WORKING	TRAVAUX	*travoh*
HIGHWAY	AUTOROUTE	*ohturoot*
SPEED LIMIT	LIMITE DE VITESSE	*leemeet duh veetehs*

TYPES OF EATING ESTABLISHMENTS IN FRANCE

Restaurant. French restaurants vary greatly, and the best way of sizing one up is to have a look at the menu, posted outside. If you order a "menu," you will get a fixed-price meal. Ordering "à la carte" means spending much more.

Brasserie. Originally "brewery" or "beershop," a brasserie nowadays is a large café that serves various types of food and drink.

Bistro. In atmosphere similar to a pub or a tavern, here you can get a tasty meal in informal but very pleasant surroundings.

Auberge, Hostellerie, Relais. Country restaurants, serving excellent food and drink, often regional in flavor.

Rôtisserie. A rather expensive place where you'll be sure to find grilled meats and chicken in addition to a variety of other dishes.

Snack-Bar, Buffet. Very informal, inexpensive places which serve "ready to eat" food.

Café. Many cafés, especially the big ones, serve complete meals in addition to sandwiches and light snacks.

Bon appétit!	**Bon appetit!**
Santé!	**Cheers!**

EATING OUT

Can you suggest a good restaurant . . . ?
Pouvez-vous me recommander un bon restaurant . . . ?
poovay voo muh ruhkumahnday eun bon rehsturahn . . . ?

for breakfast/lunch/dinner
pour le petit déjeuner/le déjeuner/le dîner
poor luh puhtee dayzheunay/luh dayzheunay/luh deenay

FRENCH

We're looking for an inexpensive restaurant. Do you know of one?
Nous cherchons un restaurant pas trop cher. Est-ce que vous en connaissez un?
noo shehrshonz eun rehsturahn pah troh shehr. ehskuh vooz ahn kunehsayz eun?

I'd like to make a reservation for two/four at eight this evening.
Je voudrais réserver une table pour deux/quatre à huit heures ce soir.
zhuh voodray rayzehrvay ün tabl poor deu/katr a hweet eur suh swar.

Good evening. We have a reservation. The name is . . .
Bonsoir. Nous avons réservé. Le nom est . . .
bonswar. nooz avon rayzehrvay. luh norn eh . . .

Do you have a table for three?
Avez-vous une table pour trois?
avay vooz ün tabl poor trwah?

Could we please have a/an/some . . . ?
Pouvons-nous avoir . . . s'il vous plaît?
poovon nooz avwar . . . seel voo pleh?

Could we have a table . . . ?
Pouvous-nous avoir une table . . . ?
poovon nooz avwar ün tabl . . . ?

> **outside/inside**
> dehors/à l'intérieur
> *duh-ur/a lehntayryeur*
>
> **in the corner**   **on the terrace**
> dans un coin   sur la terrasse
> *dahnz eun kwehn*   *sur la tehras*
>
> **by the window**
> près de la fenêtre
> *preh duh la fuhnehtr*

May I please see the menu/wine list?
Pourrais-je voir la carte/la carte des vins?
poorayzhuh vwar la kart/la kart day vehn?

fork	une fourchette	*ün foorsheht*
knife	un couteau	*eun kootoh*
spoon	une cuillère	*ün kweeyehr*
napkin	une serviette	*ün sehrvyeht*
plate	une assiette	*ün asyeht*
glass (of water)	un verre (d'eau)	*eun vehr (doh)*
bottle of mineral water/ wine	une bouteille d'eau minérale/de vin	*ün bootehyuh doh meen- ayral/duh vehn*
ashtray	un cendrier	*eun sahndreeay*
bread/butter	du pain/du beurre	*dü pehn/dü beur*
salt	du sel	*dü sehl*
pepper	du poivre	*dü pwavr*
oil	de l'huile	*duh lweel*
vinegar	du vinaigre	*dü veenehgr*
mustard	de la moutarde	*duh la mootard*

What's the specialty of the house?
Quelle est la specialité de la maison?
kehl eh la spehsyaleetay duh la mehzon?

What do you recommend?
Que nous recommandez-vous?
kuh noo ruhkumahnday voo?

I'd like something light.
Je voudrais quelque chose de léger.
zhuh voodray kehlkuh shohz duh layzhay.

Can you tell me what this is?
Pouvez-vous me dire ce que c'est
   que cela?
*poovay voo muh deer suh kuh seh
   kuh suhla?*

I'll have . . .
Je prendrai . . .
zhuh prahñdray . . .

The lady/gentleman will have . . .
Madame/Monsieur prendra . . .
madam/muhsyeu prahñdra . . .

It's very good.
C'est très bon.
seh treh boñ

I didn't order this.
Je n'ai pas commandé ceci.
zhuh nay pah kumahñday suhsee

I asked for . . .
J'ai demandé . . .
zhay duhmahñday . . .

This is . . .
Ceci est . . .
suhsee eh . . .

overcooked	**undercooked**
trop cuit	pas assez cuit
troh kwee	*pahz asay kwee*

May I have something else?
Puis-je avoir quelque chose d'autre?
pweezhuh avwar kehlkuh shohz dohtr?

Check, please.
L'addition, s'il vous plaît.
ladeesyoñ, seel voo pleh

I think there's a mistake on the bill.
Je crois qu'il y a une erreur dans
   l'addition.
*zhuh krwah keel ee a ün ehreur dahñ
   ladeesyoñ*

Is service included?
Le service est-il compris?
luh sehrvees ehteel comñpree?

**Do you take credit cards/traveler's
   checks?**
Acceptez-vous des cartes de crédit/
   des chèques de voyage?
*aksehptay voo day kart duh kraydee/
   day shehk duh vwayazh?*

We enjoyed the meal very much.
Le repas était très bon.
luh ruhpahz aytay treh boñ

Breakfast (Petit dejeuner)

The French normally have a croissant or two with a café au lait in the morning, and
you will probably raise a few eyebrows if you order a traditional American breakfast,
unless you are in a first-class hotel or other establishment that caters to Americans.
If you insist, however, you might try ordering some of the following:

Good morning. I'll have . . .
Bonjour. Je prendrai . . .
boñzhoor. zhuh prahñdray . . .

some coffee.	un café	*euñ kafay*
some coffee with milk	un café au lait	*euñ kafay oh lay*
some hot tea	un thé chaud	*euñ tay shoh*
with milk/lemon	avec du lait/citron	*avehk dü lay/seetroñ*
grapefruit/orange juice	du jus de pample- mousse/d'orange	*dü zhü duh pahñp- luhmoos/durahñzh*
bacon and eggs	des oeufs au lard	*dayz eu oh lar*
ham and eggs	des oeufs au jambon	*dayz eu oh zhahñboñ*

FRENCH

a boiled egg	un oeuf à la coque	*eun euf a la kuk*
soft/hard (boiled)	mollet/dur	*muleh/dür*
fried eggs	des oeufs au plat	*dayz eu oh pla*
scrambled eggs	des oeufs brouillés	*dayz eu brooyay*
an omelette	une omelette	*ün umleht*
bread/rolls	du pain/des petits-pains	*dü pehn/day puhtee pehn*
butter	du beurre	*dü beur*
jam	de la confiture	*duh la konfeetür*
sugar	du sucre	*dü sükr*
yoghurt	du yaourt	*dü yah-oor*
honey	du miel	*dü myehl*
fruit	des fruits	*day früee*

Hors d'oeuvres *ur deuvr* ## Appetizers

artichauts	*arteeshoh*	artichokes
asperges	*aspehrzh*	asparagus
avocat	*avohka*	avocado
chou-fleur	*shoo fleur*	cauliflower
crudités	*krüdeetay*	raw sliced vegetables
escargots	*ehskargoh*	snails
fonds d'artichauts	*fon darteeshoh*	artichoke hearts
fruits de mer	*früee duh mehr*	shellfish
jambon	*zhahnbon*	ham
jambon de pays	*zhahnbon duh pehyee*	cured dried ham
olives	*uleev*	olives
farcies/noires/vertes	*farsee/nwar/vehrt*	stuffed/black/green
ratatouille	*ratatooyuh*	simmered vegetables
truffes	*trüf*	truffles

Artichauts à la vinaigrette
arteeshoh a la veenehgreht

artichokes with vinaigrette sauce

Asperges froides en buissons
aspehrzh frwad ahn bweeson

cold asparagus rolled in ham with mayonnaise and spinach juice

Bouchées aux truffes
booshay oh trüf

truffles baked in a pastry shell

Coeurs de palmier
keur duh palmyay

palm hearts, often served with vinaigrette sauce

Crudités
krüdeetay

selection of raw sliced vegetables, usually served with vinaigrette sauce

Escargots à la bourguignonne
ehskargoh a la boorgeenyun

snails cooked in wine and baked in their shells with a butter and garlic mixture

Grenouilles
Cuisses de grenouilles frites
kwees duh gruhnooyuh freet

frog's legs
frog's legs fried in a coating of egg and breadcrumbs

Pâté
pahtay

liver purée baked in a wrapping of pastry

Quenelle *kuhnehl*	light dumpling served with a delicate sauce
Soufflé *sooflay*	baked froth of beaten egg whites, flavored with cheese, seafood, or vegetables
Terrine *tehreen*	baked loaf of chopped meat mixed with finely minced vegetables, spices, and herbs, served in its casserole

Les potages
lay putazh

Soups

Bisque *beesk*	seafood soup
Bisque de homard *beesk duh umard*	lobster soup
Bouillabaisse *booyabehs*	fish and seafood stew
Bouillon *booyoñ*	bouillon
Consommé *koñsuhmay*	clarified broth
Consommé de volaille *koñsuhmay duh vulahyuh*	chicken consommé
Crème d'asperges *krehm daspehrzh*	cream of asparagus
Crème de bolets *krehm duh buleh*	cream of mushroom
Crème de volaille *krehm duh vulahyuh*	cream of chicken
Garbure *garbür*	cabbage is the principal ingredient, along with assorted vegetables and pork, goose, or ham
Pot-au-feu *poht oh feu*	meat and vegetable stew
Potage à l'ail *puhtazh a la-ee*	garlic soup
Soupe aux choux *soop oh shoo*	cabbage soup
Soupe à l'oignon *soop a lwanyoñ*	onion soup

FRENCH

Soupe au pistou *soop oh peestoo*	vegetable soup with garlic, basil, and oil
Velouté aurore *vuhlootay ohrur*	cream of tomato and avocado
Velouté de tomate *vuhlootay duh tuhmat*	cream of tomato
Vichyssoise *veesheeswaz*	creamy cold leek and potato soup

Les oeufs
layz eu

Eggs

Oeufs Bercy *eu behrsee*	baked with sausages and tomato sauce
Oeufs Mireille *eu meerehyuh*	steamed with truffles and cream
Oeufs pochés *eu pushay*	poached, served in a variety of ways, usually with vegetables and some kind of cream sauce

Les poissons et les fruits de mer

Fish and Seafood

lay pwason ay lay frwee duh mehr

aiglefin	**haddock**	*ehgluhfehn*
anchois	**anchovies**	*ahnshwa*
anguilles	**eel**	*ahngeeyuh*
bar	**bass**	*bar*
brochet	**pike**	*brushay*
cabillaud	**cod**	*kabeeyoh*
calmar	**squid**	*kalmar*
carpe	**carp**	*karp*
crabe	**crab**	*krab*
crevettes	**shrimp**	*kruhveht*
écrevisses	**crayfish**	*aykruhvees*
escargots	**snails**	*ehskargoh*
féra	**lake salmon**	*fayra*
harengs	**herring**	*arahn*
homard	**lobster**	*umard*
huitres	**oysters**	*weetr*
langoustines	**prawns**	*lahngoosteen*
loup de mer	**sea bass**	*loo duh mehr*
marquereau	**mackerel**	*makroh*

FRENCH

morue	cod	murü
moules	mussels	mool
palourdes	clams	paloord
perche	perch	pehrsh
poulpes	octopus	poolp
rouget	red mullet	roozhay
saumon	salmon	sohmoñ
sole	sole	sohl
thon	tuna	toñ
truite	trout	trweet

Brandade de morue
brahñdad du murü

purée of salt cod, creamed with milk, oil, and garlic

Coquilles Saint-Jacques
kukeeyuh sehñ zhahk

scallops cooked in wine, lemon juice, and butter, sometimes served with mushrooms

Homard à l'américaine/l'amoricaine
umard a lamayreekehn/lamureekehn

lobster sautéed in oil and butter, simmered in wine, shallots, tomatoes, and herbs, served with rice

Matelote
matlut

fish stew, usually made with eel

Moules marinière
mool mareenyehr

cooked mussels in a mixture of their own liquid, white wine, herbs, butter, and lemon juice

Quenelles de brochet
kuhnehl duh brushay

sieved pike mixed with flour paste and eggs and poached

Rouget à la nantaise
roozhay a la nahñtehz

grilled red mullet with a sauce consisting of mullet livers, wine, and chopped shallots

Sole dugléré
sohl düglayray

sole poached in white wine with butter, onion, and tomatoes

La volaille et le gibier

Fowl and Game

*la vulahyuh
ay luh
zheebyay*

cabri	kid goat	kabree
caille	quail	kahyuh
canard sauvage	wild duck	kanar sohvazh
caneton	duckling	kantoñ
cerf	venison	sehrf
chevreuil	roe deer	shuhvreuyuh
cochon de lait	suckling pig	kohshoñ duh lay
coq de bruyère	grouse	kuk duh brüyehr
dinde	turkey	dehñd
dindonneau	young turkey	dehñdunoh
faisan	pheasant	fayzahñ

grive	**thrush**	*greev*
lapin	**rabbit**	*lapehń*
lièvre	**wild hare**	*lyehvr*
oie	**goose**	*wah*
perdrix	**partridge**	*pehrdree*
pintade	**guinea fowl**	*pehńtad*
poule	**stewing fowl**	*pool*
poulet	**chicken**	*poolay*
poussin	**spring chicken**	*poosehń*
sanglier	**wild boar**	*sahńglyay*
sarcelle	**chicken breast**	*sarsehl*
volaille	**fowl**	*vulahyuh*

Canard à l'orange
canard a lurahńzh

duck braised with oranges and orange liqueur

Coq à la bière
kuk a la byehr

chicken braised in dark beer, gin, cream, and mushrooms.

Coq au vin
kuk oh vehń

chicken stewed in red wine

Faisan à la bohémienne
fayzahń a la bu-aymyehn

pheasant cooked with goose fat and onions, stuffed with preserved goose liver, and served with rice and wine and cream sauce

Lièvre à la royale
lyehvr a la rwayal

stuffed hare wrapped in pork fat and baked with vegetables and red wine

Poularde belle aurore
poolard behl urur

pieces of chicken cooked in white wine, served in an egg, cream, and lemon sauce

Poularde châtelaine
poolard shatlehn

chicken cooked in butter in a casserole and served with chestnuts, asparagus tips, and artichokes in a brandy and white wine sauce

Poulet aux aromates
poolay ohz arumat

pieces of chicken seasoned with basil, rosemary, and tarragon, sautéed in butter with onions and mushrooms

Râble de lièvre à la cauchoise
rable de lyehvr a la kohshwaz

marinated hindquarters of hare, roasted and served in a cream and mustard sauce and garnished with sautéed apples

Selle de chevreuil Saint-Hubert
sehl duh shuhvreuy sehńt-übehr

marinated venison served in a pepper sauce with raisins and almonds

Volaille au vinaigre
vulahyuh oh veenehgr

chicken sautéed in butter and then simmered in white wine, vinegar, stock, and tomato paste

FRENCH

Les viandes	**Meat**	*lay vyahnd*
agneau	**lamb**	*anyoh*
boulettes	**meatballs**	*booleht*
côte	**rib**	*koht*
côtelettes	**chops**	*kohtleht*
épaule	**shoulder**	*aypohl*
escalope	**cutlet**	*ehskalup*
foie	**liver**	*fwah*
gigot	**leg**	*zheegoh*
jambon	**ham**	*zhahnbon*
jambonneau	**pig's knuckle**	*zhahnbunoh*
langue	**tongue**	*lahng*
médaillon	**steak (lamb, pork, or veal)**	*mayda-yon*
pieds	**feet**	*pyay*
ris de veau	**veal sweetbreads**	*ree duh voh*
rognons	**kidneys**	*runyon*
rosbif	**roast beef**	*rusbeef*
saucisses	**sausages**	*sohsees*
steak	**steak (beef)**	*stehk*

Blanquette de veau
blahnkeht duh voh

boiled veal with vegetables, mushrooms, and baby onions in a white sauce

Boeuf à la bourguignonne
beuf a la boorgueenyun

beef marinated with onions, carrots, herbs, and red wine, stewed in a casserole with onions, garlic, bacon, and mushrooms

Carbonnade à la flamande
karbunad a la flamahnd

slices of beef and onions cooked in a casserole with brown stock and beer

Cassoulet languedocien
kasoolay lahngdusyehn

casserole of white beans with pork, mutton, or duck with onions, garlic, and tomato paste

Choucroute garnie
shookroot garnee

sausage, cured pork, and sauerkraut

Cotelettes de veau marquise
kohtleht duh voh markeez

sautéed veal cutlets served in a wine sauce with truffles, cream, and preserved goose liver

Filet de boeuf Richelieu
feeleh duh beuf reeshuhlyeu

roast filet of beef with vegetables and mushrooms in a wine sauce

Foie de veau vénétienne
fwah duh voh vaynaytyen

veal liver sprinkled with bread crumbs and baked with bacon, shallots, mushrooms, and parsley

Fricassée de veau
freekasay duh voh

pieces of veal sautéed, simmered in stock, and served with a cream sauce

Gigot
zheegoh

roast leg of marinated lamb, served with a vegetable sauce

FRENCH

Ragoût
ragoo
meat and vegetable stew

Sauté de veau Marengo
sohtay duh voh marehngoh
veal, olives, crayfish, and fried eggs cooked in a casserole with garlic, shallots, mushrooms, tomatoes, onions, and white wine

Ways of Preparing Meat, Poultry, Game, and Fish

baked	au four	*oh foor*
boiled	bouilli	*booyee*
braised	braisé	*brehzay*
fried	frit	*free*
grilled	grillé	*greeyay*
marinated	mariné	*mareenay*
roasted	rôti	*rohtee*
smoked	fumé	*fümay*
stewed	à l'étoufée	*a laytoofay*
rare	saignant	*sehnyahṅ*
medium	à point	*a pwehṅ*
well-done	bien cuit	*byehṅ kwee*

Les légumes	**Vegetables**	*lay laygüm*
ail	**garlic**	*a-ee*
artichauts	**artichokes**	*arteeshoh*
asperges	**asparagus**	*aspehrzh*
aubergines	**eggplant**	*ohbehrzheen*
bolets	**mushrooms**	*buleh*
brocoli	**broccoli**	*brukulee*
carottes	**carrots**	*karut*
céleri	**celery**	*saylree*
cèpes	**mushrooms**	*sehp*
champignons	**mushrooms**	*shahṁpeenyoṅ*
chicorée	**chicory**	*sheekuray*
chou	**cabbage**	*shoo*
choucroute	**sauerkraut**	*shookroot*
chou-fleur	**cauliflower**	*shoo fleur*
choux de Bruxelles	**brussels sprouts**	*shoo duh brüksehl*
concombre	**cucumber**	*koṁkoṁbr*
courgettes	**zucchini**	*kurzheht*
cresson	**watercress**	*krehsoṅ*
endive	**chicory**	*ahṅdeev*
épinards	**spinach**	*aypeenar*
fenouil	**fennel**	*fuhnooyuh*
flageolets	**small kidney beans**	*flazhuleh*
fonds d'artichauts	**artichoke hearts**	*foṅ darteeshoh*

haricots verts	**green beans**	*areekoh vehr*
laitue	**lettuce**	*lehtü*
lentilles	**lentils**	*lahṅteeyuh*
maïs	**corn**	*ma-ees*
(pois) mange-tout	**snow peas**	*(pwah) mahṅzh too*
navets	**turnips**	*naveh*
oignons	**onions**	*wanyoṅ*
petits pois	**peas**	*puhtee pwah*
piment	**sweet chili pepper**	*peemahṅ*
poireaux	**leeks**	*pwaroh*
poivrons	**sweet peppers**	*pwavroṅ*
pommes de terre	**potatoes**	*pum duh tehr*
pommes frites	**french fries**	*pum freet*
potiron	**pumpkin**	*puteeroṅ*
radis	**radishes**	*radee*
riz	**rice**	*ree*
tomates	**tomatoes**	*tuhmat*
truffes	**truffles**	*trüf*

Artichauts à la barigoule
  arteeshoh a la bareegool

stuffed artichokes stewed in white wine and pork stock with onions and carrots

Aubergines à l'égyptienne
  ohbehrzheen a layzheeptyehn

stuffed eggplant with tomatoes and garlic

Macédoine de légumes
  masaydwehṅ duh laygüm

mixed diced vegetables

Pommes de terre
  pum duh tehr

potatoes

  Byron
    büeeroṅ

mashed, covered with cream and cheese

  Pont-Neuf
    poṅ neuf

french fries

  Purée
    püray

mashed with milk and butter

Truffes au champagne
  trüf oh shahṅpanyuh

truffles simmered in veal stock and champagne

Truffes sous la cendre
  trüf soo la sahṅdr

truffles wrapped in layers of paper and cooked in hot ashes until the paper burns away

Les salades
lay salad

Salads

Salade mêlée
  salad mehlay

mixed salad

Salade niçoise
  salad neeswaz

elaborate mixed salad with tuna and hard-boiled eggs

Salade russe
salad rüs

diced vegetable salad

Salade de thon
salad duh toñ

tuna salad

Salade verte
salad vehrt

green salad

Les fromages
lay frumazh

Cheeses

Bleu de Bresse
bleu duh brehs

soft, sharp and tangy cheese made from pasteurized cow's milk

Boursin
boorsehñ

mild, soft cheese made from cow's milk; sometimes garlic and herbs are added

Brie
bree

mild, soft cheese made from cow's milk

Camembert
kamahrñbehr

sharp, tangy, soft cheese, mildly fermented

Coulommiers
koolumyay

soft, smoth and tangy cheese made from cow's milk

Munster
munstehr

strong and soft cheese made from cow's milk

Petit-suisse
puhtee swees

fresh, unsalted cheese, mild and soft

Pont-l'évêque
poñ layvehk

soft, sharp cheese with a somewhat rubbery consistency, made from cow's milk

Port-salut
pur salüt

pressed cow's milk cheese, smooth and mild

Vacherin
vashrehñ

mild, soft cow's milk Swiss cheese, wrapped in pine bark

Valençay
valahñsay

goat's milk cheese

Les fruits et les noix	**Fruits and Nuts**	*lay frwee ay lay nwah*
abricots	**apricots**	*abreekoh*
amandes	**almonds**	*amahñd*
ananas	**pineapple**	*ananah*
banane	**banana**	*banan*
brugnons	**nectarine**	*brünyoñ*
cassis	**black currants**	*kasee*
cerises	**cherries**	*suhreez*
dattes	**dates**	*dat*

figues	**figs**	*feeg*
fraises	**strawberries**	*frehz*
framboises	**raspberries**	*frahrhbwaz*
groseilles	**red currants**	*gruzehyuh*
à maquereau	**gooseberries**	*a makroh*
mandarines	**tangerines**	*mahṅdareen*
marrons	**chestnuts**	*maroṅ*
melon	**cantaloupe**	*muhloṅ*
mûres	**blackberries**	*mür*
myrtilles	**blueberries**	*meerteel*
noisettes	**hazelnuts**	*nwazeht*
noix	**walnuts**	*nwah*
orange	**orange**	*urahṅzh*
pamplemousse	**grapefruit**	*pahrhplmoos*
pastèque	**watermelon**	*pastehk*
pêche	**peach**	*pehsh*
poire	**pear**	*pwar*
pommes	**apples**	*pum*
pruneaux	**prunes**	*prünoh*
prunes	**plums**	*prün*
raisins	**grapes**	*rehzehṅ*
raisins secs	**raisins**	*rehzehṅ sehk*
rhubarbe	**rhubarb**	*rübarb*

Les desserts
lay dehsehr

Desserts

Abricots condé
abreekoh koṅday

ring of rice pudding topped with apricots and kirsch

Bavaroise
bavarwaz

creamy pudding made with whipped egg yolks, milk, vanilla, and sugar

Bombe favorite
borhb favureet

chestnut ice cream filled with rum-flavored apricot mousse

Coupe
koop

ice-cream sundae

Crème à l'anglaise
krehm a lahṅglehz

custard

Crème caramel
krehm karamehl

custard baked in caramel syrup

Crêpes Suzette
krehp süzeht

thin pancakes topped with sugar, butter, and liqueur sauce

Gâteau
gatoh

cake

Gâteau Saint-Honoré
gatoh sehṅt unuray

a fluffy custard-filled pastry

Glace
glas

ice cream

FRENCH

Marjolaine *marzhulehn*	several layers of meringue and chocolate cream, butter cream, roasted and chopped almonds, and hazelnuts
Mille-feuilles *meel feuyuh*	thin layers of delicate pastry with a custard filling and sugar icing
Mont-Blanc *moñ blahn*	sieved roasted chestnuts with whipped cream
Oeufs à la neige *euf a la nehzh*	egg-shaped meringue puffs served in custard
Salade de fruits *salad duh frwee*	fruit cocktail
Soufflé Rothschild *sooflay rutsheeld*	cream soufflé mixed with kirsch-soaked chopped fruit

DRINKS

Non-alcoholic Drinks

Cold Beverages

I'd like a . . .
Je voudrais . . .
zhuh voodrayz . . .

glass of	bottle of
un verre de	une bouteille de
euñ vehr duh	*ün bootehyuh duh*

(mineral) water	d'eau (minérale)	*doh (meenayral)*
carbonated	gazeuse	*gahzeuz*
regular	non gazeuse	*noñ gahzeuz*
apricot juice	un jus d'abricot	*euñ zhü dabreekoh*
grapefruit juice	un jus de pamplemousse	*euñ zhü duh pahñplmoos*
lemonade	une limonade	*ün leemunad*
orangeade	une orangeade	*ün urahñzhad*
fresh-squeezed orange juice	une orange pressée	*ün urahñzh prehsay*
fresh-squeezed lemon juice	un citron pressé	*euñ seetroñ prehsay*
peach juice	un jus de pêche	*euñ zhü duh pehsh*
pear juice	un jus de poire	*euñ zhü duh pwar*
tomato juice	un jus de tomates	*euñ zhü duh tuhmat*
iced tea	un thé glacé	*euñ tay glasay*
iced coffee	un café glacé	*euñ kafay glasay*
milkshake	un frappé	*euñ frapay*
almond syrup and soda water	un Moresque	*euñ murehsk*
mint syrup and soda water	un diabolo menthe	*euñ dyabuloh mahñt*

FRENCH

Hot Beverages

espresso	un café espress	eun kafay ehsprehs
coffee with cream	un café crème	eun kafay krehm
cup of coffee	une tasse de café	ün tas duh kafay
hot chocolate	un chocolat chaud	eun shukula shoh
hot tea	un thé chaud	eun tay shoh
with milk/lemon	crème/citron	krehm/seetron

Alcoholic Drinks

I'd like a/an . . .
je voudrais . . .
zhuh voodrayz . . .

aperitif	un apéritif	eun apayreeteef
beer	une bière	ün byehr
Bourbon	un bourbon	eun boorbon
brandy	un brandy	eun brahndee
cider	un cidre	eun seedr
cognac	un cognac	eun kunyak
cordial	une liqueur	ün leekeur
gin	un gin	eun zheen
gin fizz	un gin-fizz	eun zheen feez
gin and tonic	un gin-tonique	eun zheen tuneek
liqueur	une liqueur	ün leekeur
port	un porto	eun purtoh
rum	un rhum	eun rum
Scotch	un scotch	eun skutsh
sherry	un sherry	eun shehree
vermouth	un vermouth	eun vehrmoot
vodka	une vodka	ün vudka
whiskey	un whisky	eun weeskee
whiskey and soda	un whisky soda	eun weeskee sohda

draft	pression	prehsyon
in the bottle	en bouteille	ahn bootehyuh
straight	sec	sehk
on the rocks	avec des glaçons	avehk day glason
with soda water	avec du soda	avehk dü sohda

Some Favorite Aperitifs

Amer Picon
amehr peekoṅ

a thick liqueur with a flavor of oranges and gentian, often served with soda water, grenadine, and a slice of orange

Byrrh
beer

a somewhat dry vermouth with a touch of orange quinine

Blanc Cassis
blaṅn kasee

white wine with cassis, a sweet black-currant liqueur

Cynar
seenahr

artichoke liqueur

Dubonnet
dübunay

a vermouth-type aperitif with a bittersweet, almost quinine taste

Lait de Tigre
lay du teegr

pastis and water

Martini blanc/rouge
marteenee blahṅ/roozh

dry or sweet vermouth

Noilly Prat
nwahyee prah

the best known French dry vermouth, served with soda and ice or in a dry Martini cocktail

Pastis
pastees

means "mixture"; a liqueur with a lively licorice taste

Pernod
pehrnoh

a licorice-tasting liqueur served with water and ice

Perroquet
pehrohkay

pastis, mint syrup, and water

Pimm's
peemz

a type of English gin, often served with fresh fruit

Porto
purtoh

port

Tomate
tuhmat

pastis with grenadine and water

Liqueurs and Brandies

Bénédictine
baynaydeekteen

a savory liqueur made from herbs, plants, and peels. "B and B" is Bénédictine and brandy

Calvados
kalvadohs

apple brandy

Chartreuse
shartreuz

a rich aromatic liqueur made from 130 herbs and spices

Crème de cassis
krehm duh kasee
a sweet black-currant liqueur

Crème de menthe
krehm duh mahnt
a sweet liqueur made from various kinds of mint

Grand Marnier
grahn marnyay
a cognac-based liqueur made from oranges

Marc de Bourgogne
mar duh boorgunyuh
a brandy made from grape skins, sometimes called "anti-gel," or "anti-freeze"

Eaux-de-vie (Flavored Brandies)

Kirsch
keersh
made from cherries

Poire Williams
pwar veelyahms
made from pears; easily identifiable by the pear inside the bottle

Quetsche
kwehtsh
distilled from the small and sour Switzen plum

Fraise
frehz
distilled from strawberries

Framboise
frahrhbwaz
distilled from raspberries

Mirabelle
meerabehl
distilled from the yellow mirabelle plum

Cognacs

Médaille d'Argent
mayda-yuh darzhahn
very, very old, very difficult to find, very expensive

Médaille d'Or
mayda-yuh dur
very old, somewhat easier to find

X.O.
ehks oh
fairly old

**V.S.O.P., V.S.,
Courvoisier, Hennessy,
Rémy Martin**
*vay ehs oh pay, vay ehs,
korrvwazyay, ehnehsee,
raymee martehn*
younger cognacs

FRENCH

Wine

Which wine do you recommend for us/me?
Quel vin nous/me recommandez-vous?
kehl vehn noo/muh rehkumahnday voo?

Which wine goes with this dish?
Quel vin recommandez-vous pour ce plat?
kehl vehn rehkumahnday voo poor suh pla?

I'd like a . . . wine
Je voudrais un vin . . .
zhuh voodrayz eun vehn . . .

dry	sec	sehk
sweet	doux	doo
light	léger	layzhay
sparkling	mousseux	mooseu
full-bodied	moelleux	mwaleu
red	rouge	roozh
rosé	rosé	rohzay
white	blanc	blahn

Please bring a . . . of . . .
Apportez-nous/moi . . . de . . . s'il vous plaît.
apurtay noo/mwa . . . duh . . . seel voo pleh

bottle	une bouteille	ün bootehyuh
carafe	un pichet	eun peeshay
half-bottle	une demi-bouteille	ün duhmee bootehyuh
liter	un litre	eun leetr
half liter	un demi-litre	ün duhmee leetr
glass	un verre	eun vehr

I would like to try some of the local wine.
J'aimerais goûter un vin du pays.
zhehmray gootay eun vehn dü pehyee

SIGHTSEEING

Where is the tourist office?
Où se trouve le syndicat d'initiative?
oo suh troov luh sehndeeka deeneesyateev?

We would like to see the main points of interest.
Nous voudrions voir ce qu'il y a de plus intéressant.
noo voodreeon vwar suh keel ee a duh plüz ehntayrehsahn

We will be here for . . .
Nous serons ici pour . . .
noo suhrohz eesee poor . . .

a few hours	a few days
quelques heures	quelques jours
kehlkuhz eur	*kehlkuh zhoor*

a day	a week
un jour	une semaine
euh zhoor	*ün suhmehn*

Is there a sightseeing tour?
Est-ce qu'il y a une excursion touristique?
ehs keel ee a ün ehkskürsyoh tooreesteek?

Where does it go?
Où va-t-elle?
oo vatehl?

How long is it?
Combien de temps dure-t-elle?
korhbyehh duh tahrh dürtehl?

How much is it?
À combien revient-elle?
a korhbyehh ruhvyehhtehl?

When/Where will the bus pick us up?
Quand/Où nous prendra l'autobus?
kahh/oo noo prahhdra lohtubüs?

Does the guide speak English?
Le guide parle-t-il anglais?
luh geed parlteel ahhglay?

We would like to see . . .
Nous voudrions voir . . .
noo voodreeoh vwar . . .

Could you direct me to the . . .?
Pouvez-vous me dire où se trouve/trouvent . . . ?
poovay voo muh deer oo suh troov . . . ?

art gallery	la galerie	*la galree*
castle	le château	*luh shatoh*
catacombs	les catacombes	*lay katakorhb*
cathedral	la cathédrale	*la kataydral*
cemetery	le cimetière	*luh seemtyehr*
church	l'église	*laygleez*
city center	le centre de la ville	*luh sahhtr duh la veel*
fortress	la forteresse	*la furtuhrehs*
fountain	la fontaine	*la fohtehn*
gardens	les jardins	*lay zhardehh*
harbor	le port	*luh pur*
lake	le lac	*luh lak*
monastery	le monastère	*luh munastehr*
museum	le musée	*luh müzay*
old city	la vieille ville	*la vyehyuh veel*
opera house	l'opéra	*lupayra*
palace	le palais	*luh paleh*
planetarium	le planétarium	*luh planaytehryuhm*
ruins	les ruines	*lay rüeen*
shops	les magasins	*lay magazehh*
statue	la statue	*la statü*
tomb	la tombe	*la tohb*
university	l'université	*lüneevehrseetay*
zoo	le zoo	*luh zoh*

When is the . . . open?
Quand . . . est-il/est-elle ouvert(e)?
kahh . . . ehteel/ehtehl oovehr(t)?

At what time does it close?
Quelle est l'heure de fermeture?
kehl eh leur duh fehrmuhtür?

How much is the admission?
Combien coûtent les billets?
korhbyehm coot lay beeyay?

The admission is free.
L'entrée est libre.
lahmtray eh leebr

Is there a reduction for children/ students/senior citizens?
Est-ce qu'il y a une réduction pour les enfants/étudiants/personnes agées?
ehs keel ee a ün raydüksyom poor layz ahmfahm/layz aytüdyahm/lay pehrsun azhay?

Where does one buy tickets?
Où achète-t-on les billets?
oo ashehtom lay beeyay?

When can I find . . .
Où puis-je trouver . . .
oo pweezhuh troovay . . .

a catalogue   **a guidebook**
un catalogue   un guide
eum katalug   *eum geed*

the . . . exhibit
l'exposition . . .
lehkspohzeesyom . . .

the . . . collection
la collection . . .
la kulehksyom

post cards
des cartes postales
day kart pustal

the souvenir shop
le magasin de souvenirs
luh magazehm duh soovneer

Am I allowed to take photographs?
Puis-je prendre des photos?
pweezhuh prahmdr day futoh?

HAVING FUN

Daytime Activities

Soccer

Let's go to the soccer match.
Allons au match de football.
alomz oh matsh duh futbal

Where is the stadium?
Où se trouve le stade?
oo suh troov luh stad?

Who is playing?
Qui est-ce qui joue?
kee ehs kee zhoo?

I would like two tickets . . .
Je voudrais deux billets . . .
zhuh voodray deu beeyay . . .

   in the sun
   côté soleil
   kohtay sulehyuh

   in the shade
   côté ombre
   kohtay orhbr

When does it start?
À quelle heure commence-t-il?
a kehl eur kumahmsteel?

What is the score?
Quel est le score?
kehl eh luh skur?

Tennis

Would you like to play tennis?
Voulez-vous/Veux-tu jouer au tennis?
voolay voo/veu tü zhooay oh tehnees?

Where are the tennis courts?
Où se trouvent les courts de tennis?
oo suh troov lay koor duh tehnees?

What's the charge for the use of the courts per hour/for half an hour?
Combien cela coûte-t-il de réserver un court pour une heure/pour une demi-heure?
korhbyehrh suhla kooteel duh rayzehrvay eurh koor poor ün eur/poor ün duhmee eur?

Is it possible to rent rackets?
Où peut-on louer des raquettes de tennis?
oo peutorh looay day rakeht duh tehnees?

I would like to buy some tennis balls.
Je voudrais acheter des balles.
zhuh voodrayz ashtay day bal

Let's go to the tennis tournament.
Allons au tournoi de tennis.
alorhz on toornwa duh tehnees

I want to watch/play the men's/women's singles/doubles.
Je veux voir/jouer les simples/doubles/hommes/femmes.
zhuh veu vwar/zhooay lay sehrhpl/doobl/um/fam

Golf

Where's the nearest golf course?
Où se trouve le terrain de golf le plus proche?
oo suh troov luh tehrehrh duh gulf luh plü prush?

Is it open to non-members?
Faut-il en être membre pour y avoir accès?
fohteel ahrh ehtr mahrhbr poor ee avwar akseh?

How much does it cost per hour/day/round?
Combien cela coûte-t-il par heure/jour/jeu?
korhbyehrh suhla kooteel par eur/zhoor/zheu?

I would like to rent a caddy/golf clubs.
Je voudrais louer un caddie/des clubs de golf.
zhuh voodray looay eurh kadee/day kloob duh gulf

I would like to buy some golf balls.
Je voudrais acheter des balles de golf.
zhuh voodrayz ashtay day bal duh gulf

Would you like to play a round with me?
Voulez-vous jouer avec moi?
voolay voo zhooay avehk mwa?

Where's the next tee?
Où se trouve le prochain tee?
oo suh troov luh prushehrh tee?

FRENCH

Horseback Riding

Is there a riding stable nearby?
Est-ce qu'il y a un manège par ici?
ehs keel ee a euñ manehzh par eesee?

I would like to rent a horse.
Je voudrais louer un cheval.
zhuh voodray looay euñ shuhval

What's the charge per hour?
Combien cela coûte-t-il par heure?
korñbyehñ suhla kooteel par eur?

I would like to take riding lessons.
Je voudrais prendre des leçons
   d'équitation.
*zhuh voodray prahñdr day luhsoñ
   daykeetasyoñ*

I am a beginner/experienced rider.
Je suis novice./Je sais bien monter.
*zhuh swee nuvees./zhuh say byehñ
   moñtay*

**Could you give me a gentle horse,
   please?**
Pouvez-vous me donner un cheval
   docile, s'il vous plaît?
*poovay voo muh dunay euñ shuhval
   duseel, seel voo pleh?*

I would like a jumper.
Je voudrais un sauteur.
zhuh voodrayz euñ sohteur

Skiing

Would you like to go skiing?
Voulez-vous/Veux-tu aller faire du ski?
voolay voo/veu tü alay fehr dü skee?

How do we get to the ski slopes?
Comment pouvons-nous aller aux
   pistes de ski?
*kumahñ poovoñ nooz alay oh
   peest duh skee?*

**What are the skiing conditions like
   at . . . ?**
Quelles sont les conditions pour
   aujourd'hui à . . . ?
*kehl soñ leh korñdeesyoñ poor
   ohzhoordwee a . . . ?*

Is it possible to take skiing lessons?
Y a-t-il une école de ski?
ee ateel un aykul duh skee?

**Is it possible to rent skiing
   equipment?**
Peut-on louer du matériel de ski?
peutoñ looay dü matayryehl duh skee?

These boots are too tight/loose.
Ces chaussures de ski sont trop
   petites/grandes.
*say shohsür duh skee soñ troh
   puhteet/grahñd*

Could you help me put on the skis?
Pouvez-vous m'aider à mettre les
   chaussures de ski?
*poovay voo mehday a mehtr lay
   shohsür duh skee?*

**How much are the lift tickets for a
   day/two days/a week?**
Combien coûte un forfait journalier/
   pour deux jours/hebdomadaire?
*korñbyehñ koot euñ furfeh zhoornalyay/
   poor deu zhoor/ehbdumadehr?*

**I'm looking for a beginner's/
   intermediate/advanced/expert trail.**
Je cherche une piste verte/bleu/
   rouge/noir.
*zhuh shehrsh ün peest vehrt/bleu/
   roozh/nwar*

FRENCH

Swimming

Would you like to go swimming?
Voulez-vous/Veux-tu aller nager?
voolay voo/veu tü alay nazhay?

Let's go to the beach/swimming pool.
Allons à la plage/piscine.
alonz a la plazh/peeseen.

Is it safe for swimming?
Peut-on nager sans danger?
peuton nazhay sahn dahnzhay?

I'd like to rent . . .
Je voudrais louer . . .
zhuh voodray looay . . .

a deckchair
une chaise longue
ün shehz long

a changing room
une cabine
ün kabeen

a beach umbrella
un parasol
eun parasul

Evening Activities

Would you like to go to . . . ?
Voudriez-vous/Voudrais-tu aller . . . ?
voodreeay voo/voodray tu alay . . . ?

the movies au cinéma *oh seenayma*	**the ballet** au ballet *oh baleh*
the opera à l'opéra *a lupayra*	**a concert** à un concert *a eun konsehr*
the theatre au théâtre *oh tayahtr*	

Who's in it?
Qui joue?
kee joo?

Who's singing?
Qui chante?
kee shahnt?

Who's dancing?
Qui danse?
kee dahns?

What orchestra is playing?
Quel est le nom de l'orchestre?
kehl eh luh nom duh lurkehstr?

At what time does it begin?
À quelle heure le spectacle commence-t-il?
a kehl eur luh spehktakl kumahnsteel?

I would like to reserve/buy two tickets for . . .
Je voudrais réserver/voudrais acheter deux billets pour . . .
zhuh voodray rayzehrvay/voodrayz ashtay deu beeyay poor . . .

Could you show me a seating plan of the theatre?
Pouvez-vous me montrer un plan du théâtre?
poovay voo muh montray eun plan dü tayahtr?

Please give me two orchestra/ mezzanine/box seats.
Je voudrais deux places au parterre/ au balcon/à la loge.
zhuh voodray deu plas oh partehr/ au balkon/a la luzh

Would you like to go to a night club/ a discotheque?
Voudriez-vous/Veux-tu aller à une boîte de nuit/une discothèque?
voodreeay vooz alay a ün bwat duh nwee/ün deeskutehk?

How much does it cost to get in?
À combien s'élève l'entrée?
a konbyehn saylehv lahntray?

What's the minimum?
Quel est le prix de la consommation?
kehl eh luh pree duh la komsumasyom?

Would you like a drink?
Voulez-vous/Veux-tu quelque chose
à boire?
*voolay voo/veu tu kehlkuh shohz
a bwar?*

Getting to Know People

How are you?
Comment allez-vous?
kumahmt alay voo?

Fine, thanks. And you?
Bien, merci. Et vous?
byehm, mehrsee. ay voo?

My name is . . .
Je m'appelle . . .
zhuh mapehl . . .

This is . . .
Je vous présente . . .
zhuh voo praysahmt . . .

  my wife/my husband
  ma femme/mon mari
  ma fam/mom maree

  my daughter/my son
  ma fille/mon fils
  ma feeyuh/mom fees

  my sister/my brother
  ma soeur/mon frère
  ma seur/mom frehr

  a friend of mine
  un ami/une amie à moi
  eum amee/ün amee a mwa

Glad to meet you.
Enchanté.
ahmshahmtay

Where are you from?
D'où venez-vous?
doo vuhnay voo?

I'm from . . .
Je viens de . . .
zhuh vyehm duh . . .

Are you here on vacation?
Êtes-vous ici en vacances?
eht voo eesee ahm vakahms?

No, I'm on a business trip.
Non, je suis en voyage d'affaires.
nom, zhuh sweez ahm vwayazh dafehr

I'm here for business and pleasure.
Je fais un voyage d'affaires et
d'agrément.
*zhuh feh eum vwayazh dafehr ay
dagraymahm*

Are you on your own?
Êtes-vous seul(e)?
eht voo seul?

I'm with a friend/friends/my family.
Je suis avec un(e) ami(e)/des
amis/ma famille.
*zhuh sweez avehk eum (ün) amee/dayz
amee/ma fameeyuh*

How long have you been here?
Depuis combien de temps êtes-vous ici?
*duhpwee kombyehm duh tahm eht voo
eesee?*

I just arrived today.
Je viens d'arriver aujourd'hui.
zhuh vyehm dareevay ohzhoordwee

I arrived yesterday/a few days ago.
Je suis arrivé hier/il y a quelques jours.
*zhuh sweez areevay yehr/eel ee a
kehlkuh zhoor*

**I've been here a week/two weeks/
a month.**
Je suis ici depuis une semaine/quinze
jours/un mois.
*zhuh sweez eesee duhpweez ün
suhmehn/kehmz zhoor/eum mwa*

How do you like it here?
Est-ce que vous vous plaisez ici?
ehskuh voo voo plehzay eesee?

FRENCH

I like it very much.
Oui, je m'y plais beaucoup.
wee, zhuh mee pleh bohkoo

It's a . . . place.
C'est un endroit . . .
seht euṅ ahṅdrwa . . .

beautiful très beau *treh boh*	**relaxing** paisible *pehzeebl*
fun amusant *amüzahṅ*	**interesting** intéressant *ehṅtayrehsahṅ*

I don't like it very much.
Je ne m'y plais pas beaucoup.
zhuh nuh mee pleh pah bohkoo

It's too crowded.
Il y a trop de monde.
eel ee a troh duh moṅd

It's . . .
C'est . . .
seh(t) . . .

noisy bruyant *brüyahṅ*	**ugly** laid *leh*
boring ennuyeux *ahṅweeyeu*	**depressing** déprimant *daypreemahṅ*

How long are you going to stay?
Combien de temps resterez-vous?
koṅbyehṅ duh tahṅ rehstray voo?

A few more days/weeks.
Encore quelques jours/semaines.
ahṅkur kehlkuh zhoor/suhmehn

I'm a(n) . . .
Je suis . . .
zhuh swee(z) . . .

I'm leaving tomorrow/soon.
Je pars demain/bientôt.
zhuh par duhmehn/byehṅtoh

Are you having a good time?
Est-ce que vous vous amusez ici?
ehskuh voo vooz amüzay eesee?

Yes, very much.
Oui, beaucoup.
wee, bohkoo

No, not really.
Non, pas vraiment.
noṅ, pah vrehmahṅ

Where are you staying?
Où logez-vous?
oo luzhay voo?

We're at the . . . hotel.
Nous sommes à l'hôtel . . .
noo sumz a lohtehl . . .

We're camping.
Nous faisons du camping.
noo fayzoṅ dü kahṅpeeng

We haven't found a place yet.
Nous n'avons pas encore trouvé
une chambre.
*noo navoṅ pahz ahṅkur troovay
ün shahṅbr*

**Do you know of a good hotel/
pension?**
Connaissez-vous un bon hôtel/
une pension?
*kunaysay voo euṅ boṅ ohtehl/
ün pahṅsyoṅ?*

What do you do?
Que faites-vous dans la vie?
kuh feht voo dahṅ la vee?

artist	artiste	*arteest*
businessman	homme d'affaires	*um dafehr*
doctor	médecin	*maydsehṅ*
factory worker	ouvrier	*oovreeay*
lawyer	avocat	*avuka*
secretary	secrétaire	*sehkraytehr*
student	étudiant	*aytüdyahṅ*
teacher	professeur	*prufehseur*
writer	écrivain	*aykreevehṅ*

FRENCH

Where do you live?
Où habitez-vous?
oo abeetay voo?

I live in . . .
J'habite . . .
zhabeet . . .

the United States aux États-Unis *ohz aytaz ünee*	**Australia** en Australie *ahṅ ohstralee*
Canada au Canada *oh kanadah*	
Great Britain en Grande Bretagne *ahṅ grahṅd bruhtanyuh*	

I'm interested in . . .
Je m'intéresse . . .
zhuh mehṅtayrehs . . .

Let me know if you ever go there.
Si jamais vous y allez, faites-moi savoir.
see zhamay vooz ee alay, feht mwa savwar

Here is my address/phone number.
Voici mon adresse/numéro de téléphone.
vwasee moṅ adrehs/nümayroh duh taylayfun

What are your interests?
Quels sont vos intérêts?
kehl soṅ vohz ehṅtayreh?

anthropology	à l'anthropologie	*a lahṅtrupuluzhee*
antiques	aux antiquités	*ohz ahṅteekeetay*
archeology	à l'archéologie	*a larkayuluzhee*
architecture	à l'architecture	*a larsheetehktür*
art	à l'art	*a lar*
botany	à la botanique	*a la butaneek*
chess	aux échecs	*ohz ayshehk*
cinema	au cinéma	*oh seenayma*
coins	à la numismatique	*a la nümeesmateek*
cooking	à la cuisine	*a la kweezeen*
dance	à la danse	*a la dahṅs*
foreign languages	aux langues étrangères	*oh lahṅgz aytrahṅzhehr*
gardening	au jardinage	*oh zhardeenazh*
geology	à la géologie	*a la zhayuluzhee*
history	à l'histoire	*a leestwar*
literature	à la littérature	*a la leetayratür*
medicine	à la médecine	*a la maydseen*
music	à la musique	*a la müseek*
natural history	à l'histoire naturelle	*a leestwar natürehl*
painting	à la peinture	*a la pehṅtür*
philosophy	à la philosophie	*a la feelusufee*
photography	à la photographie	*a la futugrafee*
sculpture	à la sculpture	*a la skültür*
science	à la science	*a la seeahṅs*
sociology	à la sociologie	*a la susyulozhee*
sports	au sport	*oh spur*
theatre	au théâtre	*oh tayahtr*

May I sit here?
Puis-je m'asseoir ici?
pweezhuh maswar eesee?

Yes, if you wish.
Oui, si vous voulez.
wee, see voo voolay

Would you like a cigarette?
Voulez-vous une cigarette?
voolay vooz ün seegareht?

No, thank you. I don't smoke.
Non, merci. Je ne fume pas.
noṅ, mehrsee. zhuh nuh füm pah

Could you give me a light?
Pouvez-vous me donner du feu?
poovay voo muh dunay dü feu?

Would you like to go out with me this evening?
Voudriez-vous sortir avec moi ce soir?
voodreeay voo surteer avehk mwa suh swar?

Would you like to go . . . ?
Voudriez-vous aller . . . ?
voodreeay vooz alay . . . ?

   to dinner
   dîner
   deenay

   to a discothèque
   à une discothèque
   a ün deeskutehk

   to a party
   à une fête
   a ün feht

   to a concert
   à un concert
   a euṅ koṅsehr

   to the movies
   au cinema
   oh seenayma

   for a drive
   faire une promenade en voiture
   fehr ün pruhmnad ahṅ vwatür

Yes, thank you. That would be nice.
Oui, merci, très volontiers.
wee, mehrsee, treh vuloṅtyay

No, thank you. I'm not free this evening.
Non, merci. Je ne suis pas libre ce soir.
noṅ, mehrsee. zhuh nuh swee pah leebr suh swar

What about tomorrow?
Et demain?
ay duhmehṅ?

No, I'll be busy.
Non, je serai occupé.
noṅ, zhuh suhray üküpay

Where/When shall we meet?
Où/Quand nous trouvons-nous?
oo/kahṅ noo troovoṅ noo?

Could you meet me at . . . ?
Pouvez-vous me trouver . . . ?
poovay voo muh troovay . . . ?

I'll meet you at your hotel.
Je vous trouverai à votre hôtel.
zhuh voo troovray a vutr ohtehl

May I call you?
Puis-je vous appeler?
pweezhuh vooz aplay?

What time?
À quelle heure?
a kehl eur?

What's your number?
Quel est votre numéro de téléphone?
kehl eh vutr nümayroh duh taylayfun?

I'd like to go home now.
Je voudrais rentrer maintenant.
zhuh voodray rahṅtray mehṅtnahṅ

I'm very tired.
Je suis très fatigué(e).
zhuh swee treh fateegay

Thank you for a lovely evening.
Merci pour une soirée très agréable.
mehrsee poor ün swaray trehz agrayabl

Expressions of Admiration or Dislike

What a beautiful view!
Quelle belle vue!
kehl behl vü!

What a lovely place/town/city!
Quel bel endroit/belle ville!
kehl behl ahṅdrwa/behl veel!

FRENCH

The sea/countryside is very beautiful.
La mer/Le paysage est très belle/beau.
la mehr/luh payeesazh eh treh behl/ boh

I particularly like . . .
J'aime surtout . . .
zhehm sürtoo . . .

I don't particularly like . . .
Je n'aime pas beaucoup . . .
zhuh nehm pah bohkoo . . .

I like this country/city/place very much.
Ce pays/Cette ville/Cet endroit me plaît beaucoup.
suh payee/seht veel/seht ahñdrwa muh pleh bohkoo

the architecture	l'architecture	*larsheetehktür*
the beaches	les plages	*lay plazh*
the climate	le climat	*luh kleema*
the food	la cuisine	*la kweezeen*
the landscape	le paysage	*luh payeesazh*
the night life	la vie nocturne	*la vee nuktürn*
the people	les gens	*lay zhahñ*
the restaurants/cafés	les restaurants/cafés	*lay rehsturahn/kafay*
the shops	les magasins	*lay magazehñ*
the sights	les curiosités	*lay küryohzeetay*

EVERYDAY SITUATIONS

Problems

Are you alone?
Êtes-vous seule?

Are you waiting for someone?
Attendez-vous quelqu'un?

Yes, I'm waiting for a friend.
Oui, j'attends un ami.
wee, zhatahñz euñ amee

Am I disturbing you?
Est-ce que je vous dérange?

Leave me alone.
Laissez-moi tranquille.
lehsay mwa trahñkeel

Go away or I'll call the police.
Allez-vous en ou j'appelle la police.
alay vooz ahñ oo zhapehl la pulees

The Weather

It's a lovely day, isn't it?
C'est une belle journée, n'est-ce pas?
seht ün behl zhoornay, nehs pah?

What beautiful/awful weather we're having!
Quel beau/sale temps!
kehl boh/sal tahrñ!

Do you think it's going to rain/snow/ be sunny all day?
Croyez-vous qu'il va pleuvoir/neiger/ faire beau toute la journée?
krwahyay voo keel va pleuvwar/nehzhay/ fehr boh toot la zhoornay?

It's terribly hot today.
Il fait terriblement chaud aujourd'hui.
eel fay tehreeblmahn shohd ohzhoordwee

It's rather cold today.
Il fait assez froid aujourd'hui.
eel fay asay frwa ohzhoordwee

It's windy.
Il fait du vent.
eel fay dü vahn

It looks as though it's going to rain.
Il me semble qu'il va pleuvoir.
eel muh sahnbl keel va pleuvwar

Should I take an umbrella?
Devrais-je prendre un parapluie?
duhvrayzhuh prahndr eun paraplwee?

I hope the weather will improve.
J'espère que le temps s'améliorera.
zhehspehr kuh luh tahn samaylyurehra

Using the Telephone

Where is the nearest telephone?
Où se trouve le téléphone le plus proche?
oo suh troov luh taylayfun luh plü prush?

May I use your telephone?
Puis-je me servir de votre téléphone?
pweezhuh muh sehrveer duh vutr taylayfun?

Where can I make a long-distance phone call?
Où puis-je téléphoner à l'étranger?
oo pweezhuh taylayfunay a laytrahnzhay?

A token, please.
Un jeton, s'il vous plaît.
eun zhehton, seel voo pleh

Do you have a telephone directory?
Avez-vous un annuaire téléphonique?
avay vooz eun ahnwehr taylayfuneek?

Do you speak English?
Parlez-vous anglais?
parlay vooz ahnglay?

I want to make a collect call.
Je voudrais téléphoner en P.C.V.
zhuh voodray taylayfunay ahn pay say vay

Hello. I would like Paris 000-00-00.
Bonjour. Je voudrais le 000-00-00 à Paris.
bonzhoor. zhuh voodray luh 000-00-00 a paree

Please let me know the cost of the call afterwards.
Veuillez m'indiquer le coût de la communication quand j'aurai terminé.
veuvay mehndeekay luh koo duh la kumüneekasyon kahn zhohray tehrmeenay

Hello. This is . . .
Bonjour. C'est . . . à l'appareil.
bonzhoor. seh(t) . . . a laparehyuh

May I please speak to . . . ?
Puis-je parler à . . . ?
pweezhuh parlay a . . . ?

Could you give me extension . . . ?
Pouvez-vous me donner le poste . . . ?
poovay voo muh dunay luh pust . . . ?

Is this . . . ?
Est-ce . . . ?
ehs . . . ?

He/She isn't here at the moment.
Il/Elle n'est pas là en ce moment.
eel/ehl neh pah la ahn suh mumahn

FRENCH

Could you tell him/her that I called? My name is . . . ; my number is . . .
Pourriez-vous lui dire que j'ai téléphoné? Je m'appelle . . . ; mon numéro
de téléphone est . . .
*pooryay voo lwee deer kuh zhay taylayfunay? zhuh mapehl . . . ; mon nümayroh
duh taylayfun eh . . .*

Would you take a message, please?
Pourriez-vous prendre un message,
s'il vous plaît?
*pooryay voo prahndr eun mehsazh,
seel voo pleh?*

**Do you know when he/she will be
back?**
Savez-vous quand il/elle sera de retour?
*savay voo kahnt eel/ehl suhra duh
ruhtoor?*

I'll call back later.
Je téléphonerai de nouveau plus tard.
zhuh taylayfunray duh noovoh plü tar

Operator, could you help me, please?
Monsieur/Mademoiselle, pouvez-vous
m'aider, s'il vous plaît?
*muhsyeu/madmwazehl, poovay voo
mehday, seel voo pleh?*

I don't speak French very well.
Je ne parle pas très bien français.
zhuh nuh parl pah treh byehn frahnsay

I dialed the wrong number.
Je me suis trompé en faisant le numéro.
*zhuh muh swee trompay ahn fehzahn
luh nümayroh*

I was cut off.
Nous avons été coupés.
nooz avonz aytay koopay

Who is this?
Qui est à l'appareil?
kee eht a laparehyuh?

Hold the line, please.
Ne quittez pas.

The line is busy.
La ligne est occupée.

Hang up. I will call you back.
Accrochez. Je vous rappellerai.

What's your number?
Quel est votre numéro?

What number are you calling?
Quel numéro désirez-vous?

I think you've got the wrong number.
Je crois que vous avez fait un faux
numéro.

Post Office (Bureau de poste)

Where is the nearest post office?
Où est le bureau de poste le plus
proche?
*oo eh luh büroh duh pust luh plü
prush?*

What window do I go to for . . . ?
À quel guichet puis-je . . . ?
a kehl geeshay pweezhuh . . . ?

    stamps
    acheter des timbres
    ashtay day tehrnbr

    telegrams
    envoyer un télégramme
    ahnvwa-yay eun taylaygram

    sending/cashing a money order
    encaisser/envoyer un mandat
    international
    *ahnkehsay/ahnvwa-yay eun mahndat
    ehntehrnasyunal*

parcels	**poste restante**
envoyer un paquet	trouver la poste
ahnvwa-yay eun	restante
pakay	*troovay la pust*
	rehstahnt

FRENCH

Are there any letters for me? Here is my passport.
Est-ce qu'il y a du courier pour moi? Voici mon passeport.
ehs keel ee a dü cooryay poor mwa? vwasee moñ paspur

What's the postage for . . . ?
Quel est le tarif d'une . . . ?
kehl eh luh tareef dün . . . ?

a letter to England
lettre pour l'Angleterre
lehtr poor lahñgluhtehr

a post card to the U.S.
carte postale pour les Etats-Unis
kart pustal poor layz aytahz ünee

I want to send this (by) . . .
Je voudrais envoyer ceci . . .
zhuh voodrayz ahñvwa-yay suhsee . . .

air mail
par avion
par avyoñ

express mail
par exprès
par ehksprehs

registered mail
en recommandé
ahñ rehkumahñday

Please give me . . ./. . . centime stamps.
Voulez-vous me donner . . . timbres à . . . centimes.
voolay voo muh dunay . . . tehrhbr a . . . sahnteem

I want to send this package to . . .
Je voudrais envoyer ce paquet à . . .
zhuh voodrayz ahñvwa-yay suh pakay a . . .

What does it contain?
Que contient-il?

I want to send a telegram. Could I have a form, please?
Je voudrais envoyer un télégramme. Pourrais-je avoir une formule, s'il vous plaît?
zhuh voodrayz ahñvwa-yay euñ taylaygram. poorayzhuh avvar ün furmül, seel voo pleh?

How much is it per word?
Quel est le tarif par mot?
kehl eh luh tareef par moh?

Bank (Banque)

Where's the nearest bank?
Où se trouve la banque la plus proche?
oo suh troov la bahñk la plü prush?

Where can I cash a traveler's check?
Où puis-je encaisser un chèque de voyage?
oo pweezhuh ahñkehsay euñ shehk duh vwayazh?

What is the fee?
Quelle commission prenez-vous?
kehl kumeesyoñ pruhnay voo?

What's the rate of exchange?
Quel est le cours du change?
kehl eh luh koor dü shahñzh?

Do you issue money on this credit card?
Puis-je toucher de l'argent sur cette carte de crédit?
pweezhuh tooshay duh larzhañ sür seht kart duh kraydee?

Can you cash a personal check?
Puis-je toucher un chèque à ordre?
pweezhuh tooshay euñ shehk a urdr?

I have a letter of credit/bank draft.
J'ai une lettre de crédit/un mandat.
zhay ün lehtr duh kraydee/euñ mahñda

FRENCH

I'm expecting money from . . . ; has it arrived?
Je attends de l'argent de . . . ; est-il arrivé?
zhatahm duh larzham duh . . . ; ehteel areevay?

I would like to make a deposit.
Je voudrais déposer ceci sur mon compte.
zhuh voodray daypuzay suhsee sür mom korht

I would like to open an account.
Je voudrais ouvrir un compte.
zhuh voodrayz oovreer eum korht

I would like to change some . . . for some . . .
Je voudrais changer des . . . pour des . . .
zhuh voodray shahnzhay day . . . poor day . . .

Shopping (Faire du shopping)

I'm looking for a . . .
Je cherche . . .
zhuh shehrsh . . .

bakery	une boulangerie	ün boolahmzhehree
barber shop	un coiffeur	eum kwafür
bookshop	une librairie	ün leebrehree
butcher shop	une boucherie	ün booshree
delicatessen	une charcuterie	ün sharkütree
department store	un grand magasin	eum grahm magazehm
drug store	une pharmacie	ün farmasee
fish store	un marchand de poissons	eum marshahm duh pwasom
greengrocer's	un magasin de primeurs	eum magazehm duh preemeur
hairdresser	un coiffeur (pour dames)	eum kwafür (poor dam)
hardware store	une quincaillerie	ün kehmkahyuhree
laundry/dry cleaner	une blanchisserie	ün blahmsheesree
liquor store	un magasin de spiritueux	eum magazehm duh speereetüeu
market	un marché	eum marshay
newsstand	un kiosque à journaux	eum kyusk a zhoornoh
shoe repair	un cordonnier	eum kurdunyay
shoe store	un magasin de chaussures	eum magazehm duh shohsür
sporting goods store	un magasin d'articles de sport	eum magazehm darteekl duh spur
stationery store	une papeterie	ün papuhtree
supermarket	un supermarché	eum süpehrmarshay
tobacconist's	un bureau de tabac	eum büroh duh tabak

Where can I buy . . .
Où puis-je acheter . . .
oo pweezhuh ashtay . . .

May I help you?
Puis-je vous être utile?

What would you like?
Que désirez-vous?

FRENCH

I would like . . .
Je voudrais . . .
zhuh voodray . . .

Can you show me . . .
Pouvez-vous me montrer . . .
poovay voo muh montray . . .

Do you have . . . ?
Avez-vous . . . ?
avay voo . . . ?

I'm just looking, thanks.
Je ne fais que regarder, merci.
zhuh nuh fay kuh ruhgarday, mehrsee

How much is this?
Combien coûte ceci?
kornbyehn koot suhsee?

Could you write that down, please?
Pourriez-vous l'écrire, s'il vous plaît?
pooryay voo laycreer, seel voo pleh?

Do you accept traveler's checks/
   credit cards dollars/pounds?
Acceptez-vous des chèques de voyage/
   cartes de crédit/dollars/livres?
*aksehptay voo day shehk duh vwayazh/
   kart duh kraydee/dular/leevr?*

I think there's an error on this bill.
Je crois qu'il y a une erreur dans
   l'addition.
*zhuh krwah keel ee a ün ehreur dahn
   ladeesyon*

Could you ship it to this address?
Pouvez-vous l'envoyer à cette adresse?
*poovay voo lahnvway-yay a seht
   adrehs?*

Bookstore/Newsstand/Stationer (Librairie/Vendeur de journaux/Papeterie)

I'd like to buy . . .
Je voudrais acheter . . .
zhuh voodrayz ashtay . . .

an address book	un carnet d'adresses	*eun karnay dadrehs*
an appointment book	un carnet de rendez-vous	*eun karnay duh rahnday voo*
a French-English dictionary	un dictionnaire français-anglais	*eun deeksyunehr frahnsay ahnglay*
some envelopes	des enveloppes	*dayz ahnvlup*
an eraser	une gomme	*ün gum*
a French grammar	une grammaire française	*ün gramehr frahnsehz*
a guidebook	un guide	*eun geed*
a map of the town	un plan de la ville	*eun plahn duh la veel*
a road map (of)	une carte routière (de)	*ün kart rootyehr (duh)*
an American/English newspaper	un journal américain/anglais	*eun zhoornal amayreekehn/ahnglay*
a notebook	un cahier	*eun ka-yay*
a pen	un stylo	*eun steeloh*
a pencil	un crayon	*eun krehyon*
some post cards	des cartes postales	*day kart pustal*
some Scotch tape	du Scotch	*dü skutsh*
some writing paper	du papier à lettres	*dü papyay a lehtr*

Clothing Store (Magasin d'habillement)

Could you show me a . . . like the one in the window?
Pouvez-vous me montrer . . . comme celui dans la vitrine?
poovay voo muh moṅtray . . . kum suhlwee dahṅ la veetreen?

Could you show me something . . . ?
Pouvez-vous me montrer quelque chose . . . ?
poovay voo muh moṅtray kehlkuh shohz . . .

   bigger/smaller
   de plus grand/petit
   duh plü grahṅ/puhtee

   lighter/darker
   de plus clair/foncé
   duh plü klehr/foṅsay

   in another color
   d'une autre couleur
   dün ohtr kooleur

   not so expensive
   de pas si cher
   duh pah see shehr

   of better quality
   d'une qualité meilleure
   dün kaleetay mehyeur

My size is . . .
Je porte du . . .
zhuh purt du . . .

I'm not sure what my size is.
Je ne suis pas sûr de ma taille.
zhuh nuh swee pah sür duh ma tahyuh

May I try it on?
Puis-je l'essayer?
pweezhuh lehsehyay?

It doesn't fit.
Cela ne me va pas.
suhla nuh muh va pah

It's too . . .
C'est trop . . .
seh troh . . .

   tight/loose
   étroit/large
   aytrwa/larzh

   short/long
   court/long
   koor/loṅ

Can you show me anything else?
Pouvez-vous me montrer quelque chose d'autre?
poovay voo muh moṅtray kehlkuh shohz dohtr?

Very well; I'll take it.
D'accord. Je le prends.
dakur. zhuh luh prahṅ

No, it's not really what I was looking for.
Non; ce n'est pas exactement ce que je cherchais.
noṅ; suh neh pahz ehksaktuhmahṅ suh kuh zhuh shehrshay

No, it's too expensive. I'll give you . . . for it.
Non, c'est trop cher. Je vous en donne . . .
noṅ, seh troh shehr. zhuh vooz ahṅ dun . . .

Articles of Clothing (Vêtements)

I'd like a/an/some . . .
Je voudrais . . .
zhuh voodray(z) . . .

bath robe	une robe de chambre	*ün rub duh shahṅbr*
bathing suit	un costume de bain	*euṅ kustüm duh behṅ*
blouse	un chemisier	*ün shuhmeezyay*

FRENCH

boots	des bottes	day but
bra	un soutien-gorge	euñ sootyehñ gurzh
cardigan	un gilet de tricot	euñ zheelay duh treekoh
coat	un manteau	euñ mahñtoh
dress	une robe	ün rub
evening dress	une robe du soir	ün rub dü swar
girdle	une ceinture	ün sehñtür
gloves	des gants	day gahñ
hat	un chapeau	euñ shapoh
jacket	un veston	euñ vehstoñ
nightgown	une chemise de nuit	ün shuhmeez duh nwee
pants	des pantalons	day pahntaloñ
panty-hose	des collants	day kulañ
pullover	un pull	euñ pül
pyjamas	un pyjama	euñ peezhahma
raincoat	un imperméable	euñ ehrñpehrmayabl
sandals	des sandales	day sahñdal
scarf	un foulard	euñ foolar
shirt	une chemise	ün shuhmeez
long sleeves	manches longues	mahñsh loñg
short sleeves	manches courtes	mahñsh koort
shoes	des chaussures	day shohsür
shorts	des shorts	day shur
skirt	une jupe	ün zhoop
slip	un jupon	euñ zhoopoñ
slippers	des pantoufles	day pahñtoofl
socks	des chaussettes	day shohseht
stockings	des bas	day bah
suit	un complet	euñ korñplay
sweater	un chandail	euñ shahñdahyuh
T-shirt	un teeshirt	euñ teesheurt
tennis shoes	des pantoufles de tennis	day pahñtoofl duh tehnees
tie	une cravate	ün kravat
tuxedo	un smoking	euñ smukeeng
underwear (men's)	des caleçons/un slip	day kalsoñ/euñ sleep
underwear (women's)	un slip	euñ sleep
belt	une ceinture	ün sehñtür
button	un bouton	euñ bootoñ
pocket	une poche	ün push
shoe laces	des lacets	day lasay
zipper	une fermeture-éclair	ün fehrmuhtür ayklehr

Colors

beige	beige	behzh
black	noir	nwar
blue	bleu	bleu
brown	brun	breuñ

FRENCH

gold	doré	*duray*
green	vert	*vehr*
gray	gris	*gree*
off-white	crème	*krehm*
orange	orange	*uraṅzh*
pink	rose	*rohz*
purple	violet	*vyuleh*
red	rouge	*roozh*
silver	argenté	*arzhahṅtay*
turquoise	turquoise	*türkwaz*
white	blanc	*blahṅ*
yellow	jaune	*zhohn*

Fabrics

acrylic	acrylique	*akreeleek*
corduroy	velours côtelé	*vuhloor kutlay*
cotton	coton	*kutoṅ*
felt	feutre	*feutr*
flannel	flanelle	*flanehl*
lace	dentelle	*dahṅtehl*
leather	cuir	*kweer*
linen	lin	*lehṅ*
rayon	rayon	*rehyoṅ*
satin	satin	*satehṅ*
silk	soie	*swah*
suede	daim	*dehrh*
synthetic	synthétique	*sehṅtayteek*
velvet	velours	*vuhloor*
wool	laine	*lehn*

Jewelry (Bijoux)

bracelet	un bracelet	*euṅ brasleh*
necklace	un collier	*euṅ kulyay*
ring	une bague	*ün bag*
wristwatch	une montre-bracelet	*ün moṅtr brasleh*
diamond	diamant	*dyamahṅ*
gold	or	*ur*
platinum	platine	*plateen*
silver	argent	*arzhahṅ*
stainless steel	inoxydable	*eenukseedabl*
plated	plaqué	*plakay*

Buying Food for Picnics and Snacks

I'd like (some) . . .
Je voudrais . . .
zhuh voodray(z) . . .

apples	des pommes	*day pum*
apple juice	du jus de pommes	*dü zhü duh pum*
bananas	des bananes	*day banan*
bread	du pain	*dü pehñ*
butter	du beurre	*dü beur*
cake	du gâteau	*dü gatoh*
candy	des bonbons	*day boñboñ*
carrots	des carottes	*day karut*
cereal	des céréales	*day sayrayal*
cheese	du fromage	*dü frumazh*
chocolate	du chocolat	*dü shukula*
coffee	du café	*dü kafay*
cold cuts	de la charcuterie	*de la sharkütree*
cookies	des biscuits	*day beeskwee*
crackers	des biscuits salés	*day beeskwee salay*
cucumbers	des concombres	*day koñkorñbr*
eggs	des oeufs	*dayz eu*
frankfurters	des saucisses de Francfort	*day sohsees duh frahñkfur*
grapefruits	des pamplemousses	*day pahrñplmoos*
grapefruit juice	du jus de pamplemousse	*dü zhü duh pahrñplmoos*
ham	du jambon	*dü zhahrñboñ*
ice cream	de la glace	*duh la glas*
lemons	des citrons	*day seetroñ*
lettuce	de la laitue	*duh la lehtü*
melon	des melons	*day muhloñ*
milk	du lait	*dü leh*
mustard	de la moutarde	*duh la mootard*
oil	de l'huile	*duh lweel*
oranges	des oranges	*dayz urahñzh*
orange juice	du jus d'orange	*du zhü durahñzh*
peaches	des pêches	*day pehsh*
pears	des poires	*day pwar*
pepper	du poivre	*dü pwavr*
peppers	des poivres	*day pwavr*
pickles	des cornichons	*day kurneeshoñ*
plums	des prunes	*day prün*
potato chips	des chips	*day sheep*
potatoes	des pommes de terre	*day pum duh tehr*
raspberries	des framboises	*day frahrñbwaz*
rolls	des petits pains	*day puhtee pehñ*
salad	de la salade	*duh la salad*
salami	du salami	*dü sahlahmee*
salt	du sel	*dü sehl*

FRENCH

sandwiches	des sandwiches	*day sahñdweetsh*
sausages	des saucisses	*day sohsees*
soft drinks	des boissons gazeuses	*day bwasoñ gahzeuz*
spaghetti	des spaghetti	*day spagehtee*
strawberries	des fraises	*day frehz*
sugar	du sucre	*dü sükr*
tea	du thé	*dü tay*
tomatoes	des tomates	*day tuhmat*
yoghurt	du yogourt	*dü yugoort*

a box/can of	une boite de	*ün bwat duh*
a jar of	un verre de	*euñ vehr duh*
a half kilo of	une livre de	*ün leevr duh*
a kilo of	un kilo de	*euñ keeloh duh*
a packet of	un paquet de	*euñ pakay duh*
a slice of	une tranche de	*ün trahñsh duh*

a bottle opener	un décapsuleur	*euñ daykapsüleur*
a corkscrew	un tire-bouchon	*euñ teer booshoñ*
paper napkins/plates	des serviettes/assiettes en papier	*day sehrvyeht/asyehtz ahñ papyay*
plastic utensils	de l'argenterie en plastique	*duh larzhahñtree ahñ plasteek*
a can opener	un tire-bouchon	*euñ teer booshoñ*

I'll have a little more.
J'en prendrai encore un peu.
zhahñ prahñdray ahñkur euñ peu

That's too much.
C'est trop.
seh troh

Could I have a bag, please?
Pourrais-je avoir un sac, s'il vous plaît?
poorayzhuh avwar euñ sak, seel voo pleh?

Pharmacy (Pharmacie)

Can you make up this prescription?
Pouvez-vous me préparer cette ordonnance?
poovay voo muh prehparay seht urdunahñs?

How long will it take?
Combien de temps vous faudra-t-il?
koñbyehñ duh tahm voo fohdrateel?

I'll come back in a little while.
Je reviendrai plus tard.
zhuh revyehñdray plü tar

Could you please write down the instructions in English?
Pourriez-vous écrire les instructions en anglais, s'il vous plaît?
pooryay vooz aycreer layz ehñstrüksyoñ ahñ ahñglay, seel voo pleh?

FRENCH

Can you give me something for . . .
Pouvez-vous me donner quelque chose contre . . .
poovay voo dunay kehluh shohz contr . . .

a cold	un rhume	*euh rüm*
constipation	la constipation	*la konsteepasyon*
a cough	une toux	*ün too*
a cut	une coupure	*ün koopür*
diarrhea	la diarrhée	*la dyaray*
hay fever	le rhume des foins	*luh rüm day fwehn*
a headache	le mal à la tête	*luh mal a la teht*
indigestion	les indigestions	*layz ehndeezhehstyon*
an insect bite/sting	une piqûre d'insecte	*un peekür dehnsehkt*
nausea	la nausée	*la nohzay*
a sore throat	le mal à la gorge	*luh mal a la gurzh*
a sunburn	un coup de soleil	*eun koo duh sulehyuh*
travel sickness	le mal au coeur	*luh mal oh keur*
an upset stomach	les indigestions	*layz ehndeezhehstyon*

I'd like a/an/some . . .
Je voudrais . . .
zhuh voodray(z) . . .

aspirin	de l'aspirine	*duh laspeereen*
bandage	une bande velpeau	*ün bahnd vehlpoh*
Band-aids	du sparadrap	*dü sparadra*
cough syrup	du sirop pour la toux	*dü seerup poor la too*
cough drops	des pastilles contre la toux	*day pasteeyuh kontr la too*
contraceptives	des contraceptifs	*day kontrasehpteef*
eye drops	des gouttes pour les yeux	*day goot poor layz yeu*
insect repellent	de la crème contre les insectes	*duh la krehm kontr layz ehnsehkt*
laxative	un laxatif	*euh laksateef*
sleeping pills	des somnifères	*day sumneefehr*
sanitary napkins	des serviettes hygiénique	*day sehrvyeht eezhyayneek*
tampons	des tampons périodiques	*day tahnpon payryudeek*

Toilet Articles

I'd like to buy a/an/some . . .
Je voudrais acheter . . .
zhuh voodrayz ashtay . . .

after-shave lotion	de la lotion après rasage	*duh la lusyon apreh rahzazh*
cream	une crème	*ün krehm*
cleansing cream	démaquillante	*daymakeeyahnt*
hand cream	pour les mains	*poor leh mehn*
moisturizing cream	hydratante	*eedratahnt*

FRENCH

deodorant	du déodorant	dü dayudurahñ
emery board	une lime à ongles	ün leem a oñgl
razor	un rasoir	euñ rahzwar
razor blades	des lames de rasoir	day lahm duh rahzwar
shampoo	du shampooing	dü shahrhpwehñ
shaving cream	de la crème à raser	duh la krehm a rahzay
soap	du savon	dü savoñ
suntan oil/cream	de l'huile/crème solaire	duh lweel/krehm sulehr
talcum powder	du talc	dü talk
tissues	des mouchoirs en papier	day mooshwar ahñ papay
toilet paper	du papier hygiénique	dü papyay eezhyayneek
toothbrush	une brosse à dents	ün brus a dahñ
toothpaste	de la pâte dentifrice	duh la paht dahñteefrees
tweezers	une pince à épiler	ün pehñs a aypeelay

Note: For makeup and perfume, go to a *parfumerie*.

Photography

I'd like a good/inexpensive camera, please.
Je voudrais un bon appareil/un appareil bon marché.
zhuh voodrayz euñ boñ aparehyuh/euñ aparehyuh boñ marshay

I'd like some . . . film for this camera.
Je voudrais un film pour cet appareil . . .
zhuh voodrayz euñ feelm poor seht aparehyuh . . .

black and white
en noir et blanc
ahñ nwar ay blahñ

color
en couleur
ahñ kooleur

color slide
diapositive en couleur
deeapuzeeteev ahñ kooleur

I need . . . for this camera.
J'ai besoin . . . pour cet appareil.
zhay buhzwehñ . . . poor seht aparehyuh

batteries
des piles
day peel

a lens
d'un objectif
deuñ ubzhehkteef

a flash cube
d'un flash
deuñ flash

How much do you charge for processing?
Combien coûte le développement?
korhbyehñ koot luh dayvehlupmahñ?

I'd like . . . prints/slides of each negative . . .
Je voudrais . . . copies/diapositives de chaque négatif . . .
zhuh voodray . . . cupee/deeapuzeeteev duh shak naygateef . . .

with a matt finish
sur papier mat
sür papyay mat

with a glossy finish
sur papier brillant
sür papyay breeyahñ

I would like an enlargement of this please.
Je voudrais un agrandissement de ceci, s'il vous plaît.
zhuh voodrayz euñ agrahñdeesmahñ duh suhsee, seel voo pleh

When will it be ready?
Quand est-ce que ce sera prêt?
kahñt ehskuh suh surah preh?

Tobacco Shop (Tabac)

I'd like a pack/carton of cigarettes, please.
Je voudrais un paquet/une cartouche de cigarettes, s'il vous plaît.
zhuh voodrayz euḿ pakay/ün kartoosh duh seegareht, seel voo pleh

Do you have . . . ?
Avez-vous . . .
avay voo . . . ?

I'd like . . .
Je voudrais . . .
zhuh voodray(z) . . .

    pipe tobacco
    du tabac pour pipe
    dü tabak poor peep

    a cigarette lighter
    un briquet
    euḿ breekay

lighter fluid
de l'essence à briquet
duh lehsahńs a breekay

matches
des alumettes
days alümeht

a pipe
une pipe
ün peep

Laundry/Dry Cleaner (Blanchisserie/Teinturerie)

Where is the nearest laundry/dry cleaner?
Où se trouve la blanchisserie/teinturerie la plus proche?
oo suh troov la blahńsheesree/tehńtür-ree la plü prush?

I'd like to have these clothes washed and ironed.
Je voudrais faire laver et repasser ces vêtements.
zhuh voodray fehr lavay ay ruhpasay seh vehtmahń

Please have this dry cleaned.
Faites nettoyer ceci, s'il vous plaît.
feht nehtwa-yay suhsee, seel voo pleh

Can you remove this stain?
Pouvez-vous ôter cette tache?
poovay vooz ohtay seht tash?

Can you mend this?
Pouvez-vous raccommoder ceci?
poovay voo rakumuday suhsee?

When will it be ready?
Quand sera-ce prêt?
kahń suhra suh preh?

I need it . . .
Il me le faut . . .
eel muh luh foh . . .

    this afternoon
    cet après-midi
    seht aprehmeedee

    this evening
    ce soir
    suh swar

    tomorrow
    demain
    duhmehń

Repairs

Can you fix this?
Pouvez-vous me réparer ceci?
poovay voo muh rayparay suhsee?

How long will it take?
Combien de temps faut-il compter?
korhbyehm duh tahm fohteel korhtay?

How much will it cost?
Combien cela coutera-t-il?
korhbyehm suhla kootehra-teel?

When will it be ready?
Quand est-ce que ce sera prêt?
kahmt ehskuh suh suhra preh?

HEALTH

At the Doctor

I don't feel well.
Je ne me sens pas bien.
zhuh nuh muh pah byehm

Where can I find a doctor who speaks English?
Où puis-je trouver un médecin qui parle anglais?
oo pweezhuh troovay eum maydsehm kee parl ahmglay?

Could you call a doctor for me?
Pourriez-vous m'appeler un médecin?
pooray voo maplay eum maydsehn?

Is there a doctor here?
Y a-t-il un médecin ici?
ee ateel eum maydsehm eesee?

I have (a) . . .
J'ai . . .
zhay . . .

Must I make an appointment?
Faut-il prendre rendezvous?
fohteel prahmdr rahmday voo?

I must see a doctor right away.
Il faut que je voie un médecin tout de suite.
eel foh kuh zhuh vwa eum maydsehm toot sweet

I feel ill.
Je suis malade.
zhuh swee malad

I've got a pain here.
J'ai mal ici.
zhay mal eesee

backache	mal au dos	*mal oh doh*
constipation	la constipation	*la korhsteepasyorh*
cough	une toux	*ün too*
cramps	des crampes	*day krahrhp*
diarrhea	la diarrhée	*la dyaray*
fever	la fièvre	*la fyehvr*
hemorrhoids	des hémorroïdes	*dayz aymoroeed*
headache	mal à la tête	*mal a la teht*
insect bite	une piqûre d'insecte	*ün peekür dehmsehkt*
lump	une bosse	*ün bos*
nausea	la nausée	*la nohzay*
rash	une éruption	*ün ayrüpsyorh*
swelling	une enflure	*ün ahmflür*
wound	une blessure	*ün blehsür*

I have difficulty breathing.
J'ai du mal à respirer.
zhay dü mal a rayspeeray

I feel dizzy/faint.
J'ai des vertiges/nausées.
zhay deh vehrteezh/nohzay

I've been vomiting.
J'ai eu des vomissements
zhay ü deh vumeesmahn

I can't eat/sleep.
Je ne peux pas manger/je ne dors pas.
zhuh nuh peu pah mahn̄zhay/zhuh nuh dur pah

I've cut/burned myself.
Je me suis coupé/brûlé.
zhuh muh swee koopay/brülay

I think I've sprained/broken my wrist/ankle.
Je crois que je me suis foulé/cassé/le poignet/la cheville.
zhuh krwah kuh muh swee foolay/kasay/luh pwahnyay/la shuhveeyuh

It hurts when I move . . .
J'ai mal quand je bouge . . .
zhay mal kahn̄ zhuh boozh . . .

I'm allergic to penicillin/iodine.
Je suis allergique à la penicilline/l'iode.
zhuh sweez alehrzheek a la pehneeceeleen/leeyohd

Doctor to Patient

Where does it hurt?
Où avez-vous mal?

How long have you had this trouble?
Depuis combien de temps vous sentez-vous ainsi?

Please undress (to the waist).
Déshabillez-vous (jusqu'à la taille) s'il vous plaît.

Does that hurt?
Cela vous fait-il mal?

I'll need a urine specimen/blood sample.
J'aurai besoin d'un prélèvement de votre urine/d'une prise de sang.

Are you taking any medication?
Prenez-vous des médicaments?

You have . . .
Vous avez . . .

Are you allergic to . . .?
Êtes-vous allergique à . . .?

I will prescribe some medication for you.
Je vais vous prescrire des médicaments.

Take these . . . times a day before/after each meal/every morning/evening.
Prenez-en . . . fois par jour, avant/après chaque repas/tous les matins/soirs.

You must rest/stay in bed for . . . days
Vous devez vous reposer/garder le lit pendant . . . jours.

It's nothing serious.
Ce n'est rien de grave.

You must go to the hospital.
Vous devez aller à l'hôpital.

an abscess	un abcès	**an infection**	une infection
appendicitis	une appendicite	**the flu**	la grippe
a cold	un rhume	**tonsillitis**	les amygdales
food poisoning	un empoisonnement	**an ulcer**	un ulcère
a hernia	une hernie		

At the Dentist

Can you recommend a good dentist?
Pouvez-vous me recommander un bon dentiste?
poovay voo muh ruhkumahńday euń bоń dahńteest?

I would like to see Dr. . . . as soon as possible.
Je voudrais voir le docteur . . . aussitôt que possible.
zhuh voodray vwar luh dukteur . . . ohseetoh kuh puseebl

I have a bad toothache.
J'ai très mal aux dents.
zhay treh mal oh dahń

My tooth has broken.
Une dent s'est cassée.
ün dahń seh kasay

My gums are bleeding/sore.
Mes gencives saignent/me font mal.
may zhahńseev sehńyuh/muh foń mal

I have an abscess.
J'ai un abcès.
zhay euń absehs

I've lost/broken a filling.
J'ai perdu un plombage.
zhay pehrdü euń plorhbazh

Can you give me temporary treatment?
Pouvez-vous faire un traitement provisoire?
poovay voo fehr euń trehtmahń pruveeswar?

Please don't extract it.
Ne l'arrachez pas, s'il vous plaît.
nuh larashay pah, seel voo pleh

Please give me a local anesthetic.
Je voudrais une anesthésie locale, s'il vous plaît.
zhuh voodrayz ün anehstayzee lukal, seel voo pleh

Dentist to Patient

I want you to have an X-ray.
Il vous faut un examen radiographique.

I will fill the tooth.
Je vais vous faire un plombage.

This tooth must come out.
Il faut arracher cette dent.

Optician

I have broken my glasses.
J'ai cassé mes lunettes.
zhay casay may lüneht

Can you repair them?
Pouvez-vous me les réparer?
poovay voo muh lay rayparay?

I have lost a contact lens.
J'ai perdu un verre de contact.
zhay pehrdü euń vehr duh końtakt

Could you make me another one?
Pouvez-vous m'en faire un autre?
poovay voo mahń fehr euń ohtr?

When will it/they be ready?
Quand est-qui'il(s) sera/seront prêt(s)?
kahńt ehskeel suhra/suhroń preh?

I need wetting/soaking solution for hard/soft contact lenses.
J'ai besoin d'un liquide pour la lubrification/conservation des verres de contact durs/souples.
zhay buhzwehn deun leekeed poor la lübreefeekasyon/konsehrvasyon day vehr duh kontakt dür/soopl

My contact lenses are bothering me. Would you have a look at them?
Mes verres de contact m'irritent les yeux. Pouvez-vous me les contrôler?
mayvehr duh kontakt meereet layz yeu. poovay voo muh lay kontrohlay?

Paying the Doctor/Dentist/Optician

How much do I owe you?
Combien vous dois-je?
kombyehn voo dwahzhuh?

Can you send me a bill?
Pouvez-vous m'envoyer la note, s'il vous plaît?
poovay voo mahnvwayay la nut, seel voo pleh?

I have health insurance.
J'ai une assurance.
zhay ün asurahns

EMERGENCY

Loss or Theft

Excuse me, can you help me?
Excusez-moi. Pouvez-vous m'aider?
ehksküzay mwa. poovay voo mehday?

Where's the police station?
Où se trouve le commissariat de police?
oo suh troov luh kumeesarya duh pulees?

Where's the American/British/ Canadian consulate?
Où se trouve le consulat américain/ anglais/canadien?
oo suh troov luh konsüla amayreekehn/ ahnglay/kanadyehn?

Where is the lost and found?
Où se trouve le bureau des objets trouvés?
oo suh troov luh büroh dayz ubzheh troovay?

I've lost my/Someone has stolen my . . .
J'ai perdu/Quelqu'un a volé . . .
zhay pehrdü/kehlkeun a vulay . . .

passport	mon passeport	*mon paspur*
money	mon argent	*mon arzhahn*
traveler's checks	mes chèques de voyage	*may shehk duh vwayazh*
credit cards	mes cartes de crédit	*may kart duh kraydee*
luggage	mes bagages	*may bagazh*
plane tickets	mes billets d'avion	*may beeyay davyon*
handbag	mon sac	*mon sak*

I left something in the train/taxi/bus.
J'ai laissé quelque chose dans le train/taxi/bus.
zhay lehsay kehlkuh shohz dahn luh trehn/taksee/büs

FRENCH

Asking for Help

Help!	Au secours!	*oh suhkoor!*
Police!	Police! Secours!	*pulees! suhkoor!*
Fire!	Au feu! Pompiers!	*oh feu! pornpay!*

TIME/DATES/NUMBERS

Time/Date

What time is it?		It's ...
Quelle heure est-il?		Il est ...
kehl eur ehteel?		*eel eh ...*

two o'clock	deux heures	*deuz eur*
ten past three	trois heures dix	*trwahz eur dees*
four fifteen	quatre heures et quart	*katr eur ay kar*
twenty past five	cinq heures vingt	*sehnk eur vehn*
six-thirty	six heures et demi	*seez eur ay duhmee*
quarter to eight	huit heures moins quart	*hweet eur mwehn kar*
five to eight	huit heures moins cinq	*hweet eur mwehn sehnk*

It's midnight.	Il est minuit.	*eel eh meenwee*
It's one o'clock.	Il est une heure.	*eel eht ün eur*

sunrise	l'aube	*lohb*
morning	le matin	*luh matehn*
noon	midi	*meedee*
afternoon	l'après-midi	*laprehmeedee*
sunset	le coucher de soleil	*luh kooshay duh sulehyuh*
evening	le soir	*luh swar*
night	la nuit	*la nwee*

It's early/late.		The date is ...
Il est tôt/tard.		Nous sommes le ...
eel eh toh/tar		*noo sum luh ...*

What's the date today?
Quel jour sommes-nous?
kehl zhoor sum noo?

Days of the Week

Monday	lundi	*lundee*
Tuesday	mardi	*mardee*
Wednesday	mercredi	*mehrkruhdee*
Thursday	jeudi	*zheudee*
Friday	vendredi	*vahndruhdee*
Saturday	samedi	*samdee*
Sunday	dimanche	*deemahnsh*

FRENCH

Seasons

spring	printemps	*prehṅtahṅ*
summer	été	*aytay*
autumn	automne	*ohtun*
winter	hiver	*eevehr*

Months

January	janvier	*zhaṅveeyay*
February	février	*fehvreeay*
March	mars	*mars*
April	avril	*avreel*
May	mai	*may*
June	juin	*zhwehṅ*
July	juillet	*zhweeyay*
August	août	*oo*
September	septembre	*sehptarhbr*
October	octobre	*uktubr*
November	novembre	*nuvaṅbr*
December	décembre	*daysarhbr*
this year	cette année	*seht anay*
last week	la semaine dernière	*la suhmehn dehrnyehr*
next month	le mois prochaine	*luh mwa prushehn*
today	aujourd'hui	*ohzhoordwee*
yesterday	hier	*yehr*
tomorrow	demain	*duhmehṅ*
the day before yesterday	avant-hier	*avahṅtyehr*
the day after tomorrow	après-demain	*aprayduhmehn*
Christmas	Noël	*nuehl*
Easter	Pâques	*pahk*

Numbers

0	zéro	*zayroh*
1	un	*euṅ*
2	deux	*deu*
3	trois	*trwah*

FRENCH

4	quatre	*katr*
5	cinq	*sehnk*
6	six	*sees*
7	sept	*seht*
8	huit	*hweet*
9	neuf	*neuf*
10	dix	*dees*
11	onze	*onz*
12	douze	*dooz*
13	treize	*trehz*
14	quatorze	*katurze*
15	quinze	*kehnz*
16	seize	*sehz*
17	dix-sept	*dees seht*
18	dix-huit	*dees-hweet*
19	dix-neuf	*dees-neuf*
20	vingt	*vehn*
21	vingt-et-un	*vehn ay eun*
22	vingt-deux	*vehn deu*
23	vingt-trois	*vehn trwah*
24	vingt-quatre	*vehn katr*
25	vingt-cinq	*vehn sehn*
26	vingt-six	*vehn sees*
27	vingt-sept	*vehn seht*
28	vingt-huit	*vehn hweet*
29	vingt-neuf	*vehn neuf*
30	trente	*trahnt*
40	quarante	*karahnt*
50	cinquante	*sehnkahnt*
60	soixante	*swasahnt*
70	soixante-dix	*swasahnt dees*
71	soixante et onze	*swasahnt ay onz*
72	soixante douze	*swasahnt dooz*
80	quatre-vingts	*katr vehn*
81	quatre-vingt-un	*katr vehn eun*
90	quatre-vingt-dix	*katr vehn dees*
91	quatre-vingt-onze	*katr vehn onz*
100	cent	*sahn*
101	cent un	*sahn eun*
102	cent deux	*sahn deu*
150	cent cinquante	*sahn sehnkahnt*
200	deux cents	*deu sahn*
300	trois cents	*trwah sahn*
400	quatre cents	*katr sahn*
500	cinq cents	*sehnk sahn*
600	six cents	*sees sahn*
700	sept cents	*seht sahn*
800	huit cents	*hweet sahn*
900	neuf cents	*neuf sahn*
1000	mille	*meel*
1100	mille cent	*meel sahn*

FRENCH

1200	mille deux cents	*meel deu sahn*
2000	deux mille	*deu meel*
5000	cinq mille	*sahn meel*
10,000	dix mille	*dee meel*
50,000	cinquante mille	*sehnkahnt meel*
100,000	cent mille	*sahn meel*
1,000,000	un million	*eun meelyon*

first	premier	*pruhmyay*
second	deuxième	*deuzyehm*
third	troisième	*trwahzyehm*
fourth	quatrième	*katryehm*
fifth	cinquième	*sehnkyehm*
sixth	sixième	*seezyehm*
seventh	septième	*sehtyehm*
eighth	huitième	*hweetyehm*
ninth	neuvième	*neuvyehm*
tenth	dixième	*deezyehm*
eleventh	onzième	*onzyehm*
twelfth	douzième	*doozyehm*

a half	une moitié	*ün mwatyay*
a quarter	un quart	*eun kar*
a third	un tiers	*eun tyehr*

FRENCH DICTIONARY

Only the masculine form of an adjective is shown if, as is usual, for the feminine a final *e* is added; in other cases, both forms are given. In some instances, which will be apparent, the same form is used for masculine and feminine (for example, *malade*).

A

a, an **un** (f. **une**)
able, to be **pouvoir**
about **environ**
above **au-dessus**
abroad **à l'étranger**
absent **absent**
absolutely **absolument**
accept, to **accepter**
accident **accident** (m.)
accompany, to **accompagner**
according to **selon**
accustomed **habitué**
ache **douleur** (f.)
across **à travers**
acquaintance **connaissance** (f.)
actor **acteur** (m.)
add, to **ajouter**
address **adresse** (f.)
admire, to **admirer**
admission **entrée** (f.)
advertisement **publicité** (f.)
advice **conseil** (m.)
advise, to **conseiller**
afraid, to be **avoir peur**
after **après**
afternoon **après-midi** (m.)
again **encore**
against **contre**
age **âge** (m.)
agency **agence** (f.)
ago **il y a**
agree, to **être d'accord**
agreeable **agréable**
agreed **d'accord**
ahead **en avant**
air **air** (m.)
air conditioning **climatisation** (f.)

air force **armeé de l'air** (f.)
air mail **par avion**
airplane **avion** (m.)
airport **aéroport** (m.)
alarm clock **réveil** (m.)
alike **pareil**
all **tout**
allow, to **permettre**
all right **ça va**
almost **presque**
alone **seul**
already **déjà**
also **aussi**
although **bien que**
always **toujours**
ambulance **ambulance** (f.)
America **Amérique** (f.)
American **américain**
among **parmi**
amount **somme** (f.)
amusement **divertissement** (m.)
amusement park **parc d'attractions**
    (m.)
amusing **drôle**
and **et**
angry **fâché**
animal **animal** (m.); **bête** (f.)
ankle **cheville** (f.)
announce, to **annoncer**
annoy, to **embêter**
answer **réponse** (f.)
answer, to **répondre**
antifreeze **antigel** (m.)
anxious to be **tenir à**
any **aucun**
anyone **n'importe qui; personne**
anything **quelque chose** (m.);
    n'importe quoi
anyway **en tout cas**
anywhere **n'importe où**
apartment **appartement** (m.)
appear, to **apparaître**

appetite **appétit** (m.)
appetizer **entrée** (f.)
apple **pomme** (f.)
appointment **rendez-vous**
appreciate, to **apprécier**
approach, to **s'approcher de**
approve, to **approuver**
arm **bras** (m.)
armchair **fauteuil** (m.)
around (adv.) **autour**
around (prep.) **autour de**
arrest, to **mettre aux arrêts**
arrival **arrivée** (f.)
arrive, to **arriver**
art **art** (m.)
artist **artiste** (m.)
as **comme**
ask, to **demander**
asleep, to fall **s'endormir**
assure, to **assurer**
at **à**
at all, (not) **(pas) du tout**
at once **tout de suite**
attend, to **assister**
attention **attention** (f.)
attractive **séduisant**
aunt **tante** (f.)
Austria **Autriche** (f.)
authentic **authentique**
author **auteur** (m.)
automatic **automatique**
automobile **automobile** (usually f.)
autumn **automne** (m.)
avoid, to **éviter**
awaken, to **se réveiller**
away, to go **s'en aller**

B

baby **bébé** (m.)
bachelor **célibataire** (m.)
back **dos** (m.); **derrière** (m.)
back (adv.) **en arrière**
backpack **havresac** (m.)
bad **mauvais**
badly **mal**
baggage **bagages** (m. pl.)
bakery **boulangerie** (f.)

band (music) **orchestre** (m.)
bank **banque** (f.)
bar (drinking) **café** (m.)
barber **coiffeur** (m.)
basket **panier** (m.)
bath **bain** (m.)
bathe, to **prendre un bain; se baigner**
bathing suit **costume de bain** (m.)
bathroom **salle de bain** (f.)
bathtub **baignoire** (f.)
battery **batterie** (f.)
battle **bataille** (f.)
be, to **être**
beach **plage** (f.)
bear **ours** (m.)
beard **barbe** (f.)
beat, to **battre**
beautiful **beau** or **bel** (m.), **belle** (f.)
beauty **beauté** (f.)
because **parce que**
become, to **devenir**
bed **lit** (m.)
bedroom **chambre à coucher** (f.)
beef **boeuf** (m.)
beer **bière** (f.)
before **avant**
begin, to **commencer**
behind **derrière**
believe, to **croire**
bell (church) **cloche** (f.)
bell (door) **sonnette** (f.)
belong, to **appartenir à**
below **en bas**
belt **ceinture** (f.)
beside **à côté de**
best **meilleur**
bet, to **parier**
better **mieux**
between **entre**
bicycle **bicyclette** (f.)
big **grand**
bill, invoice **note** (f.); **addition** (f.); **facture** (f.)
bird **oiseau** (m.)
birth **naissance** (f.)
birthday **anniversaire** (m.)
bite, to **mordre**
bitter **amer**
black **noir**
blanket **couverture** (f.)

blood **sang** (m.)
blouse **blouse** (f.)
blue **bleu**
boarding house **pension** (f.)
boat **bateau** (m.)
boat (small) **canot** (m.)
body **corps** (m.)
boil, to **bouillir**
book **livre** (m.)
border **frontière** (f.)
boring **ennuyeux** (m.), **ennuyeuse** (f.)
born, to be **naître**
borrow, to **emprunter**
both **tous les deux**
bother, to **déranger; embêter**
bottle **bouteille** (f.)
bottom **fond** (m.)
bowl **bol** (m.)
box **boîte** (f.)
boy **garçon** (m.)
brain **cerveau** (m.)
brake **frein** (m.)
brassiere **soutien-gorge** (m.)
bread **pain** (m.)
break, to **casser**
breakfast **petit déjeuner** (m.)
bride **mariée** (f.)
bridge **pont** (m.)
brief **bref** (m.), **brève** (f.)
bright **éclatant**
bring, to **apporter; amener**
broad **large**
broken **cassé; brisé**
broom **balai** (m.)
brother **frère**
brother-in-law **beau-frère**
brown **brun; marron**
brush **brosse** (f.)
bugs **punaises** (f. pl.)
build, to **construire; bâtir**
building **bâtiment** (m.)
bum **clochard** (m.)
bus **autobus** (m.); **bus** (m.)
bus stop **l'arrêt du bus** (m.)
business **les affaires** (f. pl.)
busy **occupé**
but **mais; pourtant**
butcher shop **boucherie** (f.)
butter **beurre** (m.)
button **bouton** (m.)

buy, to **acheter**
by **de; par**
by chance **par hasard**

C

cabbage **chou** (m.)
cake **gâteau** (m.)
calendar **calendrier** (m.)
call **appel** (m.)
call (telephone) **appel téléphonique** (m.)
call, to **appeler**
call, to (telephone) **téléphoner**
calm **calme; tranquille**
camera **appareil** (m.)
camping place **terrain de camping** (m.)
canoe **pirogue** (f.)
cap **casquette** (f.)
capable **capable**
captain **capitain** (m.)
car **voiture** (f.)
card **carte** (f.)
careful **prudent**
carrot **carotte** (f.)
carry, to **porter**
cash, to **encaisser**
cashier **caisseur** (m.)
castle **château** (m.)
cat **chat** (m.)
cathedral **cathédrale** (f.)
Catholic **catholique**
cause **cause** (f.)
cave **caverne** (f.)
ceiling **plafond** (m.)
celebrate, to **fêter**
cellar **sous-sol** (m.)
cemetery **cimetière** (m.)
center **centre** (m.)
center (city) **centre ville**
central **central**
century **siècle** (m.)
certain **certain**
certainly **certainement**
chair **chaise** (f.)
champagne **champagne** (m.)
change, to **changer**
change (alteration) **changement** (m.)

change (money) **monnaie** (f.)
charming **charmant**
cheap **bon marché**
check **chèque** (m.)
check, to **contrôler**
checkroom **consigne** (f.); **vestiaire** (m.)
cheerful **gai**
cheese **fromage** (m.)
chest **poitrine** (f.)
chicken **poulet** (m.)
child **enfant** (m. or f.)
childhood **enfance** (f.)
chocolate **chocolat** (m.)
Christian (n. and adj.) **Chrétien** (m.), **Chrétienne** (f.)
Christmas **Noël** (m.)
church **église** (f.)
cigar **cigare** (m.)
cigarette **cigarette** (f.)
circus **cirque** (m.)
city **ville** (f.)
city hall **hôtel de ville** (m.)
civilization **civilisation** (f.)
class **classe** (f.)
clean **net** (m.), **nette** (f.)
clean, to **nettoyer**
clear **clair**
clever **intelligent**
cliff **falaise** (f.)
climate **climat** (m.)
climb, to **grimper**
clock **horloge** (m.)
close **prés**
close, to **fermer**
closed **fermé**
closet **armoire** (f.)
cloth **étoffe** (f.)
clothes **vêtements** (m. pl.)
cloud **nuage** (m.)
cloudy **nuageux** (m.), **nuageuse** (f.)
club **société** (f.); **cercle** (m.)
coal **charbon** (m.)
coast **côte** (f.)
coat **manteau** (m.)
coffee **café** (m.)
cold (adj.) **froid**
cold (illness) **rhume** (m.)
collapse, to **s'écrouler**
collar **col** (m.)
collection **collection** (f.)

color **couleur** (f.)
comb **peigne** (m.)
come, to **venir**
come in, to **entrer**
comfort **confort** (m.)
comfortable **confortable**
commerce **commerce** (m.)
communism **communisme** (m.)
company **compagnie** (f.)
compartment **compartiment** (m.)
complain, to **se plaindre**
completely **complètement**
computer **ordinateur** (m.)
concert **concert** (m.)
condition **condition** (f.)
conductor (band) **chef d'orchestre** (m.)
conductor (train) **chef de train** (m.)
connection (train, etc.) **correspondance** (f.)
consist of, to **consister de**
contract **contrat** (m.)
contrary, on the **au contraire**
conversation **conversation** (f.)
convince, to **convaincre**
cook **chef** (m.)
cook, to **cuisiner**
cooked **cuit**
cool **frais** (m.), **fraîche** (f.)
copy **copie** (f.)
corner **coin** (m.)
correct **correct**
cost, to **coûter**
cotton **coton** (m.)
cough **toux** (f.)
count, to **compter**
country **pays** (m.)
couple **couple** (m.)
courage **courage** (m.)
course **cours** (m.); **course** (f.)
course, of **naturellement**
courtesy **courtoisie** (f.)
cousin **cousin** (m.), **cousine** (f.)
cover, to **couvrir**
cow **vache** (f.)
crazy **fou** (m.), **folle** (f.)
cream **crème** (f.)
credit **crédit** (m.)
criminal **criminel** (m.), **criminelle** (f.)
cross, to **traverser**

crossroads **carrefour** (m.)
cruise **croisière** (m.)
cry, to **pleurer**
cup **tasse** (f.)
curtain **rideau** (m.)
custom **coutume** (f.)
customs **douane** (f.)
cut, to **couper**

D

daily **quotidien**
damage **dommage** (m.)
damage, to **endommager**
damp **humide**
dance, to **danser**
danger **danger** (m.)
danger! **danger** (m.)
dangerous **dangereux** (m.),
  dangereuse (f.)
dark **obscur; sombre**
date (appointment) **rendez-vous** (m.)
date (time) **date** (f.)
daughter **fille** (f.)
dawn **aube** (f.)
day **jour** (m.)
dead **mort**
dear **cher**
decide, to **décider**
decision **décision** (f.)
deep **profond**
degree **degré** (m.)
delay **délai** (m.); **retard** (m.)
delicious **delicieux** (m.), **délicieuse**
  (f.)
delighted **ravi; enchanté**
deliver, to **délivrer**
dentist **dentiste** (m.)
dentures **dentier** (m.)
depart, to **partir**
departure **départ** (m.)
deposit **versement** (m.)
deposit, to **déposer**
describe, to **décrire**
description **déscription** (f.)
desire, to **désirer**

desk **bureau** (m.)
dessert **dessert** (m.)
diamond **diamant** (m.)
dictionary **dictionnaire** (m.)
die, to **mourir**
difference **différence** (f.)
different **différent**
difficult **difficile**
dine, to **dîner**
dining room **salle à manger** (f.)
dinner **dîner** (m.)
direction **direction** (f.); **sens** (m.)
directly **directement**
dirty **sale**
disappear, to **disparaître**
disappointed **déçu**
discount **rabais** (m.)
discover, to **découvrir**
dish **plat** (m.)
distance **distance** (f.)
distant **loin**
disturb, to **déranger**
divide, to **diviser**
diving (underwater sport) **plongeé
  sous-marine**
divorced **divorcé**
dizzy **étourdi**
do, to **faire**
doctor **docteur; médecin**
dog **chien** (m.)
dollar **dollar** (m.)
donkey **âne** (m.)
door **porte** (f.)
double **double**
doubt **doute** (m.)
downstairs **en bas**
draft (air) **courant d'air** (m.)
dream **rêve** (m.)
dream, to **rêver**
dress **robe** (f.)
dress, to **s'habiller**
drink, to **boire**
drive, to **conduire**
driver **chauffeur**
driver's license **permis de conduire**
  (m.)
drown, to **noyer**
drowned, to be **se noyer**
drunk **ivre**
dry **sec** (m.), **sèche** (f.)
during **pendant**

E

each **chaque**
ear **oreille** (f.)
early **tôt**
earn, to **gagner**
earth **terre** (f.)
east **est**
Easter **Pâques**
easy **facile**
eat, to **manger**
editor **rédacteur** (m.)
egg **oeuf** (m.)
either . . . or **ou . . . ou**
electric **électrique**
electricity **électricité**
elevator **ascenseur** (m.)
embark, to **s'embarquer**
embassy **ambassade** (f.)
embrace, to **embrasser**
embroidery **broderie** (f.)
emergency **cas urgent** (m.)
employee **employé** (m.)
employer **employeur** (m.)
empty **vide**
end **fin** (f.)
end, to **finir**
Englishman **Anglais** (m.)
enough **assez**
enter, to **entrer**
enthusiastic **enthousiaste**
entire **entier**
envelope **enveloppe** (f.)
equal **égal**
error **erreur**
escape, to **s'échapper**
especially **surtout**
eternal **éternel** (m.), **éternelle** (f.)
even **égal; uni**
evening **soir** (m.); **soirée** (f.)
event **évènement** (m.)
ever **jamais**
every **chaque**
everybody **tout le monde**
everything **tout**
everywhere **partout**
exact **exact**
exaggerate, to **exagérer**

examine, to **examiner**
example **exemple** (m.)
excellent **excellent**
except **sauf**
exchange **échange** (m.)
exchange, to **échanger**
excuse me **excusez-moi**
exist, to **exister**
exit **sortie** (f.)
expensive **cher**
experience **expérience** (f.)
explain, to **expliquer**
explanation **explication** (f.)
export, to **exporter**
expression **expression** (f.)
extinguish, to **éteindre**
extra **extra; supplémentaire**
eye **oeil** (m.)
eye doctor **ophtalmologiste** (m.)

F

fabric **tissu** (m.)
face **visage** (m.)
factory **usine** (f.)
faithful **fidèle**
fall, to **tomber**
fall (season) **automne** (m.)
family **famille** (f.)
famous **connu**
far **loin**
farm **ferme** (f.)
farmer **fermier** (m.)
farther **plus loin**
fashion **mode** (f.)
fast **vite**
fat **gros** (m.), **grosse** (f.)
father **père** (m.)
favorable **favorable**
fear **peur**
feel, to **sentir**
fence **clôture** (f.); **palissade** (f.)
fever **fièvre** (f.)
few **peu**
field **champ** (m.)
fight **combat** (m.); **lutte** (f.)
fight, to **combattre; lutter**
fill, to **remplir**
film **film** (m.)

finally **enfin**
find, to **trouver**
find out, to **découvrir**
fine (money) **amende** (f.)
finger **doigt** (m.)
fire **feu** (m.)
fire department **corps des pompiers** (m.)
first **premier**
fish **poisson** (m.)
fish, to **pêcher**
flame **flamme** (f.)
flight **vol** (m.)
floor **plancher** (m.)
floor (story) **étage** (m.)
flower **fleur** (f.)
fly **mouche** (f.)
fly, to **voler**
fog **brouillard** (m.)
follow, to **suivre**
food **nourriture** (f.)
foot **pied** (m.)
for **pour**
forbidden **défendu**
foreign **étrange**
foreigner **étranger**
forest **forêt** (f.)
forget, to **oublier**
forgive, to **pardonner**
fork **fourchette** (f.)
forward **en avant**
fountain **fontaine** (f.)
fox **renard** (m.)
France **France** (f.)
free **libre**
freedom **liberté** (f.)
freeze, to **geler**
Frenchman **Français** (m.)
frequently **souvent**
fresh **frais** (m.), **fraîche** (f.)
fried **frit**
friend **ami** (m.), **amie** (f.)
friendship **amitié** (f.)
frightened, to be **avoir peur**
from **de**
front of, in **devant**
frost **gelée** (f.)
fruit **fruit** (m.)
fry, to **frire**
frying pan **poêle à frire** (f.)
full **plein**

funeral **funérailles** (f. pl.)
funny **drôle**
furnish, to **meubler**
furnished **meublé**
furniture **meubles** (m. pl.)
future **avenir** (m.); **futur** (m.)

G

gamble, to **jouer**
game **jeu** (m.)
garage **garage** (m.)
garden **jardin** (m.)
gas station **station-service** (f.)
gasoline **essence** (f.)
gate **porte** (f.)
gather, to **ramasser; cueillir**
gentleman **monsieur** (m.)
genuine **véritable**
Germany **Allemagne** (f.)
get in, to **entrer**
get out, to **sortir**
get up, to **se lever**
girl **jeune fille**
give, to **donner**
glad **content**
glass **verre** (m.); **vitre** (f.)
glasses **lunettes** (f. pl.)
glove **gant** (m.)
go, to **aller**
God **Dieu**
gold **or** (m.)
good **bon** (m.), **bonne** (f.)
goodbye **au revoir; adieu**
good evening **bonsoir**
good morning **bonjour**
government **gouvernement** (m.)
granddaughter/son **petite fille** (f.); **petit fils** (m.)
grandfather/mother **grand-père** (m.); **grand'mère** (f.)
grape **raisin** (m.)
grapefruit **pamplemousse** (m.)
grateful **reconnaissant**
grave **tombe** (f.)
gray **gris**
great **grand**
green **vert**

FRENCH

greeting **salutation** (f.)
group **groupe** (m.)
grow, to **croître**
guess, to **deviner**
guest **hôte** (m.)
guide **guide** (m.)
guitar **guitare** (f.)
gun (hand) **pistolet** (m.); **revolver** (m.)
gymnasium **gymnase** (m.)
gynecologist **gynécologue** (m.)

H

hair **cheveux** (m. pl.)
half **moitié** (f.)
hallway **couloir** (m.)
hand **main** (f.)
handbag **sac à main** (m.)
handkerchief **mouchoir** (m.)
happiness **bonheur** (m.)
happy **heureux** (m.), **heureuse** (f.)
hard **dur**
hat **chapeau** (m.)
hate, to **détester**
have, to **avoir**
have to, to **devoir**
he **il**
head **tête** (f.)
heal, to **guérir**
health **santé** (f.)
health food store **magasin diététique** (m.)
health resort **station thermale** (f.)
hear, to **entendre**
heart **coeur** (m.)
heat **chaleur** (f.)
heating **chauffage** (m.)
heat stroke **coup de chaleur** (m.)
heavy **lourd**
heel **talon** (m.)
hello **allô**
help **aide** (m.)
help, to **aider**
her **elle**
here **ici**
here is **voici**
hers **son**
high **haut**
high school **lycée** (m.)
highway **autoroute** (f.)

hike, to **excursionner à pied**
hill **colline** (f.)
him **lui**
his **son**
history **histoire** (f.)
hitchhiker **auto-stoppeur** (m.)
hold, to **tenir**
hole **ouverture** (f.)
holiday **jour de fête** (m.)
holy **saint; sacré**
home of, at the **chez**
honest **honnête**
honey **miel** (m.)
honeymoon **lune de miel** (f.)
honor **honneur** (m.)
hope **espérance** (f.)
hope, to **espérer**
horn (automobile) **trompe** (f.)
horse **cheval** (m.)
hospital **hôpital** (m.)
hospitality **hôspitalité** (f.)
hot **chaud**
hotel **hôtel** (m.)
hour **heure** (f.)
house **maison** (f.)
how **comment**
humidity **humidité** (f.)
hunger **faim** (f.)
hungry, to be **avoir faim**
hunter **chassure** (m.)
hunting **chasse** (f.)
hurry, to be in a **être pressé**
husband **mari** (m.)
hut **cabane** (f.)

I

I **je**
ice cream **glace** (f.)
ice skate, to **patiner**
idea **idée** (f.)
identification **pièce d'identité** (f.)
idiot **idiot** (m.)
if **si**
ignorant **ignorant**
ill **malade**
imagine, to **imaginer; se figurer**
immediately **immediatement**
import, to **importer**
important **important**
impossible **impossible**

impression **impression**
in **dans; en**
including **compris**
incorrect **incorrect**
indeed **vraiment**
inexpensive **pas cher; bon marché**
inform, to **informer**
information **information** (f.)
inhabitant **habitant** (m.)
inquiry **question** (f.)
inside **à l'intérieur**
instead **au lieu de**
insurance **assurance** (f.)
interested **intéressé**
interesting **intéressant**
interpreter **interprète** (m. or f.)
interrupt, to **interrompre**
introduce, to **présenter**
introduction **introduction** (f.)
invite, to **inviter**
invitation **invitation** (f.)
island **île** (f.)
Italy **Italie** (f.)
itinerary **itinéraire** (m.)

J

jacket **veston** (m.)
jam **confiture** (f.)
jealous **jaloux** (m.), **jalouse** (f.)
jewelry **bijouterie** (f.)
Jew(ish) **Juif** (m.), **Juive** (f.)
job **travail** (m.)
joke **plaisanterie** (f.)
joke, to **plaisanter**
joy **joie** (f.)
judge **juge** (m.)
jump, to **sauter**
just (exactly) **juste**
just (only) **seulement**

K

keep, to **garder**
key **clef** (f.)
kind **genre** (m.); **sorte** (f.)
kind (adj.) **gentil** (m.), **gentille** (f.);
  bon (m.), **bonne** (f.)

kindness **gentillesse** (f.)
king **roi** (m.)
kiss **baiser** (m.)
kitchen **cuisine** (f.)
knife **couteau** (m.)
knock, to **frapper**
know, to (to be acquainted
  with) **connaître**
know, to (to be aware of) **savoir**
knowledge **connaissance** (f.); **savoir**
  (m.)

L

lady **dame** (f.)
lake **lac** (m.)
lamb **agneau** (m.)
lamp **lampe** (f.)
land **terre** (f.)
land (plane), to **atterrir**
language **langue** (f.)
large **grand**
last **dernier**
last, to **durer**
late **tard**
laugh, to **rire**
laundry **blanchisserie** (f.)
law **loi** (f.)
lawyer **avocat** (m.), **avocate** (f.)
learn, to **apprendre**
least **le moins; le moindre**
leather **cuir** (m.)
leave, to (abandon) **abandonner**
leave, to (go away) **partir**
left (direction) **gauche**
leg **jambe** (f.)
legal **légal**
lend, to **prêter**
less **moins**
lesson **leçon** (f.)
let, to (allow) **permettre**
letter **lettre** (f.)
lettuce **laitue** (f.)
liberty **liberté** (f.)
library **bibliothèque** (f.)
license plate **permis de circulation**
lie, to (tell a falsehood) **mentir**
lie **mensonge** (m.)
life **vie** (f.)
lifeboat **canot de sauvetage** (m.)

lifeguard **surveillant de plage** (m.)
lift, to **lever**
light, to **éclairer**
light (color) **clair**
light (illumination) **lumière** (f.)
light (weight) **léger**
light bulb **ampoule** (f.)
lightning **foudre** (f.)
like, to **aimer bien**
like, to (to be pleased by something) **se plaire**
line **ligne** (f.)
linen **lin** (m.); **linge** (f.)
lion **lion** (m.)
lip **lèvre** (f.)
list **liste** (f.)
listen, to **écouter**
literature **littérature** (f.)
little **peu; petit**
live, to **vivre; habiter**
living room **salon** (m.)
load **fardeau** (m.)
locate, to **situer**
lodging **logement** (m.)
logical **logique**
long **long** (m.), **longue** (f.)
look, to **regarder**
lose, to **perdre**
lost **perdu; égaré**
loud **fort**
love, to **aimer**
lover **amoreux** (m.), **amoreuse** (f.)
low **bas** (m.), **basse** (f.)
luck **chance** (f.); **fortune** (f.)
luggage **bagages** (m. pl.)
lunch **déjeuner** (m.)
luxury **luxe** (m.)

M

machine **machine** (f.)
magazine **revue** (f.)
magnificent **magnifique**
maid **bonne** (f.)
mail **poste** (f.); **courier** (m.)
mail box **boîte aux lettres** (f.)
make, to **faire**
man **homme**
management **direction** (f.)

manager **directeur** (m.)
manner **manière** (f.)
map **carte** (f.); **plan** (m.)
marble **marbre** (m.)
market **marché** (m.)
married **marié**
marry, to **se marier; épouser**
marvel **merveille** (f.)
marvelous **merveilleux** (m.), **merveilleuse** (f.)
mass (church) **messe** (f.)
material **matériel** (m.); **tissu** (m.)
mattress **matelas** (m.)
maybe **peut-être**
mayor **maire** (m.)
me **moi; me**
meal **repas** (m.)
mean, to **vouloir dire; signifier**
meaning **signification** (f.)
means **moyen** (m.)
meat **viande** (f.)
medicine **médecine** (f.)
Mediterranean **mediterranée (f.)**
medieval **médiéval**
meet, to **rencontrer; se rencontrer**
meeting **réunion** (f.); **rencontre** (f.)
member **membre** (m.)
menu **menu** (m.); **carte** (f.)
merchandise **marchandise** (f.)
message **message** (m.)
middle **milieu** (m.)
Middle Ages **moyen âge** (m.)
midnight **minuit** (m.)
mild **doux** (m.), **douce** (f.)
mile **mile** (m.)
milk **lait** (m.)
million **million** (m.)
mine **à moi; le mien** (m.), **la mienne** (f.)
minister **ministre** (m.)
minute **minute** (f.)
mirror **miroir** (m.); **glace** (f.)
miss **mademoiselle**
miss, to **manquer**
mistake **erreur** (f.)
misunderstanding **malentendu** (m.)
mix, to **mélanger**
model **modéle** (m.)
modern **moderne**
modest **modeste**
moment **moment** (m.)

monastery **monastère** (m.)
money **argent** (m.)
monkey **singe** (m.)
month **mois** (m.)
monthly **mensuel** (m.), **mensuelle** (f.)
monument **monument** (m.)
moon **lune** (f.)
more **encore; plus**
morning **matin** (m.)
most **la plupart** (f.)
mostly **pour la plupart**
mother **mère** (f.)
mother-in-law **belle-mère**
motor **moteur** (m.)
motorcycle **motocyclette** (f.)
mountain **montagne** (f.)
mountain climber **alpiniste**
mountain climbing **alpinisme** (m.)
mouse **souris** (f.)
mouth **bouche** (f.)
movement **mouvement** (m.)
movies **cinéma** (m.)
much **beaucoup**
mud **boue** (f.)
murder, to **assassiner**
music **musique** (f.)
musician **musicien** (m.)
must **devoir**
mustache **moustache** (f.)
mustard **moutarde** (f.)
mutton **mouton** (m.)
my **mon**
myself **moi-même; me**

N

name **nom** (m.)
napkin **serviette** (f.)
narrow **étroit**
nature **nature** (f.)
navy **marine** (f.)
near **près; proche**
necessary **nécessaire**
neck **cou** (m.)
necktie **cravate** (f.)
need, to **avoir besoin de**
needle **aiguille** (f.)
neighbor **voisin** (m.), **voisine** (f.)
neighborhood **quartier** (m.)
nephew **neveu** (m.)

nervous **nerveux** (m.), **nerveuse** (f.)
never **jamais**
new **nouveau** (m.), **nouvelle** (f.);
  neuf (m.), **neuve** (f.)
news **nouvelles** (f. pl.)
newspaper **journal** (m.)
New Year's Day **Jour de l'an**
next **prochain**
nice **gentil** (m.), **gentille** (f.);
  sympathique
niece **nièce** (f.)
night **nuit** (f.)
night club **boîte de nuit** (f.)
nightgown **chemise de nuit** (f.)
no (adv.) **non**
nobody **personne**
noise **bruit** (m.)
noon **midi** (m.)
north **nord** (m.)
nose **nez** (m.)
not **pas**
notebook **cahier** (m.)
nothing **rien**
notice, to **remarquer**
nowhere **nulle part**
number **numéro** (m.)
nurse **infirmier** (m.), **infirmiere** (f.)
nut **noix** (f.)

O

oar **rame** (f.)
object **objet** (m.)
occasion **occasion** (f.)
occasionally **de temps en temps**
occupied **occupé**
occur, to **arriver**
ocean **océan** (m.)
of **de**
offer, to **offrir**
office **bureau** (m.)
often **souvent**
oil **huile** (f.)
OK **d'accord**
old **vieux** (m.), **vielle** (f.)
on **sur**
once **une fois**
one **un** (m.), **une** (f.)
one way (street) **sens unique**

one-way ticket **aller simple** (m.)
only **seulement; uniquement**
open **ouvert**
open, to **ouvrir**
opera **opéra** (m.)
opinion **opinion** (f.)
opportunity **occasion** (f.)
opposite **opposé** (m.); **contraire** (m.)
or **ou**
orange **orange** (f.)
order, to **commander**
in order to **pour**
original **original**
other **autre**
othrwise **autrement**
our **notre**
ourselves **nous**
out of order **hors de service**
outside **dehors**
over **au-dessus de**
owe, to **devoir**
own **propre**
owner **propriétaire** (m. or f.)

P

package **paquet** (m.)
paid **payé**
pain **douleur** (f.)
painter **peintre** (m.)
painting **peinture** (f.)
pair **paire** (f.)
palace **palais** (m.)
pants **pantalon** (m.)
paper **papier** (m.)
parent **parent** (m.)
park **parc** (m.)
park, to **garer**
parking lot **parc de stationnement** (m.)
part **partie** (f.)
party **partie** (f.)
passenger **passager** (m.)
passport **passeport** (m.)
past **passé**
path **sentier** (m.)
pay, to **payer**
payment **paiement** (m.)
peace **paix** (f.)

pen **stylo** (m.)
pencil **crayon** (f.)
people **gens** (m.)
perfect **parfait**
perfume **parfum** (m.)
perhaps **peut-être**
period **périod** (f.)
permit, to **permettre**
person **personne** (f.)
photograph **photographie (f.)**
photograph, to **photographier**
photography **photographie** (f.)
piano **piano** (m.)
pick pocket **filou** (m.)
picture **image** (f.); **tableau** (m.)
piece **morceau** (m.)
pig **cochon** (m.)
pigeon **pigeon** (m.), **pigeonne** (f.)
pill **pilule** (f.)
pillow **oreiller** (m.)
pin **épingle** (f.)
pink **rose**
pitcher **cruche** (f.)
place **endroit** (m.); **lieu** (m.)
plan **plan** (m.)
plant **plante** (f.)
plate **asiètte** (f.)
platform (train) **quai** (m.)
play **pièce de théâtre**
play, to **jouer**
pleasant **agréable**
please **s'il vous plaît**
pleasure **plaisir** (m.)
pocket **poche** (f.)
poem **poème** (m.)
point **point** (m.)
point, to **indiquer**
police **police** (f.)
police station **poste** (m.)
polite **poli**
pond **étang** (m.)
poor **pauvre**
pope **pape** (m.)
popular **populaire**
pork **porc** (m.)
port **port** (m.)
possible **possible**
post card **carte postale** (f.)
post office **bureau de poste** (m.)
pot (cooking) **pot** (m.); **marmite** (f.)
potato **pomme de terre** (f.)

FRENCH

pound **livre** (f.)
powerful **puissant**
practice, to **s'exercer à**
pray, to **prier**
precise **précis**
pregnant **enceinte**
prepare, to **préparer**
prescription **ordonnance** (f.)
present **cadeau** (m.)
press (clothes), to **repasser**
pretty **joli**
price **prix** (m.)
priest **prêtre** (m.)
prison **prison** (f.)
probable **probable**
problem **problème** (m.)
profession **métier** (m.);
  profession (f.)
profit **profit** (m.); **bénéfice** (f.)
program **programme** (m.)
promise, to **promettre**
pronounce, to **prononcer**
property **propriété** (f.)
Protestant **protestant**
public **public** (m.)
publisher **editeur** (m.)
pull, to **tirer**
purchase, to **acheter**
push, to **pousser**
put, to **mettre**
put on (clothes), to **mettre**

Q

quality **qualité** (f.)
quarter **quart** (m.)
queen **reine** (f.)
question **question** (f.)
quick **rapide**
quickly **vite**
quiet **tranquille**
quite **assez; tout à fait**

R

rabbi **rabbin** (m.)
rabbit **lapin** (m.)
race (contest) **course** (f.)

radiator (car) **radiateur** (m.)
radiator (room) **radiateur** (m.)
radio **radio** (f.)
railroad **chemin de fer** (m.)
railway station **gare** (f.)
rain **pluie** (f.)
raincoat **imperméable** (m.)
raise, to **lever; élever**
rape **viol** (m.)
rapid **rapide**
rare (meat) **saignant**
rare (unusual) **rare**
rarely **rarement**
rather **plutôt; assez**
raw **cru**
razor **rasoir** (m.)
razor blade **lame de rasoir** (f.)
reach, to **s'étendre**
read, to **lire**
ready **prêt**
real **vrai**
really **vraiment**
reason **raison** (f.)
reasonable **raisonnable**
receipt **reçu** (m.)
receive, to **recevoir**
recently **récemment**
recognize, to **reconnaître**
recommend, to **recommander**
record (phonograph) **disque** (m.)
red **rouge**
refrigerator **frigo** (m.)
refuse, to **refuser**
regards **salutations** (f. pl.)
region **region** (f.)
regret, to **regretter**
regular **régulier**
religion **religion**
religious **religieux** (m.),
  religieuse (f.)
remain, to **rester**
remainder **reste** (m.)
remember, to **se rappeler; se**
  souvenir
remind, to **rappeler**
rent, to **louer**
repair, to **réparer**
repeat, to **répéter**
replace, to **remplacer**
report **reportage** (m.)
represent, to **représenter**

republic **république** (f.)
reserve, to **réserver**
reservation **réservation** (f.)
responsible **responsable**
rest, to **se reposer**
restaurant **restaurant** (m.)
retail **détail** (m.)
return, to **rentrer; retourner; rendre** (tr.)
ribbon **ruban** (m.)
rice **riz** (m.)
rich **riche**
ride (a horse), to **chevaucher**
right (a just claim) **droit** (m.)
right (direction) **droite**
right (opposed to wrong) **correct**
ring **bague** (f.)
rise, to **se lever**
river **fleuve** (m.)
road **rue** (f.); **route** (f.)
roast **rôti** (m.)
rob, to **voler**
robbery **vol** (m.)
rock **roc** (m.)
roll **petit pain** (m.)
roof **toit** (m.)
room **chambre** (f.); **salle** (f.); **pièce** (f.)
round **rond**
round trip **aller-retour** (m.)
route **route** (f.)
row, to **ramer**
row **rang** (m.)
rowboat **canot** (m.)
rug **tapis** (m.)
ruins **ruines** (f. pl.)
run, to **courir**

S

sacrifice **sacrifice** (m.)
sad **triste**
safe (secure) **sûr**
safe (strongbox) **coffre-fort** (m.)
sail, to **faire voile**
sailboat **bateau á voiles** (m.)
sailor **marin** (m.)
saint **saint** (m.), **sainte** (f.)
salad **salade** (f.)

salary **salaire** (m.)
sale **vente** (f.)
salesperson **vendeur** (m.), **vendeuse** (f.)
salt **sel** (m.)
salty **sale**
same **même**
satisfied **content**
satisfy, to **satisfaire**
sauce **sauce** (f.)
saucer **soucoupe** (f.)
save, to **sauver**
savings bank **caisse d'épargne** (f.)
say, to **dire**
science **science** (m.)
school **école** (f.)
scissors **ciseaux** (m. pl.)
scream **cri** (m.)
sculptor **sculpteur** (m.), **femme sculpteur** (f.)
sea **mer** (f.)
seashore **bord de la mer** (m.)
seasick, to be **avoir mal de mer**
season **saison** (f.)
seasoning **assaisonnement** (m.)
seat **siège** (m.); **place** (f.)
second **deuxième; second**
secretary **secrétaire**
see, to **voir**
seek, to **chercher**
seldom **rarement**
sell, to **vendre**
send, to **envoyer**
separate **séparé**
serious **sérieux** (m.), **sérieuse** (f.)
serve, to **servir**
service **service** (m.)
set, to **poser; placer; mettre**
several **plusieurs**
sew, to **coudre**
shade **ombre** (f.)
shadow **ombre** (f.)
share, to **partager**
sharp **aigu**
shave (oneself), to **se raser**
she **elle**
sheet (bed) **drap** (m.)
ship **bateau** (m.)
shirt **chemise** (f.)
shoe **chaussure** (f.)
shoelaces **lacets** (m. pl.)

shop   **magasin** (m.)
short   **court**
shorts   **short** (m.)
shoulder   **épaule** (f.)
show   **spectacle** (m.)
show, to   **montrer**
shower   **douche** (f.)
shut, to   **fermer**
sick   **malade**
side   **côte** (m.)
sidewalk   **trottoir** (m.)
sights   **curiosités** (f. pl.)
sign   **signal** (m.); **affiche** (f.)
silence   **silence** (m.)
silk   **soie** (f.)
silver   **argent** (m.)
similar   **pareil**
simple   **simple**
since   **puisque**
sing, to   **chanter**
singer   **chanteur** (m.), **chanteuse** (f.)
single   **seul; unique**
sir   **monsieur**
sister   **soeur**
sister-in-law   **belle-soeur**
sit, to   **s'asseoir**
size   **taille** (f.)
ski   **ski** (m.)
skiing, to go   **aller faire du ski**
skin   **peau** (f.)
skirt   **jupe** (f.)
sky   **ciel** (m.)
skyscraper   **gratte-ciel** (m.)
sleep, to   **dormir**
sleep, to go to   **s'endormir**
sleeping bag   **sac de couchage** (m.)
sleeve   **manche** (f.)
slip, to   **glisser**
slow   **lent**
small   **petit**
smell, to   **sentir**
smile, to   **sourire**
smoke, to   **fumer**
smooth   **lisse**
snake   **serpent** (m.)
sneeze, to   **éternuer**
snow   **neige** (f.)
so   **alors; ainsi**
soap   **savon** (m.)
sock   **chaussette** (f.)
sofa   **divan** (m.)

soft   **doux** (m.), **douce** (f.); **tendre**
soldier   **soldat** (m.)
some   **quelque**
somebody   **quelqu'un**
something   **quelque chose**
sometimes   **quelquefois**
somewhat   **assez; plutôt**
somewhere   **quelque part**
son   **fils**
song   **chanson** (f.)
soon   **bientôt**
soup   **soupe** (f.)
sour   **aigre**
south   **sud**
souvenir   **souvenir** (m.)
Spain   **Espagne** (f.)
speak, to   **parler**
special   **spécial**
speed limit   **limite de vitesse** (f.)
spend, to   **dépenser**
sponge   **éponge** (f.)
spoon   **cuillère** (f.)
sport   **sport** (m.)
sporting goods   **articles de sport** (m. pl.)
spring   **printemps** (m.)
stairs   **escalier** (m.)
stamp   **timbre** (m.)
standing (on end)   **debout**
star   **étoile** (f.)
start, to   **commencer**
station   **station** (f.); **gare** (f.)
statue   **statue** (f.)
stay, to   **rester**
stay   **séjour** (m.)
steak   **bifteck** (m.)
steal, to   **voler**
steamer (boat)   **vapeur** (m.)
stick   **bâton** (m.)
still (quiet)   **calme; tranquille**
still (yet)   **encore; toujours**
stockings   **bas** (m. pl.)
stomach   **estomac** (m.)
stone   **pierre** (f.)
stop, to   **arrêter** (m.)
stop (bus, etc.)   **arrêt du . . .** (m.)
storm   **tempête** (f.)
story   **conte** (m.); **histoire** (f.)
stove   **poêle** (f.)
straight   **droit**
strange   **étrange**

street **rue** (f.)
streetcar **tramway** (m.)
strike, to **frapper**
string **ficelle** (f.)
strong **fort**
student **étudiant** (m.), **etudiante** (f.)
study, to **étudier**
stupid **stupide; bête**
style **style** (m.)
subway **métro** (m.)
sudden **soudain**
sugar **sucre** (m.)
suit **complet** (m.)
suitcase **valise** (f.)
summer **été** (m.)
summit **sommet** (m.)
sun **soleil** (m.)
sunburn **hâle** (m.); **coup de soleil** (m.)
sunglasses **lunettes de soleil** (f.)
sunset **coucher de soleil** (m.)
sure **sûr; certain**
surf **ressac** (m.)
surprise **surprise** (f.)
supper **souper** (m.); **dîner** (m.)
supplement **supplément** (m.)
suppose, to **supposer**
sweat, to **suer**
sweater **chandail** (m.)
sweet **doux** (m.), **douce** (f.)
swim, to **nager**
swimming pool **piscine** (f.)
Switzerland **Suisse** (f.)

T

table **table** (f.)
tablecloth **nappe** (f.)
tailor **tailleur** (m.)
take, to **prendre**
take off (plane), to **décoller**
take off, to (remove) **ôter**
talk, to **parler**
tall **haut; grand**
tape **ruban** (m.); **bande** (f.)
tape recorder **magnétophone** (m.)
taste **goût** (m.)
taste, to **goûter**
tax **impôt** (m.)
taxi **taxi** (m.)
tea **thé** (m.)

teach, to **enseigner**
teacher **professeur** (m. or f.)
team **équipe** (f.)
tear (from crying) **larme** (f.)
tear, to (rip) **déchirer**
telegram **télégramme** (m.)
telephone **téléphone** (f.)
television **télévision** (f.)
tell, to **raconter; dire**
temperature **température** (f.)
temporarily **temporairement**
tent **tente** (f.)
terrible **terrible**
than **que**
thank, to **remercier**
thank you **merci**
the **le** (m.), **la** (f.)
theatre **théâtre** (m.)
then **alors; puis; donc**
there **là; y**
there is/are **il y a**
thermometer **thermomètre** (m.)
they **ils** (m.), **elles** (f.)
thief **voleur** (m.), **voleuse** (f.)
thin **mince**
thing **chose** (f.)
think, to **penser**
third **troisième**
thirst **soif** (f.)
thirsty, to be **avoir soif**
this **ce, cet, cette**
those **ceux** (m.), **celles** (f.)
thousand **mille**
thread **fil** (m.)
throat **gorge** (f.)
through **par**
throw, to **jeter; lancer**
thunder **tonnerre** (m.)
thus **ainsi**
ticket (for speeding) **papillon** (m.)
ticket (theatre, etc.) **billet** (m.)
tide **marée** (f.)
tie **cravate** (f.)
tight **étroit**
time **temps** (m.)
timetable **indicateur** (m.)
tip (money) **pourboire** (m.)
tire **pneu** (m.)
tired **fatigué**
to **à**
tobacco **tabac** (m.)
today **aujourd'hui**

together **ensemble**
toilet **toilette** (f.)
tomato **tomate** (f.)
tomorrow **demain**
tongue **langue** (f.)
tonight **ce soir**
too (also) **aussi**
tooth **dent** (f.)
toothbrush **brosse à dents** (f.)
toothpaste **dentifrice** (m.)
top, on **au-dessus**
topless **sans haut**
touch, to **toucher**
tough **dur**
tour **excursion touristique**
towel **serviette de bain** (f.)
tower **tour** (f.)
town **ville** (f.)
tow truck **dépanneuse** (f.)
toy **jouet** (m.)
trade **commerce** (m.)
trade fair **faire commerciale** (f.)
traffic **circulation** (f.)
traffic light **feu rouge** (m.)
traffic jam **embouteillage** (m.)
train **train** (m.)
translate, to **traduire**
translation **traduction** (f.)
travel, to **voyager**
travel agency **agence de voyages** (f.)
traveler **voyageur**
tree **arbre** (m.)
trip **voyage** (m.)
trouble **ennui** (m.); **souci** (m.);
  peine (f.)
truck **camion** (m.)
true **vrai**
trunk (luggage) **malle** (f.)
truth **vérité** (f.)
try, to **essayer**
try on, to **essayer**
turn off, to **éteindre; fermer; couper**
turn on, to **ouvrir, allumer**
typewriter **machine à écrire**

U

ugly **laid**
umbrella **parapluie** (m.)
uncle **oncle** (m.)
unconscious (physically) **sans
  connaissance**

unconscious (unaware) **sans
  conscience de**
under **sous; au-dessous de**
understand, to **comprendre**
underwear **sous-vêtements** (m. pl.)
undress, to **se déshabiller**
unfortunately **malheureusement**
United States **États-Unis** (m. pl.)
university **université** (f.)
unless **à moins que**
until **jusqu'à**
up **en haut**
upstairs **en haut**
urgent **urgent**
us **nous**
use **usage** (m.)
use, to **utiliser; se servir de**
useful **utile**
usual **normal**

V

vacant **libre**
vacation **vacances** (f. pl.)
valid **valable**
valuables **objets de valeur** (m. pl.)
value **valeur** (f.)
various **divers; varié**
vegetable **légume** (m.)
vehicle **véhicule** (m.)
very **très**
victory **victoire** (f.)
view **vue** (f.)
village **village** (m.)
vineyard **vignoble** (m.)
visit, to **visiter; rendre visite à**
violin **violon** (m.)
voice **voix** (f.)
voltage **tension** (f.)
voyage **voyage** (m.)

W

waist **taille** (f.); **ceinture** (f.)
wait, to **attendre**
waiter **garçon de restaurant**
waiting room **salle d'attente**
waitress **fille de salle** (f.)
wake up, to **se réveiller**
walk, to **marcher**

walk **promenade** (f.)
wall **mur** (m.)
wallet **portefeuille** (m.)
want, to **vouloir**
war **guerre** (f.)
warm **chaud**
warn, to **prévenir**
wash, to **laver**
wash basin **lavabo** (m.)
wash oneself, to **se laver**
waste, to **gaspiller**
watch, to **regarder; veiller**
watch **montre** (f.)
water **eau** (f.)
waterfront **front de mer** (m.)
water sports **sports nautiques** (m. pl.)
wave **vague** (f.)
way **manière** (f.); **façon** (f.)
we **nous**
weak **faible**
wear, to **porter**
weather **temps** (m.)
wedding **mariage** (m.)
week **semaine** (f.)
weekend **fin de semaine** (f.)
weigh, to **peser**
weight **poids** (m.)
welcome **bienvenu**
well **bien**
west **ouest**
what **quoi; qu'est-ce que; comment**
whatever **tout ce qui/que**
wheat **blé** (m.)
wheel **roue** (f.)
when **quand**
where **où**
whether **si**
which **lequel** (m.), **laquelle** (f.)
while **pendant que**
white **blanc** (m.), **blanche** (f.)
who **qui**
whole **entier**
whose **dont; duquel; de qui**
why **pourquoi**
wide **large**
widow **veuve** (f.)
widower **veuf** (m.)
wife **femme** (f.)
wilderness **étendue déserte** (f.)
win, to **gagner**
wind **vent** (m.)

window (house) **fenêtre** (f.)
window (railway station, etc.) **guichet** (m.)
windy **venteux** (m.), **venteuse** (f.)
wine **vin** (m.)
wine list **carte des vins** (f.)
wing **aile** (f.)
winter **hiver** (m.)
wish **désir** (m.)
wish, to **vouloir; désirer**
with **avec**
without **sans**
woman **femme** (f.)
wonder **merveille** (m.)
wonderful **merveilleux** (m.), **merveilleuse** (f.)
wood **bois** (m.)
wool **laine** (f.)
word **mot** (m.)
work **travail** (m.)
world **monde** (m.)
worries **soucis** (m. pl.)
worse **pire**
wrap, to **enrouler**
wrist **poignet** (m.)
write, to **écrire**
writer **écrivain**
wrong **incorrect**

Y

yacht **yacht** (m.)
year **an** (m.), **année** (f.)
yellow **jaune**
yes **oui**
yesterday **hier**
yet **encore**
you **vous; tu**
young **jeune**
your **votre**
you're welcome **de rien**

Z

zero **zéro** (m.)
zipper **fermeture éclair** (f.)
zone **zone** (f.)
zoo **zoo** (m.)

GERMAN

GERMAN

PRONUNCIATION GUIDE

Phonetic Symbol		Approximate Pronunciation	German Example	Phonetic Transcription	Meaning
Vowels					
a	ah	like a in father			
	or a	as in aunt	Abend	*ah*bent	evening
		as in met	an	an	at
ä	or a	as in rain	Geschäft	ges*hehft*	business
	ai		spät	shpait	late
e	or ai	like e in pen	Henne	*henn*e	hen
	or e	as in pain	nehmen	*nai*men	take
		in unstressed syllables			
		like e in the	bitte	*bitt*e	please
	or i	as in bit	mit	mit	with
i	or ee	as in deed	dir	deer	to you (dative)
ie	ee	as in feel	viel	feel	much
o	o	as in not	oft	oft	often
	or oh	as in note	ohne	*ohn*e	without
ö	eu	as in hors d'oeuvres	schön	sheun	beautiful
u	oo	as in foot	jung	yoong	young
	or oo	as in food	du	doo	you
ü	ew	no English equivalent; round lips and say ee	über	*ew*ber	over
		like ü above	Symphonie	zewmfon*ee*	symphony
y	ew				
Diphthongs					
ai, ay, ei, ey	ahy	like y in cry	mein	mahyn	my
au	ow	like ow in cow	aus	ows	out
äu, eu	oy	like oy in boy	Fräulein	*froy*lahyn	miss
			treu	troy	faithful
Consonants					
c,f,h,k, m,n,p,t,x		pronounced as in English			

Letter		Pronounced	Notes	German	Phonetic	English
b		p	at the end of a word or syllable like p in map otherwise as in English	gab	gahp	gave
ch		ch	like ch in Bach	ich	ich	I
				hoch	hoch	high
d	or	t	at the end of a word or syllable like t in bat otherwise as in English	Bad	baht	bath
		d				
g	or	ch	only in the ending ig like ch in Bach	billig	*bill*ich	cheap
	or	k	often pronounced like ck in tack at the end of a word	Tag	tahk	day
j		y	like y in yet	ja	ya	yes
kn		kn	both letters are pronounced	Knopf	knopf	button
ng		ng	like ng in singer	Sänger	*zeng*er	singer
qu		kv	k sound followed by v	bequem	be*kvehm*	comfortable
r		r	similar to the French r but slightly rolled	rein	rahyn	clean
s		z	before a vowel like z in zoo; or	sehen	*zai*en	see
	or	sh	before p and t like sh in shoe; or	stehen	*shtai*en	stand
				Spiel	Shpeel	game
	or	s	at the end of a word like ss in mess	das	das	the, that
sch		sh	like sh in shoe	Schein	shahyn	brilliance
ß		ss	like ss in mess	Schloß	shloss	castle
tsch		tch	like tch in Dutch	Deutsch	doytch	German
tz		ts	like ts in kits	Platz	plahts	place
v		f	like f in fur	vor	for	for
w		v	like v as in vase	wie	vee	how
z		ts	like ts in kits	Zoll	tsohl	customs

GERMAN

GERMAN GRAMMAR

The Noun with Definite and Indefinite Article and Adjective

All German nouns belong to one of three genders: masculine, feminine or neuter, and are capitalized. For example:

der Wagen	(masculine)	the car
die Tür	(feminine)	the door
das Haus	(neuter)	the house

According to their use in the sentence, German nouns, pronouns, adjectives and articles are declined; that is, their endings change. There are four cases in German: nominative or subject case; accusative or object case; genitive or possessive case; and dative or indirect object case. See the tables below:

MASCULINE with the definite article   (the)

			Plural
Nominative	der alte Mann	the old man	die alten Männer
Accusative	den alten Mann	the old man	die alten Männer
Genitive	des alten Mannes	of the old man	der alten Männer
Dative	dem alten Mann	to the old man	den alten Männern

MASCULINE with the indefinite article   (a)

Nominative	ein alter Mann
Accusative	einen alten Mann
Genitive	eines alten Mannes
Dative	einem alten Mann

MASCULINE without article

			Plural
Nominative	guter Wein	good wine	gute Weine
Accusative	guten Wein	good wine	gute Weine
Genitive	guten Weines	of good wine	guter Weine
Dative	gutem Wein	to good wine	guten Weinen

FEMININE with the definite article

			Plural
Nominative	die junge Frau	the young woman	die jungen Frauen
Accusative	die junge Frau	the young woman	die jungen Frauen
Genitive	der jungen Frau	of the young woman	der jungen Frauen
Dative	der jungen Frau	to the young woman	den jungen Frauen

FEMININE with the indefinite article

Nominative	eine junge Frau	a young woman
Accusative	eine junge Frau	a young woman
Genitive	einer jungen Frau	of a young woman
Dative	einer jungen Frau	to a young woman

FEMININE without article

			Plural
Nominative	frische Frucht	fresh fruit	frische Früchte
Accusative	frische Frucht	fresh fruit	frische Früchte
Genitive	frischer Frucht	of fresh fruit	frischer Früchte
Dative	frischer Frucht	to fresh fruit	frischen Früchten

NEUTER with the definite article

Nominative	das kleine Kind	the small child
Accusative	das kleine Kind	the small child
Genitive	des kleinen Kindes	of the small child
Dative	dem kleinen Kind	to the small child

GERMAN

NEUTER without article

			Plural
Nominative	dunkles Brot	dark bread	dunkle Brote
Accusative	dunkles Brot	dark bread	dunkle Brote
Genitive	dunklen Brotes	of dark bread	dunkler Brote
Dative	dunklem Brot	to dark bread	dunklen Broten

Demonstrative adjectives are declined in the same way as the definite article.

	Masculine	Feminine	Neuter
this	dieser	diese	dieses
that	jener	jene	jenes
every	jeder	jede	jedes
some	mancher	manche	manches
such	solcher	solche	solches
which	welcher	welche	welches
many	viele	viele	viele

	Masculine	Feminine	Neuter	Plural
my	mein	meine	mein	meine
your	dein	deine	dein	deine
his, its	sein	seine	sein	seine
her	ihrer	ihre	ihr	ihre
our	unser	unsere	unser	unsere
your	euer	eure	euer	eure
your	Ihrer	Ihre	Ihr	Ihre
their	ihrer	ihre	kein	keine
no/not any	keiner	keine	kein	keine

Personal Pronouns

	Nominative	Accusative	Dative	Genitive
I	ich	mich	mir	meiner
you[1]	du	dich	dir	deiner
he	er	ihn	ihm	seiner
she	sie	sie	ihr	ihrer
it	es	es	ihm	seiner
we	wir	uns	uns	unser
you[2]	ihr	euch	euch	euer
you[3]	Sie	Sie	Ihnen	Ihrer
they	sie	sie	ihnen	ihrer

[1]singular familiar form (for close friends, relatives, children)
[2]plural familiar form
[3]formal singular and plural form. Written with capital "S" to distinguish it from "they."

Interrogative Pronouns

Nominative	wer	who	was	what
Accusative	wen	whom	was	what
Genitive	wessen	whose	wem	of what
Dative	wem	to whom		

Relative Pronouns

The most frequently used relative pronoun is almost identical to the definite article, der-die-das, in the nominative, accusative and dative cases. The only difference is the dative plural form, which is *denen*. The corresponding forms for the genitive are: dessen, deren, dessen, and deren.

Examples: Die Lehrerin, die sehr nett ist, hat mir ein Buch gegeben.
The teacher, who is very nice, gave me a book.

Der Arzt, den ich Ihnen empfehlen kann, heisst Johann Werner.
The doctor, whom I can recommend to you, is called Johann Werner.

The comparative is formed by adding -er to the adjective (or -r if it ends in e) as in *schnell-schneller* (fast, faster); the superlative is formed by adding -st or -est to the adjective. The endings are declined like all adjectives. As in English, the adjectives gut (good) and viel (much) have special forms for the comparative and superlative:

gut-besser-best
good-better-best

viel-mehr-meist
much-more-most

GERMAN

VERBS

The two most important auxiliary verbs are *sein* (to be) and *haben* (to have).

Sein

ich bin	I am
du bist	you are
er, sie, es ist	he, she, it is
wir sind	we are
ihr seid	you are
Sie sind	you are
sie sind	they are

Haben

ich habe	I have
du hast	you have
er, sie, es hat	he, she, it has
wir haben	we have
ihr habt	you have
Sie haben	you have
sie haben	they have

Other useful auxiliary verbs

	may	*can*	*must*	*want*	*like*
ich	darf	kann	muss	will	mag
du	darfst	kannst	musst	willst	magst
er, sie, es	darf	kann	muss	will	mag
wir	dürfen	können	müssen	wollen	mögen
ihr	dürft	könnt	müsst	wollt	mögt
Sie, sie	dürfen	können	müssen	wollen	mögen

Darf ich mitkommen?   Ich kann ihn nicht verstehen.
May I come along?   I can't understand him.

Ich muss weggehen.   Ich will nicht gehen.   Ich mag dieses Bier.
I must go away   I don't want to go.   I like this beer.

GERMAN

Some other useful verbs (notice the regular endings)

	to make	*to go*	*to come*	*to see*	*to speak*
ich	mache	gehe	komme	sehe	spreche
du	machst	gehst	kommst	siehst	sprichst
er, sie, es	macht	geht	kommt	sieht	spricht
wir	machen	gehen	kommen	sehen	sprechen
ihr	macht	geht	kommt	seht	spricht
Sie, sie	machen	gehen	kommen	sehen	sprechen

The Past Tense

One form of the past tense combines the proper form of the auxiliary verb *haben* or *sein* (sein being used with verbs involving a change of position or condition that cannot take an object) with the past participle. The past participle is usually formed by adding the prefix ge- and the suffix -en or -t to the stem of the verb. Sometimes the vowel changes as well, as in *sprechen* (to speak), *gesprochen* (spoken). Note that the past participle is placed at the end of the sentence.

sprechen:	Ich habe gestern mit meiner Mutter gesprochen.
	I spoke with my mother yesterday.
finden:	Ich habe das Buch endlich gefunden.
	I finally found the book.
sehen:	Er hat viele Tiere in dem Zoo gesehen.
	He saw many animals at the zoo.
bleiben:	Wir sind den ganzen Tag in dem Haus geblieben.
	We stayed the whole day long in the house.
ausgehen:	Meine Schwester ist allein ausgegangen.
	My sister went out alone.

Imperative

| Gehen wir! | Let's go! |
| Gehen Sie! | Go! |

Negatives

Go in front of the word or idea to be negated.

| Ich will es nicht kaufen. | I don't want to buy it. |
| Ich werde es nie kaufen. | I will never buy it. |

GERMAN

GERMAN

Questions

Questions are formed by inverting the verb with the subject:

Sie wird bald ankommen.	She will arrive soon.
Wird sie bald ankommen?	Will she arrive soon?

Prepositions

The following prepositions take the accusative case:

durch	through	Er kam durch das Fenster.	He came through the window.
ohne	without		
um	round		
für	for		
gegen	against, toward		
wider	against		

The following prepositions take the dative case:

aus	out of, from	Sie ist aus dem Haus gekommen.	She came out of the house.
bei	by, near		
mit	with		
nach	to, after		
seit	since		
von	of, from		
zu	to		

The following prepositions take the genitive case:

während	during		
wegen	because of		
trotz	in spite of	Trotz des Regens werden wir hinausgehen.	
ausserhalb	outside	In spite of the rain, we'll go out.	
innerhalb	inside		
statt/anstatt	instead of		

These prepositions take the dative or accusative case, depending upon their usage. The dative case expresses action that takes place in a fixed position or location, while the accusative case expresses motion toward or into a place. In English the same differentiation is made between the prepositions *in* and *into,* or *on* and *upon.*

an	at, on, to
hinter	behind
in	in, into
unter	under, among
neben	beside, near
auf	on, upon
vor	before, in front of
über	over
zwischen	between

For example:

1) Sie ging in das Haus. (She went into the house.) The accusative case is used here because motion is involved.
2) Wir sind in dem Haus geblieben. (We stayed in the house.) The dative case is called for in this sentence because no motion is involved.

Prepositions are frequently contracted with the definite article. Both forms are acceptable. Here are some examples:

an dem → am (at the)		bei dem → beim (at the)	
an das → ans (to the)		in dem → im (in the)	
auf das → aufs (upon the)		von dem → vom (from the, of the)	
für das → fürs (for the)		zu dem → zum (to the)	
in das → ins (in the)		zu der → zur (to the)	

GERMAN

GERMAN

EXPRESSIONS FOR EVERYDAY USE

Basic

Hello
Hallo
hallo

Yes
Ja
ya

No
Nein
nahyn

Please
Bitte
bitte

Thank you
Danke
danke

Yes, thank you
Ja, danke
ya, danke

No, thank you
Nein, danke
nahyn danke

Thank you very much
Vielen Dank
feelen dank

You're welcome
Bitte
bitte

Excuse me
Verzeihung
fehrtsahyoong

Just a moment
Einen Augenblick, bitte
ahynen owgenblick, bitte

Of course
Natürlich
natewlich

How much?
Wieviel?
veefeel?

Where is the restroom?
Wo ist die Toilette?
vo ist dee twalette?

I don't understand.
Ich verstehe nicht.
ich fehrstai'e nicht.

I beg your pardon?
Wie bitte?
vie bitte?

I beg your pardon.
Entschuldigung.
entshooldigoong

That's quite all right.
Gern geschehen
gehrn geshai'en

Greetings

Good morning
Guten Morgen
gooten morgen

Good afternoon
Guten Tag
gooten tahk

Good evening
Guten Abend
gooten ahbent

Good night
Gute Nacht
goote nacht

Goodbye
Auf Wiedersehen
*owf **vee**derzai'n*

See you later.
Bis später.
bis shpaitehr

See you this evening.
Bis heute Abend.
bis hoyte ahbent

See you tomorrow.
Bis Morgen.
bis morgen

How are you?
Wie geht es Ihnen?
vee gait es eenen?

Wie geht es dir? (Informal)
vee gait es deer?

How are things?
Wie geht's?
vee gaits?

Everything's fine.
Es geht gut.
es gait goot

That's fine.
Gut.
goot

GERMAN

Communication Problems

Do you speak English?
Sprechen Sie Englisch?
shprechen zee ehnglish?

**Do you speak French/German/
    Spanish?**
Sprechen Sie Französisch/Deutsch/
    Spanisch?
*shprechen zee frantseuzish/doytch/
    shpanish?*

I don't speak German.
Ich spreche kein Deutsch.
ich shpreche kahyn doytch

I speak some French.
Ich spreche ein bißchen französisch.
*ich shpreche ahyn bisschen
    frantseuzish*

I don't understand you.
Ich verstehe Sie nicht.
ich fehrshtai'e zee nicht

Could you speak more slowly?
Könnten Sie langsamer sprechen?
keunten zee lahngzahmer shprechen?

Could you repeat that, please?
Könnten Sie das wiederholen, bitte?
keunten zee das veederholen, bitte?

Could you write that down, please?
Könnten Sie es aufschreiben, bitte?
keunten zee es owfshrahyben, bitte?

**Could you translate this for me,
    please?**
Könnten Sie mir das übersetzen, bitte?
*keunten zee meer das ewberzetsen,
    bitte?*

I understand.
Ich verstehe.
ich fehrshtai'e

Do you understand?
Verstehen Sie?
fehrshtai'en zee?

**Just a moment. I'll see if I can find it
    in this book.**
Moment, bitte. Ich schaue mal, ob ich
    es im Buch finde.
*moment, bitte Ich shahwe mal, op ich
    es im booch finde*

**Please point to your answer in this
    book.**
Zeigen Sie mir bitte ihre Antwort in
    diesem Buch.
*Tsahyg'n zee meer bitte eere
    ahntwohrt in deezem booch*

GERMAN

Is there someone here who speaks English?
Gibt es hier jemand, der Englisch spricht?
gipt es heer yaimant, der ehnglish shpricht?

What does that mean?
Was bedeutet das?
vas bedoytet das?

How do you say that in German?
Wie sagt man das auf Deutsch?
vie zagt mahn das owf doytch?

Questions

Where?
Wo?
Vo

Where is/are . . .
Wo ist/sind . . .
vo ist/zint

What?
Was?
vas

Why?
Warum?
varoom

How?
Wie?
vee

When?
Wann?
vahn

How much/many
Wieviel/wieviele
veefeel/veefeele

What time is it?
Wieviel Uhr ist es?
veefeel oor ist es?

Is there . . .
Gibt es . . .
gipt es

Are there . . .
Gibt es . . .
gipt es

Could you tell me . . .
Können Sie mir sagen . . .
keunen zee meer zahgen

Could you show me . . .
Können Sie mir zeigen . . .
keunen zee meer tsahygen

Could you tell me how to get to . . .?
Können Sie mir sagen, wie ich nach . . . komme?
keunen zee meer zahgen, vee ich nach . . . komme

It is/isn't

It is . . .
Es ist . . .
es ist

It isn't . . .
Es ist nicht . . .
es ist nicht

Isn't it . . .?
Ist es nicht . . . ?
ist es nicht?

There is/are . . .
Es gibt . . .
es gipt

There isn't/aren't
Es gibt nicht . . .
es gipt nicht

. . . , isn't it?
. . . ,nicht wahr?
nicht vahr?

Here it is/they are.
Hier ist es/hier sind sie.
heer ist es/heer zint zee

Common Adjectives and Adverbs and Their Opposites

beautiful/ugly	schön/hässlich	*sheun/**hess**lich*
before/after	bevor/nach	*be**for**/nach*
better/worse	besser/schlechter	***bess**er/**schlech**ter*
big/small	gross/klein	*gross/**klahyn***
cheap/expensive	billig/teuer	*bil**lich**/**toy**er*
clean/dirty	sauber/schmutzig	*zowber/**shmoot**zich*
cold/hot	kalt/heiss	*kalt/**hahyss***
cool/warm	kühl/warm	*kewl/**vahrm***
dangerous/safe	gefährlich/ungefährlich	*ge**fehr**lich/oonge**fehr**lich*
deep/shallow	tief/seicht	*teef/**zahycht***
early/late	früh/spät	*frew/**shpait***
easy/difficult	leicht/schwierig	*la**hycht**/**shveer**ich*
empty/full	leer/voll	*lair/**foll***
first/lastly	zuerst/zuletzt	*tsu-**ehrst**/tsu**letst***
good/bad	gut/schlecht	*goot/**shlecht***
heavy/light	schwer/leicht	*shvair/**lahycht***
here/there	hier/da, dort	*heer/da, **dort***
high/low	hoch/niedrig	*hoch/**need**rich*
ill/well	krank/gesund	*krahnk/ge**zoont***
inside/outside	drinnen/draussen	*drinnen/**drows**sen*
long/short	lang/kurz	*lahng/**koortz***
more/less	mehr/weniger	*mair/**vain**iger*
at most/at least	meistens/mindestens	*ma**hys**tens/**min**destens*
much/little	viel/wenig	*feel/**vain**ich*
narrow/wide	eng/weit	*eng/**vahyt***
near/far	nah/weit	*nah/**vahyt***
now/later	jetzt/später	*yetzt/**shpai**ter*
often/rarely	oft/selten	*oft/**zel**ten*
old/new	alt/neu	*alt/**noy***
old/young	alt/jung	*alt/**yoong***
open/closed	offen/geschlossen	***off**'n/ge**shloss**'n*
pleasant/unpleasant	angenehm/unangenehm	***an**genaim/oon**an**genaim*
quick/slow	schnell/langsam	*shnell/**lang**zam*
quiet/noisy	ruhig/geräuschvoll	*roo'ich/ge**roysh**fol*
right/left	rechts/links	*rechts/**links***
right/wrong	richtig/falsch	***rich**tich/falsh*
still/not yet	noch/noch nicht	*noch/noch nicht*
thick/thin	dick/dünn	*dick/**dewn***
under/over	unter/über	*unter/**ew**ber*
vacant/occupied	frei/besetzt	*frahy/be**zetzt***
well/badly	gut/schlecht	*goot/**shlecht***

GERMAN

GERMAN

More Useful Words

also	auch	owch
and	und	oont
enough	genug	gen**ook**
not	nicht	nicht
nothing	Nichts	nichts
or	oder	**oder**
perhaps	vielleicht	feell**ahycht**
soon	bald	bahlt
very	sehr	zair

To Help You Further in Conversation

according to	nach	nach
as you wish	wie Sie wollen	vee zee **vollen**
best wishes	herzliche Glückwünsche	**hehrt**sliche **glewk**vewnshe
certainly	gewiss	ge**viss**
entirely	völlig	**feul**lich
everyone	jedermann	**yai**der**mahn**
I don't know	ich weiß nicht	ich vah**yss** nicht
I have forgotten	ich habe vergessen	ich **habe** fehr**gessen**
indeed?	wirklich?	**veer**klich?
in any case	auf jeden Fall	owf **yaiden** fahl
in what way	in welcher Weise	in **velcher** **vahy**ze
it's not important	es macht nichts	es macht nichts
never mind	es macht nichts	es macht nichts
no one	niemand	**nee**mahnt
on the contrary	im Gegenteil	im **geh**gentahyl
precisely	genau	ge**now**
same to you	ebenfalls	**aib**'nfals
sometimes	manchmal	**manch**mal
that is to say	das heißt	das hah**ysst**
that's all	das ist alles	das ist **alles**
that's correct	das ist richtig	das ist **rich**tich
that's impossible	das ist unmöglich	das ist oon**meug**lich
that's incredible	das ist unglaublich	das ist oon**glowb**lich
that's not right	das ist nicht richtig	das ist nicht **rich**tich
that's too bad	das ist schade	das ist **shah**de
What's the matter?	Was ist los?	vas ist lohs?
Where are we going?	Wohin gehen wir?	vohin **gai**'en veer?
with pleasure	mit Vergnügen	mit fehr**gnew**gen

Asking for Something

Could you help me, please?	Können Sie mir helfen, bitte?	*keunen zee meer helfen, bitte?*
Could I have ...	Darf ich ... haben?	*darf ich ... hab'n?*
Could you give me ...	Können Sie mir ... geben?	*keunen zee meer ... gaib'n?*
Could I have one?	Darf ich eine davon haben?	*darf ich ahyne dafon hahb'n?*
I would like ...	Ich möchte ...	*ich meuchte*
I'm looking for ...	Ich suche ...	*ich zooche*
I need ...	Ich brauche ...	*ich browche*

ARRIVAL

Passport and Customs

Your passport, please.
Paß, bitte.

Here it is.
Hier ist er.
heer ist ehr.

How long will you stay here?
Wie lange bleiben Sie?

Where will you be staying?
Wo werden Sie wohnen?

What is the purpose of your visit?
Was ist der Grund Ihres Aufenthaltes?

I'll be staying ...
Ich bleibe ...
ich blahybe

a few days	**two weeks**
ein paar Tage	zwei Wochen
ahyn pahr tahge	*tsvahy vohch'n*
a week	**a month**
eine Woche	einen Monat
ahyne vohche	*ahynen monat*

I'm just passing through.
Ich bin nur auf der Durchreise.
ich bin noor owf dehr doorchrahyze

I'm on my way to ...
Ich fahre nach ...
ich fahre nach

I am visiting relatives/friends.
Ich besuche Verwandte/Freunde.
ich bezooche fehrvahnte/froynde

I'm here on vacation.
Ich bin auf Urlaub.
ich bin owf oorlahwb.

I'm here on business.
Ich bin auf Geschäftsreise.
ich bin owf geshehftsrahyze.

I'm here to study.
Ich werde hier studieren.
ich vehrde heer shtoodeeren

This is my address.
Hier ist meine Adresse.
heer ist mahyne adresse.

How much money do you have?
Wieviel Geld haben Sie?

Do you have any food or plants?
Haben Sie Nahrungsmittel oder Pflanzen?

Do you have anything to declare?
Haben Sie etwas zu verzollen?

GERMAN

No, nothing. I have only personal belongings.
Nein, nichts. Ich habe nur persönliche Dinge.
nahyn, nichts. ich hahbe noor pehrzeunliche Dinge

I have . . .
Ich habe . . .
ich hahbe

cigarettes	**perfume**
Zigaretten	Parfüm
tsigaretten	*parfewm*
liquor	**wine**
Alkohol	Wein
alkohol	*vahyn*
some gifts	
einige Geschenke	
ahynige geshenke	

It's for my personal use.
Das ist für meinen persönlichen Verbrauch.
das ist fewr mahynen pehrzeun, fehrbrowch

Open your bag, please.
Bitte öffnen Sie ihre Tasche.

You'll have to pay duty on this.
Dies is zollpflichtig.

How much do I have to pay?
Wieviel muß ich bezahlen?
veefeel mooss ich betsahlen?

I can't afford it.
Ich kann den Zoll nicht bezahlen.
ich kahn dain tsohl nicht betsahlen

May I go through?
Darf ich durchgehen?
dahrf ich doorchgai'en?

Porter/Luggage

Where can I find a luggage cart?
Wo gibt es Gepäckwagen?
vo gipt es gepeckvahg'n?

Are you using this cart?
Benutzen Sie diesen Gepäckwagen?
benutzen zee deez'n gepeckvahg'n?

Porter!
Gepäckträger!
gepecktraiger

Please take this luggage . . .
Bitte bringen Sie diese Taschen . . .
bitte bringen zee deeze tahshen

to the bus	**taxi**
zum Bus	zum Taxi
tsoom booss	*tsoom taksi*
train	
zum Zug	
tsoom tsook	
checkroom	
zur Gepäckaufbewahrung	
tsoor gepeckowfbevahrung	

Follow me, please.
Folgen Sie mir, bitte.
fohlgen zee meer, bitte

How much do I owe you?
Wieviel, bitte?
veefeel, bitte?

Changing Money

Can you change these traveler's checks?
Können Sie diese Reiseschecks einlösen?
keunen zee deeze rahyzeschecks ahynleuz'n?

I would like to change dollars/ pounds.
Ich möchte einige Dollar/Pfund/ wechseln.
ich meuchte ahynige dohlar pfoont/ vechseln

What is the exchange rate?
Wie ist der Wechselkurs?
vee ist dehr vechselkurs?

Here is my passport.
Hier ist mein Reisepaß.
heer ist mahyn rahyzepahss

Could you please give me . . .
Können Sie mir bitte . . . geben?
keunen zee meer bitte . . . gaib'n?

German marks
D-Marks
dai-mahrks

Austrian schillings
Schillinge
shillinge

Swiss francs
Schweizer Franken
shvahytser frahnken

Could you change this bill?
Können Sie mir bitte das Geld wechseln?
keunen zee meer bitte das gelt wechseln?

GETTING INTO TOWN

Taxi

Where can I find a taxi?
Wo kann ich ein Taxi kriegen?
vo kahn ich ahyn taksi kreegen?

Please call a taxi for me.
Besorgen Sie mir bitte ein Taxi.
bezohrg'n zee meer bitte ahyn taksi

Please take me to . . .
Bringen Sie mich bitte zu . . .
bring'n zee mich bitte tsoo . . .

How much will the fare be?
Wieviel wird es kosten?
veefeel veerd es kohst'n?

How far is it?
Wie weit ist es?
vee vahyt ist es?

Turn right/left . . .
Biegen Sie . . . rechts/links
beeg'n zee rechts/links

at the next corner
an der nächsten Ecke
an dehr nechsten ehke

at the stoplight
bei der Ampel
bahy dehr ahmpel

Go straight ahead.
Geradeaus
gerahde'owss

Turn the meter on, please.
Die Uhr anstellen, bitte.
dee oor anstellen, bitte

GERMAN

GERMAN

Why are you taking me this way?
Sind Sie sicher, daß dies der kürzeste
   Weg ist?
*zint zee zicher, dass deez dehr
   kewrtseste vek ist?*

Please don't drive so fast.
Nicht so schnell, bitte.
nicht zo shnell, bitte

I'm in a hurry.
Ich habe es eilig.
ich hahbe es ahylich

Let me out, please.
Aussteigen, bitte!
owsshtahygen, bitte

Stop here, please.
Halten Sie hier, bitte.
halten zee heer, bitte

Please could you wait for me here?
Können Sie hier auf mich warten, bitte?
keunen zee heer owf mich vahrten?

How much?
Wieviel, bitte?
veefeel bitte?

Bus/Train

Where can I get a bus/train to . . .
Wo kann ich einen Bus/Zug
   nach . . . bekommen?
*vo kahn ich ahynen boos/tsoogk
   nach . . . bekohmen?*

Which bus/train do I take for . . .
Welchen Bus/Zug fährt nach . . .
velchen boos/tsoogk fairt nach

When is the next bus/train for . . .
Wann fahrt der nächste Bus/Zug
   nach . . .
*vahn fairt dehr nechste boos/tsook
   nach*

Do I have to change buses/trains?
Muß ich umsteigen?
mooss ich oomshtahygen?

Where do I buy the ticket?
Wo kauft man die Fahrkarte?
vo kowft man dee fahrkarte?

Could you tell me when we reach . . .
Können Sie mir sagen, wann wir
   in . . . sind?
*keunen zee meer zahgen, vahn veer
   in . . . zint?*

Please let me off.
Aussteigen, bitte!
owsshtatiygen, bitte

Car Rental

I have a reservation for a car.
Ich habe einen Wagen reserviert.
ich hahbe ahynen vahgen rezerveert

I'd like to rent a small/large car.
Ich möchte einen kleinen/großen
   Wagen mieten.
*ich meuchte ahynen klahynen/
   grossen vahgen meeten*

   with an automatic gearshift
   mit automatischer Schaltung
   mit owtomahtisher shaltoong

I need it for . . .
Ich brauche ihn für . . .
ich browche een fewr

   a day/two days
   einen Tag/zwei Tage
   ahynen tahk/tsvahy tahge

   a week/two weeks
   eine Woche/zwei Wochen
   ahyne vohche/tsvahy vohchen

How much is it per . . .
Wieviel kostet es pro . . . ?
veefeel kohstet es pro

hour	**week**
Stunde	Woche
shtoonde	*vohche*
day	**kilometer**
Tag	Kilometer
tahk	*keelomehter*

Is gas included?
Benzin inbegriffen?
bentseen inbegriffen?

Is insurance included?
Versicherung inbegriffen?
fehrzicheroong inbegriffen?

I would like comprehensive insurance.
Ich möchte eine Vollkaskoversicherung.
ich meuchte ahyne fohlkaskofehrzicheroong

Do I have unlimited mileage?
Kilometergeld inbegriffen?
keelomehtergelt inbegriffen?

Can I pay by credit card?
Darf ich mit meiner Kreditkarte zahlen?
dahrf ich mit mahyner kredeetkarte tsahlen?

Here is my driver's license.
Hier ist mein Führerschein.
heer ist mahyn fewrershahyn

What's the deposit?
Wieviel muß ich hinterlegen?
veefeel mooss ich hinterlaig'n?

May I look at the car first, please?
Darf ich mir zuerst den Wagen ansehen, bitte?
dahrf ich meer tsueHrst dain vahgen anzai'en, bitte?

I'm not familiar with this kind of car. Please show me . . .
Ich kenne diese Art von Wagen nicht.
Würden Sie mir bitte . . . erklären?
ich kenne deeze art fon vahgen nicht. vewrden zee meer bitte . . . erklehren?

the headlights
die Scheinwerfer
dee shahynvehrfer

the directionals
die Blinker
dee blinker

the ignition
die Zündung
dee tsewndoong

the gas cap
den Tankverschluß
dain tahnkfehrshlooss

What kind of gas must I use?
Welches Benzin muß ich benutzen?
velches bentseen mooss ich benootzen?

standard/premium
Normal/Super
normahl/zooper

Could you show me how to release the hood?
Könnten Sie mir bitte erklären, wie man die Kühlerhaube öffnet?
keunten zee meer bitte ehrklehren, vee mahn dee kewlerhowbe eufnet?

Must I return it to this office?
Muß ich ihn zu diesem Büro zurückbringen?
mooss ich een tsu deezem bewro tsurewkbringen?

May I return it in another city?
Darf ich ihn in eine andere Stadt zurückbringen?
dahrf ich een in ahyne andere shtaht zurewkbringen?

Is there an extra charge (for that)?
Kostet es extra?
kostet es extra?

Have you got a branch in . . .
Haben Sie ein Büro in . . .
hahben zee ahyn bewro in

What do I do if I have car trouble?
Was muß ich tun, wenn ich eine Panne habe?
vas mooss ich toon, ven ich ahyne pahne hahbe?

ACCOMMODATIONS

Hotels—Pensions

I'm looking for . . .
Ich suche . . .
ich zooche

a good hotel
ein gutes Hotel
ahyn gootes hotel

an inexpensive hotel
ein preiswertes Hotel
ahyn prahyzvehrtes hotel

a pension
eine Pension
ahyne penzyohn

a youth hostel
eine Jugendherberge
ahyne yoogendhehrbehrge

I have a reservation.
Ich habe reserviert.
ich hahbe rezehrveert.

My name is . . .
Mein Name ist . . .
mahyn nahme ist

Do you have a room for tonight?
Haben Sie ein Zimmer für heute Nacht?
hahben zee ahyn tsimmer fewr hoyte nacht?

I would like . . .
Ich möchte . . .
ich meuchte

a single/double room
ein Einzel-/Doppel-zimmer
ahyn ahyntsel/dohppel tsimmer

a room . . .   **with twin beds**
ein Zimmer . . .   mit zwei Betten
ahyn tsimmer . . .   mit tsvahy betten

with a doublebed
mit Doppelbett
mit dohppelbett

I want a room with . . .
Ich möchte ein Zimmer mit . . .
ich meuchte ahyn tsimmer mit

a bath/shower
Bad/Dusche
baht/dooshe

running water
fließendem Wasser
fleessendem vahsser

hot water
warmem Wasser
vahrmem vahsser

a balcony   **a view of the sea**
Balkon   Blick aufs Meer
balkohn   *blick owfs mehr*

How much is the room per day? per week?
Wieviel kostet es pro Tag? pro Woche?
veefeel kostet es pro tahk? pro vohche?

That's too expensive. Do you have anything cheaper?
Das ist zuviel. Haben Sie was Billigeres?
das ist tsoofeel. hahben zee vas billigeres?

How much is the room. . .
Wieviel kostet das Zimmer . . .
veefeel kostet das tsimmer. . .

without meals
ohne Mahlzeiten
ohne mahltsahyten

with breakfast only
mit Frühstück
mit frewshtewk

with half board   **with full board**
mit Halbpension   mit Vollpension
mit halbpenziohn   *mit fohlpenziohn*

Is there a reduction for children/ a longer stay?
Gibt es eine Preisermässigung für Kinder/einen längeren Aufenthalt?
*gipt es **ahyne prahyz**ermehssigoong fewr **kinder/ahynen leng**eren owfenthalt?*

Do you have a safe?
Haben Sie einen Tresor?
hahben zee ahynen traizor?

Could I please have . . .
Darf ich . . . haben.
*dahrf ich . . . **hahben***

another pillow	ein extra Kopfkissen	*ahyn extra **kopf**kissen*
an extra blanket	eine extra Decke	*ahyne extra **dekke***
some towels	einige Handtücher	*ahynige **hant**ewcher*
some soap	Seife	*zahyfe*
a glass	ein Glas	*ahyn glahs*
toilet paper	Toilettenpapier	*twah**letten**papeer*
more hangers	noch einige Kleiderbügel	*noch ahynige **klahy**derbewgel*
writing paper	Schreibpapier	*shrahyb**papeer*
a bottle of mineral water	eine Flasche Mineralwasser	*ahyne flahshe mine**rahl**vahsser*
an ashtray	einen Aschenbecher	*ahynen **ah**shenbecher*
a light bulb	eine Birne	*ahyne **beer**ne*
fresh sheets	frische Laken	*frishe **lah**ken*

I would like to deposit my valuables.
Ich möchte meine Wertsachen deponieren.
*ich **meuch**te **meh**yne **vert**zachen daipohneeren.*

When is check-out time?
Um wieviel Uhr muß ich das Zimmer verlassen?
*oom veefeel oor moos ich das **tsim**mer fehrlahssen?*

The . . . doesn't work.
. . . funktioniert nicht.
*foonktsiyo**neert** nicht*

air conditioning	die Klimaanlage	*dee kleema-**an**lahge*
heating	die Heizung	*dee **hahyt**soong*
hot water	warmes Wasser	***vahr**mes **vas**ser*
light	das Licht	*das licht*
lock	das Schloß	*das **shlohss***
radio	das Radio	*das **rah**dio*
shower	die Dusche	*dee **doo**she*
tap	der Wasserhahn	*dehr **vahs**serhahn*
toilet	die Toilette	*dee twah**lette***

Can the heat/air conditioning be turned up/down?
Ist es möglich, die Heizung/Klimaanlage weiter aufzudrehen/etwas mehr abzudrehen?
*ist es **meu**glich, dee **hahyt**soong/kleema-**an**lahge **vahy**ter owftsudrai'en/etvas mehr aptsudrai'en?*

The mattress is too soft. May I have a firmer one?
Die Matratze ist zu weich. Darf ich eine härtere haben?
*dee ma**trat**se ist tsu vahych. dahrf ich ahyne **hehr**tere **hah**ben?*

GERMAN

Could you wake me up tomorrow morning at . . .
Können Sie mich um . . . Morgen früh wecken?
keunen zee mich oom . . . morgen frew vecken?

May we have breakfast in our room?
Können wir im Zimmer frühstücken?
keunen veer im tsimmer frewshtewken?

Until what time do you serve breakfast?
Bis wann können wir frühstücken?
bis vahn keunen veer frewshtewken?

May I see the room?
Darf ich das Zimmer sehen?
dahrf ich das tsimmer zai'en?

Yes, this room will do.
Das Zimmer ist in Ordnung.
das tsimmer ist in ordnoong.

No, this room won't do.
Nein, das Zimmer ist nicht in Ordnung.
nahyn, das tsimmer ist nicht in ordnoong.

Do you have any bigger/better rooms?
Haben Sie grössere/bessere Zimmer?
hahben zee greussere/bessere tsimmer?

This is the only room vacant right now.
Wir haben nur dieses Zimmer frei.

We'll have another room tomorrow.
Wir werden Morgen ein Anderes haben.

How long will you be staying?
Wie lange bleiben Sie?

I will be staying . . .
Ich bleibe . . .
ich blahybe . . .

   tonight only
   nur eine Nacht
   noor ahyne nacht

   two or three days   **a week**
   einige Tage   eine Woche
   ahynige tahge   *ahyne vohche*

I haven't decided yet.
Ich weiß noch nicht.
ich vahyss noch nicht

Here is my passport.
Hier ist mein Reisepaß.
Heer ist mahyn rahyzepass.

When may I have it back?
Wann kann ich ihn zurückbekommen?
vahn kahn ich een tsurewkbekommen?

May I go to the room now?
Darf ich jetzt ins Zimmer gehen?
dahrf ich yetzt ins tsimmer gai'en?

May I have the key?
Der Schlüssel, bitte.
dehr shlewssel, bitte

Shall I take the key with me when I go out or leave it with you?
Soll ich den Schlüssel mitnehmen, wenn ich ausgehe, oder ihn bei Ihnen hinterlassen?
zohl ich dain shlewssel mitnaim'n, ven ich owsgai'e, oder een bye eenen hinterlassen?

At what time do you lock the front door?
Um wieviel uhr ist die Tür abgeschlossen?
um veefeel oor ist dee tewr apgeshlohss'n?

How do I get in if I come later?
Wie kann ich hineingelangen, wenn ich später zurückkehre?
vee kahn ich hinahyn gelangen, ven ich shpaiter tsurewckkehre?

At what time is lunch/dinner?
Um wieviel Uhr gibt es Mittagessen/Abendessen?
oom veefeel oor gipt es mittakessen/ahbentessen?

Could you please have the linen changed today?
Können Sie bitte die Bettwäsche wechseln?
keunen zee bitte dee bettveshe vechseln?

Are there any letters for me?
Sind Briefe für mich da?
*zint **breefe** fewr mich da?*

I would like to call this number . . .
Ich möchte diese Nummer anrufen.
*ich meuchte **dee**ze **noo**mer **an**roofen*

Checking Out

We'll be leaving tomorrow.
Wir fahren Morgen ab.
*veer **fahren morgen** ap*

**May I have the bill,
please?**
Könnte ich bitte meine Rechnung
haben?
*keunte ich **bitte mahyne rechnoong**
hahben?*

Could you give me a receipt, please?
Könnte ich bitte eine Quittung haben?
*keunte ich **bitte ahyne kvittoong**
hahben?*

Could you explain this item?
Können Sie mir diesen Posten erklären?
*keunen zee meer **deezen pohsten**
erklehren?*

Thank you for a most enjoyable stay.
Vielen Dank für den sehr angenehmen
Aufenthalt.
*feelen dank fewr den zehr **an**genaimen
owfenthalt*

**I hope we'll be able to return some
day.**
Ich hoffe, daß wir mal wiederkommen.
*ich **hoffe**, dass veer mahl
veederkommen*

Youth Hostel

Are there any rooms available?
Haben Sie ein Zimmer frei?
*hahben zee ahyn **tsimmer**
frahy?*

When is the curfew?
Wann schliessen Sie die
Jugendherberge?
*vahn shleessen zee dee
yoogendhehrbehrge?*

Do we have to do chores?
Müssen wir Hausarbeit machen?
*mewssen veer **hows**arbahyt **machen?***

**Is there a limit on the number of days
we can stay?**
Gibt es eine zeitliche Beschränkung des
Aufenthaltes?
*gipt es ahyne **tsahyt**liche be**shren**kung
des **owfenthaltes?***

When is checkout time?
Um wieviel Uhr müssen wir das
Zimmer verlassen?
*oom veefeel oor **mews**sen veer das
tsimmer fehrlahssen?*

Camping

Is there a campsite nearby?
Gibt es hier in der Nähe einen
Campingplatz?
*gipt es heer in dehr **nai**'e **ahynen**
kempingplahtz?*

May we camp here?
Können wir hier zelten?
*keunen veer heer **tselten?***

GERMAN

What's the charge?
Wieviel kostet es?
veefeel kostet es?

Are there . . .
Gibt es . . .
gipt es

  baths
  Bädewannen
  behdevahnen

  showers   **toilets**
  Duschen   Toiletten
  dooshen   *twahletten*

Are there cooking/washing facilities?
Gibt es hier Kochgelegenheiten/
  Waschräume?
*gipt es heer kochgelaigenhahyten/
  vashroyme?*

Is it possible to rent a tent/ bungalow?
Kann man Zelte/Bungalows mieten?
kann mahn tselte/boongalows meeten?

Where can we find drinking water?
Wo können wir Trinkwasser finden?
vo keunen veer trinkvasser finden?

May we light a fire?
Dürfen wir ein Feuer machen?
dewrfen veer ahyn foyer machen?

Where can we find . . .
Wo kann man . . . finden?
vo kahn mahn . . . finden?

  a camping equipment store
  ein Campinggeschäft
  ahyn kemping-gesheft

  elecric plugs
  Steckdosen
  shtekdohzn

  a laundry
  eine Wäscherei
  ahyne vesherahy

  a restaurant
  ein Restaurant
  ahyn restoran

  shops
  ein Einkaufszentrum
  ahyn ahynkowfstsentrum

  telephones
  Telephone
  telefone

Signs

NO CAMPING	ZELTEN VERBOTEN
NO FIRES	ES IST VERBOTEN, FEUER ANZUZÜNDEN
NO TRAILERS	KEINE WOHNWAGEN
NO TRESPASSING	KEIN DURCHGANG, EINTRITT VERBOTEN, UNBEFUGTES BETRETEN BEI STRAFE VERBOTEN
PRIVATE PROPERTY	PRIVATES EIGENTUM
VICIOUS DOG	BISSIGER HUND
WATER NOT DRINKABLE	KEIN TRINKWASSER

TRAVELING

Signs

ARRIVALS	ANKUNFT
DEPARTURES	ABFAHRT/ABFLUG
ENTRANCE	EINGANG
EXIT	AUSGANG
TICKETS	FAHRKARTEN
INFORMATION	AUSKUNFT
BAGGAGE CHECK	GEPÄCKAUFBEWAHRUNG
CHANGE	WECHSEL
TO THE PLATFORMS	ZU DEN GLEISEN/BAHNSTEIGEN
CUSTOMS	ZOLL
NO SMOKING	RAUCHEN VERBOTEN
WAITING ROOM	WARTERAUM
TOILETS	TOILETTEN

GERMAN

Traveling by Air

To the airport, please.
Zum Flughafen, bitte!
*tsoom **flook**hafen, bitte*

Is there a bus/train to/from the airport?
Gibt es ein Bus/Zug, der zum/vom Flughafen Fährt?
*gipt es ahyn boos/tsook, der tsoom/fom **flook**hafen fairt?*

Where? When?
Wo? Wann?
Vo? Vahn?

Is there a flight to . . .
Gibt es ein Flug nach . . .
gipt es ahyn flook nach

At what time?
Um wieviel Uhr?
om veefeel oor?

Is there an earlier/later one?
Gibt es ein Flug zu einem früheren Zeitpunkt?
*gipt es ahyn flook tsu **ahyn**em frew'eren **tsahyt**punkt?*

When is check-in time?
Wann muβ ich mich melden?
*vahn mooss ich mich **mel**den?*

When does it arrive?
Wann kommt der Flug an?
vahn kommt der flook an?

How much is the fare to . . .
Was kostet ein Flug nach . . .
*vas **kos**tet ahyn flook nach*

What's the flight number?
Welche Flugnummer?
***vel**she **flook**noommer?*

I'd like to book a seat on the next flight to . . .
Ich möchte den nächsten Flug nach . . .
*ich **meuch**te den **nechs**ten flook nach*

    one way
    einfacher Flug
    ***ahyn**facher flook*

    round trip
    Rückflug
    ***rewck**flook*

GERMAN

I'd like a seat . . .
Ich möchte einen Platz
ich meuchte ahynen plahtz

in the aisle	**in the front**
am Gang	vorne
am gahng	*forne*
at the window	**in the back**
biem Fenster	hinten
bahym fenster	*hinten*

in the nonsmoking section
im Nichtraucherabteil
im nichtrowcheraptahyl

in the smoking section
im Raucherabteil
im rowcheraptahyl

Is it a nonstop flight?
Ist es ein Direktflug?
ist es ahyn direktflook?

Will it be necessary to change planes?
Muβ ich umsteigen?
mooss ich oomshtahygen?

How many bags am I allowed?
Wieviele Taschen darf ich mitnehmen?
veefeele tahshen dahrf ich mitnai'men?

How much is charged for excess weight?
Wieviel muß man für Übergewicht des Gepäcks bezahlen?
veefeel mooss man fewr ewbergevicht des gepecks betsahlen?

How long is the flight delayed?
Wie lange hat der Flug Verspätung?
vee lahnge hat dehr flook fehrshpaitoong?

Traveling by Train

When is the next train to . . .
Wann fährt der nächste Zug nach . . .
vahn fairt dehr nechste tsook nach

I would like to reserve/buy a one way/round trip ticket to . . .
Ich möchte eine einfache Fahrkarte/Rückfahrkarte nach . . . reservieren/kaufen.
ich meuchte ahyne ahynfache fahrkarte/rewckfahrkarte nach . . . rezerveeren/kowfen

first/second class
erste/zweite Klasse
ehrste/tsvahyte klahsse

What is the fare to . . .
Wieviel kostet es nach . . .
veefeel kostet es nach

How much is it for a child of . . . years?
Wieviel kostet es für ein . . .-jahriges Kind?
veefeel kostet es fewr ahyn -yahriges kint?

What time does the train leave?
Um wieviel Uhr fährt der Zug ab?
oom veefeel oor fairt dehr tsook ap?

When does it arrive?
Um wieviel Uhr kommt er an?
om veefeel oor kommt ehr ahn?

At which platform?
Auf welchem Gleis?
owf velchem glahyss?

Do I have to change trains? Where?
Muß ich umsteigen? Wo?
mooss ich oomshtahygen? vo?

When will there be a connection to . . . ?
Wann habe ich Anschluss nach . . . ?
vahn hahbe ich ahnshlooss nach . . . ?

Is there a sleeping car?
Gibt es ein Schlafwagen?
gipt es ahyn shlahfvahgen?

Are there couchettes?
Gibt es Liegen?
gipt es leegen?

Is this train going to . . .
Fährt dieser Zug nach . . .
fairt deezer tsook nach

Which car for . . . ?
Welcher Wagen fährt nach . . . ?
velcher vahgen fairt nach . . . ?

Could you tell me where car number . . . is?
Können Sie mir sagen, wo der Wagen Nummer . . . ist?
keunen zee meer zahgen, vo der vahgen noomer . . . ist?

I have a reservation.
Ich habe einen Platz reserviert.
ich hahbe ahynen plahtz rezerveert

Where is my couchette?
Wo ist meine Liege?
vo ist mahyne leege?

Is this seat taken?
Ist dieser Platz besetzt?
ist deezer plahtz bezehtzt?

Excuse me. I think this is my seat.
Verzeihung. Ich glaube, das ist mein Platz.
lehrtsahyoong. ich glahwbe, das ist mahyn plahtz

May I get by?
Durchlassen, bitte!
doorchlahssen, bitte

Where is the dining car?
Wo ist der Speisewagen?
vo ist dehr shpahyzevahgen?

May I open/close the window/the curtains?
Darf ich das Fenster/den Vorhang öffnen/schliessen?
dahrf ich das fenster/dain forhang eufnen/shleessen?

Can the heating be turned off/down/ higher?
Kann man die Heizung ausmachen/ etwas mehr abdrehen/aufdrehen?
kahn mahn dee hahytsoong owsmachen/etvas mehr apdrai'en/ owfdrai'en?

Could you refrain from smoking, please?
Würden Sie bitte das Rauchen unterlassen?
vewrden zee bitte das rahwchen oonterlassen?

This is a nonsmoking compartment.
Dies ist ein Nichtraucher.
dees ist ahyn nichtrahwcher

What station is this?
Welche Station ist dies?
velche statsiyon ist deez?

Is this where I change for a train to . . .
Muß ich hier umsteigen, um nach . . . zu fahren?
mooss ich heer oomshtahygen, oom nach . . . tsu fahren?

GERMAN

Traveling by Boat

Is there a boat to . . . ?
Fährt ein Schiff von hier nach . . . ?
fairt ahyn shif fon heer nach?

When does the next boat leave?
Wann fährt das nächste Schiff ab?
vahn fairt das nechste shif ap?

I would like to buy a roundtrip/one- way ticket in first/second class.
Ich möchte eine Rückfahrkarte/einfache Fahrkarte erster/zweiter Klasse.
ich meuchte ahyne rewckfahrkarte/ ahyne fahrkarte ehrster/tsvahyter klahsse.

When does it arrive?
Wann kommt es an?
vahn kommt es an?

When does it return?
Wann kommt es zurück?
vahn kommt es tsurewk?

When must I go on board?
Wann muß ich an Bord gehen?
vahn mooss ich an bohrd gai'en?

Where can I find pills for seasickness?
Wo kann ich Tabletten für Reisekrankheit finden?
vo kahn ich tabletten fewr rahyzekrahnkhahyt finden?

Traveling by Bus/Streetcar/Subway

Where is the bus station?
Wo ist der Omnibus-Bahnhof?
vo ist dehr omneebooss bahnhof?

Where is the nearest bus stop/ subway station/streetcar stop?
Wo ist die nächste Bushaltestelle/ U-Bahnstation?
vo ist dee nechste boos-halteshtelle/ oo-bahnstahtseeohn?

Where can I get a bus/train to . . .
Wo hält der Bus/Zug, der nach . . . fährt?
vo hehlt dehr booss/tsook, dehr nach . . . fairt?

How long does it take?
Wie lange dauert die Fahrt?
vee lahnge dowehrt dee fahrt?

Does this bus/train go to . . . ?
Fährt dieser Bus/Zug nach . . . ?
fairt deezer boos/tsook nach?

Which line do I take for . . . ?
Mit welcher Linie muß ich nach . . . fahren?
mit velcher leeneeya mooss ich nach . . . fahren?

Where do I buy a ticket?
Wo kauft man die Fahrkarte?
vo kowft mahn dee fahrkarte?

What is the fare to . . . ?
Was kostet es nach . . . ?
vas kostet es nach?

Do I get off here for . . . ?
Wo muß ich für . . . aussteigen?
vo mooss ich fewr . . . ows-shtahygen?

Could you tell me when we reach . . . ?
Können Sie mir bitte sagen, wenn wir in . . . sind?
keunen zee meer bitte zahgen, vehn veer in . . . zint?

Let me off, please.
Aussteigen, bitte!
ows-shtahygen, bitte

Traveling by Car

Where can I find a gas station/ garage?
Wo kann ich eine Tankstelle/ Reparaturwerkstatt finden?
vo kahn ich ayhne tahnkshtelle/ reparatoorvehrkshtatt finden?

How much is gas per liter?
Was kostet das Benzin pro Liter?
vas kostet das bentseen pro leeter?

Please . . .

fill her up
Volltanken, bitte!
folltahnken, bitte

**give me . . . liters of standard/
premium**
. . . Liter Normal/Super, bitte
. . . leeter normahl/super

give me a liter of oil
Geben Sie mir . . . Liter Öl.
gaib'n zee meer . . . leeter eul

**check the oil/water/battery/tires/
brake fluid**
Kontrollieren Sie das Öl/das Wasser/
die Batterie/den Reifendruck/die
Bremsflüssigkeit
*kontrolleeren zee das eul/das
vasser/dain rahyfendruk/dee
bremsflewssigkahyt*

clean the windshield
Bitte reinigen Sie die
Windschutzscheibe
*bitte rahynigen zee dee
vintshutzchahybe*

adjust the brakes
Bitte stellen Sie die Bremsen ein
bitte shtellen zee dee bremsen ahyn

In Case of a Breakdown

Excuse me. My car has broken down. May I use your phone?
Entschuldignug. Mein Wagen hat eine Panne. Darf ich Ihr Telephon
benutzen?
*entshooldigoong. mahyne vahgen hat ahyne pahne darf ich eer telefown
benootzen?*

I've had a breakdown at . . . Can you send a mechanic/tow truck?
Ich habe eine Panne in . . . Können Sie einen Mechaniker/einen
Abschleppwagen schicken?
*ich hahbe ahyne pahne in . . . keunen zee ahynen mechaniker/ahynen
apshleppvahgen shicken?*

How long will you be?
Wie lange dauert es?
vee lahnge dowehrt es?

**Thank you for stopping. Could you
help me?**
Vielen Dank, daß Sie anhalten. Würden
Sie mir bitte helfen?
*feelen dank, das zee anhalten.
vewrden zee meer bitte helfen?*

I have a flat tire.
Ich habe eine Reifenpanne.
ich hahbe ahyrie rahyfenpahne.

The battery is dead.
Die Batterie ist leer.
dee batteree ist leer

Do you have a jack/jumper cables?
Haben Sie einen Wagenheber/
Batteriekabel?
*hahben zee ahynen vahgenhaiber/
battereekahbel?*

I've run out of gas.
Ich habe kein Benzin mehr.
ich hahbe kahyn bentseen mehr

**Would you please notify the next
garage?**
Würden Sie bitte die nächste
Reparaturwerkstatt
benachrichtigen?
*vewrden zee bitte dee nechste
reparatoorvehrkshtatt
benachrichtigen?*

GERMAN

GERMAN

Could you have a look at my car?
Können Sie sich bitte meinen Wagen ansehen?
keunen zee zich bitte mahynen vahgen anzai'en?

**There's something
wrong with the . . .**
. . . ist/sind nicht in Ordnung.
ist/zint nicht in ohrdnung

accelerator	das Gaspedal	das **gahs**pedahl
brakes	die Bremsen	dee **brem**zen
carburetor	der Vergasser	dehr fehr**gahs**ser
clutch	die Kupplung	dee **kupp**loong
engine	der Motor	dehr mo**tohr**
fan	der Ventilator	dehr fenteela**tohr**
gears	die Gänge	dee **gehn**ge
hand brake	die Handbremse	dee **hant**bremze
headlights	die Scheinwerfer	dee **shahyn**vehrfer
horn	die Hupe	dee **hoope**
ignition	die Zündung	dee **tsewn**doong
spark plugs	die Zündkerzen	dee **tsewnt**kehrtsen
turn signals	die Blinker	dee **blinker**

I don't know what's wrong with it.
Ich weiß nicht, was mit dem Wagen
los ist.
*ich vahyss nicht, vas mit dain **vah**gen
los ist*

A light went out on the dashboard.
Ein kleines Licht ist am Amaturenbrett
angegangen.
*ahyn **klah**ynes licht ist am
ama**toor**enbrett **an**gegangen*

**Will spare parts be needed? Do you
have them?**
Brauche ich Ersatzteile? Haben Sie sie?
***brow**che ich ehr**zatz**tahyle? **hah**ben
zee zee?*

How long will it take to repair?
Wie lange wird die Reparatur dauern?
*vee **lahn**ge veert dee repara**toor**
dowehrn?*

How much will it cost?
Wie teuer ist es?
*vee **toy**er ist es?*

When will the car be ready?
Wann kann ich den Wagen abholen?
*vahn kahn ich dain **vah**gen **ap**holen?*

**Where's the nearest garage that can
fix it?**
Wo ist die nächste Werkstatt, die das
reparieren kann?
*vo ist dee **nechs**te **vehrk**shtaht, dee
das repa**ree**ren kahn?*

Is the car repaired?
Ist der Schaden behoben?
*ist dehr **shah**den be**hoben**?*

How much do I owe you?
Was schulde ich Ihnen?
*vas **shool**de ich **ee**nen?*

**Could you give me an itemized bill,
please?**
Geben Sie mir bitte eine ausführliche
Rechnung.
***gaib**'n zee meer **bitte** **ahyne**
ows**fewr**liche **rech**noong*

Trouble with the Police

Your identification please.
Ihren Ausweis, bitte!

I don't speak German very well.
Ich spreche nur wenig Deutsch.
ich shpreche noor vainich doytch

Do you speak English?
Sprechen Sie Englisch?
sprechen zee english?

I'm sorry, I don't understand
Entschuldigen Sie bitte, aber ich
   verstehe nicht.
*entshooldigen zee bitte, ahber ich
   fehrshtai'e nicht*

Here's my driver's license.
Hier ist mein Führerschein.
heer ist mahn fewhrershein

Was I driving too fast?
Bin ich zu schnell gefahren?
bin ich tsu shnell gefahren?

What did I do wrong?
Was habe ich falsch gemacht?
vas hahbe ich falsh gemacht?

Must I pay a fine?
Muß ich Bußgeld bezahlen?
mooss ich boosgelt betsahlen?

How much is it?
Wie viel?
veefeel?

Traveling by Bicycle/Moped

Where can I rent a bicycle/moped?
Wo kann ich ein Fahrrad/Moped
   mieten?
*vo kahn ich ahyn fahrrat/moped
   meeten?*

I'd like to rent a Moped.
Ich möchte ein Moped mieten.
ich meuchte ahyn moped meeten

How much is it per hour/day?
Was kostet es pro Stunde/pro Tag?
vas kostet es pro shtoonde/pro tahk?

At what time must I return it?
Um wieviel Uhr muß ich es
   zurückbringen?
*oom veefeel oor mooss ich es
   tsurewckbringen?*

This bicycle is too big/small.
Dieses Fahrrad ist zu groß/klein.
deezes fahrrat ist tsu gross/klahyn

This tire needs air.
Dieser Reifen braucht Luft.
deezer rahyfen browcht looft

The motor keeps stalling.
Der Motor stottert.
der motohr shtohtehrt

**Something's wrong with the brake/
   headlight.**
Die Bremse/der Scheinwerfer ist nicht
   in Ordnung.
*dee bremse/der shahynvehrfer ist nicht
   in ohrdnoong*

GERMAN

GERMAN

Hitchhiking

Are you going to . . .
Fahren Sie nach . . .
fahren zee nach?

I'm only going as far as . . .
Ich fahre nur bis . . .

I can take you as far as . . .
Ich kann Sie bis . . . fahren:

Get in.
Steigen Sie ein.

Asking the Way

Excuse me. Could you tell me . . .
Entschuldigung. Können Sie mir
sagen . . .
*entshooldigoong. keunen zee meer
zahgen*

  how to get to . . .
  wie komme ich nach . . .
  vee komme ich nach

  how far is it to . . .
  wie weit ist es nach . . .
  vee vahyt ist es nach

  am I on the right road for . . .
  bin ich auf der richtigen Straße
  nach . . .
  *bin ich owf der richtigen strasse
  nach . . .*

  what is the name of this town
  wie heißt diese Stadt
  vee hahysst deeze shtaht

Could you direct me to . . . ?
Können Sie mir bitte den Weg
nach . . . erklären?
*keunen zee meer bitte dain vehk
nach . . . erklehren?*

**Could you show me where we are on
this map?**
Können Sie mir auf der Karte zeigen,
wo wir sind?
*keunen zee meer owf dehr kahrte
tsahygen, vo veer zint?*

It's not far from here.
Es ist nicht weit von hier.

It's a fair distance from here.
Es ist ziemlich weit von hier

Go straight ahead.
Fahren Sie geradeaus.

Turn left/right . . .
Biegen Sie links/rechts . . .

  at the first/second traffic light
  bei der ersten/zweiten Ampel ab

  at the next corner
  bei der nächsten Ecke ab

  at the next intersection
  bei der nächsten Kreuzung ab

  at the traffic circle
  am Verteilerkreis ab

Follow the signs for . . .
Folgen Sie den Schildern nach . . .

GERMAN

Highway Signs

EXIT	AUSFAHRT
ENTRANCE	EINFAHRT
ONE WAY	EINBAHNSTRASSE
NO ENTRY	KEINE ZUFAHRT
NO PARKING	PARKEN VERBOTEN
DETOUR	UMLEITUNG
DANGER	GEFAHR
MERGING TRAFFIC	SPURZUSAMMENFÜHRUNG
HIGHWAY	AUTOBAHN
SPEED LIMIT	GESCHWINDIGKEITSGRENZE
RESTSTOP	RASTSTELLE
RAILROAD CROSSING	BAHNÜBERGANG

TYPES OF EATING ESTABLISHMENTS IN GERMANY, AUSTRIA AND SWITZERLAND

Restaurant/Gastätte: usually found in cities; here you can have a full meal and enjoy local specialties.

Ratskeller/Rathauskeller: originally for students. Much of the fare consists of traditional specialties at reasonable prices.

Gasthaus/gasthof: often found in the country. An inn that offers modest home-cooked meals in cozy surroundings.

Bierstube: literally a "beer room." Here you can have simple meals and snacks while you enjoy your beer.

Weinstube: a "wine room." Found in wine-producing regions. Like the Bierstube, it provides simple hot dishes and snacks.

Bierhalle: in addition to beer or wine, you can enjoy hot and cold food.

Café: serves coffee and other hot and cold drinks as well as pastries and snacks.

Milchbar/Milchstübl: serves milk drinks and pastries.

Konditorei: serves pastry, coffee and hot chocolate.

Schnellimbiβ: snack bar that serves mostly beer and sausages.

Würstchenstand: a stand where you can buy various types of sausage as well as french fries and bread.

Guten Appetit!	**Bon appetit!**
Zum Wohl/Prost!	**Cheers!**

EATING OUT

Can you suggest a good restaurant . . .
for breakfast/lunch/dinner?
Können Sie mir ein gutes Restaurant für das Frühstück/Mittagessen/
Abendessen empfehlen?
*keunen zee meer ahyn **goo**tes restau**rah**n fewr das **frew**shtewk **mitt**akessen/
ahbentessen empf**ai**len?*

Do you know if there's an inexpensive restaurant around here?
Wissen Sie, ob es hier in der Nähe ein preiswertes Restaurant gibt?
***viss**en zee, op es heer in dehr **nai**'e ahyn **prah**yz vehrtes restau**rah**n gipt?*

I'd like to make a reservation for two/four at 8:00 this evening.
Ich möchte einen Tisch für zwei/vier Personen um acht Uhr heute abend
reservieren.
*ich **meuch**te **ahy**nen tish fewr tsvahy/feer pehr**zo**nen oom acht oor **hoy**te **ah**bent
rezeh**rvee**ren*

Good evening. We have a reservation.
The name is . . .
Guten Abend. Wir haben reserviert.
Der Name ist . . .
***goo**ten **ah**bent. veer **hah**ben
rezeh**rveer**t. dehr **nah**me ist*

on the terrace
auf der Terrasse
*auf dehr teh**rass**e*

by the window
beim Fenster
*bahym **fen**ster*

Do you have a table for three?
Haben Sie einen Tisch für drei
Personen?
***hah**ben zee **ahy**nen tish fewr drahy
pehr**zo**nen?*

Could we have a table with more
privacy?
Könnten wir einen Tisch haben, wo wir
ungestört sein können?
***keun**ten veer **ahy**nen tish **hah**ben, vo
veer **oong**eshteurt zahyn **keun**en?*

Could we have a table . . .
Könnten wir einen Tisch . . . haben?
***keun**ten veer **ahy**nen tish . . . **hah**ben?*

May I please see the menu/wine list?
Darf ich bitte die Speisekarte/
die Weinkarte sehen?
*dahrf ich **bitt**e dee **shpah**yzekarte/
dee **vahyn**karte zai'en?*

outside/inside
draussen/drinnen
***drow**ssen/**drinn**en

in the corner
in der Ecke
*in dehr **ehk**e*

Waiter, could we please have a/an/some . . .
Herr Ober, könnten wir . . . haben, bitte?
*hehr **oh**ber, **keun**ten veer . . . **hah**ben, **bitt**e?*

fork	eine Gabel	*ahyne **gah**bel*
knife	ein Messer	*ahyn **Mess**er*
spoon	einen Löffel	*ahynen **leuff**el*
napkin	eine Serviette	*ahyne sehr**viyeh**te*
plate	einen Teller	*ahynen **tell**er*
glass (of water)	ein Glas (Wasser)	*ahyn glas **vah**sser*
bottle of mineral water/wine	eine Flasche Mineralwasser/Wein	*ahyne **flah**she mine**rahl**vasser/vahyn*
ashtray	einen Aschenbecher	*ahynen **ahsh**enbecher*

GERMAN

bread/butter	Brot/Butter	brot/**boot**ter
salt	Salz	zalts
pepper	Pfeffer	**pfeff**er
oil	Öl	eul
vinegar	Essig	**ess**ich
mustard	Senf	zenf

What's the specialty?
Was ist die Spezialität?
*vas ist dee shpetsiyalee**tait**?*

What do you recommend?
Was empfehlen Sie?
*vas emp**fai**len zee?*

I'd like something light.
Ich möchte etwas Leichtes.
*ich **meuch**te etvas **laych**tes*

Can you tell me what this is?
Können Sie mir das ... erklären, bitte?
*keunen zee meer das ... er**kleh**ren, bitte?*

I'll have ...
Ich möchte ...
*ich **meuch**te*

The lady/gentleman will have ...
Die Dame/der Herr möchte ...
*die **dah**me/dehr hehr **meuch**te*

It's very good.
Es schmeckt sehr gut.
es shmeckt zehr goot

I didn't order this. I asked for ...
Ich habe dies nicht bestellt.
Ich wollte ...
*ich **hah**be deez nicht be**shtellt**.
ich **voll**te*

I've already ordered.
Ich habe schon bestellt.
*ich **hah**be shohn be**shtellt***

This is ...
Dies ist ...
deez ist ...

  overcooked
  zu stark gekocht
  *tsu shtahrk ge**kocht***

undercooked	**not good**
nicht genug gekocht	nicht gut
*nicht ge**nook** ge**kocht***	*nicht goot*

May I have something else?
Darf ich etwas anderes haben?
*dahrf ich etvas **ahn**deres **hah**ben?*

Waitress, the check, please.
Fräulein, zahlen, bitte!
*froy**lahn**, **tsah**len, **bit**te*

I think there's a mistake.
Ich glaube, da ist ein Irrtum.
*ich **glahw**be, da ist ahyn **eer**toom*

Is service included?
Bedienung inbegriffen?
*be**dee**nung **in**begriffen?*

Do you take credit cards/traveler's checks?
Kann ich mit Kreditkarten/
Reiseschecks bezahlen?
*kahn ich mit kre**deet**karten/
rahyzesheks be**tsah**len?*

We enjoyed the meal very much.
Es hat sehr gut geschmeckt.
*es hat zehr goot ge**shmekt***

GERMAN

GERMAN

Breakfast   Frühstück   *frewstewk*

Normally, a breakfast in Germany consists of coffee or tea, rolls (called Brötchen) or some kind of pastry, usually croissants (called Hörnchen) with jam.

Good morning. I'd like ...
Guten Morgen. Ich hätte gern ...
gooten mohrgen. ich hette gehrn

coffee	Kaffee	*kaffai*
coffee with milk	Kaffee mit Milch	*kaffai mit milch*
hot tea	Tee	*tai*
with milk/lemon	mit Milch/Zitrone	*mit milch/tsitrone*
grapefruit/orange juice	Pampelmusensaft/	*pahmpelmoozenzahft/*
	Apfelsinensaft	*ahpfelzeenenzaft*
ham and eggs	Schinken und Eier	*shinken und ahyer*
a boiled egg	ein gekochtes Ei	*ahyn gekochtes ahy*
soft/hard	weich/hart	*vahych/hahrt*
fried eggs	Spiegeleier	*shpeegelahyer*
scrambled eggs	Rühreier	*rewrahyer*
an omelette	ein Omelett	*ahyn omlett*
bread/rolls	Brot/Brötchen	*brot/breutchen*
butter	Butter	*booter*
jam	Marmelade	*marmelahde*
sugar	Zucker	*tsoocker*
yoghurt	Joghurt	*yogurt*
honey	Honig	*honich*
fruit	Frucht	*froocht*

Vorspeisen   Appetizers   *forspahysen*

Aal	**eel**	*ahl*
Aal in Gelee	**jellied eel**	*ahl in zhelé*
Appetithäppchen	**canapes**	*apeteethepchen*
Artischocken	**artichokes**	*artishokken*
Austern	**oysters**	*owstern*
Fleischpastete	**meat pâté**	*flahyshpastaite*
Gänseleberpastete	**goose liver pâté**	*genselaiber-pastaite*
Hering	**herring**	*hehring*
Lachs	**salmon**	*lahchs*
Muscheln	**mussels**	*moosheln*
Pilze	**mushrooms**	*piltse*
Sardellen	**anchovies**	*sahrdellen*
Sardinen	**sardines**	*sahrdeenen*
Schinken	**ham**	*shinken*
Spargelspitzen	**asparagus tips**	*shpahrgel-shpitzen*

Brathering
(brathehring)

baked herring fillet, marinated and served cold

Bündnerfleisch
(bewndnerfleish)

very thin slices of dried cured beef

Heringsalat
(hehringzalat)

pickled herrings, with chopped beets, apples, potatoes and onion in a sour cream dressing

Hoppel-Poppel
(hoppel poppel)

scrambled eggs with sausage

Königinpastete
(keuniginpastaite)

pastry filled with ragout fin

Leberkäs
(laiberkaiz)

meat loaf

Ragout Fin
(ragoo fehn)

pastry filled with chopped veal and sweetbreads in a herb and cream sauce

Rohkost
(ro'kost)

assorted raw vegetables

Russische Eier
(roosishe ahyer)

hard-boiled eggs with mayonnaise

Wurst
(voorst)

sausage

Suppen
(zoopen)

Soups

Aalsuppe
(ahlzooppe)

eel soup made with vegetables, dumplings and beer

Bauernsuppe
(bowernzooppe)

sausage and cabbage soup

Brotsuppe
(brotzooppe)

soup made with black and white bread, apple juice, raisins, spices and wine

Erbensuppe
(ehrpsenzooppe)

pea soup

Flädlesuppe
(flaidlezooppe)

clear soup made with bits of pancake

Frühlingssuppe
(frewlingzooppe)

spring vegetable soup

Fleischbrühe
(flahyshbrew'e)

clear meat broth served with noodles or dumplings

GERMAN

Gulashsuppe *(**goo**lashzooppe)*	a thin beef gulash
Kaltschale *(**kalt**shahle)*	cold fruit soup
Königinsuppe *(**keu**niginzooppe)*	beef soup with sour cream and almonds
Leberknödelsuppe *(**lai**berk'neudelzooppe)*	soup made with liver dumplings
Linsensuppe *(**lin**zenzuppe)*	thick lentil soup served with sausage
Ochsenschwanzsuppe *(**ock**zenshvantszooppe)*	oxtail soup
Zwiebelsuppe *(**tsvee**belzooppe)*	onion soup

Fisch	**Fish**	*feesh*
Aal	**eel**	*ahl*
Austern	**oysters**	*ows**tern***
Barsch	**freshwater perch**	*bahrsh*
Flunder	**flounder**	*floon**der***
Forelle	**trout**	*forelle*
Garnelen	**prawns**	*gar**nailen***
Hecht	**pike**	*hecht*
Heilbutt	**halibut**	*hahylboot*
Hering	**herring**	*heh**ring***
Hummer	**lobster**	*hoommer*
Jacobsmuscheln	**scallops**	*yah**kopsmoosheln***
Kabeljau	**cod**	*kah**belyow***
Karpfen	**carp**	*kahr**pfen***
Krebs	**crab**	*kreps*
Lachs, Salm	**salmon**	*lachs/zahlm*
Makrele	**mackerel**	*makrehle*
Matjeshering	**salted herring filets**	*maht**yeshehring***
Muscheln	**mussels/clams**	*moosheln*
Rotbarsch	**red sea-bass**	*rohtbahrsh*
Sardellen	**anchovies**	*sahr**dellen***
Schellfisch	**haddock**	*shellfish*
Seebarsch	**bass**	*zai**bahrsh***
Seezunge	**sole**	*zaitsunge*
Thunfisch	**tuna**	*toonfish*
Zander	**pike-perch**	*tsahn**der***

Wurst
(voorst)

Sausage

Aufschnitt
(owfshnitt)

assorted sliced sausages

Blutwurst
(blootvoorst)

blood sausage

Bratwurst
(brahtvoorst)

spiced pork frying sausage

Frankfurter Würstchen
(frahnkfoorter vewrstchen)

small boiled sausages served with bread and mustard

Himmel und Erde
(himmel oont ehrde)

fried blutwurst with potato and apple purée

Knackwurst
(knackvoorst)

thick, short sausages

Leberwurst
(laibervoorst)

liver sausage

Mettwurst
(mettvoorst)

red-skinned, smoked pork sausage

GERMAN

Geflügel und Wild

Fowl and Game

geflewgel unt vilt

Ente	**duck**	*ehnte*
Fasan	**pheasant**	*fazahn*
Gans	**goose**	*gahns*
Hase	**hare**	*hahze*
Hirsch	**venison**	*heersh*
Huhn	**chicken**	*hoon*
Hühnchen	**chicken**	*hewnchen*
Kaninchen	**rabbit**	*kaneenchen*
Rebhuhn	**partridge**	*raibhoon*
Reh	**venison**	*rai*
Taube	**pigeon**	*towbe*
Truthahn	**turkey**	*troothahn*
Wachtel	**quail**	*vachtel*
Wildschwein	**wild boar**	*viltshvahyn*

GERMAN

Fleisch	Meat	flahysh
Deutsches Beefsteak	—	*doytches beefstaik*
Filetsteak	**steak**	*fillaisteak*
Kalbfleisch	**veal**	*kalpflahysh*
Kasseler Kotelett	**pork chop**	*kasseler kotelett*
Kotelett	**cutlet, chop**	*kotelett*
Lammfleisch	**lamb**	*lahmflahysh*
Leber	**liver**	*laiber*
Nieren	**kidneys**	*neeren*
Schinken	**ham**	*shingken*
Schnitzel	**cutlet**	*shnitzel*
Schweinefleisch	**pork**	*shvahyhneflahysh*
Spanferkel	**suckling pig**	*shpahnfehrkel*
Speck	**bacon**	*shpeck*
Wurst	**sausage**	*voorst*
Zunge	**tongue**	*tsoonge*

Bauernfrühstück
(bowehrnfrewshtewck)
literally, a "farmer's breakfast," an omelette with potato and bacon

Frikadellen
(freekahdellen)
cold meatballs

Gulasch
(goolahsh)
spicy beef stew

Kalbkotelett
(kalpkotelett)
veal chop

Kalbleber
(kalplaiber)
calf's liver

Kalbrouladen
(kalproolahden)
rolled fillet of veal stuffed with ground pork

Königsbergerklopse
(keunigsbehrgerklopse)
poached dumplings or meatballs served in a sour cream and caper sauce

Wiener Schnitzel
(veener shnitzel)
fried escalopes of breaded veal

Ways of Preparing Meat, Fish, Poultry and Game

baked	gebacken	*gebacken*
boiled	gekocht	*gekocht*
braised	geschmort	*geshmort*
broiled	vom Rost	*fom rost*
fried	gebraten	*gebrahten*

grilled	gegrillt	*gegrillt*
marinated	mariniert	*marineert*
roasted	(im Ofen) gebraten	*im ohfen gebrahten*
smoked	geräuchert	*geroychert*
steamed	gedämpft	*gedempft*
stewed	gedämpft	*gedempft*
rare	blutig	*blootich*
medium	mittel	*mittel*
well done	gut durchgebraten	*goot doorchgebrahten*

Gemüse	**Vegetables**	*gemewse*
Auberginen	**eggplant**	*obehrzheenen*
Blumenkohl	**cauliflower**	*bloomenkohl*
Bohnen	**beans**	*bohnen*
Bratkartoffeln	**fried potatoes**	*brahtkartoffeln*
Braunkohl	**broccoli**	*brownkohl*
Champignons	**mushrooms**	*sharhpeenyon*
Chicoree	**endives**	*sheekoré*
Endiven	**endives**	*endeeven*
Erbsen	**peas**	*ehrpsen*
Erdäpfel	**potatoes**	*ehrdehpfel*
Fisolen	**green beans**	*fizolen*
Gemischtes Gemüse	**mixed vegetables**	*gemishtes gemewze*
Grüner Salat	**green salad**	*grewner zalaht*
Gurken	**cucumber**	*goorken*
Karfiol	**cauliflower**	*kahrfyol*
Karotten	**carrots**	*karotten*
Kartoffeln	**potatoes**	*kartoffeln*
Kohl	**cabbage**	*kohl*
Kopfsalat	**lettuce salad**	*kopfzalaht*
Lauch	**leeks**	*lowch*
Linsen	**lentils**	*linzen*
Mais	**sweet corn**	*mahyss*
Mohrrüben	**carrots**	*morewben*
Pilze	**mushrooms**	*piltze*
Rosenkohl	**brussels spouts**	*rozenkohl*
Spargel	**asparagus**	*shpargel*
Spinat	**spinach**	*shpinaht*
Tomaten	**tomatoes**	*tomahten*
Weißkohl	**cabbage**	*vahysskohl*
Zwiebeln	**onions**	*tsveebeln*

GERMAN

Grünkohl (**grewn**kohl)	a green winter vegetable served with baked potatoes or fried bratwurst
Kartoffelknödeln (kahr**toffelk**'neudeln)	potato dumplings
Kartoffelpuffer (kahr**toffel**poofer)	potato pancakes served with cranberry or apple sauce
Kartoffelsalat (kar**toffel**zalaht)	hot or cold potato salad with a dressing of vinegar and oil or sour cream
Leipziger Allerei (**lahypt**siger alle**rahy**)	mixture of carrots, peas, cauliflower, asparagus tips and mushrooms
Linsen auf Schwäbische Art (**linzen** owf **shvehb**ishe ahrt)	lentils and noodles stewed with onions, bacon, meat and sausage
Rösti (**reustee**)	Swiss roast potatoes
Rotkohl (**roht**kohl)	red cabbage stewed with wine vinegar, onions, sliced apple and spices, sometimes served with roast pork and potato dumplings

Früchte	**Fruit**	*frewchte*
Ananas	**pineapple**	*ahnanas*
Apfel	**apple**	*ahpfel*
Apfelsine	**orange**	*ahpfelzeene*
Aprikosen	**apricots**	*ahprikohzen*
Banane	**banana**	*banahne*
Birne	**pear**	*beerne*
Blaubeeren	**blueberries**	*blahwbehren*
Brombeeren	**blackberries**	*brombehren*
Datteln	**dates**	*dahteln*
Erdbeeren	**strawberries**	*ehrdbehren*
Feigen	**figs**	*fahygen*
Hazelnüsse	**hazel nuts**	*hahzelnewsse*
Heidelbeeren	**blueberries**	*hahydelbehren*
Himbeeren	**raspberries**	*himbehren*
Kirschen	**cherries**	*keershen*
Kokosnuβ	**coconut**	*kokosnooss*
Mandarine	**tangerine**	*mandareene*
Mandeln	**almonds**	*mandeln*
Marillen	**apricots**	*marillen*
Mirabellen	**plums**	*meerabellen*
Melone	**melon**	*melohne*
Nüsse	**nuts**	*noosse*
Pampelmuse	**grapefruit**	*pahmpelmooze*
Pfirsich	**peach**	*pfeerzich*

Pflaumen	plums	*pflahwmen*
Preiselbeeren	cranberries	*prahyzelbehren*
Rhabarber	rhubarb	*rabarber*
Trauben	grapes	*trahwbem*
Walnüße	walnuts	*vahlnewsse*
Wassermelone	watermelon	*vassermelohne*
Zwetschgen	black plums	*tsvetshgen*

Käse
(kaise)

Cheese

Allgäuer, Emmentaler
(ahlgoyer, ementahler)

Swiss cheese, mild

Bierkäse
(beerkaizeh)

low-fat cottage cheese

Käseteller
(kaizeteller)

a plate of assorted cheeses

Kümmelkäse
(kewmelkaizeh)

mild cheese with caraway seeds

Quark
(kvahrk)

low-fat cottage cheese with a somewhat sour taste

Rahmkäse, Sahnekäse
(rahmkaizeh, zahnekaizeh)

cream cheese

Räucherkase
(roycherkaizeh)

smoked cheese

Thüringer Käse
(tewringer kaizeh)

sausage shaped cheese made from curd

Tilsiter
(tilziter)

mild, yellow, creamy cheese

Wilstermarschkäse
(vilstermarshkaizeh)

a sour-tasting cheese with a smooth yellow skin

Nachspeisen
(nachspahysen)

Desserts

Apfelstrudel
(ahpfelshtroodel)

apple pastry with cinnamon and raisins

Arme Ritter
(ahrme ritter)

fried bread sprinkled with cinnamon and sugar; served with apple sauce

Eis
(eiss)

ice cream

GERMAN

Faschingskrapfen *(fahshingskrapfen)*	deep-fried dough buns filled with apricot jam and dusted with vanilla sugar
Fruchtsalat *(froochtzalat)*	fruit salad
Kaiserschmarren *(kahyzershmahren)*	shredded white raisin pancake served with fruit purée
Kasnudeln *(kahsnoodeln)*	noodles filled with fruit and poppy seeds
Lebkuchen *(laibkoochen)*	honey cakes
Marmorgugelhupf *(mahrmorgoogelhoopf)*	chocolate yeast cake covered with vanilla sugar and blanched almonds
Mozartkugeln *(motsahrtkoogeln)*	chocolate balls with a rum-flavored filling
Pfannkuchen *(pfahnkoochen)*	pancake
Nusstorte *(noosstorte)*	walnut cake
Rehrücken *(rairewken)*	chocolate cake with blanched almonds
Sachertorte *(zahchertorte)*	chocolate cake filled with apricot jam and covered with chocolate icing
Schokoladenpudding *(shokolahdenpudding)*	chocolate pudding
Schokoladentorte *(shokolahdentorte)*	chocolate cake

DRINKS

Nonalcoholic Drinks

Cold Beverages

I'd like a . . .
Ich hätte gern . . .
ich hette gehrn

glass of ein Glas *ahyn glahs*	bottle of eine Flasche *ahyne flahshe*	carbonated mit Kohlensäure *mit kohlenzoyre*
(mineral) water (mineral) wasser *minerahlvasser*		**regular** ohne Kohlensäure *ohne kohlenzoyre*

apricot juice	einen Aprikosensaft	*ahynen ahprikozenzahft*
grapefruit juice	einen Pampelmusensaft	*ahynen pahmpelmuzenzahft*
lemonade	eine Zitronenlimonade	*ahyne tsitronenlimonahde*
orangeade	eine Orangeade	*ahyne oranjzhahde*
orange juice	einen Apfelsinensaft	*ahynen ahpfelzeenenzahft*
peach juice	einen Pfirsichsaft	*ahynen pfeerzichzahft*
tomato juice	einen Tomatensaft	*ahynen tomahtenzahft*
ice tea	einen Eistee	*ahynen ahystai*
iced coffee	einen Eiskaffee	*ahynen ahyskaffai*
milkshake	ein Milchmixgetränk	*ahyn milchmixgetrenk*
soda	einen Sprudel	*ahynen shproodel*
orange soda mixed with Coca-Cola	ein Diesel	*ahyn deezl*

Hot Beverages

espresso	einen Espresso	*ahynen espresso*
coffee	einen Kaffee	*ahynen kaffai*
with cream	mit Sahne	mit *zahne*
with milk	mit Milch	mit milch
black coffee	einen schwarzen Kaffee	*ahynen shvahrtsen kaffai*
decaffeinated coffee	einen koffeinfreien Kaffee	*ahynen koffahynfrahyen kaffai*
Mokka	einen Mokka	*ahynen moka*
lemon tea	einen Zitronentee	*ahynen tsitronentai*
peppermint tea	einen Pfefferminztee	*ahynen pfaifermintstai*

Alcoholic Drinks

aperitif	ein Aperitif	*ahyn ahperiteef*
beer	ein Bier	*ahyn beer*
Bourbon	ein Bourbon	*ahyn boorbon*
brandy	ein Weinbrand	*ahyn vahynbrant*
cider	ein Apfelwein	*ahyn ahpfelvahyn*
cognac	ein Kognak	*ahyn konyak*
cordial	ein Likör	*ahyn likeur*
gin	ein Gin	*ahyn jin*
gin fizz	ein Gin-fizz	*ahyn jin fizz*
gin and tonic	ein Gin mit Tonic	*ahyn jin mit tonik*
liqueur	ein Likör	*ahyn likeur*
mulled wine	ein Glühwein	*ahyn glewvahyn*
port	ein Portwein	*ahyn port*
rum	ein Rum	*ahyn room*
Scotch	ein Scotch	*ahyn scotch*
sherry	ein Sherry	*ahyn sherry*

GERMAN

GERMAN

vermouth	ein Wermut	*ahyn vehrmoot*
vodka	ein Wodka	*ahyn vodka*
whiskey and soda	ein Whiskey mit Soda	*ahyn whisky mit soda*
straight	pur	*poor*
on the rocks	mit Eis	*mit ahyss*
with soda water	mit Soda	*mit soda*

Some Favorite Aperitifs

Damengedeck
(dahmengedeck)
sparkling wine with orange juice

Herrengedeck
(hehrrengedeck)
sparkling wine with beer

Kir
(keer)
wine with cassis (blackcurrant liqueur)

Kir Royale
(keer rwahyahl)
champagne with cassis

Portwein
(pohrtvahyn)
port

Weinscharle
(vahynshahrle)
wine and mineral water

You may want to try these after-dinner drinks:

Liqueurs and Brandies

Aprikosenlikör
(ahprikohzenlikeur)
apricot

Calvados
(kahlvahdos)
apple

Doornkaat
(doornkaht)
juniperberry

Himbeergeist
(himbehrgahyst)
raspberry

Himbeerlikör
(himberhrlikeur)
raspberry

Kirschwasser
(keershvahsser)
cherry

Obstler
(ohpstler)
fruit

Steinhäger   juniperberry
  (shtahynhehger)

Träsch   pear and apple
  (trehsh)

Zwetschgenwasser   plum
  (tsvetshgenvahsser)

Williamine   pear
  (villyahmeene)

Schnapps (shnahps) is a clear grain spirit.

Wine-distilled Brandies

Asbach-Uralt
  (ahsbach-oorahlt)

Chantré
  (shahntré)

Dujardin
  (dewzhahrdehn)

Whiskey

Doppelkorn
  (doppelkorn)

Weizenkorn
  (vahytsenkorn)

Beer

Altbier   dark beer of medium strength
  (altbeer)

Berliner Weiße   pale golden beer brewed from wheat
  (behrleener vahysse)   grain

Berliner Weiße mit Schuß   the above with a shot of raspberry juice
  (behrleener vahysse mit shooss)

Bock   rich, strong malt beer with a high alco-
  (bock)   holic content

Doppelbock   extra-strong Bock
  (doppelbock)

Gespritzter   light beer mixed with a soft drink
  (geshpritzter)

GERMAN

GERMAN

Kölsch *(keulsh)*		pale golden beer of medium strength
Malzbier *(maltsbeer)*		dark and somewhat sweet, with low alcoholic content
Pils, Pilsener *(pils, pilzner)*		pale golden lager beer
Radlermaß, Alsterwasser *(rahdlermass, alstervasser)*		light beer with lemonade
Weißbier *(vahyssbeer)*		light summer beer from Bavaria
Weizenbier *(vahytsenbeer)*		sparkling Bavarian wheat beer, medium in strength

draft	vom Faß	*fom fahss*
bottle	eine Flasche	*ahyne flahshe*
glass	ein Glas	*ahyn glahs*
a small glass	ein halbes	*ein halbes*
a large glass	ein großes	*ein grosses*
mug	eine Maß	*ahyne mahss*
dark	(ein) Dunkles	*(ahyn) doonkles*
light	(ein) Helles	*(ahyn) helles*

Wine

Which wine do you recommend?	**Which wine goes with this dish?**
Was für Wein empfehlen Sie?	Welchem Wein empfehlen Sie zu diesem Gericht?
vas fehr vahyn empfailen zee?	*velchem vahyn empfailen zee tsu deezem gericht?*

I'd like a . . . wine.
Ich möchte einen . . . Wein.
ich meuchte ahynen . . . vahyn

very dry	sehr trockenen	*zair trokkenen*
dry	trockenen	*trokkenen*
sweet	süßen	*zewssen*
light	leichten	*lahychten*
full-bodied	vollmundigen	*fohlmoondigen*
red	roten	*roten*
white	weißen	*vahyssen*
open, by the glass	offenen	*ohffenen*
mulled	Glüh-	*glewvahyn*

Please bring a . . . of
Bitte bringen Sie . . .
bitte bringen zee

bottle	eine Flasche	*ahyne flahshe*
carafe	eine Karaffe	*ahyne karahffe*
half bottle	eine halbe Flasche	*ahyne halbe flahshe*
liter	einen Liter	*ahynen leeter*
a quarter liter (glass)	ein Viertel	*ahyn feertel*
an eighth liter (glass)	ein Achtel	*ahyn achtel*

I'd like to try a local wine.
Ich möchte ein Wein aus dieser Gegend probieren.
ich meuchte ahyn vahyn ows deezer gaigent probeeren

SIGHTSEEING

Where is the tourist office?
Wo ist das Fremdenverkehrsbüro?
vo ist das fremdenfehrkehrsbewro?

We would like to see the main points of interest.
Wir möchten die Hauptsehenswürdigkeiten sehen.
veer meuchten dee howptzai'enzvewrdichkahyten zai'en

We will be here for . . .
Wir sind für . . . hier.
veer zint fewr . . . heer

a few hours	a day
einige Stunden	einen Tag
ahynige shtoonden	*ahynen tahk*

a few days	a week
einige Tage	eine Woche
ahynige tahge	*ahyne vohche*

We would like to see . . .
Wir möchten gern . . . sehen
veer meuchten gehrn . . . zai'en

Could you direct me to the . . .
Können Sie mir sagen, wo . . . ist/sind?
keunen zee meer zahgen, vo . . . ist/zint?

Is there a sightseeing tour?
Gibt es eine Stadtrundfahrt?
gipt es ahyne shtatroontfahrt?

Where does it go?
Wohin Führt sie?
vohin fewrt zee?

How long is it?
Wie lange dauert sie?
vee lahnge dowehrt zee?

How much is it?
Was kostet es?
vas kostet es?

When/where will the bus pick us up?
Wann/wo holt uns der Bus ab?
vann/vo holt oons dehr boos ap?

Does the guide speak English?
Spricht der Fremdenführer Englisch?
shpricht dehr fremdenfewrer english?

art gallery	die Kunstgalerie	*dee kunstgaleree*
castle	das Schloß/die Burg	*das shloss/dee boorg*
catacombs	die Katakomben	*dee katakohmben*
cathedral	die Kathedrale/der Dom	*dee katedrahle/dehr dohm*

GERMAN

cemetery	der Friedhof	*dehr **freedhof***
church	die Kirche	*dee **keerche***
city center	die Stadtmitte	*dee **shtatmitte***
fortress	die Festung	*dee **festoong***
fountain	der Brunnen	*dehr **broonen***
gardens	die Grünanlagen	*dee **grewnanlahgen***
harbor	der Hafen	*dehr **hafen***
lake	der See	*dehr zai*
monastery	das Kloster	*das **kloster***
museum	das Museum	*das **moozai'oom***
old city	die Altstadt	*dee **ahltshtaht***
opera house	das Opernhaus	*das **opehrnhows***
palace	der Palast/das Schloß	*dehr **palast**/das **shloss***
planetarium	das Planetarium	*das **plahnetahrioom***
ruins	die Ruinen	*dee **rueenen***
shops	das Einkaufszentrum	*das **ahynkowfstsentroom***
statue	die Statue	*dee **shahtu'e***
theater	das Theater	*das **taiater***
tomb	die Gruft	*dee **grooft***
university	die Universität	*dee **uneevehrseetait***
zoo	der Zoo	*dehr **tso***

When is the . . . open?
Wann ist . . . geöffnet?
*vann ist . . . ge-**euffnet**?*

At what time does it close?
Um wieviel Uhr schließt es?
*oom veefeel oor **shleest** es?*

How much is the admission?
Was kostet der Eintritt?
*vas kostet dehr **ahyntritt**?*

The admission is free.
Der Eintritt ist frei.
*dehr **ahyntritt** ist **frahy***

**Is there a reduction for children/
students/senior citizens?**
Gibt es Ermäßigung für Kinder/
Studenten/Pensionäre?
*gipt es ehr**mes**sigoong fewr **kinder**/
shtu**denten**/pensiyo**nehr**e?*

Where does one buy tickets?
Wo kauft man die Eintristtskarten?
*vo kowft man dee **ahyn**trittskarten?*

Where can I find . . .
Wo kann ich . . . finden?
*vo kann ich . . . **finden**?*

a catalogue
einen Katalog
*ahynen kata**lohk***

a guidebook
einen Reiseführer
*ahynen **rahy**zefewrer*

the . . . exhibit
die . . . Ausstellung
*dee . . . **ows**shtelloong*

the . . . collection
die . . . Sammlung
*dee . . . **zahm**loong*

postcards
Ansichtskarten
ahnzichtskahrten

the souvenir shop
den Souvenirladen
*dain souvee**neer**lahden*

Am I allowed to take photographs?
Darf ich fotografieren?
*dahrf ich fotogra**fee**ren?*

HAVING FUN

Daytime Activities

Soccer

Let's go to the football game.
Laß uns zum Fußballspiel gehen.
*lass oons tsoom **foos**ballshpeel **gai**'en*

Where is the stadium?
Wo ist das Stadion?
*vo ist das **shtah**diyen?*

Who is playing?
Wer spielt gegen wen?
*vehr shpeelt **gaig**'n wain?*

I would like two tickets in the sun/ in the shade
Ich möchte zwei Eintrittskarten in der Sonne/im Schatten
*ich **meuch**te tsvahy **ahyn**trittskarten in dehr **zon**ne/im **shah**tten*

When does it start?
Wann beginnt es?
*vahn be**ginn**t es?*

What is the score?
Wie steht es?
vee shtait es?

Tennis

Would you like to play tennis?
Möchten Sie/möchtest du Tennis spielen?
***meuch**ten zee/**meuch**test doo tennis **shpee**len?*

Where are the tennis courts?
Wo sind die Tennisplätze?
*vo zint dee **tennis**plehtse?*

What's the charge for the use of the courts per hour/for half an hour?
Wieviel kostet es, den Platz pro Stunde/ für eine halbe Stunde zu benutzen?
*veefeel **kos**tet es, dain plahtz pro **shtoon**de/fewr ahyne **hal**be **shtoon**de tsu be**noo**tzen?*

Is it possible to rent tennis rackets?
Kann man Tennisschläger mieten?
*kann man **tennis**schlaiger **mee**ten?*

I would like to buy tennis balls.
Ich Würde gerne Tennisbälle kaufen.
*ich **vewr**de **gehr**ne **tennis**belle **kow**fen*

Let's go to the tennis tournament.
Laß uns zum Tennisturnier gehen.
*lass oons tsoom **tennis**toornyai **gai**en*

I want to watch/play the men's/ women's singles/doubles
Ich möchte gerne die Männer/Frauen- einzel/doppel anschauen/spielen.
*ich **meuch**te dee **mehn**er/**frow**en **ahyn**tsel/**dop**pel **an**shahwen/ **shpee**len*

GERMAN

GERMAN

Golf

Where is there a golf course around here?
Wo gibt es einen Golfplatz in der Nähe?
*vo gipt es ahynen **golf**platz in dehr nai'e?*

Is it open to nonmembers?
Ist es auch für Nicht-Mitglieder offen?
*ist es auch fewr **nicht**mitgleeder offen?*

How much does it cost per hour/day/round?
Wie teuer ist das Spielen pro Stunde/Tag/Runde?
*vee **toy**er ist das **shpee**len pro **shtoon**de/tak/**roon**de?*

I would like to rent a caddy/golf clubs.
Ich möchte einen Caddie/Golfschläger mieten.
*ich **meuch**te ahynen **cad**dy/**golf**shlaiger meeten.*

I would like to buy some golfballs.
Ich möchte einige Golfbälle kaufen.
*ich **meuch**te ahynige **golf**behle kowfen*

Would you like to play a round with me?
Würden Sie eine Runde mit mir spielen?
***vewr**den zee ahyne **roon**de mit meer **shpee**len?*

Where's the next tee?
Wo ist das nächste Abschlagmall?
*vo ist das **nech**ste apshlagmal?*

Horseback Riding

Is there a riding stable nearby?
Gibt es einen Reitstall in der Nähe?
*gipt es ahynen **rahyt**shtahl in der nai'e?*

I would like to rent a horse.
Ich möchte ein Reitpferd mieten.
*ich **meuch**te ahyn **rahyt**pferd **mee**ten.*

What's the charge per hour?
Wie teuer ist es pro Stunde?
*vee **toy**er ist es pro **shtoon**de?*

I would like to take riding lessons.
Ich möchte Reitstunden nehmen.
*ich **meuch**te **rahyt**shtoonden **nai**men*

I am a beginner/experienced rider.
Ich bin Neuling/Ich kann gut reiten.
*ich bin **noy**ling/ich kann goot **rahy**ten*

Could you give me a gentle horse, please?
Könnten Sie mir bitte ein ruhiges Pferd geben?
***keun**ten zee meer **bit**te ahyn **roo**higes pfehrd **gai**ben?*

I would like a jumper.
Ich möchte ein Springer.
*ich **meuch**te ahyn **shpring**er*

Skiing

Would you like to go skiing?
Möchten Sie/möchtest du Skifahren gehen?
***meuch**ten zee/**meuch**test doo **shee**fahren gai'en?*

How do we get to the slopes?
Wie kommen wir zu den Pisten?
*vee **kom**men veer tsu dain **pis**ten?*

What are the skiing conditions at . . .
Wie sind die Schneeverhältnisse in . . .
vee zint dee shnaifehrhaltnisse in . . .

Is it possible to take skiing lessons?
Ist es möglich, Skiunterricht
zu nehmen?
*ist es meuglich, sheeoonterricht
tsu naimen?*

**Is it possible to rent skiing
equipment?**
Ist es möglich, Skiausrüstungen
zu mieten?
*ist es meuglich, sheeowsrewstoongen
tsu meeten?*

These boots are too tight/loose.
Diese Stiefel sind zu eng/zu weit.
deeze shteefel zint tsu eng/vahyt

Could you help me put on the skis?
Können Sie mir bitte helfen, die Stiefel
anzuziehen?
*keunen zee meer bitte helfen, dee
shteefel ahntsootsee'en?*

**How much are the lift tickets for
a day/two days/a week?**
Wieviel kostet eine Liftkarte für
zwei Tage/für eine Woche?
*veefeel kostet ahyne liftkarte fewr
tsvahy tahge/fewr ahyne voche?*

**I'm looking for a beginner's/
intermediate/advanced trail.**
Ich suche eine Piste für Anfänger/
Fortgeschrittene/gute Fahrer.
*ich zooche ahyne piste fewr anfenger/
fortgeshrittene/goote fahrer*

Swimming

Would you like to go swimming?
Möchten Sie/möchtest du schwimmen
gehen?
*meuchten zee/meuchtest doo
shvimmen gai'en?*

**Let's go to the beach/swimming
pool**
Laß uns zum Strand/Schwimmbad
gehen.
*lahss oons tsoom shtrahnt/shvimbaht
gai'en*

Is it safe for swimming?
Ist es ungefährlich, jetzt
zu schwimmen?
*ist es oongefehrlich, yetzt
tsu shvimmen?*

I'd like to rent
Ich möchte . . . mieten.
ich meuchte . . . meeten

  a deckchair
  einen Liegestuhl
  ahynen leegeshtool

  a changing room
  ein Umkleiderraum
  ahyn oomklahyderahwm

  a beach umbrella
  einen Sonnenschirm
  ahynen zonnensheerm

Evening Activities (der Abend)

Would you like to go to . . .
Möchten Sie/möchtest du . . . gehen?
*meuchten zee/meuchtest doo . . .
gai'en*

the movies	the opera
ins Kino	in die Oper
ins keeno	*in dee ohper*

GERMAN

the ballet   a concert
ins Ballett   in ein Konzert
ins ballett   *in ahyn kontsehrt*

Who's in it?
Wer spielt mit?
vehr shpeelt mit?

Who's singing?
Wer singt?
vehr zingt?

Who's dancing?
Wer tanzt?
vehr tantzt?

What orchestra is playing?
Welches Orchester spielt?
velches orkester shpeelt?

At what time does it begin?
Wann beginnt die Vorstellung?
vann beginnt dee forstelloong?

I would like to reserve/buy two tickets for . . .
Ich möchte zwei Karten für . . . vorbestellen/kaufen.
ich meuchte tsvahy kahrten fewr . . . forbeshtellen/kowfen

Could you show me a seating plan of the theater?
Können Sie mir bitte einen Sitzplan des Theaters zeigen?
keunen zee meer bitte ahynen zitzplahn des tai-ahters tsahygen?

Please give me two orchestra/ mezzanine/box seats.
Geben Sie mir bitte zwei Plätze im Parkett/im ersten Rang/in der Loge.
gaiben zee meer bitte tsvahy plehtze im parkett/im ehrsten rahng/ in dehr lozhe

Would you like to go to a nightclub/ discotheque?
Möchten Sie/möchtest Du in ein Nachtlokal/eine Discothek gehen?
meuchten zee/meuchtest doo in ahyn nachtlokahl/ahyne discotaik gai'en?

How much does it cost to get in?
Was kostet der Eintritt?
vas kostet dehr ahyntritt?

What's the minimum?
Was ist der Mindestpreis?
vas ist dehr mindestprahyss?

Would you like a drink?
Möchten Sie/möchtest du etwas zu trinken?
or
Trinken Sie etwas?
meuchten zee/meuchtest doo etvas tsu trinken?
trinken zee etvas?

Getting to Know People

Hello
Hallo
hallo

How are you?
Wie geht es Ihnen?
vie gait es eenen?

Fine, thanks. And you?
Gut, danke. Und Ihnen?
goot, danke, oont eenen?

My name is . . .
Ich heiße . . .
ich hahysse . . .

This is
Das ist . . .
das ist . . .

    my wife/husband
    meine Frau/mein Mann
    mahyne frow/mahyn mahn

my daughter/son
meine Tochter/mein sohn
mahyne tochter/mahyn sohn

my sister/my brother
meine Schwester/mein Bruder
mahyne shvester/mahyn brooder

a friend of mine
ein Freund/eine Freundin von mir
ahyn froynt/ahyne froyndin fon meer

Glad to meet you.
Sehr erfreut.
zehr erfroyt

Where are you from?
Woher kommen Sie?
vohehr kommen zee?

I'm from . . .
Ich komme aus . . .
ich komme aus

Are you here on vacation?
Machen Sie Ferien?
machen zee fehriyen?

No, I'm on a business trip.
Nein, ich bin auf einer Geschäftsreise.
nahyn, ich bin owf ahyner geshehftsreize

I'm here for business and pleasure.
Ich bin hier wegen Geschäften und aus Vergnügen.
ich bin heer vaigen geshehften oont ows fehrgnewgen

Are you on your own?
Sind Sie allein(e)?
zint zee allahyn(e)?

I'm with a friend//my family
Ich bin hier mit einem Freund/meiner Familie.
ich bin heer mit ahynem froynt/mahyner fameelee-ye

How long have you been here?
Wie lange sind Sie schon hier?
vee lahnge zind zee shohn heer?

I've just arrived today.
Ich bin gerade heute angekommen.
ich bin gerahde hoyte angekommen

I arrived yesterday/a few days ago.
Ich bin gestern/vor einigen Tagen angekommen.
ich bin gestern/for ahynigen tahgen angekommen

I've been here a week/two weeks/ a month.
Ich bin seit einer Woche/zwei Wochen/ einem Monat hier.
ich bin zahyt ahyner vohche/tsvahy vohchen/ahynem monat heer

How do you like it here?
Gefällt es Ihnen hier?
gefellt es eenen heer?

I like it very much.
Es gefällt mir sehr gut.
es gefellt meer zehr goot

It's a . . . place
Es ist ein . . . Ort.
es ist ahyn . . . ohrt

wonderful	**beautiful**
wunderbarer	herrlicher
voonderbarer	*hehrlicher*
fun	**interesting**
lustiger	interessanter
loostiger	*interessahnter*
	toller
	toller

I don't like it very much.
Es gefällt mir nicht sehr.
es gefellt meer nicht sehr

It's . . . too crowded
Es ist . . . überfüllt
es ist . . . ewberfewllt

noisy	**ugly**
geräuschvoll	hässlich
geroyshfohl	*hesslich*
boring	**depressing**
langweilig	deprimierend
lahngvahylich	*depreemeerent*

How long are you going to stay?
Wie lange bleiben Sie?
vee lahnge blahyven zee?

GERMAN

A few more days/weeks.
Noch ein paar Tage/Wochen
noch ahyn paar tahge/vochen

I'm leaving tomorrow/soon.
Ich fahre morgen/bald ab.
ich fahre mohrgen/balt ap

Are you having a good time?
Amüsieren Sie sich gut?
amewzeeren zee zich goot?

Yes, very much.
Ja, sehr.
ya, zehr.

No, not really.
Nein, nicht besonderes.
nahyn, nicht bezonderes

Where are you staying?
Wo wohnen Sie?
vo vohnen zee?

We're at the . . . hotel.
Wir wohnen im Hotel . . .
veer vohnen im hotel

I'm a(n) . . .
Ich bin ein . . .
ich bin ahyn

We're camping.
Wir zelten.
veer tselten

We haven't found a place yet.
Wir haben noch keine Unterkunft
gefunden.
*veer hahben noch kahyne
oonterkoonft gefoonden*

Do you know a good hotel/pension?
Kennen Sie ein gutes Hotel/eine gute
Pension?
*kennen ze ahyn gootes hotel/ahyne
goote penziyohn?*

Do you have brothers and sisters?
Haben Sie Geschwister?
hahben zee geshvister?

What do you do?
Was machen Sie?
vas machen zee?

artist	Künstler	*kewnstler*
businessman	Geschäftsmann	*geshehftsmahn*
doctor	Arzt	*artzt*
factory worker	Arbeiter	*arbahyter*
lawyer	Anwalt	*anvalt*
secretary	Sekretär(in)	*sekretehr(in)*
student	Student	*shtudent*
teacher	Lehrer	*lehrer*
writer	Schriftsteller	*shriftshteller*

Where do you live?
Wo leben Sie?
vo laib'n zee?

I live in . . .
Ich lebe . . .
ich laibe

the United States
in den Vereinigten Staaten
in den fehrahynigten shtahten

in Canada
in Kanada
in kanada

Great Britain
in Groβ Britannien
in gross britahniyen

Australia
in Australien
in owstraliyen

Let me know if you ever go there.
Lassen Sie mich es wissen, wenn
  Sie dorthin kommen.
lassen zee mich es vissen, venn
  zee dorthin kommen

Here is my address/phone number.
Dies ist meine Adresse/
  Telefonnummer.
deez ist mahyne adresse/
  telefohnoomer

What are your interests?
Für was interessieren Sie sich?
fewr vas interesseeren zee zich?

I'm interested in . . .
Ich interessiere mich für . . .
ich interesseere mich fewr

anthropology	Anthropologie	*antropologhee*
antiques	Antiquitäten	*anteekveetaiten*
archeology	Archaeologie	*archai-ologhee*
architecture	Architektur	*archeetektoor*
art	Kunst	*koonst*
botany	Botanik	*botaneek*
chess	Schach	*shahch*
cinema	Filme	*filme*
coins	Münzen	*mewntsen*
cooking	Kochen	*kochen*
dance	Tanz	*tantz*
foreign languages	Fremdsprachen	*fremtshprachen*
gardening	Gärtnerei	*gehrtnerahy*
geology	Geologie	*gai-ologhee*
history	Geschichte	*geshichte*
literature	Literatur	*literatoor*
medicine	Medizin	*medeetseen*
music	Musik	*moozeek*
natural history	Naturgeschichte	*natoorgeshichte*
painting	Malerei	*mahlerahy*
philosophy	Philosophie	*filozofee*
photography	Photos	*fotos*
sculpture	Bildhauerei	*bilthowerahy*
science	Wissenschaft	*vissenshahft*
sociology	Soziologie	*sohtsiologhee*
sports	Sport	*shport*
theater	Theater	*taiahter*

GERMAN

May I sit here?
Darf ich mich hier setzen?
dahrf ich mich heer zetzen?

Yes, if you wish.
Ja, wenn Sie wollen.
ya, venn zee vohlen.

Would you like a cigarette?
Möchten Sie eine Zigarette?
meuchten zee ahyne tseegarette?

No, thank you. I don't smoke.
Nein, danke. Ich rauche nicht.
nahyn, dahnke. ich rahwche nicht

Could you give me a light?
Haben Sie Feuer?
hahben zee foyer?

Would you like to go out with me this evening?
Hätten Sie Lust, mit mir heute Abend auszugehen?
hetten zee loost, mit meer hoyte ahbent owstsoogai'en?

Would you like to go . . .
Hätten Sie Lust . . .
hetten zee loost

to dinner
zum Essen
tsoom essen

to the movies
ins Kino
ins keeno

to a party
zu einer Party
tsu ahyner pahrtee

to a discotheque
in eine Diskothek
in ahyne discotaik

to a concert
zu einem Konzert
tsu ahynem kontsehrt

. . . **zu gehen?**
. . . *tsu gai'en?*

Yes, thank you. That would be nice.
Ja, gerne. Das wäre nett.
ya, gehrne. das vehre nett

No, thank you. I'm not free this evening.
Nein, danke. Ich bin heute Abend nicht frei.
nahyn, danke. ich bin hoyte ahbent nicht frahy

What about tomorrow?
Was ist mit morgen?
vas ist mit mohrgen?

No, I'll be busy.
Morgen bin ich beschäftigt.
mohrgen bin ich besheftict

Where/when shall we meet?
Wo/wann wollen wir uns treffen?
vo/vann vohlen veer oons treffen?

Could you meet me at . . .
Könnten Sie/könntest du mich an . . . treffen?
keunten zee/keuntest doo mich an . . . treffen?

I'll meet you at your hotel.
Ich treffe Sie in Ihrem Hotel.
ich treffe zee in eerem hotel

May I call you?
Darf ich Sie anrufen?
dahrf ich zee anroofen?

At what time?
Um wieviel Uhr?
oom veefeel oor?

What's your number?
Wie ist Ihre Telefonnummer?
vee ist eere telefohnnoomer?

I'd like to go home now.
Ich möchte jetzt nach Hause gehen.
ich meuchte yetzt nach howze gai'en

I'm very tired.
Ich bin sehr müde.
ich bin zehr mewde

Thank you for a lovely evening.
Danke für den schönen Abend.
danke fewr dain sheunen ahbent

Expressions of Admiration or Dislike

What a beautiful view!
Was für eine schöne Aussicht!
vas fewr ahyne sheune owszicht

What a lovely place/ town/city!
Was für ein schöner Ort/eine schöne Stadt!
vas fewr ahyn sheuner ohrt/ahyne sheune shtaht

The sea/countryside is very beautiful.
Das Meer/die Landschaft ist sehr schön.
das mehr/dee lahntshahft ist zehr sheun

I like this country/city/place very much.
Ich liebe dieses Land/diese Stadt/ diesen Ort sehr.
ich leebe deezes lahnt/deese shtaht/ deezen ohrt zehr

I particularly like . . .
Ich liebe speziell . . .
ich leebe sphetsyel

I don't particularly like . . .
Ich mag nicht ausgesprochen . . .
ich mahk nicht owsgeshprochen

the architecture	die Architektur	*dee archeetektoor*
the beaches	den Strand	*dain shtrahnt*
the climate	das Klima	*das kleema*
the food	das Essen	*das essen*
the landscape	die Landschaft	*dee lahntshahft*
the night life	das Nachtleben	*das nachtlaib'n*
the people	die Leute	*dee loyte*
the restaurants/cafés	die Restaurants/Cafés	*dee restaurans/cafés*
the shops	die Geschäfte	*dee geshehfte*
the sights	die Sehenswürdigkeiten	*dee zai'ensvewrdichkahyten*

GERMAN

EVERYDAY SITUATIONS

Problems

Are you alone?
Sind Sie alleine?
zint zee ahlahyne?

Am I disturbing you?
Störe ich Sie?
shteure ich zee?

Are you waiting for someone?
Erwarten Sie jemanden?
ehrvahrten zee yaimahnden?

Leave me alone.
Lassen Sie mich alleine.
lahssen zee mich ahlahyne

Yes, I'm waiting for a friend.
Ja, ich warte auf einen Freund.
ya, ich vahrte owf ahynen froynt

Go away or I'll call the police.
Gehen Sie oder ich rufe die Polizei.
gai'en zee oder ich roofe dee politsahy

The Weather

It's a lovely day, isn't it?
Ist das nicht ein schöner Tag?
ist das nicht ahyn sheuner tahk?

What beautiful/awful weather we are having!
Was für schönes/schlechtes Wetter!
vas fewr sheunes/schlechtes vetter

Do you think it's going to rain/snow/be sunny all day?
Glauben Sie, daß es den ganzen Tag regnen/schneien/wird? daß wir den ganzen Tag Sonne haben werden?
glahwben zee, dass es dain gantsen tahk raignen/shnahyen veert? das veer dain gantsen tahk zonne haben vehrden?

It's terribly hot today.
Es ist sehr heiß heute.
es ist zehr hahyss hoyte

It's rather cold today.
Es ist ziemlich kalt heute.
es ist tseemlich kahlt hoyte

It's windy.
Es ist windig.
es ist vindik

It looks as though it's going to rain.
Es sieht nach Regen aus.
es zeet nach raigen ows

Should I take an umbrella?
Soll ich einen Regenschirm mitnehmen?
zoll ich ahynen raigensheerm mitnaimen?

I hope the weather will improve.
Ich hoffe, daß das Wetter besser wird.
ich hoffe, das das vetter besser veert

Telephoning

Where is the nearest telephone?
Wo ist die nächste Telefon?
vo ist dehr nechste telefohn?

May I use your telephone?
Darf ich Ihr Telefon benutzen?
dahrf ich eer telefohn benootzen?

Where can I make a long-distance phone call?
Wo kann ich ein Ferngespräch führen?
vo kann ich ahyn fehrngeshprech fewren?

Do you have a telephone directory?
Haben Sie ein Telefonbuch?
hahben zee ahyn telefohnbooch?

Do you speak English?
Sprechen Sie Englisch?
shprechen zee ehnglish?

I want to make a collect call.
Ich möchte ein R-Gespräch anmelden.
ich meuchte ahyn ehr-geshprech anmelden

Hello. I would like Berlin 0000.
Guten Tag. Ich möchte Berlin 0000.
gooten tahk. ich meuchte behrleen 0000.

Could you let me know the cost of the call afterwards, please?
Könnten Sie mir bitte anschließend die Gebühr mitteilen?
keunten zee meer bitte anshleessent dee gebewr mittahylen?

Hello. This is . . .
Hallo. Hier spricht . . .
hallo. heer shpricht

May I please speak to . . .
Darf ich . . . sprechen?
dahrf ich . . . shprechen?

Could you give me extension . . .
Könnten Sie mir Nebenanschluß . . . geben, bitte?
keunten zee meer naibenanshlooss . . . gaiben, bitte?

Is this . . . ?
Ist dort . . . ?
ist dort?

He/she isn't here at the moment.
Er/sie ist im Augenblick nicht da.
ehr/zee ist im owgenblick nicht da

Could you tell him/her that I called? My name is . . . ; my number is . . .
Könnten Sie ihm bitte sagen, daß ich angerufen habe? Ich heiße . . . Meine Nummer ist . . .
keunten zee eem bitte zahgen, dass ich angerroofen hahbe? ich hahysse . . . mahyne noomer ist

Would you take a message, please?
Würden Sie bitte etwas ausrichten?
vewrden zee bitte etvas owsrichten?

Do you know when he/she will be back?
Wissen Sie, wann er/sie zurückkommt?
vissen zee, vahn ehr/zee tsurewkkommt?

I'll call back later.
Ich rufe später wieder an.
ich roofe shpaiter veeder an

Operator, could you help me, please?
Fräulein, könnten Sie mir helfen, bitte?
froylein, keunten zee meer helfen, bitte?

I don't speak German very well.
Ich spreche nur wenig Deutsch.
ich shpreche noor vainich doytch

I dialed the wrong number.
Ich habe falsch gewählt.
ich hahbe falsh gevalt

I was cut off. Could you connect me again, please?
Ich wurde unterbrochen. Können Sie mich wieder verbinden, bitte?
ich voorde oonterbrochen. keunen zee mich veeder fehrbinden, bitte?

Who is this?
Wer ist das?

Hold the line, please.
Bleiben Sie bitte am Apparat.

The line is busy.
Die Linie ist besetzt.

Hang up. I will call you back.
Legen Sie auf. Ich rufe Sie wieder an.

What's your number?
Wie ist Ihre Nummer?

What number are you calling?
Welche Nummer haben Sie gewählt?

I think you've got the wrong number.
Ich glaube, Sie sind falsch verbunden.

How much was the call?
Was hat das Gespräch gekostet?
vas hat das geshprech gekostet?

Post Office

Where is the nearest post office?
Wo ist das nächste Postamt?
vo ist das nechste postahmt?

What window do I go to for . . .
An welchen Schalter soll ich für . . . gehen?
an velchen shalter zoll ich fewr . . . gaien?

stamps Briefmarken *breefmahrken*	**telegrams** ein Telegramm *ahyn telegrahm*
money orders Postanweisungen *pohstanvahyzoongen*	**parcels** Pakete *pakaite*
poste restante postlagernde Sendungen *postlagehrnde zendoongen*	

GERMAN

GERMAN

Are there any letters for me? Here is my passport.
Ist Post für mich da? Hier ist mein Reisepaß.
ist pohst fewr mich da? heer ist mahyn rahyzepass

What's the postage for
Was kostet . . .
vas kostet

　　a letter to England
　　ein Brief nach England
　　ahyn breef nach ehnglahnt

　　a postcard to the U.S.
　　eine Postkarte in die Vereinigten Staaten
　　ahyne postkahrte in dee fehrahynigten shtahten

I want to send this (by)
Ich möchte dies . . . senden.
ich meuchte deez . . . zenden

　　air mail　　　　**express mail**
　　per Luftpost　　　per Eilboten
　　pehr looftpohst　*pehr ahylboten*

　　registered mail
　　eingeschrieben
　　ahyngeshreeben

Please give me . . . -Pfennig stamps.
Geben Sie mir bitte . . . Briefmarken zu . . . Pfennig.
gaiben zee meer bitte breefmahrken tsu pfehnich

I want to send this package to . . .
Ich möchte dieses Paket nach . . . aufgeben.
ich meuchte deezes pakait nach . . . owfgaiben

What does it contain?
Was ist der Inhalt?

I want to send a telegram. Could I have a form, please?
Ich möchte ein Telegramm aufgeben. Darf ich bitte ein Formular haben?
ich meuchte ahyn telegrahm Owfgaiben. dahrf ich bitte ahyn formoolar hahben?

How much is it per word?
Was kostet es pro Wort?
vas kostet es pro vohrt?

Bank

Where's the nearest bank?
Wo ist die nächste Bank?
vo ist dee nechste bahnk?

Where can I cash a travelers check?
Wo kann ich einen Reisescheck einlösen?
vo kahn ich ahynen rahyzesheck einleuzen?

What is the fee?
Wie hoch ist Ihre Gebühr?
vee hoch ist eere gebewr?

What's the rate of exchange?
Wie ist der Wechselkurs?
vee ist dehr vechselkoors?

Do you issue money on this credit card?
Geben Sie Bargeld auf diese Kreditkarte?
gaiben zee bahrgelt owf deeze kredeetkahrte?

Can you cash a personal check?
Können Sie einen Barscheck einlösen?
keunen zee ahynen bahrsheck ahynleuzen?

I have a letter of credit/bank draft.
Ich habe einen Kredit-brief/eine Tratte.
ich hahbe ahynen kredeet-breef/ ahyne trahte.

EVERYDAY SITUATIONS—SHOPPING **169**

I'm expecting money from . . .
Has it arrived?
Ich erwarte Geld aus . . . Ist es schon
angekommen?
*ich ervahrte gelt ows . . . ist es shohn
angekommen?*

I would like to make a deposit.
Ich möchte Geld auf mein Konto
einzahlen.
*ich meuchte gelt owf mahyn konto
ahyntsahlen*

I would like to open an account.
Ich möchte ein Konto eröffnen.
ich meuchte ahyn konto ereuffnen

I would like to change some . . .
for some . . .
Ich möchte . . . für . . . einwechseln.
*ich meuchte . . . fewr . . .
ahynvechseln*

Shopping

I'm looking for a . . .
Ich suche . . .
ich zooche . . .

bakery	eine Bäckerei	*ahyne beckerahy*
barbershop	einen Friseur	*ahynen freezeur*
bookshop	eine Buchhandlung	*ahyne boochhandloong*
butcher shop	eine Fleischerei	*ahyne flahysherahy*
delicatessen	ein Delikatessengeschäft	*ahyn deleekatessengesheft*
department store	ein Warenhaus	*ahyn vahrenhaus*
drugstore	eine Apotheke	*ahyne ahpotaike*
fish store	eine Fischhandlung	*ahyne fishhandloong*
grocery store	eine Gemüsehandlung	*ahyne gemewzehandloong*
hairdresser	einen Damenfriseur	*ahynen dahmenfreezeur*
hardware store	eine Eisenwarenhandlung	*ahyne ahysenvahrenhantloong*
laundry/dry cleaner	einen Waschsalon	*ahynen vahshsalon*
liquor store	eine Spirituosenhandlung	*ahyne shpirituozenhantloong*
market	ein Markt	*ahyn mahrkt*
newsstand	einen Zeitungsstand	*ahynen tsahytoongs-shtahnt*
shoe repair	einen Schuhmacher	*ahynen shoomacher*
shoestore	ein Schuhgeschäft	*ahyn shoogesheft*
sporting goods store	ein Sportgeschäft	*ahyn shporhtgesheft*
stationery store	ein Schreibwarengeschäft	*ahyn shrahybvahrengesheft*
supermarket	einen Supermarkt	*ahynen soopermarkt*
tobacco shop	einen Tabakladen	*ahynen tabaklahden*

Where can I buy . . . ?
Wo kann ich . . . kaufen?
vo kahn ich . . . kowfen?

May I help you?
Darf ich Ihnen helfen?

What would you like?
Was darf es sein?

I would like . . .
Ich möchte . . . *ich meuchte*
Ich hätte gern . . . *ich hette gehrn*

GERMAN

GERMAN

Can you show me . . .
Könnten Sie mir bitte . . . zeigen?
keunten zee meer bitte . . . tsahygen?

Do you have . . . ?
Haben Sie . . . ?
hahben zee?

I'm just looking, thanks.
Ich möchte mich nur umsehen, danke.
ich meuchte mich noor oomzai'en danke

How much is this?
Was kostet dies?
vas kostet deez?

Could you write that down, please?
Könnten Sie es mir aufschreiben, bitte?
keunten zee es meer owfshrahyben bitte?

Do you accept traveler's checks/ credit cards/dollars/pounds?
Nehmen Sie Reiseschecks/ Kreditkarten/Dollar/Pfund/an?
naimen zee rahyzeshecks kredeetkahrten/dohlar/pfoond an?

I think there's an error on this bill.
Ich glaube, da ist ein Irrtum in dieser Rechnung.
ich glahwbe, da ist ahyn eertoom in deezer rechnoong

Could you ship it to this address?
Könnten Sie es bitte an diese Adresse senden?
keunten zee es bitte an deeze adresse zenden?

Bookstore/Newsstand/Stationer (Buchhandlung/Zeitungskiosk/ Schreibwarenhandlung)

I'd like to buy . . .
Ich möchte . . . kaufen.
ich meuchte . . . kowfen

an address book	ein Adressenbüchlein	*ahyn adressenbewchlein*
an appointment book	ein Notizbuch	*ahyn notitzbooch*
a German-English dictionary	ein deutsch-englisches Wörterbuch	*ahyn doytch-ehnglishes veurterbooch*
envelopes	Umschläge	*oomshlaige*
an eraser	einen Radiergummi	*ahynen radeergoomee*
a German grammar	eine Deutsche Grammatik	*ahyne doytche grahmatik*
a guidebook	einen Reiseführer	*ahynen rahyzefewrer*
a map of the town	einen Stadtplan	*ahynen shtahtplahn*
a road map (of)	eine Straßenkarte (von)	*ahyne shtrassenkahrte*
an American/English newspaper	eine amerikanische/englische Zeitung	*ahyne amehrikanishe/ ehnglishe tsahytoong*
a notebook	ein Schreibheft	*ahyn shrahybheft*
a pen	einen Kugelschreiber	*ahynen koogelshrahyber*
a pencil	einen Bleistift	*ahynen blahyshtift*
postcards	Postkarten	*pohstkahrten*
Scotch tape	durchsichtigen Klebestreifen	*doorchzichtigen klai- bes-shtrahyfen*
writing paper	einen Schreibblock	*ahynen shrahybblock*

I

Clothing Store (Herrenkleider, Damenkleider)

Could you show me a . . . like the one in the window?
Können Sie mir ein/eine . . . wie das im Fenster zeigen?
keunen zee meer ahyn/ahyne . . . vee das im fenster tsahygen?

Could you show me something . . . ?
Können Sie mir etwas . . . zeigen?
keunen zee meer etvas . . . tsahygen?

bigger/smaller
Grösseres/Kleineres
greusseres/klahyneres

lighter/darker
Helleres/Dunkleres
helleres/doonkleres

of another color
in einer anderen Farbe
in ahyner anderen fahrbe

not so expensive   **of better quaity**
nicht so teuer   Besseres
nicht zo toyer   *besseres*

My size is . . .
Ich brauche Grösse
ich browche greusse

I'm not sure what my size is.
Ich weiß nicht was meine Grösse ist.
ich vahys nicht vas mahyne greusse ist

May I try it on?
Kann ich es probieren?
kahn ich es probeeren?

It doesn't fit.
Es paßt nicht.
es pahsst nicht

It's too . . .
Es ist zu . . .
es ist tsu . . .

tight/loose   **short/long**
eng/weit   kurz/lang
ehng/vahyt   *koorts/lahng*

Can you show me anything else?
Können Sie mir etwas anderes zeigen?
keunen zee meer etvas anderes tsahygen?

Very well; I'll take it.
Ja, gut; ich nehme es.
ya, goot; ich naime es

No, it's not really what I was looking for.
Nein, es ist nicht wirklich was ich gesucht habe.
nahyn, es ist nicht veerklich vas ich gezoocht hahbe

No, it's too expensive. I'll give you . . . for it.
Nein, es ist zu teuer. Ich gebe Ihnen . . . dafür.
nahyn, es ist tsu toyer. ich gaibe eenen . . . dafewr

Articles of Clothing (Kleidung)

I'd like . . .
Ich möchte . . .
ich meuchte . . .

bathrobe	einen Bademantel	*ahynen bahdemahntel*
bathing suit	einen Badeanzug	*ahynen bahde-ahntsook*
blouse	eine Bluse	*ahyne blooze*
boots	Stiefel	*shteefel*

GERMAN

GERMAN

bra	einen Büstenhalter	*ahyne bewstenhalter*
cardigan	eine Wollweste	*ahyne vohlveste*
coat	einen Mantel	*ahynen mahntel*
dress	ein Kleid	*ahyn klahyt*
evening dress	ein Abendkleid	*ahyn ahbentklahyt*
girdle	einen Hüfthalter	*ahynen hewfthalter*
gloves	Handschuhe	*hahntshooh'e*
hat	einen Hut	*ahynen hoot*
jacket	eine Jacke	*ahyne yahke*
nightgown	ein Nachthemd	*ahyn nachthemt*
pants	eine Hose	*ahyne hoze*
panty-hose	eine Strumpfhose	*ahyne shtroompfhoze*
pullover	einen Pulli	*ahynen pullee*
pyjamas	einen Schlafanzug	*ahynen shlafantsook*
raincoat	einen Regenmantel	*ahynen raigenmahntel*
sandals	Sandalen	*sandalen*
scarf	ein Halstuch	*ahyn halstooch*
shirt	ein Hemd	*ahyn hemt*
long sleeves	mit langen Ärmeln	*mit lahngen ehrmeln*
short sleeves	mit kurzen Ärmeln	*mit koortsen ehrmeln*
shoes	Schuhe	*shoo'e*
shorts	Shorts	*shorts*
skirt	einen Rock	*ahynen rock*
slip	einen Unterrock	*ahynen oonterrock*
slippers	Hausschuhe	*howsshoo'e*
socks	Socken	*zocken*
stockings	Strümpfe	*shtrewmpfe*
suit (mens/womens)	einen Anzug/ein Kostüm	*ahynen ahntsook/ahyn kostewm*
sweater	einen Pullover	*ahynen pullover*
T-shirt	ein T-Shirt	*ahyn t-shirt*
tennis shoes	Tennisschuhe	*tehnisshoo'e*
tie	eine Krawatte	*ahyne kravahte*
tuxedo	einen Smoking	*ahynen smoking*
underwear (men's)	eine Unterhose	*ahyne oonterhoze*
underwear (women's)	einen Schlüpfer	*ahynen shlewpfer*
belt	einen Gürtel	*ahynen gewrtel*
buttons	Knöpfe	*kneupfe*
pocket	die Tasche	*dee tashe*
shoelaces	Schnürsenkel	*shnewrzenkel*
zipper	ein Reißverschluß	*ahyn rahyssfehrshlooss*

Colors (Farben)

beige	beige	*beige*
black	schwarz	*shvahrtz*
blue	blau	*blahw*
brown	braun	*brown*
gold	golden	*golden*
green	grün	*grewn*

gray	grau	*grahw*
off-white	creme	*crehme*
orange	orangenfarbig	*oranzhenfahrbich*
pink	rosa	*roza*
purple	purpur	*poorpoor*
red	rot	*roht*
silver	silbern	*zilbehrn*
turquoise	türkisfarben	*turkeesfahrben*
white	weiss	*vahyss*
yellow	gelb	*gelp*

Fabrics (Stoffe)

acrylic	Acryl	*akrewl*
corduroy	Kord	*kohrt*
cotton	Baumwolle	*bowmvohle*
felt	Filz	*filtz*
flannel	Flanell	*flanell*
lace	Spitze	*shpitze*
leather	Leder	*laider*
linen	Leinen	*lahynen*
rayon	Kunstseide	*kunstzahyde*
satin	Satin	*zateen*
silk	Seide	*zahyde*
suede	Wildleder	*viltlaider*
synthetic	synthetisch	*zewntaitish*
velvet	Samt	*zahmt*
wool	Wolle	*vohle*

Jewelry (Schmuck)

bracelet	ein Armband	*ahyn ahrmbant*
necklace	eine Halskette	*ahyne halskette*
ring	einen Ring	*ahynen ring*
wristwatch	eine Armbanduhr	*ahyne ahrmbantoor*
diamond	Diamant	*dyamahnt*
gold	Gold	*golt*
platinum	Platin	*plateen*
silver	Silber	*zilber*
stainless steel	Edelstahl	*ehdelstahl*
plated: gold plated	vergoldet	*fehrgoldet*
silver plated	versilbert	*fehrzilbehrt*

GERMAN

GERMAN

Buying Food for Picnics and Snacks

I'd like some . . .
Ich möchte bitte . . .
*ich **meuch**te bitte*

apples	Äpfel	*ehpfel*
apple juice	Apfelsaft	*ahpfelzahft*
bananas	Bananen	*banahnen*
bread	Brot	*broht*
butter	Butter	*booter*
cake	Kuchen	*koochen*
candy	Konfekt	*konfekt*
carrots	Karotten	*karotten*
cheese	Käse	*kaize*
chocolate	Schokolade	*shokolahde*
coffee	Kaffee	*kaffai*
cold cuts	Aufschnitt	*owfshnitt*
cookies	Kekse	*kaize*
crackers	Cräckers	*krehckers*
cucumbers	Gurken	*goorken*
eggs	Eier	*ahyer*
frankfurters	Frankfurter Würstchen	*frahnkfoorter vewrstchen*
grapefruit	Pampelmusen	*pahmpelmoozen*
grapefruit juice	Pampelmusensaft	*pahmpelmoozenzaft*
ham	Schinken	*shinken*
ice cream	Eis	*ahys*
lemons	Zitronen	*tsitronen*
lettuce	Kopfsalat	*kopfsalaht*
melon	Melone	*melone*
milk	Milch	*milch*
mustard	Senf	*zehnf*
oil	Öl	*eul*
oranges	Apfelsinen	*ahpfelzeenen*
orange juice	Apfelsinensaft	*ahpfelzeenenzahft*
peaches	Pfirsich	*pfeerzish*
pears	Birnen	*beernen*
pepper	Pfeffer	*pfeffer*
peppers	Pepperoni	*pepperonee*
pickles	Pökel	*peuk'l*
plums	Pflaumen	*pflahwmen*
potato chips	Kartoffelchips	*kahrtoffelchips*
potatoes	Kartoffeln	*kahrtoffeln*
raspberries	Himbeeren	*himbehren*
rolls	Brötchen	*breutchen*
salad	Salat	*zalaht*
salami	Salami	*zalahmee*
salt	Salz	*zalts*
sandwiches	Butterbrote	*booterbrohte*

sausages	Würstchen	*vewrstchen*
soft drinks	Fruchtsaft	*fruchtzahft*
spaghetti	Spaghetti	*spaghettee*
strawberries	Erdbeeren	*ehrdbehren*
sugar	Zucker	*tsooker*
tea	Tee	*tai*
tomatoes	Tomaten	*tomahten*
yoghurt	Jogurt	*yogurt*
a box of	eine Schachtel	*ahyne shachtel*
a can of	eine Büchse/Dose	*ahyne bewchze/doze*
a jar of	ein Glas	*ahyn glahs*
a half kilo of	ein halbes Kilo	*ahyn halbes keelo*
a kilo of	ein Kilo	*ahyn keelo*
a packet of	eine Packung	*ahyne packoong*
a slice of	eine Scheibe	*ahyne shahybe*
a bottle opener	einen Flaschenöffner	*ahynen flasheneuffner*
a corkscrew	einen Korkenzieher	*ahyne korkentsee'er*
paper napkins	Papierservietten	*papeerzehrvyehten*
paper plates	Papierteller	*papeerteller*
plastic utensils	Plastikbesteck	*plastikbeshteck*
a tin (can) opener	einen Büchsenöffner	*ahynen bewchseneuffner*

I'll have a little more.
Etwas mehr, bitte!
etvas mehr, bitte

That's too much.
Das ist zuviel.
das ist tsu feel

A bag, please.
Eine Tüte, bitte.
ahyne tewte, bitte

Pharmacy (Apotheke)

Can you make up this prescription?
Können Sie mir dieses Rezept machen?
keunen zee meer deezes retsept machen?

How long will it take?
Wie lange dauert es?
vee lahnge dowehrt es?

Can you give me something for . . .
Ich brauch ein Mittel gegen . . .
ich browche ahyn mittel gaigen

I'll come back in a little while.
Ich komme gleich zurück.
ich komme glahych tsurewk

Could you please write down the instructions in English?
Könnten Sie bitte die Gebrauchsanweisung auf Englisch schreiben?
keunten zee bitte dee gebrowchsanvahyzoong owf ehnglish shrahyben?

a cold	Erkältung	*ehrkeltoong*
constipation	Verstopfung	*fehrshtopfoong*
a cough	Husten	*hoosten*

GERMAN

a cut	Schnittwund	*shnittvoond*
diarrhea	Durchfall	*doorchfahl*
hay fever	Heuschnupfen	*hoyshnoopfen*
a headache	Kopfschmerzen	*kopfshmehrtsen*
hemorrhoids	Hämorrhoiden	*haimoroyden*
indigestion	Magenverstimmung	*mahgenfehrshtimmoong*
insect bites	Insektenstiche	*insektenshtiche*
nausea	Übelkeit	*ewbelkahyt*
a sore throat	Halsschmerzen	*halsshmehrtzen*
sunburn	Sonnenbrand	*zohnenbrahnt*
travel sickness	Reisekrankheit	*rahyzekrahnkhahyt*

I'd like a/an/some . . .
Ich möchte . . .
*ich **meuch**te*

aspirin	Aspirin	*aspireen*
bandage	Verband	*fehrbant*
Band-aid	Pflaster	*pflahster*
contraceptives	Verhütungsmittel	*fehrhewtoongsmittel*
cough syrup	Hustensirup	*hoostenseeroop*
cough drops	Hustentabletten	*hoostentabletten*
eyedrops	Augentropfen	*owgentropfen*
insect repellent	eine Salbe gegen Insekten	*ahyne zalbe gaigen insekten*
laxative	ein Abführmittel	*ahyn apfewrmittel*
sleeping pills	Schlaftabletten	*shlahftabletten*
sanitary napkins	Damenbinden/Monatsbinden	*dahmenbinden/ monatsbinden*
tampons	Tampons	*tampons*
tranquilizers	Sedativum	*saidateevum*

Toilet Articles

I'd like to buy . . .
Ich möchte . . .
*ich **meuch**te*

after-shave lotion	Rasierwasser	*razeervahsser*
cream	eine Creme	*ahyne craime*
cleansing cream	Reinigungsmilch	*rahynigoongsmilch*
hand cream	Handcreme	*hantcraime*
moisturizing cream	Feuchtigkeitscreme	*foychtichkahytscraime*
deodorant	ein Desodorant	*ahyn dezodorahn*
emery board	eine Sandpapierfeile	*ahyne zantpapeerfahyle*
razor	einen Rasierapparat	*ahynen razeerahparaht*
razor blades	Rasierklingen	*razeerklingen*
shampoo	ein Haarwaschmittel	*ahyn hahrvashmittel*

GERMAN

shaving cream	Rasiercreme	*razeercraime*
soap	Seife	*zahyfe*
suntan oil/cream	Sonnenöl/Sonnencreme	*zohneneul/ zohnencraime*
talcum powder	Talkumpuder	*talkoompooder*
tissues	Papiertücher	*papeertewcher*
toilet paper	Toilettenpapier	*twahlettenpapeer*
toothbrush	eine Zahnbürste	*ahyne tsahnbewrste*
toothpaste	Zahnpasta	*tsahnpasta*
tweezers	eine Pinzette	*ahyne pintsette*

N.B.: for other toilet articles and cosmetics, you should go to a "Drogerie."

Photography (Photographie)

I'd like a good/inexpensive camera, please.
Eine gute/ preiswerte Kamera, bitte.
ahyne goote/prahyzvehrte kahmera, bitte

I'd like some film for this camera.
Ich möchte einen Film für diese Kamera.
ich meuchte ahynen film fewr deeze kahmera

black and white	color
schwarzweiß	Farbfilm
shvahrtzvahyss	*fahrpfilm*

color slide	
Farbdiapositive	
fahrpdeeaposeeteeve	

I need . . . for this camera.
Ich brauche . . . für diese Kamera.
ich browche . . . fewr deeze kahmera

batteries	a flash cube
Batterien	ein Blitzlicht
batteree'en	*ahyn blitzlicht*

a lens	
ein Objektiv	
ahyn obyekteef	

How much do you charge for processing?
Was kostet das Entwickeln?
vas kostet das entvickeln?

I'd like . . . prints/slides of each negative.
Ich hätte gerne . . . Abzüge von jedem Negativ.
ich hette gehrne . . . aptsewge fon yaidem negateef

with a matt finish
matt
mahtt

with a glossy finish
Hochglanz
hochglantz

I would like an enlargement of this, please.
Können Sie das bitte vergrößern?
keunen zee das bitte fehrgreussehrn?

When will it be ready?
Wann ist es fertig?
vahn ist es fehrtich?

Tobacco Shop (Tabakladen)

I'd like a pack/carton of cigarettes, please.
Eine Schachtel/Stange Zigaretten, bitte.
ahyne shachtel/shtahnge tsigaretten, bitte

GERMAN

Do you have . . . ?
Haben Sie . . . ?
hahben zee

I'd like . . .
Ich hätte gerne . . .
ich hette gehrne

   pipe tobacco
   Pfeifentabak
   pfahyfentabahk

   a cigarette lighter
   ein Feuerzeug
   ahyn foyertsoyg

   lighter fluid
   Feuerzeugbenzin
   foyertsoygbentseen

   matches
   Streichhölzer
   shtrahych-heultser

   a pipe
   eine Pfeife
   ahyne pfahyfe

   cigars
   Zigarren
   tsigaren

Laundry/Dry Cleaner

Where is the nearest laundry/dry cleaner?
Wo ist die nächste Wäscherei/chemische Reinigung?
vo ist dee nechste vesherahy/chemishe rahynigoong?

I'd like to have these clothes washed and ironed.
Ich möchte diese Kleider waschen und bügeln lassen.
ich meuchte deeze klahyder vahshen oont bewgeln lassen

Please have this dry cleaned.
Bitte reinigen Sie dies.
bitte rahynigen zee deez

Can you remove this stain?
Können Sie diesen Flecken rausmachen?
keunen zee deezen flecken rowsmachen?

Can you mend this?
Können Sie dies ausbessern?
keunen zee dees owsbessehrn?

When will it be ready?
Wann ist es fertig?
vahn ist es fehrtich?

I need it . . .
Ich brauche es . . .
ich browche es

   this afternoon
   heute nachmittag
   hoyte nachmittahk

   this evening   **tomorrow**
   heute Abend   morgen
   hoyte ahbent   *mohrgen*

Repairs

Can you fix this?
Können Sie dies flicken?
keunen zee dees flicken?

How long will it take?
Wie lange dauert es?
vee lahnge dowehrt es?

How much will it cost?
Was wird es kosten?
vas veert es kosten?

When will it be ready?
Wann ist es fertig?
vahn ist es fehrtich?

GERMAN

HEALTH

At the Doctor's

| **Office hours:**
"Sprechstunden"

I don't feel well.
Ich fühle mich nicht wohl.
ich fewle mich nicht vohl

I feel ill.
Ich bin krank.
ich bin krahnk

Where can I find a doctor who speaks English?
Wo kann ich einen Arzt finden, der Englisch spricht?
vo kann ich ahynen artzt finden, dehr ehnglish shpricht?

I have (a) . . .
Ich habe . . .
ich hahbe

Could you call a doctor for me?
Könnten Sie mir einen Arzt anrufen?
keunten zee meer ahynen artzt anroofen?

Is there a doctor here?
Gibt es hier einen Arzt?
gipt es heer ahynen artzt?

Must I make an appointment?
Muß ich mich anmelden?
mooss ich mich anmelden?

I must see a doctor right away.
Ich brauche sofort einen Arzt.
ich browche zofohrt ahynen artzt

I've got a pain here.
Ich habe hier Schmerzen.
ich hahbe heer shmehrtzen

backache	Rückenschmerzen	*rewkenshmehrtzen*
constipation	Verstopfung	*fehrshtopfoong*
cough	Husten	*hoosten*
cramps	Krämpfe	*krehmpfe*
diarrhea	Durchfall	*doorchfahl*
fever	Fieber	*feeber*
headache	Kopfschmerzen	*kopfshmehrtsen*
hemorrhoids	Hämorrhoiden	*hemmoroyden*
insect bite	einen Insektenstich	*ahynen insektenshtich*
lump, blister	eine Beule	*ahyne boyle*
nausea	Übelkeit	*ewbelkahyt*
nervous breakdown	Nervenzusammenbruch	*nehrfen-tsuzahmen-brooch*
rash	einen Ausschlag	*ahynen owsshlahk*
sexual complaint	Geschlechtskrankheit	*geshlechts-krahnkhayt*
swelling	eine Schwellung	*ahyne shvelloong*
wound	eine Wunde	*ahyne voonde*

I have difficulty breathing.
Ich habe Schwierigkeiten beim Atmen.
ich hahbe shveerigkahyten bahym ahtmen

I feel dizzy/faint.
Ich fühle mich schwindlig/Ich werde ohnmächtig
ich fewle mich shvindlich/ich vehrde ohnmechtich

GERMAN

I've been vomiting.
Ich habe mich übergeben.
*ich **hahbe** mich ewbergaiben*

I can't eat/sleep.
Ich mag nicht essen. Ich schlafe nicht.
ich mahk nicht essen ich shlahfe nicht

I've cut/burned myself.
Ich habe mich geschnitten/verbrannt.
*ich **hahbe** mich geshnitten/
fehrbrahnt*

**I have sprained/broken my wrist/
ankle.**
Ich habe mein Handgelenk/mein
Fußgelenk verstaucht/gebrochen.
*ich hahbe mahyn **hahnt**gelenk/mahyn
foosgelenk fehrshtahwcht/
.gebrochen*

I'm allergic to penicillin/iodine.
Ich bin allergisch gegen Penizillin/Jod.
*ich bin al**lehr**gish **gai**gen penitsilleen/
eeyot.*

Doctor to Patient

What's wrong?
Was fehlt Ihnen?

Where does it hurt?
Wo tut es weh?

How long have you had this trouble?
Seit wann haben Sie diese
Beschwerden?

Please undress (to the waist).
Bitte machen Sie den Oberkörper frei.

Does that hurt?
Tut das weh?

**I'll need a urine specimen/blood
sample.**
Ich brauche eine Urinprobe/Blutprobe.

Are you taking any medication?
Nehmen Sie Medikamente?

Are you allergic to . . .
Sind Sie allergisch gegen . . .

You have . . .
Sie haben . . .

I will prescribe some pills for you.
Ich werde Ihnen Pillen verschreiben.

**Take these . . . times a day before/
after each meal every morning/
evening.**
Nehmen Sie diese . . . pro Tag vor/nach
jeder Mahlzeit morgens/abends

You are fatigued.
Sie sind übermüdet.

You must stay in bed for . . . days.
Sie müssen für . . . Tage im Bett
bleiben.

It's nothing serious.
Es ist nichts Ernstes.

You are very sick.
Sie sind sehr krank.

You must go to the hospital.
Sie müssen ins Krankenhaus.

an abscess	ein Abszess
appendicitis	eine Blinddarmentzündung
a cold	eine Erkältung
food poisoning	eine Lebensmittelvergiftung
a hernia	eine Hernia
an infection	eine Infektion
the flu	eine Grippe
tonsillitis	Mandelentzündung
an ulcer	ein Geschwür

GERMAN

At the Dentist's

Can you recommend a good dentist?
Können Sie mir einen guten Zahnarzt empfehlen?
keunen zee meer ahynen gooten tsahnartzt empfailen?

I would like to see Dr. . . . as soon as possible.
Ich möchte Herrn Doktor . . . so bald wie möglich sehen.
ich meuchte hehrn doktor zo bahlt vee meuglich zai'en

I have a toothache.
Ich habe Zahnschmerzen.
ich hahbe tsahnshmehrtzen

My tooth has broken.
Ich habe mir einen Zahn abgebrochen.
ich hahbe meer ahynen tsahn apgebrochen

My gums are bleeding/sore.
Mein Zahnfleisch blutet/ist entzündet.
mahyn tsahnflahysh blootet/ ist entsewndet

I have an abscess.
Ich habe einen Abszess.
ich hahbe ahynen apsess

I've lost/broken a filling.
Ich habe eine Füllung verloren.
ich hahbe ahyne fewloong fehrloren.

Can you give me temporary treatment?
Können Sie mich provisorisch behandeln?
keunen zee mich provizorish behahndeln?

Please don't extract it.
Bitte ziehen Sie den Zahn nicht.
bitte tsee'en zee dain tsahn nicht

Please give me a local anesthesia.
Bitte geben Sie mir eine lokale Betäubung.
bitte gaiben zee meer ahyne lokahle betoyboong

Dentist to Patient

I want you to have an X ray.
Ich muß Sie röntgen.

I will fill the tooth.
Ich mache Ihnen eine Füllung.

This tooth must come out.
Dieser Zahn muß gezogen werden.

Optician (Optiker)

I have broken my glasses.
Ich habe meine Brille zerbrochen.
ich hahbe mahyne brille tsehrbrochen

Can you repair them?
Können Sie sie reparieren?
keunen zee zee repareeren?

I have lost a contact lens.
Ich habe eine Kontaktlinse verloren.
ich hahbe ahyne kontahktlinze fehrloren

Could you make me another one?
Können Sie mir eine neue machen?
keunen zee meer ahyne noye machen?

When will they/it be ready?
Wann sind sie/ist sie fertig?
vahn zint zee/ist zee fehrtich?

GERMAN

I need wetting/soaking solution for hard/soft contact lenses.
Ich brauche Benetzungsflüssigkeit/aüfbewahrungsflüssigkeit für harte/
weiche Kontaktlinsen.
*ich **brow**che benetsoongs-flewssigkahyt/**ewf**bevahroongz-flewssigkakyt fewr
harte/**vahy**che kontahklinzen*

My contact lenses are bothering me. Could you have a look at them, please?
Meine Kontaktlinsen stören mich. Könnten Sie sie kontrollieren, bitte?
*mahyne kontahktlinzen shteuren mich. **keun**ten zee zee kontrol**lee**ren, bitte?*

Paying the Doctor/Dentist/Optician

How much do I owe you?
Was schulde ich Ihnen?
*vas **shool**de ich eenen?*

Can you send me a bill?
Könnten Sie mir eine Rechnung
   schicken?
*keunten zee meer **ahy**ne **rech**noong
   shicken?*

I have health insurance.
Ich bin versichert.
*ich bin fehr**zich**ert*

EMERGENCY

Loss or Theft

Excuse me, can you help me?
Entschuldigung, können Sie mir helfen?
*entshool**di**goong. **keu**nen zee meer
   helfen?*

Where's the police station?
Wo ist die Polizeiwache?
*vo ist dee polee**tsahy**vahche?*

**Where's the American/British/
   Canadian consulate?**
Wo ist das amerikanische/britische/
   kanadische Konsulat?
*vo ist das amehri**kah**nishe/**bri**tishe/
   kana**di**she konsu**lat**?*

Where is the lost and found?
Wo ist das Fundbüro?
*vo ist das **foont**bewro?*

I've lost my . . . Someone has stolen my . . .
Ich habe . . . verloren. Jemand hat . . . gestohlen.
*ich **hah**be . . . fehr**lor**en. **yai**mant hat . . . ge**shto**len*

passport	meinen Reisepaß	*mahynen **rahy**zepass*
money	mein Geld	*mahyn gelt*
travelers checks	meine Reiseschecks	*mahyne **rahy**zeshecks*
credit cards	meine Kreditkarten	*mahyne kre**deet**kahrten*
luggage	mein Gepäck	*mahyn ge**peck***
plane tickets	meine Flugbillets	*mahyne **flook**bilyets*
handbag	meine Tasche	*mahyne **tah**she*
keys	meine Schlüßel	*mahyne **shlew**sel*

I left something on the train/taxi/bus.
Ich habe etwas im Zug/Taxi/Bus verlassen.
*ich **hah**be etvas im tsook taksi/boos fehr**lah**ssen*

Asking for Help

Help!	Hilfe!	*hilfe!*
Police!	Polizei!	*poleetsahy!*
Fire!	Feuer!	*foyehr!*
Thief!	Dieb!	*deep!*
Look out!	Achtung!	*achtoong!*
Stop!	Halt!	*halt!*

TIME, DATES, NUMBERS

Time, Dates

What time is it?
Wieviel Uhr ist es?
veefeel oor ist es?

It's . . .
Es ist . . .
es ist . . .

two o'clock	zwei Uhr	*tsvahy oor*
ten past three	zehn nach drei	*tsain nach drahy*
four fifteen	viertel nach vier	*feertel nach feer*
twenty past five	zwanzig nach fünf	*tsvahntsich nach fewnf*
six thirty	halb sieben	*halp zeeben*
quarter to eight	viertel vor acht	*feertel for acht*
five to eight	fünf vor acht	*fewnf for acht*
It's midnight.	Es ist Mitternacht.	*es ist mitternacht*
It's one o'clock.	Es ist ein Uhr.	*es ist ahyn oor*
sunrise	Sonnenaufgang	*zohnenowfgahng*
morning	Morgen	*mohrgen*
noon	Mittag	*mittahk*
afternoon	Nachmittag	*nachmittahk*
sunset	Sonnenuntergang	*zohnenoontergahng*
evening	Abend	*ahbent*
night	Nacht	*nacht*

It's early/late.
Es ist früh/spät.
es ist frew/shpait

What's the date today?
Welches Datum haben wir heute?
velches dahtum hahben veer hoyte?

The date is . . .
Heute haben wir . . .
hoyte hahben veer

GERMAN

GERMAN

Days of the Week

Monday	Montag	*montahk*
Tuesday	Dienstag	*deenstahk*
Wednesday	Mittwoch	*mittvoch*
Thursday	Donnerstag	*donnerstahk*
Friday	Freitag	*frahytahk*
Saturday	Samstag	*zahmztahk*
Sunday	Sonntag	*zohntahk*

Seasons

Spring	Frühling	*frewling*
Summer	Sommer	*zommer*
Autumn	Herbst	*hehrpst*
Winter	Winter	*vinter*

The Months

January	Januar	*yanuar*
February	Februar	*faibruar*
March	März	*mehrtz*
April	April	*april*
May	Mai	*mahy*
June	Juni	*yoonee*
July	Juli	*yoolee*
August	August	*owgoost*
September	September	*zeptember*
October	Oktober	*oktober*
November	November	*november*
December	Dezember	*detsember*

this year	dieses Jahr	*deezes yahr*
last week	letzte Woche	*letzte vohche*
next month	im nächsten Monat	*im nechsten monaht*

today	heute	*hoyte*
yesterday	gestern	*gestehrn*
tomorrow	morgen	*mohrgen*

| the day before yesterday | vorgestern | *forgestehrn* |
| the day after tomorrow | übermorgen | *ewbermohrgen* |

Numbers

0	null	*nool*
1	eins	*ahyns*
2	zwei	*tsvahy*
3	drei	*drahy*
4	vier	*feer*
5	fünf	*fewnf*
6	sechs	*sechs*
7	sieben	*zeeb'n*
8	acht	*acht*
9	neun	*noyn*
10	zehn	*tsehn*
11	elf	*elf*
12	zwölf	*tsveulf*
13	dreizehn	***drahy**tsehn*
14	vierzehn	***feer**tsehn*
15	fünfzehn	***fewnf**tsehn*
16	sechszehn	***zech**tstsehn*
17	siebzehn	***zeeb**tsehn*
18	achtzehn	***acht**tsehn*
19	neunzehn	***noyn**tsehn*
20	zwanzig	***tsvantsich***
21	einundzwanzig	***ahyn**oon-tsvantsich*
22	zweiundzwanzig	***tsvahy**oon-tsvantsich*
23	dreiundzwanzig	***drahy**oon-tsvantsich*
24	vierundzwanzig	***feer**oon-tsvantsich*
25	fünfundzwanzig	***fewnf**oon-tsvantsich*
26	sechsundzwanzig	***zechs**oon-tsvantsich*
27	siebenundzwanzig	***ziebe**noon-tsvantsich*
28	achtundzwanzig	***acht**oon-tstvanzich*
29	neunundzwanzig	***noyn**oon-tsvanzich*
30	dreißig	***drahys**sich*
40	vierzig	***feer**tsich*
50	fünfzig	***fewnf**tsich*
60	sechzig	***zecht**sich*
70	siebzig	***zeeb**tsich*
80	achtzig	***acht**sich*
90	neunzig	***noyn**tsich*
100	(ein)hundert	***ahyn**hoordert*
101	hunderteins	*hoordert**ahyns***
102	hundertzwei	*hoordert**svahy***
150	hundertfünfzig	*hoordert**fewnf**zich*
200	zweihundert	***tsvahy**hoordert*
300	dreihundert	***drahy**hoordert*
400	vierhundert	***feer**hoordert*
500	fünfhundert	***fewnf**hoordert*
600	sechshundert	***zechs**hoordert*
700	siebenhundert	***zee**benhoordert*

GERMAN

GERMAN

800	achthundert	***ach*hoondert**
900	neunhundert	***noyn*hundert**
1000	(ein)tausend	***ahyn*tauzent**
1100	tausendeinhundert	***tahw*zendahynhoondert**
2000	zweitausend	***tsvahy*tahwzent**
5000	fünftausend	***fewnft*ahwzent**
10,000	zehntausend	***tsenh*tahwzent**
50,000	fünfzigtausend	***fewnf*sigtahwzent**
100,000	hunderttausend	***hund*ertahwzent**
1,000,000	eine Million	***ahyne Meel*yon**

first	erste	***ehr*ste**
second	zweite	***tsvahy*te**
third	dritte	***dritt*e**
fourth	vierte	***feer*te**
fifth	fünfte	***fewnf*te**
sixth	sechste	***zech*ste**
seventh	siebte	***zeep*te**
eighth	achte	***ach*te**
ninth	neunte	***noyn*te**
tenth	zehnte	***tsain*te**
eleventh	elfte	***elf*te**
twelfth	zwölfte	***tsveulf*te**

a half	ein halber	*ahyn **halber***
	ein halbes	*ahyn **halbes***
	eine halbe	*ahyne **halbe***
a half	eine Hälfte	*ahyne **helfte***
a third	ein Drittel	*ahyn **drittel***
a quarter	ein Viertel	*ahyn **feertel***

GERMAN DICTIONARY

Only the base, or masculine, form of adjectives and nouns is given.

The feminine form of the noun is made by adding the ending -in, as in Freund/Freundin.

For the declension of adjectives, see page 108.

Where it is obvious (as in Mann) the gender of a word is not shown.

A

a, an **ein/eine/ein**
able, to be **können**
about **ungefähr**
above **über**
abroad **im Ausland**
absent **nicht da**
absolutely **unbedingt**
accept, to **annehmen**
accident **Unfall** (m.)
accompany, to **begleiten**
according to **gemäß**
accustomed **gewöhnt**
ache **Schmerz** (m.)
across **über, jenseits**
acquaintance **Bekannte** (m.)
actor **Schauspieler**
add, to **hinzufügen**
address **Adresse** (f.)
admire, to **bewundern**
admission **Eintritt** (m.)
advertisement **Anzeige** (f.)
advertising **Werbung** (f.)
advice **Rat** (m.)
advise, to **raten**
afraid, to be **Angst haben**
after **nach**
afternoon **Nachmittag** (m.)
again **wieder**
against **gegen**
age **Alter** (n.)
agency **Agentur** (f.)
ago **vor**
agree, to **übereinstimmen**
agreeable **angenehm**
agreed **abgemacht**
ahead **vorne**
air **Luft** (f.)

air conditioning **Klimaanlage** (f.)
air force **Luftwaffe** (f.)
air mail **Luftpost** (f.)
airplane **Flugzeug** (n.)
airport **Flugplatz** (m.)
alarm clock **Wecker** (m.)
alike **ähnlich**
all **alle, Alles**
allow, to **erlauben**
all right **in Ordnung, gut, ok**
almost **beinahe, fast**
alone **allein**
already **schon**
also **auch**
although **obwohl**
always **immer**
ambulance **Krankenwagen** (m.)
America **Amerika**
American **amerikanisch**
among **zwischen, unter**
amount **Betrag** (m.)
amusement **Unterhaltung** (f.)
amusement park **Vergnügungspark**
  (m.)
amusing **amüsant**
ancient **sehr alt**
and **und**
angry **böse, ärgerlich**
animal **Tier** (n.)
ankle **Fußknöchel** (m.)
announce, to **ankündigen**
annoy, to **belästigen, stören**
answer, to **antworten**
answer **Antwort** (f.)
antifreeze **Frostschutzmittel** (n.)
anxious, to be **ängstlich sein**
any **irgendein**
anyone **irgendeiner**
anything **irgend etwas**
anyway **jedenfalls**

GERMAN

187

GERMAN

anywhere **irgendwo**
apartment house　**Miethaus** (n.)
appear, to　**erscheinen**
appetite　**Appetit** (m.)
appetizer　**Vorspeise** (f.)
apple　**Apfel** (m.)
appointment　**Verabredung** (f.)
appreciate　**schätzen**
approach, to　**sich nähern**
approve, to　**billigen**
arm　**Arm** (m.)
armchair　**Lehnstuhl** (m.)
around　**rings herum**
arrest, to　**verhaften**
arrival　**Ankunft** (f.)
arrive, to　**ankommen**
art　**Kunst** (f.)
artist　**Künstler**
as　**wie**
ask, to　**fragen**
asleep, to fall　**einschlafen**
assure　**versichern**
at　**an/zu/bei/um**
at all, not　**gar nicht**
at once　**sofort**
attack　**angreifen**
attention　**Aufmerksamkeit** (f.)
attractive　**reizend**
aunt　**Tante** (f.)
Austria　**Österreich** (n.)
authentic　**authentisch**
author　**Autor**
automatic　**automatisch**
automobile　**Auto** (n.), **Wagen** (m.)
autumn　**Herbst** (m.)
avoid, to　**vermeiden**
awaken, to　**erwachen**
away, to go　**weggehen**

B

baby　**Baby** (n.)
bachelor　**Junggeselle**
backward　**zurück**
back　**Rücken** (m.)
backpack　**Rucksack** (m.)
bad　**schlecht**
badly　**schlecht**
baggage　**Gepäck** (n.)
bakery　**Bäckerei** (f.)

band (music)　**Kapelle** (f.)
bank　**Bank** (f.)
bar (drinking)　**Bar** (f.)
barber　**Friseur** (m.)
basket　**Korb** (m.)
bath　**Bad** (n.)
bathe, to　**baden**
bathing suit　**Badeanzug** (m.)
bathroom　**Badezimmer** (n.)
bathtub　**Badewanne** (f.)
battery　**Batterie** (f.)
battle　**Schlacht** (f.)
be, to　**sein**
beach　**Strand** (m.)
beans　**Bohnen** (pl.)
bear　**Bär** (m.)
beard　**Bart** (m.)
beat, to　**schlagen**
beautiful　**schön**
beauty　**Schönheit** (f.)
because　**weil**
become　**werden**
bed　**Bett** (n.)
bedroom　**Schlafzimmer** (n.)
beef　**Rindfleisch** (n.)
beer　**Bier** (n.)
before　**vorher**
begin, to　**anfangen**
behind　**hinter**
believe, to　**glauben**
bell (church)　**Glocke** (f.)
bell (door)　**Klingel** (f.)
belong, to　**gehören**
below　**unter**
belt　**Gürtel** (m.)
beside　**neben**
best　**das Beste**
bet, to　**wetten**
better　**besser**
between　**zwischen**
bicycle　**Fahrrad** (n.)
big　**groß**
bill　**Rechnung** (f.)
bird　**Vogel** (m.)
birth　**Geburt** (f.)
birthday　**Geburtstag** (m.)
bite, to　**beissen**
bitter　**bitter, herb**
black　**schwarz**
blanket　**Decke** (f.)
blood　**Blut** (n.)

blouse **Bluse** (f.)
blue **blau**
boarding house **Pension** (f.)
boat **Boot** (n.)
boat(small) **Kahn** (m.)
body **Körper** (m.)
boil, to **sieden**
book **Buch** (n.)
border **Grenze** (f.)
boring **langweilig**
born, to be **geboren sein**
borrow, to **borgen**
both **beide**
bother, to **stören, belästigen**
bottle **Flasche** (f.)
bottom **Boden** (m.)
bowl, to **kegeln**
box **Schachtel** (f.)
boy **Junge, Knabe**
brain **Gehirn** (n.)
brake **Bremse** (f.)
brassiere **Büstenhalter** (m.)
bread **Brot** (n.)
break, to **brechen**
breakfast **Frühstück** (n.)
bride **Braut** (f.)
bridge **Brücke** (f.)
brief **kurz**
bring, to **bringen**
broad **breit**
broken **gebrochen, kaputt**
broom **Besen** (n.)
brother **Bruder**
brother-in-law **Schwager**
brown **braun**
brush **Bürste** (f.)
bugs **Ungeziefer, Wanzen**
build, to **bauen**
building **Gebäude** (n.)
bum **Gammler**
bus **Bus** (m.)
bus stop **Bushaltestelle** (f.)
business **Geschäft** (n.)
busy **beschäftigt**
but **aber**
butcher shop **Metzgerei** (f.)
butter **Butter** (f.)
button **Knopf** (m.)
buy, to **kaufen**
by **bei, von**
by chance **Zufällig**

C

cabbage **Kohl** (m.)
cake **Kuchen** (m.)
calendar **Kalender** (m.)
call, to **rufen**
call, to (telephone) **anrufen**
call (telephone) **Anruf** (m.)
calm **ruhig**
camera **Kamera** (f.)
campingplace **Campingplatz** (m.)
cancer **Krebs** (m.)
canoe **Kanu** (n.)
cap **Mütze** (f.)
capable **fähig**
captain **Kapitän** (m.)
car **Wagen** (m.)
card **Karte** (f.)
careful **vorsichtig**
carrot **Mohrrübe** (f.)
carry, to **bringen, tragen**
cash, to **einlösen**
cashier **Kassierer** (m.)
Catholic **katholisch**
castle **Schloβ**, (n.), **Burg** (f.)
cat **Katze** (f.)
cathedral **Dom** (m.)
cause **Grund** (m.)
cave **Höhle** (f.)
ceiling **Decke** (f.)
celebrate, to **feiern**
cellar **Keller** (m.)
cemetery **Friedhof** (m.)
center (city) **Zentrum** (n.)
central **zentral**
century **Jahrhundert** (n.)
certain **sicher**
certainly **gewiβ**
chair **Stuhl** (m.)
champagne **Sekt** (m.)
change, to (money) **wechseln**
charming **charmant**
cheap **billig**
check, to **kontrollieren**
check **Scheck** (m.)
checkroom **Gepäckannahme,**
   Garderobe (f.)
cheerful **heiter**

GERMAN

GERMAN

cheese **Käse** (m.)
chest **Brust** (f.)
chicken **Hühnchen** (n.)
child **Kind** (n.)
childhood **Kindheit** (f.)
children **Kinder**
chocolate **Schokolade** (f.)
Christian **Christ**
Christmas **Weihnachten** (pl.)
Christmas tree **Weinachtsbaum** (m.)
church **Kirche** (f.)
club **Lokal** (n.)
cigar **Zigarre** (f.)
cigarette **Zigarette** (f.)
circus **Zirkus** (m.)
city **Stadt** (f.)
city hall **Rathaus** (n.)
civilization **Zivilisation** (f.)
class **Klasse** (f.)
clean **sauber** (f.)
clean, to **reinigen**
clear **klar**
clever **gescheit, klug**
cliff **Felsen** (m.), **Kliff** (n.)
climate **Klima** (n.)
climb **steigen**
climbing expedition **Bergtour** (f.)
clock **Uhr** (f.)
close **nahe**
close, to **schließen**
closed **geschlossen**
closet **Wandschrank** (m.)
cloth **Stoff** (m.)
clothes **Kleider** (f.)
cloud **Wolke** (f.)
cloudy **wolkig**
coal **Steinkohle** (f.)
coast **Küste** (f.)
coat **Mantel** (m.)
coffee **Kaffee** (m.)
cold (adj.) **kalt**
      (n.) **Erkältung**
collapse, to **einfallen**
collar **Kragen** (m.)
collection **Sammlung** (f.)
color **Farbe** (f.)
comb **Kamm** (m.)
come, to **kommen**
to come in **hereinkommen**
comfort **Bequemlichkeit** (f.)
comfortable **bequem, gemütlich**

commerce **Handel** (m.)
communism **Kommunismus** (m.)
company **Firma, Gesellschaft** (f.)
compartment **Abteil** (m.)
complain, to **sich beschweren**
completely **ganz**
computer **Computer** (m.)
concert **Konzert** (n.)
condition **Zustand** (m.)
conductor (streetcar, etc.) **Schaffner**
congratulate, to **gratulieren**
connection (train, etc.) **Anschluß**
consist of, to **bestehen aus**
contract **Vertrag** (m.)
contrary, on the **im Gegenteil**
conversation **Unterhaltung** (f.)
convince, to **überzeugen**
cook, to **kochen**
cook **Koch** (m.)
cooked **gekocht**
cool **kühl**
copy **Kopie** (f.)
corner **Ecke** (f.)
correct **richtig**
cost, to **kosten**
cotton **Baumwolle** (f.)
cough **Husten** (m.)
count **zählen**
country **Land** (n.)
couple **Paar** (n.)
courage **Mut** (m.)
course **Lauf, Weg, Kurs** (m.)
of course **gewiß**
courtesy **Höflichkeit** (f.)
cousin **Vetter** (m.) **Kusine** (f.)
cover, to **bedecken**
cow **Kuh** (f.)
crazy **verrückt**
cream **Rahm** (m.) **Sahne** (f.)
credit **Kredit** (m.)
criminal **Verbrecher**
crook **Schwindler**
cross, to **hinübergehen, überqueren**
crossroads **Kreuzung** (f.)
cruise **Kreutzfahrt** (f.)
cry, to **schreien**
cup **Tasse** (f.)
curtain **Vorhang** (m.)
custom **Gewohnheit** (f.)
customs **Zoll** (m.)
cut, to **schneiden**

D

daily **täglich**
damage, to **beschädigen**
damp **feucht**
dance, to **tanzen**
danger **Gefahr** (f.)
danger! **Achtung!**
dangerous **gefährlich**
dark **dunkel**
date (rendezvous) **Verabredung** (f.)
date (time) **Datum** (n.)
daughter **Tochter** (f.)
dawn **Sonnenaufgang** (m.)
day **Tag** (m.)
dead **gestorben, tot**
decide, to **entscheiden**
decision **Entscheidung** (f.)
deep **tief**
degree **Grad** (m.)
delay **Aufschub** (m.) **Verspätung** (f.)
delicious **köstlich**
delighted **sehr erfreut**
deliver, to **liefern**
dentist **Zahnarzt** (m.)
dentures **Gebiß** (n.)
depart, to **abfahren**
departure **Abfahrt** (f.)
deposit, to **deponieren**
deposit **Einlage** (f.)
describe, to **beschreiben**
description **Beschreibung** (f.)
desire, to **wollen, wünschen**
desk **Schreibtisch** (m.)
dessert **Nachtisch** (m.)
diamond **Diamant** (m.)
dictionary **Wörterbuch** (n.)
die, to **sterben**
difference **Unterschied** (m.)
different **verschieden**
difficult **schwer**
dine, to **speisen**
dining room **Eßzimmer** (n.)
dinner **Abendessen** (n.)
direction **Richtung** (f.)
directly **direkt**
dirty **schmutzig**
disappear, to **verschwinden**

disappointed **enttäuscht**
discount **Preisnachlass, Rabatt** (m.)
discover **entdecken**
disgusting **ekelhaft**
dish **Teller** (m.)
distance **Entfernung** (f.)
distant **entfernt**
disturb, to **stören**
divide, to **teilen**
diving (underwater sport) **Tauchen** (n.)
divorced **geschieden**
dizzy **schwindlig**
do, to **tun**
doctor **Arzt** (m.)
dog **Hund** (m.)
dollar **Dollar** (m.)
donkey **Esel** (m.)
door **Tür** (f.)
double **doppel**
doubt **Zweifel** (m.)
downstairs **unten**
draft (air) **Zugluft** (f.)
dream, to **träumen**
dream **Traum** (m.)
dress, to **sich anziehen**
dress **Kleid** (n.)
drink, to **trinken**
drive, to **fahren**
driver **Fahrer** (m.)
driver's license **Führerschein** (m.)
drown, to **ertrinken**
drunk **betrunken**
dry **trocken**
during **während**

E

each **jeder**
ear **Ohr** (n.)
early **früh**
earn, to **verdienen**
earth **Erde** (f.)
east **Osten** (m.)
Easter **Ostern** (n.)
East Germany **Deutsche Demokratische Republik (DDR)** (f.)
easy **leicht**
eat, to **essen**

GERMAN

editor **Redakteur**
egg **Ei** (n.)
either . . . or **entweder . . . oder**
electric **elektrisch**
electricity **Elektrizität** (f.)
elevator **Aufzug, Lift** (m.)
embark, to **sich einschiffen**
embassy **Botschaft** (f.)
embrace, to **sich umarmen**
embroidery **Stickerei** (f.)
emergency **Notfall** (m.)
employee **Angestellte**
employer **Arbeitgeber**
empty **leer**
end **Ende** (n.)
to end **enden**
Englishman **Engländer**
enough **genug**
enter **hineintreten**
enthusiastic **begeistert**
entire **ganz**
envelope **Umschlag** (m.)
equal **gleich, gleichmäßig**
error **Fehler** (m.)
escape, to **entkommen**
especially **besonders**
eternal **ewig**
even **eben, gleichmäßig**
evening **Abend** (m.)
event **Vorfall** (m.)
ever **immer, nie**
every **jeder**
everybody **jedermann**
everything **alles**
everywhere **überall**
exact **genau**
exaggerate, to **übertreiben**
examine, to **prüfen, untersuchen**
example **Beispiel** (n.)
excellent **ausgezeichnet**
except **ausser**
exchange, to **wechseln**
exchange **Geldwechsel** (m.)
excuse me **entschuldigen Sie**
exist, to **existieren**
exit **Ausgang** (m.)
expensive **teuer**
experience **Erfahrung** (f.)
explain, to **erklären**
explanation **Erklärung**
export, to **ausführen**

expression **Ausdruck** (m.)
extinguish **auslöschen**
extra **Extra . . .**
eye **Auge** (n.)
eye doctor **Augenarzt**

F

fabric **Stoff** (m.)
face **Gesicht** (n.)
factory **Fabrik** (f.)
faithful **treu**
fall (season) **Herbst** (m.)
fall, to **fallen**
family **Familie** (f.)
famous **berühmt**
far **entfernt; weit**
farm **Bauernhof** (m.), **Farm** (f.)
farmer **Bauer** (m.)
farther **weiter**
fashion **Mode** (f.)
fast **schnell**
fat **dick**
father **Vater**
favorable **günstig**
fear **Angst** (f.)
feel, to **fühlen**
fence **Zaun** (m.)
fever **Fieber** (f.)
few **wenig**
field **Feld** (n.)
fight, to **streiten**
fight **Kampf** (m.)
fill, to **füllen**
film **Film** (m.)
finally **endlich**
find, to **finden**
find out, to **entdecken**
fine (money) **Bußgeld** (n.)
finger **Finger** (m.)
fire **Feuer** (n.)
fire department **Feuerwehr** (f.)
first **erster**
fish, to **fischen**
fish **Fisch** (m.)
fishing tackle **Fischzeug** (n.)
flame **Flamme** (f.)
flight **Flug** (m.)
floor (ground) **Boden** (m.)
floor (of building) **Stock** (m.)

flower   **Blume** (f.)
fly, to   **fliegen**
fly (insect)   **Fliege** (f.)
fog   **Nebel** (m.)
follow, to   **folgen**
food   **Essen** (n.)
foot   **Fuss** (m.)
for   **für**
forbidden   **untersagt, verboten**
foreign   **fremd**
foreigner   **Ausländer**
forest   **Wald** (m.)
forget, to   **vergessen**
forgive, to   **vergeben**
fork   **Gabel** (f.)
forward   **vorwärts**
fountain   **Springbrunnen** (m.)
fox   **Fuchs** (m.)
France   **Frankreich** (n.)
free   **frei**
freedom   **Freiheit** (f.)
freeze, to   **frieren**
Frenchman   **Franzose**
frequently   **häufig, oft**
fresh   **frisch**
fried   **gebraten**
friend   **Freund**
friendship   **Freundschaft** (f.)
frightened, to be   **Angst haben**
from   **von**
front of, in   **vor**
frost   **Frost** (m.)
fruit   **Frucht** (f.)
fry   **braten**
frying pan   **Bratpfanne** (f.)
full   **voll**
funeral   **Beerdigung** (f.)
funny   **komisch**
furnish, to   **möbilieren**
furnished   **möbiliert**
furniture   **Möbel** (pl.)
future   **Zukunft** (f.)

G

gamble, to   **spielen**
game   **Spiel** (n.)
garage   **Garage** (f.)
garden   **Garten** (m.)
gasoline   **Benzin** (n.)

gas station   **Tankstelle** (f.)
gate   **Tor** (n.)
gather   **versammeln**
gentleman   **Herr** (m.)
genuine   **echt**
German   **deutsch**
Germany   **Deutschland** (n.)
get in, to (car, etc.)   **einsteigen**
get out, to   **aussteigen**
get up, to   **aufstehen**
girl   **Mädchen** (n.)
give, to   **geben**
glad   **froh**
glass   **Glas** (n.)
glasses   **Brille** (pl.)
glove   **Handschuh** (m.)
go   **gehen**
God   **Gott**
good   **gut**
goodbye   **Auf Wiedersehen**
good evening   **Guten Abend**
good morning   **Guten Morgen**
government   **Regierung** (f.)
granddaughter/son   **Enkelin/Enkel**
grandfather/mother   **Großvater/
   -mutter**
grapefruit   **Pampelmuse** (f.)
grapes   **Trauben, Weinbeeren**
grateful   **dankbar**
grave   **Grab** (n.)
gray   **grau**
Greece   **Griechenland**
green   **grün**
greeting   **Begrüßung** (f.) **Gruß** (m.)
group   **Gruppe** (f.)
grow, to   **wachsen**
guess, to   **raten**
guest   **Gast** (m.)
guide   **Führer** (m.)
guitar   **Gitarre** (f.)
gun   **Feuerwaffe** (f.)
gymnasium   **Turnhalle** (f.)
gynecologist   **Frauenarzt** (m.)

H

hair   **Haar** (n.)
half   **halb**
hallway   **Flur** (m.)
hand   **Hand** (f.)

GERMAN

handbag **Handtasche** (f.)
handkerchief **Taschentuch** (n.)
happiness **Glückseligkeit** (f.)
happy **glücklich**
hard **hart**
hat **Hut** (m.)
hate, to **hassen**
have, to **haben**
have to, to **müssen**
he **er**
head **Kopf** (m.)
health **Gesundheit** (f.)
healthfood store **Reformhaus** (n.)
health resort **Kurort** (m.)
hear, to **hören**
heart **Herz** (n.)
heat **Hitze** (f.)
heating **Heizung** (f.)
heatstroke **Hitzschlag** (m.)
heal **heilen**
heavy **schwer**
heel **Ferse** (f.)
Hello **Hallo, Guten Tag**
help, to **helfen**
help **Hilfe** (f.)
her, her **sie, ihr**
here **hier**
here is **hier ist**
high **hoch**
high school **Gymnasium** (n.)
highway **Autobahn** (f.)
hike **wandern**
hill **Hügel** (m.)
him, his **ihn, ihm; sein** (possessive)
history **Geschichte** (f.)
hitchhiker **Anhalter**
hold, to **(fest)halten**
hole **Loch** (n.)
holiday **Feiertag** (m.)
holy **heilig**
home, at the — of **bei . . .**
honest **ehrlich**
honey **Honig** (m.)
honeymoon **Flitterwochen** (pl.)
honor **Ehre** (f.)
hope, to **hoffen**
hope **Hoffnung** (f.)
horn (auto) **Hupe** (f.)
horse **Pferd** (n.)
hospital **Krankenhaus** (n.)
hospitality **Gastfreundschaft** (f.)

hot **heiß**
hotel **Hotel** (n.)
hour **Stunde** (f.)
house **Haus** (n.)
how **wie**
humidity **Feuchtigkeit** (f.)
hunger **Hunger** (m.)
hungry, to be **hungrig sein**
hurry, to be in a **Eile haben** (f.)
hunter **Jäger**
hunting **Jagd** (f.), **Jagen** (n.)
husband **Mann**
hut **Hütte** (f.)

I

I **ich**
ice cream **Eis** (n.)
ice skate **Schlittschuk laufen**
idea **Idee** (f.)
identification **Ausweiß** (m.)
idiot **Idiot** (m.)
if **wenn**
ignorant **unwissend**
ill **krank**
imagine, to **sich vorstellen**
immediately **sofort**
import, to **einführen**
important **wichtig**
impossible **unmöglich**
impression **Eindruck** (m.)
identification **Ausweis** (m.)
in **in**
including **einschließlich**
incorrect **falsch**
indeed **tatsächlich**
inexpensive **billig, preiswert**
inform, to **benachrichtigen**
information **Auskunft** (f.)
inhabitant **Bewohner**
inquiry **Erkundigung** (f.)
inside **innen**
instead **anstatt**
insurance **Versicherung** (f.)
interested **interessiert**
interesting **interessant**
interpreter **Dolmetscher** (m.)
interrupt, to **unterbrechen**
introduce (person) **vorstellen**
introduction **Einführung, Vorstellung**
   (f.)

invitation **Einladung** (f.)
invite, to **einladen**
island **Insel** (f.)
Italy **Italien** (n.)
itinerary **Reiseroute** (f.)

J

jacket **die Jacke**
jam **Marmelade** (f.)
jealous **eifersüchtig**
Jew **Juden**
jewelry **Schmuck** (m.)
Jewish **jüdisch**
job **Arbeit** (f.)
joke, to **scherzen**
joke **Witz** (m.)
joy **Freude** (f.)
judge **Richter** (m.)
jump, to **springen**
just (only) **nur**
    (now) **eben**

K

keep, to **behalten**
key **Schlüssel** (m.)
kind (adj.) **gütig, liebenswürdig**
kind (n.) **Art, Weise** (f.)
kindness **Freundlichkeit** (f.)
king **König**
kiss **Kuß** (m.)
kitchen **Küche** (f.)
knife **Messer** (n.)
knock, to **klopfen**
know, to **wissen**
know, to (to be acquainted
    with) **kennen**
knowledge **Kenntnis** (f.)

L

lady **Dame**
lake **See** (m.)
lamb **Lamm** (n.)
lamp **Lampe** (f.)

land, to (plane) **landen**
land **Land** (n.)
language **Sprache** (f.)
large **groß**
last, to **dauern**
last **letzt**
late **spät**
laugh, to **lachen**
laundry **Wäscherei** (f.)
law **Gesetz** (n.)
lawyer **Rechtsanwalt**
learn **lernen**
least **mindest-, wenigst-**
leather **Leder** (n.)
leave, to (go away) **abfahren**
    (abandon) **verlassen**
left **links**
leg **Bein** (n.)
legal **gesetzlich, legal**
lend, to **verleihen**
less **weniger**
lesson **Stunde** (f.)
let, to **lassen**
letter **Brief** (m.)
lettuce **Kopfsalat** (m.)
liberty **Freiheit** (f.)
library **Bibliothek** (f.)
license plate **Nummernschild** (n.)
lie, to **lügen**
lie **Lüge** (f.)
life **Leben** (n.)
lifeboat **Rettungsboot** (n.)
lifeguard **Bademeister**
lift, to **heben**
light, to **beleuchten**
light (color) **hell**
light (illumination) **Licht** (n.)
light (weight) **leicht**
light bulb **Birne** (f.)
lightning **Blitz** (m.)
like, to **gerne haben, mögen**
line **Linie** (f.)
linen **Leinen** (n.)
lion **Löwe** (m.)
lip **Lippe** (f.)
list **Liste** (f.)
listen, to **zuhören**
literature **Literatur** (f.)
little **klein**
live, to **leben, wohnen**
living room **Wohnzimmer** (n.)

GERMAN

load **Ladung** (f.)
lodging **Unterkunft** (f.)
logical **logisch**
long **lang**
look, to **schauen**
lose, to **verlieren**
lost **verloren**
loud **laut**
love, to **lieben**
lover **Liebhaber**
low **niedrig**
luck **Glück** (n.)
luggage **Gepäck** (n.)
lunch **Mittagessen** (n.)
luxury **Luxus** (m.)

M

machine **Maschine** (f.)
magazine **Zeitschrift** (f.)
magnificent **herrlich, prächtig**
maid **Dienstmädchen** (n.), **Putzfrau**
mail **Post** (f.)
mailbox **Briefkasten** (m.)
make, to **machen**
man **Mann**
management **Aufsicht, Direktion** (f.)
manager **Direktor**
manner **Art, Weise** (f.)
map **Karte** (f.)
marble **Marmor** (m.)
market **Markt** (m.)
married **verheiratet**
marry, to **sich verheiraten**
marvel **Wunder** (n.)
marvelous **wunderbar**
Mass **Messe** (f.)
material **Material** (n.) **Stoff** (m.)
mattress **Matratze** (f.)
maybe **vielleicht**
mayor **Bürgermeister** (m.)
me **mich, mir**
meal **Mahlzeit** (f.)
mean, to (word) **bedeuten**
meaning **Bedeutung** (f.)
meat **Fleisch** (n.)
medicine **Arznei, Medizin** (f.)
Mediterranean **Mittelmeer** (n.)
medieval **mittelalterlich**

meet, to **treffen**
meeting **Zusammentreffen** (n.)
member **Mitglied** (n.)
menu **Speisekarte** (f.)
merchandise **Waren** (pl.)
message **Nachricht** (f.)
middle **Mitte** (f.)
Middle Ages **Mittelalter** (n.)
midnight **Mitternacht** (f.)
mile **Meile** (f.)
milk **Milch** (f.)
million **Million** (f.)
mine **mein**
minister **Geistliche, Pfarrer** (m.)
minute **Minute** (f.)
mirror **Spiegel** (m.)
miss, to (a train, etc.) **verpassen**
Miss **Fräulein** (n.)
mistake **Fehler** (m.)
misunderstanding **Mißverständnis** (n.)
mix, to **vermischen**
model **Modell** (n.)
modern **modern**
modest **bescheiden**
moment **Augenblick** (m.)
monastery **Kloster** (n.)
money **Geld** (n.)
monkey **Affe** (m.)
month **Monat** (m.)
monthly **monatlich**
monument **Denkmal** (n.)
moon **Mond** (m.)
more **mehr**
morning **Morgen** (m.)
most **meist, die meisten**
mostly **meistens**
mother **Mutter** (f.)
mother-in-law **Schwiegermutter**
motor **Motor** (m.)
motorcycle **Motorrad** (n.)
mountain **Berg** (m.)
mountain climbing **Bergsteigen** (n.)
mouse **Maus** (f.)
mouth **Mund** (m.)
movement **Bewegung** (f.)
movies **Kino** (n.)
much **viel**
mud **Schlamm** (m.)
murder, to **umbringen**
music **Musik** (f.)

musician **Musiker**
must **müssen**
mustache **Schnurrbart** (m.)
mustard **Senf** (m.)
mutton **Hammelfleisch** (n.)
my **mein**
myself **mich**

N

name **Name** (m.)
napkin **Serviette** (f.)
narrow **eng**
nature **Natur** (f.)
navy **Marine** (f.)
near **nahe**
necessary **notwendig**
neck **Hals** (m.)
necktie **Krawatte** (f.)
need, to **brauchen**
needle **Nadel** (f.)
neighbor **Nachbar**
neighborhood **Nachbarschaft** (f.),
    Viertel (n.)
nephew **Neffe** (m.)
nervous **nervös**
never **nie, niemals**
new **neu**
news **Nachrichten** (f.)
newspaper **Zeitung** (f.)
New Year's Eve **Silvesterabend** (m.)
next **nächst**
nice **nett**
niece **Nichte**
night **Nacht** (f.)
nightclub **Nachtlokal** (n.)
nightgown **Nachthemd** (n.)
no **nein**
    (not a/any) **kein**
nobody **niemand**
noise **Lärm** (m.)
noon **Mittag** (m.)
north **Norden** (m.)
nose **Nase** (f.)
not **nicht**
notebook **Heft** (n.)
nothing **nichts**
notice, to **bemerken**
nowhere **nirgends**

number **Nummer** (f.)
nurse **Krankenschwester**
nut **Nuß** (f.)

O

oar **Ruder** (n.)
object **Gegenstand** (m.)
occasion **Gelegenheit** (f.)
occasionally **dann und wann**
occupied **besetzt**
occur, to **passieren**
ocean **Meer** (n.), **Ozean** (m.)
of **von**
offer **anbieten**
office **Büro** (n.)
often **oft**
oil **Öl** (n.)
OK **in Ordnung**
old **alt**
on **auf, an**
once **einmal**
one **ein**
one way (ticket) **einfach**
one-way street **Einbahnstraße** (f.)
only **nur**
open, to **öffnen**
open **offen, geöffnet**
opera **Oper** (f.)
opinion **Meinung** (f.)
opportunity **Gelegenheit** (f.)
opposite **gegenüber liegend**
or **oder**
orange **Apfelsine** (f.)
order, to **bestellen**
in order to **um . . . zu**
original **ursprünglich**
other **anderer**
otherwise **sonst**
our **unser**
ourselves **uns**
out of order **außer Betrieb, kaputt**
outside **draußen**
over **über**
owe, to **schulden**
own **eigen**
owner **Eigentümer**

GERMAN

GERMAN

P

package **Paket** (n.)
paid **bezahlt**
pain **Schmerz** (m.)
painter **Maler**
painting **Gemälde** (n.)
pair **Paar** (n.)
palace **Palast** (m.)
pants **Hose** (f.)
paper **Papier** (n.)
parents **Eltern**
park **Park** (m.)
park, to **parken**
parking lot **Parkplatz** (m.)
part **Teil** (m.)
party **Gesellschaft, Party** (f.)
passenger **Fahrgast, Fluggast**
  (plane), **Passagier** (plane, ship)
passport **Pass** (m.)
past **Vergangenheit** (f.)
path **Pfad** (m.)
pay, to **bezahlen**
payment **Bezahlung** (f.)
peace **Friede** (m.)
pen **Kugelschreiber** (m.)
pencil **Bleistift** (m.)
people **Leute** (pl.)
perfect **tadellos**
perfume **Parfüm** (n.)
perhaps **vielleicht**
period **Periode** (f.)
permit, to **erlauben**
person **Person** (f.)
photograph, to **photographieren**
photograph **Aufnahme** (f.)
photography **Photographie** (f.)
piano **Klavier** (n.)
pickpocket **Taschendieb** (m.)
picture **Bild** (n.)
piece **Stück** (n.)
pig **Schwein** (n.)
pigeon **Taube** (f.)
pill **Pille** (f.)
pillow **Kissen** (n.)
pin **Stecknadel** (f.)
pink **rosa**
pitcher **Krug** (m.)

place **Ort** (m.)
plan **Plan** (m.)
plant **Pflanze** (f.)
plate **Teller** (m.)
platform (train) **Bahnsteig** (m.)
play, to **spielen**
play **Schauspiel** (n.)
pleasant **angenehm**
please **bitte**
pleasure **Vergnügen** (n.)
pocket **Tasche** (f.)
poem **Gedicht** (n.)
point, to **zeigen**
point **Punkt** (m.)
police **Polizei** (f.)
policeman **Polizist** (m.)
police station **Polizeirevier** (n.)
polite **höflich**
pond **Teich** (m.)
poor **arm**
pope **Papst**
popular **beliebt**
pork **Schweinefleisch** (n.)
port **Hafen** (m.)
possible **möglich**
postcard **Ansichtskarte, Postkarte**
  (f.)
post office **Post** (f.)
pot (cooking) **Topf** (m.)
potato **Kartoffel** (f.)
pound **Pfund** (n.)
powerful **mächtig, stark**
practice, to **üben**
pray, to **beten**
precise **genau**
pregnant **schwanger**
prepare, to **vorbereiten**
prescription **Rezept** (n.)
present **Geschenk** (n.)
press, to **drücken**
pretty (adj.) **hübsch**
price **Preis** (m.)
priest **Priester** (m.)
prison **Gefängnis** (n.)
probable **wahrscheinlich**
problem **Problem** (n.)
profession **Beruf** (m.)
profit **Gewinn, Profit** (m.)
program **Programm** (n.)
promise, to **versprechen**
pronounce, to **aussprechen**

property **Eigentum** (n.)
Protestant **evangelisch**
public **öffentlich; staatlich**
publisher **Herausgeber, Verlag** (m.)
pull, to **ziehen**
purchase, to **kaufen**
push, to **schieben**
put, to **tun**
put on, to **anziehen**

Q

quality **Qualität** (f.)
quarter **Viertel** (n.)
queen **Königin**
question **Frage** (f.)
quickly **schnell**
quiet **ruhig, still**
quite **ganz**

R

rabbi **Rabbiner** (m.)
rabbit **Kaninchen** (n.)
race (contest) **Wettrennen** (n.)
radiator (car) **Kühler** (m.)
radiator (room) **Heizung** (f.)
radio **Radio** (n.)
railroad **Eisenbahn** (f.)
railway station **Bahnhof** (m.)
rain **Regen** (m.)
raincoat **Regenmantel** (m.)
raise, to **heben**
rape **Vergewaltigung** (f.)
rapid **schnell**
rare **selten**
rare (meat) **blutig**
rarely **selten**
rather **ziemlich**
raw **roh**
razor **Rasierapparat** (m.)
razor blades **Rasierklingen** (pl.)
reach **erreichen**
read, to **lesen**
ready **bereit, fertig**
real **wahr**
really **wirklich**
reason **Grund** (m.)

reasonable **vernünftig**
receipt **Quittung** (f.)
receive, to **bekommen**
recently **neulich, vor kurzem**
recognize **erkennen**
recommend, to **empfehlen**
record (phonograph) **Schallplatte** (f.)
red **rot**
refrigerator **Kühlschrank** (m.)
refuse, to **verweigern, abschlagen**
regards **Grüße** (pl.)
region **Gegend** (f.)
regret, to **bedauern**
regular **regelrecht**
religion **Religion** (f.)
religious **religiös**
remain, to **bleiben**
remainder **Rest** (m.)
remember, to **sich erinnern**
remind, to **erinnern**
rent, to **mieten**
repair, to **reparieren**
repeat, to **wiederholen**
replace, to **ersetzen**
report **Bericht** (m.)
represent, to **repräsentieren**
republic **Republik** (f.)
reserve, to **reservieren**
reservation **Reservierung** (f.)
responsible **verantwortlich**
rest, to **sich ausruhen**
restaurant **Restaurant** (n.)
retail **Einzelhandel** (m.)
return, to **zurückgeben, zurückkehren**
return trip **hin und zurück**
ribbon **Band** (n.)
rice **Reis** (m.)
rich **reich**
ride, to (horseback) **reiten**
ride, to (travel) **fahren**
right (correct) **richtig**
right (direction) **rechts**
right **Recht** (n.)
rise, to **sich erheben**
river **Fluss** (m.)
road **Strasse** (f.)
roast **Braten** (m.)
rob **rauben**
robbery **Überfall** (m.)
roll **Brötchen** (n.)

GERMAN

rock **Stein** (m.)
roof **Dach** (n.)
room **Zimmer** (n.)
round **rund**
round trip **Rundfahrt** (f.)
route **Weg** (m.)
row, to **rudern**
row (theater) **Reihe** (f.)
rowboat **Ruderboot** (n.)
rug **Teppich** (m.)
ruins **Ruinen** (f.)
run, to **laufen**
Russia **Rußland** (n.)
Russian **Russe**

S

sacrifice **Opfer** (n.)
sad **traurig**
safe **sicher**
safe (strongbox) **Tresor,
  Geldschrank** (m.)
sail, to **segeln**
sailboat **Segelboot** (n.)
sailor **Matrose, Seemann**
saint **Heilige, sankt**
salad **Salat** (m.)
salary **Gehalt** (n.)
sale **Verkauf** (m.)
salesman **Kaufmann, Vertreter**
salt **Salz** (n.)
salty **salzig**
same **der-, die- dasselbe**
satisfied **zufrieden**
satisfy **befriedigen**
sauce **Soße** (f.)
saucer **Untertasse** (f.)
save, to (rescue) **retten**
savings bank **Sparkasse** (f.)
say, to **sagen**
school **Schule** (f.)
science **Wissenschaft** (f.)
scissors **Schere** (f.)
scream **schreien**
sculptor **Bildhauer**
sea **Meer** (n.), **See** (f.)
seashore **Seeküste** (f.)
seasick **seekrank**
season **Jahreszeit** (f.)

seasoning **Würze** (f.)
seat **Platz** (m.)
second **zweite**
secretary **Sekretär**
see, to **sehen**
seek, to **suchen**
seldom **selten**
sell, to **verkaufen**
send, to **schicken**
separate **getrennt**
serious **ernst**
serve **bedienen**
service **Bedienung** (f.)
set, to **setzen**
several **mehrere**
sew, to **nähen**
shade **Schatten** (m.)
shadow **Schatten** (m.)
shallow **nicht tief**
share, to **teilen**
sharp **scharf**
shave, to **rasieren**
she **sie**
sheet (bed) **Laken** (m.)
ship **Boot, Schiff** (n.)
shirt **Hemd** (n.)
shoe **Schuh** (m.)
shoelaces **Schnürsenkel**
shop **Laden** (m.)
short **kurz**
shorts **Shorts** (pl.)
shoulder **Schulter** (f.)
show, to **zeigen**
show **Schau** (m.)
shower **Dusche** (f.)
shut, to **schliessen**
sick **krank**
side **Seite** (f.)
sidewalk **Bürgersteig** (m.)
sights **Sehenswürdigkeiten** (pl.)
silence **Schweigen** (n.)
silk **Seide** (f.)
silver **Silber** (n.)
similar **ähnlich, gleich**
simple **einfach**
since **seit; da**
sing, to **singen**
singer **Sänger**
single (unmarried) **unverheiratet,
  ledig**
sir **mein Herr**

sister **Schwester**
sister-in-law **Schwägerin**
sit, to **sitzen**
size **Größe** (f.)
ski **Ski** (m.)
skiing **Skilaufen** (n.)
skin **Haut** (f.)
skirt **Rock** (m.)
sky **Himmel** (m.)
skyscraper **Wolkenkratzer** (m.)
sleep, to **schlafen**
to go to sleep **einschlafen**
sleeping bag **Schlafsack** (m.)
sleeve **Ärmel** (m.)
slip, to **schlüpfen**
slow **langsam**
small **klein**
smell, to **riechen**
smile, to **lächeln**
smoke, to **rauchen**
smooth **glatt**
snake **Schlange** (f.)
sneeze, to **niesen**
snow **Schnee** (m.)
so **so**
soap **Seife** (f.)
sock **Socke** (f.)
sofa **Sofa** (n.)
soft **weich**
soldier **Soldat** (m.)
some **einige, etwas**
somebody **jemand**
something **etwas**
sometimes **manchmal**
somewhat **etwas, ziemlich**
somewhere **irgendwo**
son **Sohn**
song **Lied** (n.)
soon **bald**
soup **Suppe** (f.)
sour **sauer**
south **Süden** (m.)
South America **Südamerika**
souvenir **Andenken** (n.)
Spain **Spanien** (n.)
speak, to **sprechen**
special **besonder-**
speed limit
   Geschwindigkeitsbegrenzung (f.)
spend **ausgeben**
sponge **Schwamm** (m.)

spoon **Löffel** (m.)
sport **Sport** (m.)
sporting goods **Sportausrüstung**
spring **Frühling** (m.)
stairs **Treppen** (pl.)
stamp **Briefmarke** (f.)
standing **stehend**
star **Stern** (m.)
start, to **anfangen**
station **Bahnhof** (m.)
statue **Statue** (f.)
stay, to **bleiben**
stay **Aufenthalt** (m.)
steak **Beefsteak** (n.)
steal, to **stehlen**
steamer (boat) **Dampfer** (m.)
stick **Stock** (m.)
still (adj) **still**
   (yet) **noch**
stockings **Strümpfe** (m. pl.)
stomach **Magen** (m.)
stone **Stein** (m.)
stop, to **anhalten**
stop (bus, etc.) **Haltestelle** (f.)
storm **Sturm** (m.)
story **Geschichte** (f.)
stove **Ofen** (m.)
straight **gerade**
strange **fremd, sonderbar**
street **Straße** (f.)
streetcar **Straßenbahn** (f.)
strike, to **schlagen**
string **Strang** (m.)
strong **stark**
student **Student**
study, to **studieren**
stupid **dumm**
style **Stil** (m.)
subway **Untergrund** (m.), **U-Bahn** (f.)
sudden **plötzlich**
sugar **Zucker** (m.)
suit **Anzug** (m.)
suitcase **Koffer** (m.)
summer **Sommer** (m.)
summit **Gipfel** (m.)
sun **Sonne** (f.)
sunburn **Sonnenbrand** (m.)
sunglasses **Sonnenbrille** (f.)
sunset **Sonnenuntergang** (m.)
supper **Abendessen** (n.)
supplement **Zuschlag** (m.)

GERMAN

GERMAN

sure **sicher**
surf **Brandung** (f.)
surprise **Überraschung** (f.)
sweat **schwitzen**
sweater **Pulli** (m.)
sweet **süß**
swim, to **schwimmen**
swimming pool **Badeanstalt** (f.)
Switzerland **Schweiz** (f.)
synagogue **Synagoge** (f.)

T

table **Tisch** (m.)
tablecloth **Tischtuch** (n.)
tailor **Schneider** (m.)
take, to **nehmen**
take off, to (clothing) **ausziehen**
take off, to (plane) **abfliegen**
talk, to **sprechen**
tall **groß**
tape **Band** (n.)
tape recorder **Tonbandgerät** (n.)
taste, to **schmecken**
taste **Geschmack** (m.)
tax **Steuer** (f.)
taxi **Taxi** (n.)
tea **Tee** (m.)
teach, to **lehren**
teacher **Lehrer**
team **Mannschaft** (f.)
tear, to **reißen**
tear (from crying) **Träne** (f.)
telegram **Telegramm** (n.)
telephone **Telephon** (n.)
television **Fernsehen** (n.)
tell, to **erzählen**
temperature **Temperatur** (f.)
temporarily **vorübergehend**
tent **Zelt** (n.)
terrible **furchtbar**
than **als**
thank, to **danken**
thank you **danke schön**
the **der, die, das**
theater **Theater** (n.)
them **sie**
then **dann**
there **dort, da**

there is/are **es gibt**
thermometer **Thermometer** (n.)
they **sie**
thief **Dieb**
thin **dünn**
thing **Ding** (n.), **Sache** (f.)
think, to **denken**
third **dritte**
thirst **Durst** (m.)
thirsty, to be **durstig sein**
this **dieser**
those **diese**
thousand **tausend**
thread **Faden** (m.)
throat **Gurgel** (f.)
through **durch**
throw **werfen**
thunder **Donner** (m.)
ticket (for speeding) **Strafmandat** (m.)
ticket (theater, etc.) **Karte** (f.)
tide **Flut** (f.)
tie **Krawatte** (f.)
tight **eng**
time **Zeit** (f.)
timetable **Fahrplan** (m.)
tip (money) **Trinkgeld** (n.)
tire **Reifen** (m.)
tired **müde**
to **nach, zu**
tobacco **Tabak** (m.)
today **heute**
together **zusammen**
toilet **Toilette** (f.)
tomato **Tomate** (f.)
tomorrow **morgen**
tongue **Zunge** (f.)
tonight **heute abend**
too (also) **auch**
tooth **Zahn** (m.)
toothbrush **Zahnbürste** (f.)
toothpaste **Zahnpaste** (f.)
top, on **oben, auf**
touch, to **rühren**
tough **zäh**
tour **Rundreise** (f.)
towel **Handtuch** (n.)
tower **Turm** (m.)
town **Dorf** (n.)
tow truck **Abschleppwagen** (m.)
toy **Spielzeug** (n.)

trade **Handel** (m.)
trade fair **Handelsmesse** (f.)
traffic **Verkehr** (m.)
traffic jam **Stau** (m.),
  Verkehrstöpfung (f.)
traffic light **Verkehrsampel** (f.)
train **Zug** (m.)
translate, to **übersetzen**
translation **Übersetzung**
travel, to **reisen**
travel agency **Reisebüro**
traveler **Reisende**
tree **Baum** (m.)
trip **Ausflug** (m.), **Fahrt** (f.), **Reise** (f.)
troubles **Sorgen** (pl.)
truck **Lastwagen** (m.)
true **wahr**
trunk **Koffer** (m.)
truth **Wahrheit** (f.)
try, to **versuchen**
try on, to **probieren**
Turkey **Türkei** (f.)
turn off, to **abstellen, ausmachen**
turn on, to **anstellen**
typewriter **Schreibmaschine** (f.)

U

ugly **hässlich**
umbrella **Regenschirm** (m.)
uncle **Onkel** (m.)
unconscious **ohnmächtig**
under **unter**
understand **verstehen**
underwear **Unterkleider, Wäsche**
  (pl.)
undress, to **sich ausziehen**
unfortunately **leider**
United States **Vereinigten Staaten**
  (pl.)
university **Universität** (f.)
unless **wenn nicht, außer wenn**
until **bis**
up **auf**
upstairs **oben**
urgent **dringend**
us **uns**
use, to **gebrauchen**

use **Gebrauch** (m.)
useful **nützlich**
usual **gewöhnlich**

V

vacant **frei**
vacation **Ferien** (pl.), **Urlaub** (m.)
valid **gültig**
valuables **Wertsachen** (pl.)
value **Wert** (m.)
various **verschiedene**
vegetable **Gemüse** (n.)
vehicle **Fahrzeug** (n.)
very **sehr**
victory **Sieg** (m.)
Vienna **Wien**
view **Blick** (m.)
village **Dorf** (n.)
vineyard **Weinberg** (m.)
violin **Geige** (f.)
visit, to **besuchen**
voice **Stimme** (f.)
voltage **Spannung** (f.)
voyage **Reise** (f.)

W

waist **Taille** (f.)
wait, to **warten**
waiter **Ober**
waiting room **Warteraum** (m.)
waitress **Fräulein** (n.)
wake up, to **aufwachen**
walk, to **spazierengehen**
walk **Spaziergang** (m.)
wall (as in Berlin) **Mauer** (f.)
wall (room) **Wand** (f.)
wallet **Geldbeutel** (m.)
want, to **wollen**
war **Krieg** (m.)
warm **warm**
warn, to **warnen**
wash, to **waschen**
wash oneself, to **sich waschen**
washbasin **Waschbecken** (n.)
waste, to **verschwenden**
watch, to **anschauen**

GERMAN

GERMAN

watch **Uhr** (f.)
water **Wasser** (n.)
waterfront **Hafenviertel** (n.)
watersports **Waßersport** (m.)
waves **Wellen** (pl.)
way **Weg** (m.)
we **wir**
weak **schwach**
wear, to **tragen**
weather **Wetter** (n.)
wedding **Hochzeit** (f.)
week **Woche** (f.)
weekend **Wochenende** (n.)
weigh, to **wiegen**
weight **Gewicht** (n.)
welcome **wilkommen**
west **Westen** (m.)
West Germany **Bundesrepublik** (f.)
well **gut**
what **was**
wheat **Weizen** (m.)
wheel **Rad** (n.)
when **wann, wenn**
where **wo**
whether **ob**
which **welcher**
while **während**
white **weiß**
who **wer**
whole **ganz**
whose **wessen**
why (question) **warum**
wide **breit**
widow **Witwe**
widower **Witwer**
wife **Frau**
wilderness **Wildnis** (f.)
win, to **gewinnen**
wind **Wind** (m.)
windy **windig**
window (house) **Fenster** (n.)
window (railway station,
  etc.) **Schalter** (m.)
wine **Wein** (m.)
wine list **Weinkarte** (f.)
wing **Flügel** (m.)

winter **Winter** (m.)
wish, to **wünschen**
wish **Wunsch** (m.)
with **mit**
without **ohne**
woman **Frau**
wonder **Wunder** (n.)
wonderful **wunderbar**
wood **Holz** (n.)
wool **Wolle** (f.)
word **Wort** (n.)
work **Arbeit** (f.)
world **Welt** (f.)
worries **Sorgen** (pl.)
worse **schlechter**
wrap, to **wickeln**
wrist **Handgelenk** (n.)
write, to **schreiben**
writer **Schriftsteller**
wrong **falsch**

Y

yacht **Jacht** (f.)
year **Jahr** (n.)
yellow **gelb**
yes **ja**
yesterday **gestern**
yet **noch**
you **Sie, du**
young **jung**
your **Ihr, dein**
you're welcome **bitte sehr**

Z

zero **null**
zipper **Reissverschluss** (m.)
zone **Zone** (f.)
zoo **Tiergarten, Zoo** (m.)

ITALIAN

ITALIAN

PRONUNCIATION GUIDE

Vowels

	Phonetic Symbol	Approximate Pronunciation	Italian Example	Phonetic Transcription	Meaning
a	ah	like a in father	palazzo	pah*lah*tso	palace
e	ay	like ay in pay	cena	*chay*na	dinner
or	e	like e in fell	bello	*bel*lo	beautiful
			c'è	che	there is
i	ee	like i in Pauline	viso	*vee*zo	face
o	aw	as in law or cost	costo	*caw*sto	cost
or	o	as in vote	volo	*vo*lo	flight
u	oo	as in food	luna	*loo*nah	moon

Diphthongs

	Phonetic Symbol	Approximate Pronunciation	Italian Example	Phonetic Transcription	Meaning
au	ow	as in now	autobus	*ow*toboos	bus
ia	eeah	as in Maria	lavanderia	lahvandereeah	laundry
or	ya	as in Sonia	chiave	*kyah*vay	key
ie	ye	as in yes	fieno	*fye*no	straw
io	eeo	as in Rio	mio	*mee*o	my
or	yo	as in yoke	stazione	stahts*yo*nay	station
iu	yoo	as in Yule	più	pyoo	more
ai	ah-ee	like y in why	mai	*mah*-ee	never
ei	e-ee	like ey in they	vorrei	vorre-ee	I'd like

Consonants

b, d, f, k, l, m, n, p, q, t, v   are pronounced as in English

c	ch	like ch in cheese before e and i	cena	**chay**nah	dinner
	or k	like k in kiss or c in class before all consonants and a, o, and u	cibo	**chee**bo	food
			camicia	kah**mee**chah	shirt
ch	k	like ch in chemical	caro	**kah**ro	dear
			che	kay	what
			chiamare	kyah**mah**ray	to call
g	j	like g in gem before e and i	giallo	**jah**llo	yellow
g	g	like g in game before all consonants and a, o, and u	gente	**jen**tay	people
gh	g	like g in ghetto	gallo	**gah**llo	rooster
gl	ly	like lli in million	ghiaccio	**gyah**tcho	ice
gn	ny	like ny in canyon	moglie	**mol**yay	wife
h	_	always silent	bagno	**bah**nyo	bath
			ho	aw	I have
			ha	ah	he/she has
qu	kw	as in quick	quanto	**kwahn**to	how much
r	r	trilled	rosso	**ros**so	red
s	s	like s in see	sera	**say**rah	evening
	or z	like z in zoo	rosa	**raw**zah	rose
sc	sh	like sh before e and i	scimmia	**sheem**myah	monkey
	or sk	like sk before all consonants and a, o, and u	scala	**skah**lah	stairs
			scritto	**skreet**to	written
z	ts	like ts in kits	pezzo	**pet**so	piece
	or dz	like ds in roads	benzina	bend**zee**nah	gasoline

Note: wherever there is a double consonant, give it particular emphasis; otherwise, in certain cases, the entire meaning of the word may change!

ITALIAN

ITALIAN GRAMMAR

Nouns and Articles

There are two genders in Italian, masculine and feminine.

Masculine nouns usually end in *o* and their plural is formed by changing the *o* to *i*. Note that there are five forms of the masculine definite article, three for the singular and two for the plural:

The Definite Article (the) *with the Masculine Noun*

singular				plural
il		il ragazzo	the boy	i ragazzi
lo	(before nouns beginning with s + consonant or z)	lo spillo	the pin	gli spilli
		lo zio	the uncle	gli zii
l'	(before nouns beginning with a vowel)	l'amico	the friend	gli amici
		l'uomo	the man	gli uomini

Feminine nouns usually end in *a* and their plural is formed by changing the *a* to *e*. Note the three forms of the feminine definite article:

The Definite Article (the) *with the Feminine Noun*

la	(before a consonant)	la donna	the woman	le donne
l'	(before a vowel)	l'alba	the dawn	le albe

Some nouns that end in *e* are masculine, while others are feminine. All these nouns form their plural by changing the *e* to *i*:

il bicchiere	the glass	i bicchieri
la luce	the light	le luci

The Indefinite Article (a, an) *with the Masculine Noun*

un		un albero	a tree
uno	(before s + consonant or z)	uno studente	a student

The Indefinite Article (a, an) *with the Feminine Noun*

una		una porta	a door
un'	(before a vowel)	un'idea	an idea

The Partitive (some, any)

Note that *di* + definite article not only means *some* or *any*, but can also mean *of the*.

-with masculine nouns

	singular			**plural**
dell'	before a vowel	dell'antipasto	some antipasto	degli antipasti
dello	before s + consonant or z	dello zucchero	some sugar	degli zuccheri
del	before other consonants	del vino	some wine	dei vini

-with feminine nouns

	singular			**plural**
dell'	before a vowel	dell'acqua	some water	delle acque
della	before a consonant	della birra	some beer	delle birre

Adjectives

The adjective agrees in gender and number with the noun it modifies. In the singular, it ends in *o*, *a*, or *e*, and usually follows the noun. To form the plural, the final *o* or *e* changes to *i*, and the final *a* changes to *e*.

il cane nero	the black dog	i cani neri
il vestito verde	the green dress	i vestiti verdi
la borsa rossa	the red bag	le borse rosse
la valigia pesante	the heavy suitcase	le valige pesanti

Demonstrative Adjectives (this, that, these, those)

this	questo/questa	(*quest'* before a vowel)
	questo quadro	this painting
	questa mela	this apple
	quest'albero	this tree
these	questi/queste	
	questi quadri	these paintings
	queste mele	these apples
	questi alberi	these trees
that	quel, quello, quella	note that the forms of *quel* follow the same pattern as *del, dello, della*, etc.

ITALIAN

those	quei, quegli, quelle	
	quello sbaglio	that mistake
	quella signora	that lady
	quegli scrittori	those writers
	quelle persone	those persons

Personal Pronouns

	Subject	Indirect object	Direct object	Disjunctive (used after a preposition)
I, me	io	mi	mi	me
you (familiar)	tu	ti	ti	te
she; her/it	lei/essa	le	la	lei, essa
you (formal)	Lei	Le	La	Lei
he; him/it	lui/egli	gli	lo	lui
we/us	noi	ci	ci	noi
you (plural)	voi	vi	vi	voi
they (masc.)/ them	loro, essi	loro	li	loro
they (fem.)/ them	loro, esse	loro	le	loro

Note that the *tu* (familiar) form is used with children, relatives, young people and good friends. The *Lei* form is used with people you don't know very well or wish to remain on rather formal terms with.

The subject pronouns are often omitted. When they are used, it is where there is a need for emphasis. For example, it is more common to say: *vado a scuola* (I go to school) than to say *io vado a scuola*. The latter places the emphasis on the subject rather than the action.

Possessive Adjectives and Pronouns

	singular		plural	
	masculine	feminine	masculine	feminine
my	il mio	la mia	i miei	le mie
your	il tuo	la tua	i tuoi	le tue
his, her, its	il suo	la sua	i suoi	le sue
our	il nostro	la nostra	i nostri	le nostre
your	il vostro	la vostra	i vostri	le vostre
their	il loro	la loro	i loro	le loro

Possessive adjectives and pronouns agree with their corresponding nouns. The definite article is always used except in the case of reference to close relatives (hence, *la mia macchina*—my car— but *mia sorella*—my sister). Note also that *il suo, i suoi,* etc. can mean his, her, or your (formal).

ITALIAN

Interrogative Pronouns

che, che cosa, cosa	what
chi	who, whom
quale	which

Interrogative Adjectives

che	what
quale	which
quanto	how much/many

Relative Pronouns

quel che	that which
quello che	that which
ciò che	that which
che	that, who

The comparative is formed by placing the word *più* (more) in front of the adjective: *più importante* (more important). The superlative is formed by placing the article before the adjective: il *più* importante (the most important). As in English, the adjectives *buono* and *cattivo* (good and bad) have special forms to denote better-best and worse-worst: *buono: migliore-il migliore; cattivo: peggiore-il peggiore.*

Verbs

The two most important auxiliary verbs are *essere* (to be) and *avere* (to have).

essere (to be)		avere (to have)	
io sono	I am	io ho	I have
tu sei	you are	tu hai	you have
lui, lei è	he, she is	lui, lei ha	he, she has
Lei è	you are	Lei ha	you have
noi siamo	we are	noi abbiamo	we have
voi siete	you are	voi avete	you have
loro sono	they are	loro hanno	they have

ITALIAN

Regular verbs are formed in one of three ways, according to their endings:

Present Indicative

infinitive ending in	-are parlare to speak	-ere vendere to sell	-ire partire to leave
io	parlo	vendo	parto
tu	parli	vendi	parti
lui, lei	parla	vende	parte
noi	parliamo	vendiamo	partiamo
voi	parlate	vendete	partite
loro	parlano	vendono	partono

Some of the most common verbs do not follow the above pattern:

	to go andare	to do fare	to understand capire	to see vedere	to be able potere	to know sapere
io	vado	faccio	capisco		posso	so
tu	vai	fai	capisci		puoi	sai
lui, lei	va	fa	capisce		può	sa
noi	andiamo	facciamo	capiamo		possiamo	sappiamo
voi	andate	fate	capite		potete	sapete
loro	vanno	fanno	capiscono		possono	sanno

Past Tense

One form of the past tense combines the proper form of the auxiliary verb *essere* or *avere* (*essere* being used with verbs of motion, state of being, and reflexive verbs) with the past participle. The past participle is formed by adding one of three endings to the stem of the verb: *-ato* for *-are* verbs; *-ito* for *-ire* verbs; and *-uto* for *-ere* verbs. Like the adjective, the past participle agrees in number and gender with the noun modified.

parlare:	ho parlato	I spoke, I have spoken
finire:	ho finito	I finished, I have finished
vendere	ho venduto	I sold, I have sold
stare:	sono stato/stata	I was, I have been
partire:	sono partito/partita	I left, I have left
crescere:	sono cresciuto/cresciuta	I grew, I have grown

Negatives

Negatives are formed by placing *non* in front of the verb:

Ho fame.   I'm hungry.   Non ho fame.   I'm not hungry.

ITALIAN

Questions

Questions are formed generally by using the affirmative word order and merely inflecting the voice at the end. For example:

Dobbiamo andare a Roma.   We have to go to Rome.
Dobbiamo andare a Roma?   Do we have to go to Rome?

Questions can also be formed by placing the subject at the end of the sentence:

Roberto va al cinema stasera.   Roberto is going to the cinema tonight.
Va al cinema stasera Roberto?   Is Roberto going to the cinema tonight?

Prepositions

A number of prepositions contract with the definite article, like the partitive *di* (some/any, or of the). Here are some common prepositions and their contractions:

article:	il	lo	la	l'	i	gli	le
a (to, at)	al	allo	alla	all'	ai	agli	alle
da (from)	dal	dallo	dalla	dall'	dai	dagli	dalle
di (of)	del	dello	della	dell'	dei	degli	delle
in (in)	nel	nello	nella	nell'	nei	negli	nelle
su (on)	sul	sullo	sulla	sull'	sui	sugli	sulle

Here are some other useful prepositions:

for	per
after	dopo
before	prima (di)
in front of	davanti (a)
with	con
without	senza
towards	verso
through	attraverso
during	durante
until	fino a
inside	dentro
outside	fuori
up/upstairs	su, in alto
down/downstairs	giù, in basso
against	contro

ITALIAN

EXPRESSIONS FOR EVERYDAY USE

Basic

Yes.
Sì.
see

No.
No.
naw

Please.
Per piacere.
Per favore.
per pyahchayray
per favoray

Thank you.
Grazie.
grahtsyay

Yes, thank you.
Sì, grazie.
see, grahtsyay

No, thank you.
No, grazie.
naw, grahtsyay

Thank you very much.
Tante grazie.
tahntay grahtsyay

You're welcome.
Prego.
praygo

Excuse me.
Mi scusi.
mee skoozee

Just a moment.
Un momento.
oon momaynto

Of course.
Certamente.
chertahmayntay

How much?
Quanto?
kwahnto?

Where is the restroom?
Dov'è il gabinetto?
dove eel gahbeenetto?

I don't understand.
Non capisco.
non kapeesko

What did you say?
Prego?
praygo?

I beg your pardon.
La prego di scusarmi.
la praygo dee skoozahrmee

That's quite all right.
Non si preoccupi.
non see prayawkoopee

Greetings

Good morning.
Buon giorno.
bwawn jorno

Good afternoon.
Buona sera.
bwawnah sayrah

Good evening.
Buona sera.
bwawnah sayrah

Good night.
Buona notte.
bwawnah nawtay

ITALIAN

Goodbye.
Arrivederci.
Ciao. (informal)
ahreevayderchee
chow

See you later.
A più tardi.
ah pyoo tahrdee

See you this evening.
A stasera.
ah stahsayrah

See you tomorrow.
A domani.
ah domahnee

How are you?
Come sta?
Come stai? (informal)
komay stah?
komay stahee?

How are things?
Come va?
komay vah

Everything's fine.
Tutto va bene.
tootto vah benay

That's fine.
Va bene.
vah benay

Communication Problems

Do you speak English?
Parla inglese?
pahrlah eenglayzay?

**Do you speak French/German/
Spanish?**
Parla francese/tedesco/spagnolo?
*pahrlah frahnchayzay/taydesko/
spahnyolo?*

I don't speak Italian.
Non parlo italiano.
non pahrlo eetahlyahno

I speak some French.
Parlo un po' di francese.
pahrlo oon paw dee franchayzay

I don't understand you.
Non La capisco.
non la kahpeesko

Could you speak more slowly?
Può parlare più lentamente?
pwaw pahrlahray pyoo lentamayntay?

Could you repeat that, please?
Può ripetere, per favore?
pwaw reepayteray per fahvoray?

Could you write that down, please?
Può scriverlo, per piacere?
pwaw skreeverlo per pyahchayray?

**Could you translate this for me,
please?**
Mi può tradurre questo, per favore?
*mee pwaw trahdoorray kwesto per
favoray?*

I understand.
Capisco.
kahpeesko

Do you understand?
Capisce?
kahpeeshay?

**Just a moment. I'll see if I can find it
in this book.**
Un momento. Vedo se lo trovo in
questo libro.
*oon momaynto. Vaydo say (say) lo
trawvo een kwesto leebro*

**Please point to your answer in this
book.**
Per favore, mi indichi la sua risposta su
questo libro.
*per fahvoray mee eendeekee lah
sooah reespawstah soo kwesto
leebro*

ITALIAN

Is there someone here who speaks English?
C'è qualcuno qui che parli inglese?
*che kwahlkoono kwee kay **pahrlee** eenglayzay?*

What does that mean?
Cosa vuol dire questo?
*kawzah vwawl **deeray** kwesto?*

How do you say that in Italian?
Come si dice in italiano?
*komay see **deechay** een eetahlyahno?*

Questions

Where?
Dove?
dovay?

What time is it?
Che ora è?
kay orah e?

Where is/are . . . ?
Dov'è/Dove sono . . . ?
*dove/**dovay** sono . . . ?*

Is there . . . ?
C'è . . . ?
che . . . ?

What?
Cosa, che cosa, che?
*kawzah, kay **kawzah**, kay?*

Are there . . . ?
Ci sono . . . ?
Chee sono . . . ?

Why?
Perchè?
perkay?

Could you tell me . . . ?
Mi può dire . . . ?
*mee pwaw **deeray** . . . ?*

How?
Come?
komay?

Could you show me . . . ?
Mi può mostrare . . . ?
mee pwaw mostrahray . . . ?

When?
Quando?
kwahndo?

Could you tell me how to get to . . . ?
Mi può dire come arrivare a . . . ?
*mee pwaw **deeray** komay ahrreevahray ah . . . ?*

How much/many?
Quanto/Quanti?
kwahnto/kwahntee?

It Is/Isn't

It is . . .
È . . .
e . . .

There isn't/aren't . . .
Non c'è/ci sono . . .
non che/chee sono . . .

It isn't . . .
Non è . . .
non e . . .

. . . , isn't it?
. . . , non è vero?
*. . . non e **vayro**?*

Isn't it . . . ?
Non è . . . ?
non e . . . ?

Here it is/they are.
Eccolo/eccoli.
*ekko-lo/**ekko**-lee*

There is/are . . .
C'è/ci sono . . .
che/chee sono . . .

ITALIAN

Common Adjectives and Adverbs and Their Opposites

beautiful/ugly	bello/brutto	*bello/brootto*
before/after	prima/dopo	*preemah/dawpo*
better/worse	meglio/peggio	*melyo/pedjo*
big/small	grande/piccolo	*grahnday/peekkolo*
cheap/expensive	a buon mercato/caro	*a bwawn merkahto/kahro*
clean/dirty	pulito/sporco	*pooleeto/spawrko*
cold/hot	freddo/caldo	*frayddo*
cool/warm	fresco/caldo	*fraysko/kahldo*
deep/shallow	profondo/poco profondo	*profondo/pawko*
early/late	presto/tardi	*presto/tahrdee*
easy/difficult	facile/difficile	*fahcheelay/ deeffeecheelay*
empty/full	vuoto/pieno	*vwawto/pyeno*
first/last	primo/ultimo	*preemo/oolteemo*
good/bad	buono/cattivo	*bwawno/kahtteevo*
heavy/light	pesante/leggero	*payzahntay/layjero*
here/there	qua/là	*kwah/lah*
high/low	alto/basso	*ahlto/bahsso*
ill/well	malato/sano	*mahlahto/sahno*
inside/outside	dentro/fuori	*dayntro/fwawree*
long/short	lungo/corto	*loongo/korto*
more/less	più/meno	*pyoo/mayno*
the most/the least	il massimo/ill minimo	*ell mahsseemo/eel meeneemo*
much/little	molto/poco	*molto/pawko*
narrow/wide	stretto/largo	*straytto/lahrgo*
near/far	vicino/lontano	*veecheeno/lontahno*
now/later	adesso/più tardi	*ahdesso/pyoo tahrdee*
often/rarely	spesso/raramente	*spesso/rahramayntay*
old/new	vecchio/nuovo	*vekkyo/nwauvo*
old/young	vecchio/giovane	*vekkyo/jovahnay*
open/closed	aperto/chiuso	*ahperto/kyoozo*
pleasant/unpleasant	gradevole/sgradevole	*grahdayvohlay/ zgrahdayvolay*
quick/slow	veloce/lento	*vaylochay/laynto*
quiet/noisy	tranquillo/rumoroso	*trahnqueello/roomorozo*
right/left	destra/sinistra	*destrah/seeneestrah*
right/wrong	giusto/sbagliato	*joosto/zbahlyahto*
still/not yet	ancora/non ancora	*ahnkorah/non ahnkorah*
thick/thin	spesso/sottile	*spesso/soteelay*
under/over	sotto/sopra	*sawtto/soprah*
vacant/occupied	libero/occupato	*leebero/awkoopahto*
well/badly	bene/male	*benay/mahlay*

ITALIAN

More Useful Words

also	anche	*ahnkay*
and	e	*ay*
enough	abbastanza	*ahbbah**stahn**tsah*
not	non	*non*
nothing	niente; nulla	***nyen**tay; **nool**lah*
or	o; oppure	*o; op**poo**ray*
perhaps	forse	***for**say*
soon	presto	***pres**to*
very	molto	***mol**to*

To Help You Further in Conversation

according to	secondo	*say**kon**do*
as you wish	come vuole	***ko**may v**waw**lay*
best wishes	auguri	*aw**goo**ree*
certainly	certamente	*chertah**mayn**tay*
entirely	completamente	*komplaytah**mayn**tay*
everyone	tutti	***too**tee*
I don't know	non lo so	*non lo saw*
I have forgotten	ho dimenticato	*aw deementee**kah**to*
indeed?	davvero?	*dah**vay**ro?*
in any way	in qualsiasi modo	*een kwahl**see**ahsee **mo**do*
in what way	in che modo	*een kay **mo**do*
it's not important	non importa	*non eem**por**tah*
never mind	lasci perdere	***lah**shee **per**dayray*
no one	nessuno	*nes**soo**no*
on the contrary	al contrario	*ahl kon**trah**reeo*
precisely	appunto	*ap**poon**to*
same to you	altrettanto	*ahltrayt**tahn**to*
sometimes	ogni tanto	***on**yee **tahn**to*
that's all	è tutto	*e **too**tto*
that is to say	cioè	*cho-**e***
that's correct	è giusto	*e **joo**sto*
that's impossible	è impossibile	*e eempos**see**beelay*
that's incredible	è incredibile	*e eenkray**dee**beelay*
that's not right	non è giusto	*non e **joo**sto*
that's too bad	peccato	*pek**kah**to*
What's the matter?	che c'è?	*kay che?*
Where are we going?	dove andiamo?	***do**vay ahn**dyah**mo?*
with pleasure	con piacere	*kon pyahc**hay**ray*

ITALIAN

Asking for Something

Could you help me, please?	Mi può aiutare, per favore?	*mee pwaw ahyootahray, per fahvoray?*
Could I have . . . ?	Posso avere . . . ?	*pawsso ahvayray . . . ?*
Could you give me . . . ?	Mi può dare . . . ?	*mee pwaw dahray . . . ?*
Could I have one . . . ?	Posso avere uno . . . ?	*pawsso ahvayray oono . . . ?*
I would like . . .	Vorrei . . .	*vorre-ee . . .*
I'm looking for . . .	Sto cercando . . .	*staw cherkahndo . . .*
I need . . .	Ho bisogno di . . .	*aw beezonyo dee . . .*

ARRIVAL

Passport and Customs

Your passport, please.
Il suo passaporto, prego.

Here it is.
Eccolo.
ekkolo

How long will you stay here?
Quanto tempo resterà?

Where will you be staying?
Quale sarà il suo domicilio?

What is the purpose of your visit?
Qual'è lo scopo della sua visita?

I'll be staying . . .
Resterò . . .
resteraw . . .

a few days	a month
qualche giorno	un mese
kwalkay jorno	*oon mayzay*

a week
una settimana
oonah setteemahnah

a fortnight
quindici giorni
kweendeechee jornee

I'm just passing through.
Sono di passaggio.
sono dee pahssahdjo

I'm on my way to . . .
Vado a . . .
vahdo ah . . .

I am visiting relatives/friends.
Faccio una visita a dei parenti/degli amici.
fahtcho oonah veezeetah ah de-ee pahrentee/delyee ahmeechee

I'm here on vacation.
Sono qui in vacanza.
sono kwee een vahkahntsah

I'm here on business.
Sono qui per affari.
sono kwee per ahffahree

I'm here to study.
Sono qui per studiare.
sono kwee per stoodyahray

This is my address.
Questo è il mio indirizzo.
kwesto e eel meeo eendeereetso

How much money do you have?
Quanto denaro ha?

ITALIAN

ITALIAN

Do you have any food or plants?
Ha dei cibi o delle piante?

Do you have anything to declare?
Ha qualcosa da dichiarare?

No, nothing. I have only personal belongings.
No, niente. Ho solo degli effetti personali.
naw nyentay. aw solo delyee effettee personahlee

I have . . .
Ho . . .
aw . . .

cigarettes	wine
delle sigarette	del vino
dellay seegahrettay	*del veeno*
liquor	
degli alcolici	
delyee ahlkawleechee	

perfume	some gifts
del profumo	qualche regalo
del profoomo	*kwahlkay raygahlo*

It's for my personal use.
È per uso personale.
e per oozo personahlay

Open your bag, please.
Apra la borsa, per piacere.

You'll have to pay duty on this.
Per questo deve pagare una tassa.

How much do I have to pay?
Quanto devo pagare?
kwahnto devo pahgahray?

I can't afford it.
Non posso pagarlo.
non pawsso pahgahrlo

May I go through?
Posso passare?
pawsso pahssahray?

Porter/Luggage

Where can I find a luggage cart?
Dove si può trovare un carrello?
dovay see pwaw trovahray oon kahrrello?

Are you using this cart?
Sta usando questo carrello?
stah oozahndo kwesto kahrrello?

Porter!
Facchino!
fahkkeeno

Please take this luggage . . .
Porti per piacere questi bagagli . . .
portee per pyahchayray kwestee bahgahlyee . . .

to the bus	taxi
all'autobus	al tassì
ahllowtoboos	*ahl tahssee*
train	
al treno	
ahl treno	
checkroom	
al deposito bagagli	
ahl daypawzeeto bahgahlyee	

Follow me, please.
Mi segua, per cortesia.
mee segwah per kortayzeeah

How much do I owe you?
Quanto Le devo?
kwanto lay devo?

Changing Money

Can you change these traveler's checks?
Può cambiare questi traveler's checks?
pwaw kambyahray kwestee traveler's checks?

I would like to change dollars/pounds.
Vorrei cambiare dei dollari/delle sterline.
vorre-ee kambyahray de-ee dawllahree/dellay sterleenay

What is the exchange rate?
Qual'è il cambio di oggi?
kwahle eel kahmbyo dee awjjee?

Here is my passport.
Ecco il mio passaporto.
ekko eel meeo pahssahporto

Could you please give me . . .
Mi può dare . . .
mee pwaw dahray . . .

    Swiss/Belgian/French francs
    dei franchi svizzeri/belgi/francesi
    de-ee frahnkee sveetseree/beljee/ / frahnchayzee?

    large bills
    un taglio grande
    oon tahlyo grahnday

    small bills
    un taglio piccolo
    oon tahlyo peekolo

Could you change this bill?
Può cambiare questa banconota?
pwaw kahmbyahray kwestah bahnkonawtah?

GETTING INTO TOWN

Taxi

Where can I find a taxi?
Dove si può trovare un tassì?
dovay see pwaw trovahray oon tahssee?

Please call a taxi for me.
Per piacere, mi trovi un tassì.
per pyahchayray mee trawvee oon tahssee

Please take me to . . .
Per favore, mi conduca a . . .
per fahvoray, mee kondookah ah . . .

How much will the fare be?
Quanto costerà la corsa?
kwanto kawstayrah lah korsah?

How far is it?
Quanto dista?
kwahnto deestah?.

Turn right/left . . .
Giri a destra/sinistra . . .
jeeree a destrah/seeneestrah . . .

    at the next corner
    al prossimo angolo
    ahl prawsseemo ahngolo

    at the stoplight
    al semaforo
    ahl semahforo

Go straight ahead.
Vada sempre diritto.
vahdah sempray deereetto

Why are you taking me this way?
Perchè stiamo andando da questa parte?
perkay styahmo ahndahndo dah kwestah pahrtay?

Please don't drive so fast.
Per favore, non guidi così veloce.
per fahvoray non gweedee kozee vaylochay

I'm in rather a hurry.
Ho piuttosto fretta.
aw pyoottawsto frayttah

Let me out please.
Per favore, mi faccia scendere.
per fahvoray mee fahtchah shendayray

ITALIAN

Turn the meter on.
Faccia scattare il tassametro.
fahtchah scahttahray eel tahssahmetro

Stop here, please.
Si fermi qui, per cortesia.
see fermee kwee, per kortayzeeah

Could you wait for me here?
Mi può attendere qui?
mee pwaw ahttendayray kwee?

How much do I owe you?
Quanto Le devo?
kwahnto lay devo?

Bus/Train

Where can I get a bus/train to . . . ?
Dove posso trovare un autobus/treno che va a . . . ?
dovay pawsso trovahray oon owtoboos/treno kay vah ah . . . ?

Which bus/train do I take for . . . ?
Quale autobus/treno devo prendere per . . . ?
kwahlay owtoboos/treno devo prendayray per . . . ?

When is the next bus/train for . . . ?
Quando parte il prossimo autobus/treno per . . . ?
kwahndo pahrtay eel prawseemo owtoboos/treno per . . . ?

Do I have to change buses/trains?
Devo cambiare autobus/treno?
devo kahmbyahray owtoboos/treno?

Where do I buy the ticket?
Dove si comprano i biglietti?
dovay see komprahno ee beelyettee?

Could you tell me when we reach . . . ?
Mi può dire quando arriviamo a . . . .?
mee pwaw deeray kwahndo arreevyahmo ah . . . ?

Please let me off.
Per favore, mi faccia scendere.
per fahvoray, mee fahtchah shendayray

Car Rental

I have a reservation for a car.
Ho prenotato una macchina.
aw praynotahto oonah mahkeenah

I'd like to rent a small/large car.
Vorrei noleggiare una macchina piccola/grande.
vorre-ee nolejjahray oonah mahkkeenah peekkolah/grahnday

   with an automatic gearshift
   con cambio automatico
   kon kahmbyo owtomahteeko

I need it for . . .
Ne ho bisogno per . . .
nay aw beezonyo per . . .

   a day/two days
   un giorno/due giorni
   oon jorno/dooay jornee

   a week/two weeks
   una settimana/due settimane
   oonah setteemahnah/dooay setteemahnay

How much is it per . . . ?
Qual'è la tariffa . . . ?
kwahle lah tahreeffah . . . ?

hour	**kilometer**
all'ora	al chilometro
ahllorah	*ahl keelawmetro*
day	
giornaliera	
jornahlyerah	
week	
per una settimana	
per oonah setteemahnah	

Is gas included?
È compresa la benzina?
*e kom**pray**zah lah ben**dzee**nah?*

Is insurance included?
È compresa l'assicurazione?
*e kom**pray**zah lahsseekoorahts**yo**nay?*

**I would like comprehensive
   insurance.**
Vorrei l'assicurazione completa.
*vorre-ee lahsseekoorahts**yo**nay
   kom**play**ta*

Do I have unlimited mileage?
È illimitato il chilometraggio?
*e eeleemee**tah**to eel keelome**trahj**jo?*

Can I pay by credit card?
Posso pagare con una carta di credito?
***paws**so pah**gah**ray kon **oo**nah **kahr**tah
   dee **kray**deeto?*

Here is my driver's license.
Ecco la mia patente.
***ek**ko lah **mee**ah pah**ten**tay*

What's the deposit?
Quant'è la cauzione?
*kwahn**te** lah kowts**yo**nay?*

May I look at the car first, please?
Posso vedere la macchina prima,
   per favore?
***paws**so vay**day**ray lah **mahk**keenah
   preemah per fa**vo**ray?*

**I'm not familiar with this type of car.
   Please show me . . . ?**
Non conosco questo tipo di macchina.
   Mi faccia vedere per piacere . . .
*non ko**nos**ko **kwes**to **tee**po dee
   mahkkeenah. Mee **fah**tchah
   vay**day**ray per pya**chay**ray . . .*

   the headlights
   i fari anteriori
   *ee **fah**ree ahntereeoree*

   the indicators
   le frecce di direzione
   *lay **frayt**che dee deeretsyonay*

   the ignition
   l'accensione
   *lahchens**yo**nay*

   hood release
   la leva del cofano
   *lah **lay**vah del **kaw**fahno*

   gas cap
   il tappo della benzina
   *eel **tahp**po **del**lah ben**dzee**nah*

What kind of gas should I use?
Che benzina ci metto?
*kay ben**dzee**nah chee **mayt**to?*

   regular/super
   normale/super
   *nor**mah**lay/**soo**per*

Must I return it to this office?
La devo restituire a quest'ufficio?
*lah **day**vo resteetoo-**ee**ray ah
   kwestoof**fee**cho?*

May I return it in another city?
La posso restituire in un'altra città?
*lah **paws**so resteetoo-**ee**ray een oon
   ahltrah cheet**tah**?*

Is there an extra charge (for that)?
C'è un sovrapprezzo?
*che un sovrah**pret**so?*

Have you got a branch in . . . ?
Avete un ufficio a . . . ?
*a**vay**tay oon oof**fee**cho ah . . . ?*

What do I do if I have car trouble?
Cosa devo fare se il motore mi dà delle
   noie?
***kaw**za **day**vo **fah**ray say eel mo**to**ray
   mee dah **del**lay **naw**yay?*

ACCOMMODATIONS

I'm looking for . . .
Sto cercando . . .
*staw cher**kahn**do . . .*

   a good hotel
   un buon'albergo
   *oon b**wawn** ahl**ber**go*

ITALIAN

an inexpensive hotel
un albergo che abbia un prezzo
ragionevole
*oon ahlbergo kay ahbbyah oon
pretso rajonayvolay*

a pension
una pensione
oonah pensyonay

a youth hostel
un ostello della gioventù
oon awstello dellah joventoo

Hotel / Pension

I have a reservation.
Ho prenotato.
aw praynotahto

My name is . . .
Mi chiamo . . .
mee kyahmo . . .

Do you have a room for tonight?
Avete una camera per stasera?
*avaytay oonah kahmerah per
stasayrah?*

I would like . . .
Vorrei . . .
vorre-ee . . .

a single/double room
una camera singola/doppia
*oonah kahmerah seengolah/
doppyah*

a room with twin beds
una camera con due letti
oonah kahmerah kon dooay lettee

a room with a double bed
una camera con un letto matrimoniale
*oonah kahmerah kon oon letto
mahtreemonyahlay*

I want a room with . . .
Vorrei una camera con . . .
vorre-ee oonah kahmerah kon . . .

a bath/shower
bagno/doccia
bahnyo/dotchah

running water
l'acqua corrente
lahkwa korrentay

hot water
l'acqua calda
lahkwah kaldah

a balcony
terrazzo
terrahtso

a view of the sea
vista sul mare
veestah sool mahray

**How much is the room per day?
per week?**
Qual'è il prezzo della camera per un
giorno? per una settimana?
*kwahle eel pretso dellah kahmerah per
oon jorno? per oonah setteemahnah?*

**That's too expensive. Do you have
anything cheaper?**
È troppo caro. Avete qualche cosa di
più economico?
*e trawppo kahro. avaytay kwalkay
kawzah dee pyoo ekonawmeeko?*

How much is the room . . . ?
Qual'è il prezzo . . . ?
kwahle eel pretso . . . ?

without meals
pasti esclusi
pahstee eskloozee

with breakfast only
con la colazione
kon lah kolahtsyonay

with half board
con mezza pensione
kon medzah pensyonay

with full board
con pensione completa
kon pensyonay komplaytah

**Is there a reduction for children/
a longer stay?**
C'è una riduzione per i bambini/un
soggiorno più lungo?
*che oonah reedootsyonay per ee
bahmbeenee/oon sojjorno pyoo
loongo?*

You can get help fast with the easy-to-use phrases (in French, German, Italian, and Spanish) printed on both sides of this tear-out card. On the reverse side you'll also find a blank currency exchange table to help you get used to spending money abroad. Fill in the foreign currency values at the rate prevailing when you change money. This card can also serve as a handy place marker as you use this book. *Bon voyage!*

FRENCH

Excusez-moi. Je ne parle pas français. Pourriez-vous m'aider, s'il vous plaît.

GERMAN

Verzeihung. Ich spreche kein Deutsch. Können sie mir helfen, bitte?

[Pardon me. I do not speak French/German. Will you please help me?]

ITALIAN

Mi scusi. Non parlo italiano. Mi può aiutare, per favore?

SPANISH

Perdóneme. No hablo español. ¿Me puede ayudar, por favor?

[Pardon me. I do not speak Italian/Spanish. Will you please help me?]

CURRENCY CONVERSIONS

Fill in the foreign currency values at the rate prevailing when you change money.

U.S. $	FRANCS	MARKS	LIRE	PESETAS
50¢				
1.00				
5.00				
10.00				
15.00				
20.00				
50.00				

1 Franc = $._____   1 Lira = $._____

1 Mark = $._____   1 Peseta = $._____

May I see the room?
Posso vedere la camera?
pawsso vaydayray lah kahmerah?

Yes, this room will do.
Sì, andrà bene questa.
see ahndrah baynay kwestah

No, this room won't do.
No, non va bene questa.
naw, non va benay kwestah

Do you have any better/bigger rooms?
Avete qualche camera migliore/più grande?
ahvaytay kwalkay kahmerah meelyoray/pyoo grahnday?

This is the only room vacant right now.
Questa è l'unica camera disponibile.

We'll have another room tomorrow.
Avremo un'altra camera domani.

How long will you be staying?
Quanto tempo intende fermarsi?

I will be staying . . .
Rimarrò . . .
reemahrraw . . .

   tonight only
   una notte
   oonah nawttay

   two or three days
   due o tre giorni
   dooay o tray jornee

   a week
   una settimana
   oonah setteemahnah

Could I please have . . . ?
Per favore, potrei avere . . . ?
per fahvoray potre-ee ahveray . . . ?

I haven't decided yet.
Non ho ancora deciso.
non aw ahnkorah daycheezo

Here is my passport.
Ecco il mio passaporto.
ekko eel meeo pahssahporto

When may I have it back?
Quando posso riaverlo?
kwahndo pawsso reeahverlo?

May I go to the room now?
Posso andare adesso alla camera?
pawsso ahndahray ahdesso ahllah kahmerah?

May I have the key?
Posso avere la chiave?
pawsso ahveray lah kyahvay?

Shall I take the key with me when I go out or leave it with you?
Prendo la chiave quando esco oppure la lascio a Lei?
prendo lah kyahvay kwando esko oppooray lah lahsho ah le-ee?

At what time do you lock the front door at night?
A che ora di sera chiudete il portone?
ah kay orah dee sayrah kyoodaytay eel portonay?

How do I get in if I come later?
Come posso entrare se torno più tardi?
komay pawsso entrahray say torno pyoo tahrdee?

When is check-out time?
A che ora bisogna lasciare la camera?
ah kay orah beezonyah lahshahray lah kahmerah?

ITALIAN

another pillow	un'altro guanciale	*oon ahltro gwahnchahlay*
an extra blanket	una coperta in più	*oonah kopertah een pyoo*
some towels	degli asciugamani da bagno	*delyee ahshoogahmahnee dahbahnyo*
some soap	del sapone	*del sahponay*

a glass	un bicchiere	*oon beekyeray*
toilet paper	della carta igenica	*della kahrtah eejeneekah*
more hangers	degli attaccapanni	*delyee ahttahkkahpahnnee*
writing paper	della carta da lettere	*dellah kahrtah dah letteray*
a bottle of mineral water	una bottiglia di acqua minerale	*oonah botteelyah dee ahkwah meenerahlay*
an ashtray	un portacenere	*oon portahchayneray*
a light bulb	una lampadina	*oonah lahmpadeenah*

The . . . doesn't work
Non funziona . . .
non foontsyonah . . .

air conditioning	l'aria condizionata	*lahreeah kondeetsyonahtah*
heating	il riscaldamento	*eel reeskahldahmaynto*
hot water	l'acqua calda	*lahkwah kahldah*
light	la luce	*lah loochay*
lock	la serratura	*lah serrahtoorah*
radio	la radio	*lah rahdyo*
shower	la doccia	*lah dotchah*
tap	il rubinetto	*eel roobeenetto*
toilet	il gabinetto	*eel gahbeenetto*

Can the heat/air conditioning be turned up/down?
Si può alzare/abbassare il riscaldamento/l'aria condizionata?
see pwaw ahltsahray/ahbbahs-sahray eel reeskahldamaynto/lahreeah kondeetsyonahtah?

The mattress is too soft. May I have a firmer one?
Il materasso è troppo morbido. Posso averne uno più duro?
eel mahterahsso e trawppo morbeedo. pawsso ahvernay oono pyoo dooro?

Could you wake me up tomorrow morning at . . . ?
Mi può svegliare domani mattina alle . . . ?
mee pwaw zvelyahray domahnee mahtteenah ahllay . . . ?

May we have breakfast in our room?
Servite la colazione in camera?
serveetay lah kolahtsyonay een kahmerah?

Until what time do you serve breakfast?
Fino a che ora è servita la colazione?
feeno a kay orah e serveetah lah kolahtsyonay?

At what time is lunch/dinner?
A che ora è servito il pranzo/la cena?
ah kay orah e serveeto eel prahndzo/lah chaynah?

Could you please have the linen changed today?
Può fare cambiare le lenzuola oggi, per piacere?
pwaw fahray kahmbyahray lay lentswawlah awjjee per pyahchayray?

Are there any letters for me?
C'è posta per me?
che pawstah per may?

I would ilke to call this number . . .
Vorrei telefonare a questo numero . . .
vorre-ee taylayfonahray ah kwesto noomero . . .

ITALIAN

Checking Out

We'll be leaving tomorrow.
Partiremo domani.
pahrteeraymo domahnee

May I have the bill, please?
Posso avere il conto, per piacere?
pawsso ahveray eel konto per pyahchayray?

Could you give me a receipt, please?
Mi può dare una rice-vuta, per piacere?
mee pwaw dahray oonah reechay vootah per pyachayray?

Could you explain this item?
Mi può spiegare a cosa si riferisce qui?
mee pwaw spyegahray ah kawzah see reefereeshay kwee?

Thank you for a most enjoyable stay.
La ringrazio per un soggiorno molto piacevole.
lah reengrahtsyo per oon sojjorno molto pyahchayvolay

I hope we'll be able to return some day.
Spero che potremo tornare un giorno.
spayro kay potraymo tornahray oon jorno

Youth Hostel

Do you have dormitory accommodations?
Avete dei posti letto?
avaytay de-ee pawstee letto?

Is there a curfew?
Si deve rientrare entro una certa ora?
see dayvay ree-entrahray entro oonah chertah orah?

Do I have to do chores?
C'è un contributo in lavoro?
che oon kontreebooto een lahvoro?

Is there a limit on the number of days we can stay?
Per quanto tempo si può rimanere? C'è un limite massimo?
per kwanto tempo see pwaw reemahneray? che oon lee meetay mahsseemo?

Camping

Is there a camp site nearby?
C'è una zona di campeggio qui vicino?
che oonah dzawnah dee kahmpejjo kwee veecheeno?

May we camp here?
Possiamo accamparci qui?
pawssyahmo ahccahmpahrchee kwee?

What's the charge?
Quanto costa?
kwanto kawstah?

Are there . . . ?
Ci sono . . . ?
chee sono . . . ?

baths	**showers**
i bagni	le docce
ee bahnyee	*lay dotchay*

toilets	
i gabinetti	
ee gahbeenettee	

Are there cooking/washing facilities?
C'è la possibilità di cucinare/lavare?
che lah posseebeeleetah dee coocheenahray/lahvahray?

Is it possible to rent a tent/bungalow?
È possibile affittare una tenda/un bungalow?
e posseebeelay ahffeettahray oonah tendah/oon boongahlo?

Where can we find drinking water?
Dove si può trovare dell'acqua potabile?
dovay see pwaw trovahray dellakwah potahbeelay?

May we light a fire?
Si può accendere un fuoco?
see pwaw ahchenderay oon fwawko?

Where can we find . . . ?
Dove si trova . . . ?
dovay see trawvah . . . ?

a camping equipment store
un negozio da attrezzatura per campeggiatori
oon negawtsyo dah ahttretsahtoorah per kahmpejjahtoree

a laundry
una lavanderia
oonah lahvahndereeah

a restaurant
un ristorante
oon reestorahntay

shops
dei negozi
de-ee negawtsee

telephones
dei telefoni
de-ee taylayfonee

electric hook-ups
delle prese elettriche
dellay prayzay aylettreekay

Signs

NO CAMPING	VIETATO CAMPEGGIARE
NO TRAILERS	ROULOTTE VIETATE
NO TRESPASSING	VIETATO L'INGRESSO
PRIVATE PROPERTY	PROPRIETÀ PRIVATA
NO FIRES	VIETATO ACCENDERE FUOCHI

TRAVELING

Signs

ARRIVALS	ARRIVI
DEPARTURES	PARTENZE
ENTRANCE	ENTRATA
EXIT	USCITA
TICKETS	BIGLIETTI
INFORMATION	INFORMAZIONI
BAGGAGE CHECK	DEPOSITO BAGAGLI
CURRENCY EXCHANGE	CAMBIO
TO THE PLATFORMS	AI BINARI
CUSTOMS	DOGANA
NO SMOKING	VIETATO FUMARE
WAITING ROOMS	SALE D'ATTESA

ITALIAN

Traveling by Air

Is there a bus/train to/from the airport?
C'è un'autobus/treno all'/dall' aeroporto?
*che oon **owtoboos**/**treno** all/dahll ahero**porto**?*

Where? When is there a flight to . . . ? What time? Is there an earlier/later one?
Dove? quando c'è un volo per . . . ? A che ora? Ce n'è uno che parte prima/più tardi?
*dovay? **kwand**o che oon **volo** per . . . ? ah kay **orah**? chay ne **oono** kay **pahr**tay preemah/pyoo **tahr**dee?*

When is check-in time?
A che ora è il check-in?
*ah kay **orah** e eel check-in?*

When does it arrive?
A che ora arriva?
*ah kay **orah** ahr**ree**vah?*

How much is the fare to . . . ?
Quanto costa il biglietto per . . . ?
***kwahn**to **kaws**tah eel beel**yetto** per . . . ?*

What's the flight number?
Qual'è il numero del volo?
***kwahle** eel **noo**mero del **vol**o?*

I'd like to book a seat on the next flight to . . .
Vorrei prenotare un posto sul prossimo volo per . . .
*vorre-ee **prayno**tahray oon **pawst**o sool **praws**seemo **vol**o per . . .*

one way	round trip
andata	andata e ritorno
*ahn**dahtah***	*ahn**dahtah** ay ree**torno***

I'd like a seat . . .
Vorrei un posto . . .
*vorre-ee oon **pawst**o . . .*

on the aisle
dalla parte del corridoio
*dahl**lah pahr**tay del korree**doyo***

at the window
al finestrino
*ahl feenes**treeno***

in the front
davanti
*dah**vahn**tee*

in the back
in coda
*een **kaw**dah*

in the non-smoking section
non-fumatori
*non-foomah**toree***

in the smoking section
fumatori
*foomah**toree***

Is it a non-stop flight?
È un volo diretto?
*e oon **vol**o dee**retto**?*

Will it be necessary to change planes?
Sarà necessario cambiare aereo?
*sah**rah** neches**sahr**yo kam**byahray** ahereo?*

How many bags am I allowed?
Quanti colli sono permessi?
***kwahn**tee **kawl**lee **so**no per**messee**?*

How much is charged for excess weight?
Quanto si paga per il sovrapeso?
***kwahn**to see **pahg**ah per eel sovrah**payzo**?*

How long is the flight delayed?
Quanto ritardo porta il volo?
***kwahn**to ree**tahr**do **port**ah eel **vol**o?*

ITALIAN

Traveling by Train

When is the next train to . . . ?
Quando è il prossimo treno per . . . ?
kwahndo e eel prawsseemo treno per . . . ?

**I would like to buy/reserve a one way/round trip ticket to . . .
in first/second class**
Vorrei comprare/prenotare un'andata/un'andata e ritorno a . . .
prima/seconda classe
*vorre-ee komprahray praynotahray oon ahndahtah/
oon ahndahtah ay reetorno ah . . .
preema/sekondah klahssay*

What is the fare to . . . ?
Quanto costa il biglietto per . . . ?
*kwahnto kawstah eel beelyetto
per . . . ?*

**How much is it for a child of . . .
years?**
Quanto costa il biglietto per un bambino
di . . . anni?
*kwahnto kawstah eel beelyetto per oon
bahmbeeno dee . . . ahnnee?*

What time does the train leave?
A che ora parte il treno?
ah kay orah pahrtay eel treno?

When does it arrive?
A che ora arriva?
ah kay orah ahrreevah?

At which platform?
Da che binario parte?
dah kay beenahryo pahrtay?

Do I have to change trains? Where?
Devo cambiare treno? Dove?
dayvo kambyahray treno? dovay?

When will there be a connection . . . ?
Quando ci sarà una coincidenza
per . . . ?
*kwahndo chee sahrah oonah
coeencheedentsah per . . . ?*

Is there a sleeping car?
C'è un vagone-letto?
che oon vahgonay letto?

Are there couchettes?
Ci sono delle cuccette?
chee sono dellay koochettay?

Is this train going to . . . ?
Va a . . . questo treno?
vah ah . . . kwesto treno?

Which car for . . . ?
Quale vagone per . . . ?
kwahlay vahgonay per . . . ?

**Could you tell me where car
number . . . is?**
Mi può dire dov'è il vagone numero . . . ?
*mee pwaw deeray dove eel vahgonay
noomero . . . ?*

I have a reservation.
Ho un posto riservato.
aw oon pawsto reezervahto

Where is my couchette?
Dov'è la mia cuccetta?
dove lah meeah koochettah?

Is this seat taken?
È occupato questo posto?
e awkkoopahto kwesto pawsto?

Excuse me. I think this is my seat.
Mi scusi. Penso che questo sia il mio
posto.
*mee skoozee. penso kay kwesto seeah
eel meeo pawsto*

May I get by?
Permesso?
permaysso?

Where is the dining car?
Dov'è il vagone-ristorante?
dove eel vahgonay-reestorahntay?

May I open/close the window/the curtains?
Posso aprire/chiudere il finestrino/le tendine?
*paws*so ah*pree*ray/*kyoo*deray eel feenes*tree*no/lay ten*dee*nay?

Can the heating be turned down/off/higher?
Si può abbassare/chiudere/alzare il riscaldamento?
see pwaw abbahs*sah*ray/*kyoo*deray/ahlt*sah*ray eel reeskahldah**mayn**to?

Could you refrain from smoking, please?
Potrebbe evitare di fumare, per favore?
*potreb*bay ayveet**ah**ray dee foo**mah**ray, per fah**vo**ray?

This is a non-smoking compartment.
È uno scompartimento per non fumatori.
e **oo**no skompahrteem**ayn**to per non fooma**ht**oree

What station is this?
Che stazione è questa?
kay staht**syo**nay e **kwes**tah?

Is this where I change for a train to . . . ?
È qui che c'è la coincidenza per . . . ?
*e kwee kay che lah koeencheed*ent*sah per . . . ?

Traveling by Boat

Is there a boat to . . . ?
C'è una nave per . . . ?
che **oo**nah **nah**vay per . . . ?

When does the next boat leave?
Quando parte la prossima nave?
*kwahn*do **pahr**tay lah **praws**seemah **nah**vay?

I would like to buy a round-trip/one-way ticket in first/second class.
Vorrei comprare un' andata e ritorno/un' andata in prima/seconda.
vorre-ee kom**prah**ray oon ahn**dah**tah ay reet**or**no/oon ahn**dah**tah een **pree**mah/se**kon**dah

When does it arrive? When does it return?
Quando arriva? Quando torna?
*kwahn*do ahr**ree**vah? **kwahn**do **tor**nah?

When must I go on board?
Quando devo salire a bordo?
*kwahn*do **day**vo sah**lee**ray ah **bor**do?

Where can I find pills for seasickness?
Dove posso trovare delle pillole per il mal di mare?
dovay **paws**so trov**ah**ray **del**lay **pee**lolay per eel mahl dee **mah**ray?

Traveling by Bus/Streetcar/Subway

Where is the bus station?
Dov'è la stazione degli autobus?
dove lah staht**syo**nay **del**yee ow**to**boos?

Where is the nearest bus stop/subway station/streetcar stop?
Dov'è la fermata dell' autobus/della metropolitanta/del tram più vicina?
dove lah fehr**mah**tah dello**w**toboos/**del**lah maytropolee**tah**nah del trahm pyoo vee**chee**nah?

Where can I get a bus/train to . . . ?
Dove posso prendere un autobus/treno a . . . ?
*dovay paws*so *prenderay oon owtoboos/treno ah . . . ?*

How long does it take?
Quanto ci vuole?
*kwahn*to *chee vwaw*lay?

Does this bus/train go to . . . ?
Va a . . . quest' autobus/treno?
vah ah . . . kwestowtoboos/treno?

Which line do I take for . . . ?
Quale linea devo prendere per . . . ?
*kwah*lay *lee*nayah *day*vo *prenderay
per . . . ?*

Where do I buy a ticket?
Dove si comprano i biglietti?
dovay see komprahno ee beelyettee?

What is the fare to . . . ?
Quanto costa a . . . ?
*kwahn*to *kaws*tah *ah . . . ?*

Do I get off here for . . . ?
Scendo qui per . . . ?
*shayn*do *kwee per . . . ?*

**Could you tell me when we
    reach . . . ?**
Mi può dire quando arriviamo a . . . ?
*mee pwaw deeray kwahn*do
    ahrreevyahmo ah . . . ?

Let me off, please.
Mi faccia scendere, per favore!
*mee fahtchah shayn*deray *per fahvoray*

Traveling by Car

Where can I find a gas station/garage?
Dove posso trovare una stazione di rifornimento/un garage?
*dovay paws*so *trovahray oonah staht*syonay *dee reeforneemaynto/oon gahrahzh?*

How much is gas per liter?
Quanto costa la benzina al litro?
*kwahn*to *kaws*tah *lah bendzeena ahl leetro?*

Please . . .
Per favore . . .
per fahvoray . . .

fill her up	faccia il pieno	*fahtchah eel pyeno*
give me . . . liters	mi dia . . . litri	*mee deeah . . . leetree*
of standard/premium	di normale/super	*dee normahlay/sooper*
give me a liter of oil.	mi dia un litro di olio.	*mee deeah oon leetro dee awlyo*
check the oil/water	controlli l'olio/l'acqua	*contrawllee lawlyo/*
battery/tires	la batteria/le gomme	*lakwah/lah bahttereeah/*
brake fluid	l'olio dei freni	*lay gommay/lawlyo de-ee fraynee*
clean the windshield	pulisca il cristallo	*pooleeska eel kreestahllo*
adjust the brakes	aggiusti i freni	*ahdjoostee ee fraynee*

ITALIAN

In Case of a Breakdown

Excuse me. My car has broken down.
Mi scusi. Ho avuto un guasto.
mee skoozee. aw avooto oon gwahsto

May I use your phone?
Posso usare il suo telefono?
pawsso oozahray eel soo-o taylefono?

I've had a breakdown at . . . Can you send a mechanic/tow truck?
Ho avuto un guasto a . . . Può mandare un meccanico/carro attrezzi?
aw ahvooto oon gwahsto ah . . . pwaw mahndahray oon mekkahneeko/kahrro ahttraytsee?

How long will you be?
Quanto tempo impiegherete?
kwahnto tempo eempyaygeraytay?

Thank you for stopping. Could you help me?
Grazie di essersi fermato. Mi potrebbe aiutare?
grahtsyay dee essersee fermahto. mee potraybbay ahyootahray?

There's something wrong with the . . .
Non funziona/funzionano . . .
non foontsyonah/foontsyonahno . . .

I have a flat tire.
Ho una gomma sgonfiata.
aw oonah gommah zgonfyahtah

The battery is dead.
È scarica la batteria.
e skahreekah la bahttereeah

Do you have a jack/jumper cables?
Ha un crick/dei fili per ricaricare la batteria?
ah oon kreek/de-ee feelee per reekahreekahray lah bahttereeah?

I've run out of gas.
Sono rimasto senza benzina.
sono reemahsto sentsah bendzeenah

Could you please notify the next garage?
Potrebbe gentilmente notificare il prossimo garage?
potraybbay jenteelmayntay noteefeekahray eel prawseemo gahrahzh?

Could you have a look at my car?
Può dare un'occhiata alla mia macchina?
pwaw dahray oon awkkyahtah ahllah meeah mahkkeenah?

accelerator	l'acceleratore	*lahcheleratoray*
brakes	i freni	*ee fraynee*
carburetor	il carburatore	*eel kahrboorahtoray*
clutch	la frizione	*le freetsyonay*
engine	il motore	*eel motoray*
fan	il ventilatore	*eel venteelahtoray*
gears	le marce	*lay mahrchay*
hand brake	il freno a mano	*eel frayno ah mahno*
headlights	i fari anteriori	*ee fahree ahnteryoree*
horn	il clacson	*eel klahkson*
ignition	l'accensione	*lahchensyone*
spark plugs	le candele	*lay kahndaylay*
turn signals	le frecce di direzione	*lay fraytchay dee deeretsyone*

ITALIAN

ITALIAN

I don't know what's wrong with it.
Non so dove sia il guasto.
non saw dovay seeah eel gwahsto

A light on the dashboard went on.
Si è accesa una spia sul cruscotto.
see e ahchayzah oonah speeah sool krooskawtto

Will spare parts be needed? Do you have them?
Ci vorrano pezzi di ricambio? Ce li avete?
chee vorrahnno petsee dee reekahmbyo? chay lee ahvaytay?

How long will it take to repair?
Quanto tempo impiegherete per ripararla?
kwahnto tempo eempyay geraytay per reepahrahlah?

How much will it cost?
Quanto costerà?
kwahnto kosterah?

When will the car be ready?
Quando sarà pronta la macchina?
kwahndo sahrah prontah lah mahkkeenah?

Where's the nearest garage that can fix it?
Dov'è il garage più vicino che possa ripararla?
dove eel gahrahzh pyoo veecheeno kay pawssah reepahrahrlah?

Is the car repaired?
È a posto la macchina?
e ah pawsto lah mahkkeenah?

How much do I owe you?
Quanto le devo?
kwahnto lay dayvo?

Could you give me an itemized bill, please?
Mi può dare una fattura dettagliata, per favore?
mee pwaw dahray oonah fahttoorah dayttahlyahtah per fahvoray?

Trouble with the Police

I don't speak Italian very well.
Non parlo bene l'italiano.
non pahrlo benay leetahlyahno

Do you speak English?
Parla inglese lei?
pahrlah eenglayzay le-ee?

I'm sorry, I don't understand.
Mi dispiace, non capisco.
mee deespyahchay, non kahpeesko

Here's my driver's license.
Ecco la mia patente.
ekko lah meeah pahtentay

Was I driving too fast?
Stavo guidando troppo veloce?
stahvo gweedahndo trawppo velochay?

What did I do wrong?
Che cosa ho fatto?
kay kawzah aw fahtto?

Must I pay a fine?
Devo pagare una multa?
dayvo pahgahray oonah mooltah?

How much is it?
Quant'è?
kwahnte?

Traveling by Bicycle/Moped

Where can I rent a bicycle/moped?
Dove posso noleggiare una bicicletta/un motorino?
dovay pawsso nolejjahray oonah beecheekklettah/oon motoreeno?

I'd like to rent a moped.
Vorrei noleggiare un motorino.
vorre-ee nolejjahray oon motoreeno

How much is it per hour/day?
Quant'è all'ora/per una giornata?
kwahnte ahllorah/per oonah jornahtah?

At what time must I return it?
A che ora la devo restituire?
ah kay orah lah dayvo resteetooeeray?

This bicycle is too big/small.
Questa bicicletta è troppo grande/
  piccola.
*kwestah beecheeklettah e trawppo
  grahnday/peekkolah*

This tire needs air.
Questa gomma ha bisogno di essere
  gonfiata.
*kwestah gommah ah beezonyo dee
  esseray gonfyahtah*

The motor keeps stalling.
Il motore continua a fermarsi.
*eel motoray konteenoo-ah ah
  fermahrsee*

**Something's wrong with the brake/
  headlight.**
Non funziona il freno/il faro anteriore.
*non foontsyonah eel frayno/eel fahro
  ahnteryoray*

Hitchhiking

Could you please give me a lift to . . . ?
Mi può dare un passaggio a . . . , per piacere?
mee pwaw dahray oon pahssahjjo a . . . , per pyahchayray?

I'm only going as far as . . .
Vado solo fino a . . .

I can take you as far as . . .
Posso accompagnarla fino a . . .

Asking the Way

Excuse me. Could you tell me . . . ?
Mi scusi. Mi può dire . . . ?
mee skoozee. mee pwaw deeray . . . ?

how to get to . . .
come si va a . . .
komay see vah ah . . .

how far is it to . . .
quanto dista . . .
kwahnto deestah . . .

am I on the right road for . . .
sono sulla strada giusta per . . .
sono soollah strahdah joostah per . . .

which road do I take for . . .
che strada devo prendere per . . .
*kay strahdah dayvo prenderay
  per . . .*

what is the name of this town
come si chiama questa città
*komay see kyahmah kwestah
  cheettah*

Could you direct me to . . . ?
Mi può indicare la strada per . . . ?
*mee pwaw eendeekahray lah strahdah
  per . . . ?*

**Could you show me where we are on
  this map?**
Mi può indicare sulla carta dove siamo?
*mee pwaw eendeekahray soollah
  kahrtah dovay syahmo?*

It's not far from here.
Non è lontano da qui.

ITALIAN

It's a fair distance from here. Dista parecchio da qui.	**at the next intersection.** al prossimo incrocio.
Go straight ahead. Vada diritto.	**at the next corner.** al prossimo angolo.
Turn left/right . . . Giri a sinistra/destra . . .	**at the traffic circle.** alla circonvallazione.
at the first/second traffic light. al primo/secondo semaforo.	**Follow the signs for . . .** Segua i cartelli per . . .

Highway Signs

EXIT	USCITA
ENTRANCE	ENTRATA
ONE WAY	SENSO UNICO
NO ENTRY	DIVIETO D'ENTRATA
NO PARKING	DIVIETO DI SOSTA
DETOUR	DEVIAZIONE
DANGER	PERICOLO
MERGING TRAFFIC	VEICOLI IN IMMISSIONE
HIGHWAY	AUTOSTRADA
SPEED LIMIT	LIMITE DI VELOCITÀ

TYPES OF EATING ESTABLISHMENTS IN ITALY

Ristorante: Restaurant. The most sophisticated and expensive type of eating establishment. The dishes tend to be less regionally oriented.

Trattoria: A small restaurant that serves simple meals at very reasonable rates; many dishes are of a local character.

Taverna: A still more modest version of a Trattoria.

Buco: Literally "hole," it usually designates a cellar trattoria, most often frequented by young people.

Locanda/Osteria: Usually in a rural setting, an establishment that serves wine and simple food.

Pizzeria: Serves pizza, obviously, but also pasta and other dishes.

Tavola calda: A snack bar that serves hot meals.

Rosticceria: Serves entire meals, hot and cold, to be eaten on the premises or to take out.

Caffè/Bar: A "café" that serves coffee, tea, alcoholic and non-alcoholic beverages, ready-made sandwiches, rolls, and occasionally hamburgers or grilled sandwiches.

Gelateria: Ice cream parlor.

Buon appetito!	**Bon appétit!**
Cin-cin!	**Cheers!**

ITALIAN

EATING OUT

Can you suggest a good restaurant . . . ? for breakfast/lunch/dinner
Può consigliarmi un buon ristorante . . . ? per la colazione/il pranzo/la cena
pwaw konseelyahrmee oon bwawn reestorahntay . . . ? per lah kolahtsyonay/eel prahndzo/lah chaynah

We're looking for an inexpensive restaurant. Do you know of one?
Cerchiamo un ristorante che non costi troppo. Ne conosce uno?
cherkyahmo oon reestorahntay kay non kawstee trawppo. nay konoshay oono?

I'd like to make a reservation for two/four at 8:00 this evening.
Vorrei riservare un tavolo per due/quattro alle otto stasera.
vorre-ee reeservahray oon tahvolo per dooay/kwattro ahllay awtto stahsayrah

Good evening. We have a reservation. The name is . . .
Buona sera. Abbiamo prenotato. Il nome è . . .
bwawnah sayrah. ahbbyahmo praynotahto. eel nomay e . . .

Do you have a table for three? Avete un tavolo per tre? *ahvaytay oon tahvolo per tray?*	**by the window** vicino alla finestra *veecheeno ahllah feenestrah*
Could we have a table . . . ? Potremmo avere un tavolo . . . ? *potremmo ahvayray oon tahvolo . . . ?*	**with more privacy** un po' più tranquillo *oon paw pyoo trahnkweello*
outside/inside **in the corner** fuori/dentro d'angolo *fwawree/dentro* *dahngolo*	**May I please see the menu/wine list?** Per favore, posso vedere il menu/la lista dei vini *per fahvoray, pawsso vaydayray eel menoo/lah leestah de-ee veenee?*
on the terrace sulla terrazza *soollah terrahtsah*	

Could you please bring me some/a/an . . . ?
Per favore, mi può dare . . . ?
per fahvoray, mee pwaw dahray . . . ?

ashtray	un portacenere	*oon portachayneray*
fork	una forchetta	*oonah forkettah*
knife	un coltello	*oon koltello*
spoon	un cucchiaio	*oon kookkyahyo*
napkin	un tovagliolo	*oon tovahlyawlo*
plate	un piatto	*oon pyahtto*
glass	un bicchiere	*oon beekkyeray*
glass of water	un bicchier d'acqua	*oon beekkyer dahkwah*
bottle of mineral water/ wine	una bottiglia di acqua minerale/vino	*oonah botteelyah dee ahkwah meenerahlay/veeno*
bread/butter	del pane/del burro	*del pahnay/del boorro*
salt	il sale	*eel sahlay*
pepper	il pepe	*eel paypay*

ITALIAN

oil	dell'olio	*dellawlyo*
vinegar	dell'aceto	*dellahchayto*
mustard	della senape	*dellah senahpay*

What's the specialty of the house?
Qual'è la specialità della casa?
kwahle la spaychahleetah dellah kahzah?

What do you recommend?
Che cosa raccomanda lei?
kay kawzah rahkkomahndah le-ee?

I'd like something light.
Vorrei qualcosa di leggero.
vorre-ee kwahl kawzah dee lejjayro

Can you tell me what this is?
Mi può dire che cos'è questo?
mee pwaw deeray kay kawze kwesto?

I'll have . . .
Prenderò . . .
prenderaw . . .

The lady/gentleman will have . . .
La signora/il signore prenderà . . .
lah seenyorah/eel seenyoray prenderah . . .

It's very good.
È molto buono.
e molto bwawno

I didn't order this. I asked for . . .
Non ho ordinato questo. Ho chiesto . . .
non aw ordeenahto kwesto. aw kyaysto . . .

This is . . .
È troppo . . .
e trawppo . . .

overcooked	undercooked
cotto	poco cotto
kawtto	*pawko kawtto*

May I have something else?
Posso avere qualcos' altro?
pawsso ahvayray kwahlcawzahltro?

Check, please.
Il conto, per favore.
eel konto, per fahvoray

I think there's a mistake on the bill.
Penso che ci sia un errore nel conto.
penso kay chee see-a oon erroray nel konto

Is service included?
È compreso il servizio?
e komprayzo eel serveetsyo?

Do you take credit cards/traveler's checks?
Accettate le carte di credito/i traveler's check?
achettahtay lay kahrtay dee kraydeeto/ee traveler's check?

We enjoyed the meal very much.
Abbiamo gustato molto il pranzo.
ahbbyahmo goostahto molto eel prahndzo

Breakfast (Colazione)

Good morning. I'd like . . .
Buongiorno. Vorrei . . .
bwawn jorno. Vorre-ee . . .

some coffee.	un caffè	*oon kahffe*
some coffee with milk	un caffelatte	*oon kahffelahttay*
some hot tea	un tè caldo	*oon te kahldo*
with milk/lemon	con latte/limone	*kon lahttay/leemonay*
grapefruit/orange juice	un succo di pompelmo/arancia	*oon sookko dee pompelmo arahnchah*
bacon and eggs	uova e pancetta	*wawvah ay pahnchettah*
ham and eggs	uova e prosciutto	*wawvah ay proshootto*

a boiled egg	un uovo alla coque	*oon wawvo ahllah kawk*
a soft/hard boiled egg	molle/sodo	*mawlay sawdo*
fried eggs	uova fritte	*wawvah freettay*
scrambled eggs	uova strapazzate	*wawvah strahpahtsahtay*
an omelette	una frittata	*oonah freettahtah*
bread/rolls	del pane/delle rosette	*del pahnay/dellay rozettay*
butter	del burro	*del boorro*
jam	la marmellata	*lah mahrmellahtah*
sugar	lo zucchero	*lo dzookkero*
yoghurt	lo yoghurt	*lo yawgoort*
honey	del miele	*del myelay*
fruit	la frutta	*la froottah*

In Italy, a typical breakfast consists of a *caffelatte* or a *cappuccino* with a *brioche*, any of a number of different kinds of pastry, eaten standing up at the nearest *caffè*, or *bar*. What Italians would consider a quite substantial breakfast would be what we call a continental one, with rolls, butter, and jam. Only in luxury and first-class hotels will you find a typical American breakfast.

Antipasti / **Appetizers** / *ahnteepahstee*

Antipasti	**Appetizers**	*ahnteepahstee*
acciughe	**anchovies**	*ahchoogay*
affettati misti	**cold cuts of pork**	*ahffetahtee meestee*
antipasto misto	**assorted appetizers**	*ahnteepahsto meesto*
carciofi	**artichokes**	*kahrchawfee*
caviale	**caviar**	*kahvyahlay*
frutti di mare	**mixed seafood**	*frootee de mahray*
gamberetti	**shrimps**	*gahmberettee*
mortadella	**Bolognese sausage**	*mortahdellah*
olive	**olives**	*oleevay*
ostriche	**oysters**	*awstreekay*
prosciutto	**ham**	*proshootto*
affumicato	smoked	*ahffoomeekahto*
cotto	cooked	*kawtto*
crudo	cured	*kroodo*
salame	**salami**	*sahlahmay*
tartufi/trifoli	**white truffles**	*tahrtoofee/treefolee*

Antipasto misto
(ahnteepahsto meesto) — assorted appetizers

Bresaola
(brezaholah) — dried beef served with oil and lemon

Caponata
(kahponahtah) — fried eggplant with celery, onions, olives, and anchovies

Cozze in salsa piccante
(kawtse een sahlsah peekkahntay) — mussels in a sauce of anchovies, white wine and vinegar

ITALIAN

Crostini di fegato
(krosteenee dee faygahto)
chicken liver paste with capers and anchovies, served on fried bread or polenta (corn meal).

Fagiolini toscani con tonno
(fahjjoleenee toskahnee kon tawnno)
sauteed string beans with seasoned tuna and white beans

Insalata di frutti di mare
(eensahlahtah dee froottee dee mahray)
squid and prawns with lemon, pickles and olives

Melanzane ripiene
(melahntsahnay reepyaynay)
stuffed eggplant

Prosciutto e melone
(proshootto ay melonay)
cured ham with melon

Torta pasqualina
(tortah pahskwahleenah)
artichoke pie with eggs, mushrooms and Parmesan cheese

Pizze
(peetze)

Pizza

Capricciosa
(kahpreechozah)
filled with whatever the chef fancies

Margherita
(mahrgereetah)
made with tomatoes, basil, mozzarella and Parmesan

Napoletana
(nahpoletahnah)
made with tomatoes, anchovies, mozzarella, and oregano

Quattro stagioni
(kwahttro stahjonee)
four sections representing the four seasons: seafood; cheese with tomato and oregano; tomato, anchovies, capers, and oregano; tomato and anchovies.

Riso
(reezo)

Rice

Risotto alla milanese
reezawtto ahllah meelahnayzay
Rice cooked in beef marrow and wine, with onions, Parmesan, and saffron

Risi e bisi
(reezee ay beezee)
thick soup with bacon, fresh peas, onion, and rice, served with Parmesan cheese

Riso in binaco giallo
(reezo een byahnko jahllo)
boiled saffron rice with butter and parmesan

Riso di frutti di mare
(reezo dee froottee dee mahray)
rice cooked in fish stock with seafood

Riso ai funghi
(reezo ahee foongee)

rice with mushrooms

Riso alla veneziana
(reezo ahllah venetsyahnah)

a black risotto, made with cuttlefish and its ink sac and Swiss chard.

Pasta e farinacei
(pahstah ay fahreenahche-ee)

Pasta

Agnolotti
(ahnyolawttee)

see ravioli

Cannelloni
(kahnnellonee)

big tubes of home-made egg pasta, filled with ragù or a creamy spinach stuffing, baked in tomato sauce and topped with bechamel

-**alla partenopea**
(ahllah pahrtenopayah)

stuffed with mozzarella, ham, and ricotta, baked in seasoned tomato sauce

Fettuccine
(fettoocheenay)

flat, long strips of egg pasta, also called tagliatelle

-**al doppio burro**
(ahl doppyo boorro)

cooked in a mixture of butter, cream, and cheese

Gnocchi
(nyawkkee)

tiny dumplings usually made with potato and flour

-**alla genovese**
(ahllah jenovayzay)

served with tomato sauce and Parmesan cheese

-**in brodo**
(een brawdo)

in beef or chicken consomme

Lasagne
(lazahnyay)

large flat egg pasta, sometimes made with spinach, baked in layers with a ragù or spinach filling

-**pasticciate**
(pahsteechahtay)

spinach lasagne baked with ragù and bechamel

Linguine
(leengweenay)

flat, narrow pasta without egg

-**alle vongole**
(ahllay vongolay)

served with a sauce of baby clams, parsley, and tomato

Maccheroni
(mahkkeronee)

small tube-shaped pasta (macaroni)

-**Pasticcio di maccheroni**
(pahsteecho dee mahkeronee)

a sweet pastry pie filled with macaroni and spices

ITALIAN

Penne (maltagliati)
(pennay)

short, tube-shaped, ribbed or smooth pasta

-all'arrabbiata
(ahllahrrahbyahtah)

served with a sauce of tomato and hot red peppers with bacon

Ravioli
(rahvyawlee)

small squares of pasta filled with spinach, herbs, and ricotta, and served with cream or beef sauce

Spaghetti

-alla matriciana
(ahllah mahtreechahnah)

with bacon, tomatoes, onion, cheese, and chili pepper

-alla bolognese
(ahllah bolonyayzay)

served with a sauce made with ground beef and pork, prosciutto, tomatoes, vegetables, mushrooms, garlic, and herbs.

-alla carbonara
(ahllah kahrbonahrah)

served with bits of fried bacon, eggs, Parmesan and cream, to which should be added black pepper.

Tagliatelle
(tahlyahtellay)

see fettuccine

Tortellini
(tortelleenee)

small, stuffed pasta usually served in stock or a cream sauce. The stuffing is made with chopped ham, mortadella, chicken, pork, and veal, eggs, nutmeg, and Parmesan.

-alla panna
(ahllah pahnnah)

served with heavy cream and Parmesan

Trenette al Pesto
(traynette ahl pesto)

a smaller version of fettuccine, served with a savory sauce of basil, pine nuts, garlic, and grated pecorino.

Minestre
(meenesstray)

Soups

Brodetto
(brodetto)

fish broth served with clams, eel, squid, and white fish

Brodo
(brawdo)

consommé

  di manzo
  (dee mahntso)

beef consommé

  di pollo
  (dee pawllo)

chicken consommé

Minestra di bavette
(meenestrah dee bahvette)

broth with noodles, oregano, and cheese

ITALIAN

Minestrone alla milanese
(meenestronay ahllah meelahnayzay)

minestrone with vegetables, macaroni, and pork

Passatelli in brodo
(pahssatellee een brawdo)

chicken or beef consomme with noodles made of breadcrumbs, cheese, egg, nutmeg, and lemon.

Passato di verdura
(pahssahto dee vehrdoorah)

sieved green vegetable soup

Pasta e fagioli
(pahstah ay fahjjawlee)

thick white bean soup with pork and pasta

Ribollita alla fiorentina
(reebolleeta ahllah fyorenteenah)

thick soup made with white beans, vegetables, bread, cheese, and olive oil

Stracciatella
(strachatellah)

beef or chicken broth with egg, cheese paste, and semolina

Zuppa
(dzooppah)

soup

  di pesce
  (dee payshay)

spicy fish soup

  di verdura
  (dee verdoorah)

vegetable soup

  di vongole
  (dee vongolay)

clam soup

Pesce	**Fish and Seafood**	*payshay*
aragosta	lobster	*ahrahgawstah*
aringa	herring	*ahreengah*
capesante	scallops	*kahpaysahntay*
baccalà	dried salt cod	*bahkkahlah*
branzino	sea bass	*brahndzeeno*
calamaretti	baby squid	*kahlamahrettee*
calamari	squid	*kahlamahree*
carpa	carp	*kahrpah*
cozze	mussels	*kawtsay*
gamberetti	shrimps	*gahmberettee*
gamberi	crayfish	*gahmberee*
granchi	crabs	*grahnkee*
luccio	pike	*loocho*
lumache di mare	sea snails	*loomahkay dee mahray*
merluzzo	cod	*merlootso*
ostriche	oysters	*awstreekay*
pesce persico	perch	*payshay perseeko*

ITALIAN

pesce spada	swordfish	*payshay spahdah*
polipo	octopus	*pawleepo*
ricci	sea urchins	*reechee*
salmone	salmon	*sahlmonay*
sardine	sardines	*sahrdeenay*
scampi	prawns	*skahmpee*
sgombro	mackerel	*zgombro*
seppia	cuttlefish	*sayppyah*
sogliola	sole	*sawlyolah*
spigola	sea bass	*speegolah*
storione	sturgeon	*storyohnay*
tonno	tuna	*tawno*
triglia	red mullet	*treelyah*
trota	trout	*trawtah*
vongole	clams	*vongolay*

Anguilla in umido
(ahngweellah een oomeedo)

eel browned in oil and butter, simmered in white wine, lemon, tomato paste, and garlic

Baccalà alla vicentina
(bahkkahlah ahllah vee-chenteenah)

cod cooked in wine, oil and milk, with onion, garlic, anchovies, and herbs

Branzino ai ferri
(brahndzeeno ahee ferree)

sea bass, grilled

Calamaretti in umido
(kahlahmahrettee een oomeedo)

rings of squid stewed with onion, tomatoes, red wine, tomato paste, herbs, and garlic

Cernia ai ferri
(chernee-ah ahee fehrree)

grouper fish, grilled

Fritto misto di mare
(freetto meesto dee mahray)

deep fried assortment of seafood served with lemon juice

Pesce spada ai ferri
(payshay spahdah ahee ferree)

swordfish, grilled

Polipo affogato
(pawleepo ahffogahto)

octopus, poached and served in a tomato sauce

Sarde a beccafico
(sahrday ah bekkahfeeco)

stuffed sardines baked in lemon juice

Sogliola al burro e salvia
(sawlyolah ahl boorro ay sahlvyah)

sole sautéed in butter and sage

Triglia alla livornese
(treelyah ahllah leevornayzay)

red mullet, baked

Trota in bianco con maionese
*(**traw**tah een **byahn**ko kon mahyo**nay**zay)*

trout, boiled, served with mayonnaise

Vongole alla marinara
*(**von**golay **ahl**lah mahree**nah**rah)*

clams served in tomato sauce with basil

Pollame e cacciagione	**Fowl and Game**	*paw**l**lahmay ay kachee-ahjeeonay*
anatroccolo	**duckling**	*ahnah**trawk**kolo*
anitra	**duck**	*ah**nee**trah*
capretto	**kid goat**	*kah**pret**to*
cervo	**deer**	*cher**vo*
cinghiale	**wild boar**	*cheen**gyah**lay*
coniglio	**wild rabbit**	*ko**nee**lyo*
fagiano	**pheasant**	*fah**jah**no*
faraona	**guinea hen**	*fahrah**o**nah*
gallina	**hen**	*gah**llee**nah*
lepre	**hare**	*lay**pray*
oca	**goose**	*aw**ka*
pollo	**chicken**	*paw**llo*
pollo novello	**spring chicken**	*paw**llo novello*
porcellino da latte/porchetta	**suckling pig**	*porche**llee**no dah **laht**tay/ por**ket**tah*
quaglia	**quail**	*kwah**lyah*
tacchino	**turkey**	*tah**kkee**no*
tordo	**thrush**	*tor**do*

Coniglio alla cacciatora
*(ko**nee**lyo **ahl**lah kahchah**to**rah)*

rabbit, cooked in oil with vegetables, herbs, garlic, and wine

Faraona alla piemontese
*(fahrah**o**nah **ahl**lah pyaymon**tay**zay)*

guinea hen, stuffed with herbs, liver, and breadcrumbs, cooked with white wine and vegetables

Fagiano in caseruola
*(fah**jah**no een kahsser**waw**lah)*

pheasant, cooked in cognac and butter

Filetti di tacchino alla bolognese
*(fee**let**tee dee tah**kkee**no **ahl**lah bolon**yay**zay)*

turkey breasts fried with white truffles, ham and cheese

ITALIAN

Lepre in salmì
(laypray een sahlmee)

hare marinated in wine, herbs, garlic, and anchovies

Palombacci alla perugina
(pahlombahchee ahllah peroojeenah)

roast squab in red wine sauce with olives, juniper berries, sage, and sometimes with their intestines

Petti di pollo
(pettee dee pawllo)

chicken breasts

-alla valdostana
(ahllah vahldostahnah)

cooked with cheese, white truffles, white wine, and brandy

-alla bolognese
(ahllah bolonyayzay)

baked with ham, cheese, and white truffles

Pollo
(pawllo)

chicken

-alla cacciatora
(ahllah kahchahtorah)

cooked with tomatoes, mushrooms, and herbs; sometimes with black olives and anchovies

-alla diavola
(ahllah dyahvolah)

grilled

-alla romana
(ahllah romahnah)

braised with sweet peppers, tomatoes, rosemary, onion, ham, oil, and butter

Quaglie arroste con polenta
(kwahlyay ahrrawstay kon polentah)

quails, roasted with polenta (a cornmeal mush)

Tacchino arrosto ripieno
(tahkkeeno ahrrawsto reepyayno)

turkey, roasted and stuffed

Tordi in salmì
(tordee een sahlmee)

thrushes served with a sauce of pureed thrush meat, oil, Marsala wine, olives, and juniper berries

Uccelletti
(oochelettee)

small birds, usually skewered and roasted

Carne	Meats	*kahrnay*
agnello	lamb	*ahnyello*
animelle di vitello	sweetbreads	*ahneemellay dee veetello*
bistecca	steak	*beestaykkah*
bistecca di filetto	rib steak	*beestaykkah dee feeletto*
braciola	chop	*brahcholah*
costola	rib	*kawstolah*
costolette	cutlet	*kawstolette*
cervello	brains	*chervello*
fegato	liver	*faygahto*

ITALIAN

filetto	filet	feeletto
lingua	tongue	leengwah
maiale	pork	mahyahlay
manzo	beef	mahndzo
montone	mutton	montonay
polpette	meatballs	polpettay
porchetta	suckling pig	porkettah
rognoni	kidneys	ronyonee
salumi	assorted pork	sahloomee
salsicce	sausages	sahlseechay
scaloppina	scallop	skahloppeenah
trippe	tripe	treeppay
vitello	veal	veetello
zampa	pig's foot	dzahmpah

Carne
(*kahr*nay)

Meat Dishes

Abbacchio al forno
(ahb*bahk*kyo ahl *for*no)

roast lamb

Bistecca alla fiorentina
(bee*stayk*kah *ahl*lah
fyoren*tee*nah)

large rib steak, grilled and sometimes flavored with parsley and lemon juice

Bollito misto
(bol*leet*o *mees*to)

an assortment of boiled meats (beef,
chicken, veal, sausage, and tongue)
served with a green sauce

**Bracciolette a scotta-
dito**
(brahcho*let*tay a scawt-
tah*dee*to)

grilled lamb cutlets

Brasato alla genovese
(brah*zah*to *ahl*lah
jenoh*vay*zay)

beef braised in red wine with tomatoes,
carrots, onions, and mushrooms

Carpaccio
(kahr*pah*cho)

thin slices of raw beef with a mustard
sauce; sometimes served with olive oil
and lemon juice

Cima di vitello
(*chee*ma dee vee*tel*lo)

rolled veal stuffed with vegetables,
sweetbreads, eggs, and nuts, served cold.

Cotechino con lenticchie
(kotek*kee*no kon
len*teek*kyay)

boiled pork sausage served with lentils

Costoletta alla milanese
(kawsto*let*tah *ahl*lah
meelah*nay*zay)

veal cutlet, breaded and fried

ITALIAN

Fegato alla veneziana
(faygahto ahllah venetsyahnah)

thinly sliced calf's liver cooked with onions

Involtini alla cacciatora
(eenvolteenee ahllah kahchahtorah)

thin slices of veal rolled and stuffed with a chicken liver filling, skewered in butter

Osso buco alla milanese
(awsso booko ahllah meelahnayzay)

veal knuckle braised in white wine and a savory tomato sauce

Noce di vitello arrosto
(nochay dee veetello arrawsto)

roast top round of veal served with bechamel

Porchetta
(porkettah)

roasted suckling pig seasoned with rosemary and garlic

Saltimbocca alla romana
(sahlteembokkah ahllah romahnah)

rolled or flat escalope of veal, layered with ham and sage and braised in butter and Marsala wine

Scaloppine
(skahlohppeenay)

escalopes of veal sauteed in butter and Marsala wine, served with a white cream and mushroom sauce

    alla marsala
    (ahllah mahrsahlah)

    alla crema con funghi
    (ahllah kraymah kon foongee)

Spezzatino di vitello
(spetsahteeno dee veetello)

veal stew including wine, sweet peppers, and tomato

Trippa alla fiorentina
(treeppah ahllah fyorenteenah)

braised tripe served with a savory tomato sauce

Vitello tonnato
(veetello tonnahto)

cold veal served with a sauce of tuna fish

Zampone di Modena
(dzahmponay dee mawdenah)

pork meat stuffed into a pig's foot and boiled

Ways of Preparing Meat, Poultry, Game, and Fish

baked	al forno	*ahl forno*
barbecued	alla graticola	*ahllah grahteecolah*
boiled	lesso	*lesso*
braised	brasato	*brahzahto*
broiled	allo spiedo	*ahllo spyaydo*
en casserole	in casseruola	*een kahsserwawlah*
fried	fritto	*freetto*
grilled	ai ferri, alla griglia	*ahee ferree*
marinated	marinato	*mahreenahto*
roasted	arrostito	*arrawsto*

smoked	affumicato	*ahffoomeekahto*
stewed	in umido	*een oomeedo*
stuffed	farcito, ripieno	*fahrcheeto, reepyayno*
rare	al sangue	*ahl sahngway*
medium	a puntino	*ah poonteeno*
well-done	ben cotto	*ben cawtto*

Contorni, legumi, verdure	**Vegetables**	*kontornee, laygoomee, verdooray*
asparagi	**asparagus**	*ahspahrahjee*
carciofi	**artichokes**	*kahrchawfee*
cavolfiore	**cauliflower**	*kahvolfyoray*
cavoli	**cabbage**	*kahvolee*
cavolini di Bruxelles	**brussels sprouts**	*kahvoleenee dee brewksell*
ceci	**chick-peas**	*chaychee*
cetrioli	**cucumbers**	*chetree-awlee*
cicoria	**chicory**	*cheekoreeah*
cipolle	**onions**	*cheepawllay*
fagioli	**white beans**	*fahjawlee*
fagiolini	**string beans**	*fahjoleenee*
finocchio	**fennel**	*feenawkkyo*
funghi	**mushrooms**	*foongee*
lattuga	**lettuce**	*lahttoogah*
lenticchie	**lentils**	*lenteekkyay*
mais dolce	**corn**	*maheess dolchay*
melanzane	**eggplant**	*melahntsahnay*
patate	**potatoes**	*pahtahtay*
peperoni	**peppers**	*paypayronee*
piselli	**peas**	*peezellee*
pomodori	**tomatoes**	*pawmodoree*
radicchio	**red lettuce**	*rahdeekkyo*
rape	**turnips**	*rahpay*
ravanelli	**radishes**	*rahvahnellee*
sedano	**celery**	*saydahno*
spinaci	**spinach**	*speenahchee*
tartufi	**truffles**	*tahrtoofee*
verdura mista	**mixed vegetabes**	*verdoorah meestah*
zucca	**pumpkin**	*dzookkah*
zucchini	**zucchini**	*dzookkeenee*

Asparagi alla fiorentina
(ahspahrahjee ahllah fyorenteenah)
asparagus boiled and served with melted butter and fried eggs

Carciofi alla giudia
(kahrchawfee ahllah joodeeah)
artichokes deep fried in oil

ITALIAN

Fagioli con le cotiche
(fahjawlee kon lay koteekay)
white beans cooked with pork rind and tomato sauce

Fagioli all'uccelletto
(fahjawlee ahlloochelletto)
white beans boiled and cooked in tomato sauce with oil, sage, and garlic

Fagiolini
(fahjoleenee)
string beans, usually served cold with lemon juice and olive oil.

Finocchio al forno
(feenawkkyo ahl forno)
fennel, boiled and baked with butter and grated cheese

Fiori di zucca
(fyoree dee dzookkah)
squash flowers fried in batter

Funghi trifolati
(foongee treefolahtee)
mushrooms sliced and fried in oil and garlic, served with chopped anchovies, parsley, lemon and butter

Melanzane ripiene
(maylahntsahnay reepyaynay)
stuffed eggplant

Patatine novelle fritte
(pahtahteenay novellay freettay)
new potatoes, fried

Piselli alla romana
(peezellee ahllah romahnah)
peas cooked with butter and bits of onion and ham

Spinaci alla parmigiana
(speenahchee ahllah pahrmeejahnah)
spinach served with butter and parmesan cheese

Salads

Insalata
(eensahlahtah)
salad

  mista *(meestah)* — mixed
  di pomodori *(dee pawmodoree)* — sliced tomatoes
  verde *(verday)* — green

Formaggi
(formahjjee)

Cheese

Bel paese
(bel pahayzay)
made from cow's milk, it is soft and bland

Caciotta
(cahchawttah)
made from various kinds of milk, it is soft and mild

Fontina
(fonteenah) · bland cheese made from cow's milk

Gorgonzola
(gorgondzawlah) · a veined blue cheese

Mascarpone
(mahskahrponay) · unsalted cream cheese

Mozzarella
(motsahrellah) · white cheese made from buffalo or cow's milk

Parmigiano
(pahrmeejahno) · sharp and salty

Pecorino romano
(pekoreeno romahno) · made from ewe's milk; hard and sharp

Provolone
(provolonay) · spicy sharp cheese

Ricotta
(reekawttah) · fresh, moist cottage cheese made from ewe's milk

Stracchino
(strahkkeeno) · soft white cheese

Taleggio
(tahlejjio) · mild, creamy cheese

Frutta · Fruit
(froottah)

albicocche
(ahlbeekawkkay) · apricots

arance
(ahrahnchay) · oranges

banane
(bahnahnay) · bananas

cocomero
(kokomero) · watermelon

fichi
(feekkee) · figs

fragole
(frahgolay) · strawberries

lamponi
(lahmpohnee) · raspberries

mandarino
(mahndahreeno) · mandarine

mele
(maylay) · apples

melone
(melonay) · melon

mirtilli
(meerteellee) · blueberries

more
(mawray) · blackberries

pere
(payray) · pears

pesche
(peskay) · peaches

prugne
(proonyay) · blue plums

susine
(soozeenay) · red plums

uva
(oovah) · grapes

ITALIAN

Dolci (dolchee)	Desserts
bongo-bongo (bongo-bongo)	small cream puffs covered with chocolate sauce
budino (boodeeno)	pudding
cannoli (kahnnawlee)	horns of pastry filled with sweet ricotta
composta di frutta (kompawstah dee frootah)	stewed fruit
crema (kraymah)	custard
gelato (jelahto)	ice cream
macedonia di frutta (mahchedawneeah dee froottah)	fruit cocktail
millefoglie (meellayfawlyay)	thin layers of delicate pastry with a custard filling and icing sugar
meringa (mereengah)	meringue
monte bianco (montay byahnko)	sieved roasted chestnuts with whipped cream
torta di riso (tortah dee reezo)	sweet rice pudding cake
zuppa inglese (dzooppah eenglayzay)	trifle with sponge cake, cream, and liqueur

DRINKS

Non-alcoholic Drinks

Cold Beverages

I'd like a . . .	Vorrei . . .	*vorre-ee . . .*
glass of	un bicchiere di	*oon beekkyeray dee*
bottle of	una bottiglia di	*oonah botteelyah dee*
(mineral) water	acqua (minerale)	*ahkwah meenerahlay*
carbonated	gassata	*gahssahtah*
regular	naturale	*nahtoorahlay*

ITALIAN

apricot juice	un succo di albicocca	oon **sook**ko dee ahlbee**kawk**kah
grapefruit juice	un succo di pompelmo	oon **sook**ko dee pompelmo
lemon soda	una limonata	**oo**nah leemoh**nah**tah
orange soda	un'aranciata	oonahrahn**chah**tah
fresh-squeezed orange/lemon juice	una spremuta di arancia/limone	**oo**nah spray**moo**tah dee ah**rahn**chah/lee**moh**nay
peach juice	un succo di pesca	oon **sook**ko dee **pay**skah
pear juice	un succo di pera	oon **sook**ko dee **pay**rah
tomato juice	un succo di pomodoro	oon **sook**ko dee paw**mo**doro
milkshake with fresh fruit	un frullato di frutta	oon froo**llah**to dee **froo**ttah
iced tea	un tè freddo	oon te **frayd**do
iced coffee	un caffè freddo	oon kahffe **frayd**do

Hot Beverages

an expresso	un espresso	oon es**press**o
very strong expresso	un ristretto	oon ree**stray**tto
somewhat less concentrated expresso	un caffè lungo	oon kahffe **loon**go
espresso with a drop of milk	un caffè macchiato	oon kahffe mahk**kyah**to
espresso coffee with steamed milk, dusted with cocoa.	un cappuccino	oon kahppoo**chee**no
coffee with hot milk	un caffelatte	oon kahffela**htt**ay
steamed milk with a small amount of coffee	un latte macchiato	oon **lah**ttay mahk**kyah**to
espresso with liqueur	un caffè corretto	oon kahffe ko**rre**tto
decaffeinated coffee	un Hag	oon ahg
hot chocolate	un cioccolato	oon chokko**lah**to
hot tea	un tè caldo	oon te **kahl**do
with milk/lemon	con latte/limone	kon **lah**ttay/lee**moh**nay

ITALIAN

Alcoholic Drinks

The following alcoholic beverages have the same names in Italian:

bourbon	gin & tonic	vermouth
brandy	rum	vodka
cognac	Scotch	whisky
gin/gin fizz	sherry	whisky and soda

Others:

aperitif	un aperitivo	*oon ahpereeteevo*
beer	una birra	*oonah beerrah*
light/dark	chiara/scura	*kyahrah/skoorah*
bottle/draft	bottiglia/alla spina	*botteelyah/ahllah speenah*
cordial	un liquore	*oon leekworay*
port	un porto	*oon porto*
straight	liscio	*leesho*
on the rocks	con ghiaccio	*kon gyahcho*
with soda water	con soda	*kon sawda*

Some Favorite Aperitifs:

Americano
(ahmereekahno)
vermouth with Campari, club soda, and lemon peel

Aperol
(ahperol)
non-alcoholic, somewhat bitter

Campari con soda
(kahmpahree kon sawdah)
a reddish-brown quinine-tasting drink, to which herbs and orange peel are added; mixed with club soda

Cinzano
(cheentsahno)
a sweet or dry vermouth made from wine and herbs

Cynar
(cheenahr)
made with artichoke extract, may be mixed with club soda

Martini
(mahrteenee)
a type of vermouth, not to be confused with the American mixed drink

Negroni
(negrohnee)
sweet vermouth mixed with Campari and gin or vodka

And Some Favorite Digestivi, or After-dinner Drinks:

Amaro Averna
(ahmahro ahverna)
a Sicilian liqueur made from bitter herbs

Amaretto di Saronno
(ahmahretto dee sahrawnno)
a sweet liqueur made from almonds

Anisetta
(ahneezaytta)
a sweet liqueur made from aniseed, has a strong licorice taste

Galliano
(gahllyahno)
a sweet liqueur, golden in color, made from flowers, spices, and herbs

ITALIAN

Fernet-Branca
(fernet-brahnkah)

to many, a cure-all for any problems associated with digestion; it is made from aloes, gentian, rhubarb, myrrh, camomile, saffron, peppermint oil, and various herbs; *very* bitter. Beware: an overdose may produce a laxative effect.

Fra Angelico
(frah ahnjeleeko)

a liqueur made from hazel nuts, berries, and flowers

Sambuca
(sahmbookah)

a sweet licorice-flavored liqueur, often taken with espresso

Strega
(straygah)

a sweet and spicy liqueur made from more than 70 herbs

Tuaca
(tooahkah)

a sweet liqueur made from herbs

You may want to try these Italian brandies, or cognacs:

Grappa
(grahppah)

distilled grape residue, made from grapes grown in the northern regions of Italy

Stock 84
(stok ottahntah-kwahttro)

another type of *acqua vitae*, also made from grapes

Wine

Which wine do you recommend?
Quale vino ci suggerisce?
*kwahlay **veeno** chee soojereeshay?*

I'd like a . . . wine
Vorrei un vino . . .
*vorre-ee oon **veeno** . . .*

Which wine goes with this dish?
Quale vino va con questo piatto?
*kwahlay **veeno** vah kon **kwesto pyaht**to?*

dry	secco	**say**kko
sweet	dolce	**dohl**chay
light	leggero	le**jero**
sparkling	spumante	spoo**mahn**tay
full-bodied	pieno	**pyay**no
red	rosso	**rohs**so
rosé	rosatello, rosato	rawza**tello**, rawza**hto**
white	bianco	**byahn**ko

ITALIAN

Please bring a . . . of . . .
Per favore, mi porti . . . di . . .
Per fahvoray, mee portee . . . dee . . .

bottle	una bottiglia	*oonah botteelyah*
carafe	una caraffa	*oonah kahrahffah*
half-bottle	una mezza bottiglia	*oonah medzah botteelyah*
liter	un litro	*oon leetro*
half liter	un mezzo litro	*oon medzo leetro*
quarter-liter	un quartino	*oon kwahrteeno*
glass	un bicchiere	*oon beekyeray*

I'd like to try some of the local wine.
Vorrei provare un vino del posto.
vorre-ee provahray oon veeno del pawsto

SIGHTSEEING

Where is the tourist office?
Dov'è l'ufficio turistico?
dove looffeecho tooreesteeko?

We would like to see the main points of interest.
Vorremmo vedere i principali punti di interesse.
vorremmo vaydayray ee preencheepahlee poontee dee eentayressay

We will be here for . . .
Siamo qui per . . .
syahmo kwee per . . .

a few hours
qualche ora
kwahlkay orah

a few days
qualche giorno
kwahlkay jorno

a day
un giorno
oon jorno

a week
una settimana
oonah setteemahnah

Is there a sightseeing tour?
C'è un giro turistico?
che oon jeero tooreesteeko?

Where does it go?
Dove va?
dovay vah?

We would like to see . . .
Vorremmo vedere . . .
vorremmo vaydayray . . .

Could you direct me to the . . . ?
Mi può dire dov'è/dove sono . . . ?
Mee pwaw deeray dove/dovay sono . . . ?

How long is it?
Quanto dura?
kwahnto doorah?

How much is it?
Quanto costa?
kwahnto kawstah?

When/where will the bus pick us up?
Quando/dove ci viene a prendere l'autobus?
kwahndo/dove chee vyenay ah prendayray lowtoboos?

Does the guide speak English?
Parla inglese la guida?
pahrlah eenglayzay lah gweedah?

art gallery	la galleria d'arte	*lah gahllereeah dahrtay*
castle	il castello	*eel kahstello*
catacombs	le catacombe	*lay kahtahkombay*

ITALIAN

cathedral	la cattedrale	*kahttedrahlay*
cemetery	il cimitero	*eel cheemeetayro*
church	la chiesa	*lah kyayzah*
city center	il centro città	*eel chentro cheettah*
fortress	la fortezza	*lah fortetsah*
fountain	la fontana	*lah fontahnah*
gardens	i giardini	*ee jahrdeenee*
harbor	il porto	*eel porto*
lake	il lago	*eel lahgo*
monastery	il monastero	*eel monastero*
museum	il museo	*eel moozayo*
old city	la città vecchia	*lah cheettah vekkyah*
opera house	il teatro dell'opera	*eel tayahtro dellawperah*
palace	il palazzo	*eel pahlahtso*
planetarium	il planetario	*eel plahnetahryo*
ruins	le rovine	*lay roveenay*
sanctuary	il santuario	*eel sahntooahryo*
shops	i negozi	*ee negawtsee*
statue	la statua	*lah stahtooah*
tomb	la tomba	*lah tombah*
university	l'università	*looneeverseetah*
zoo	lo zoo	*lo dzo*

When is the . . . open?
Quando è aperto/a il/la . . . ?
kwahndo e ahperto/ah eel/lah . . . ?

At what time does it close?
A che ora si chiude?
ah kay orah see kyooday?

How much is the admission?
Quant'è l'entrata?
kwahnte lentrahtah?

The admission is free.
L'entrata è libera.

Is there a reduction for children/ students/senior citizens?
C'è una riduzione per bambini/studenti/ persone anziane?
Che oonah reedootsyonay per bahmbeenee/stoodentee/personay ahntsyahnay?

Where does one buy tickets?
Dove si comprano i biglietti?
Dovay see komprahno ee beelyettee?

Where can I find . . . ?
Dove posso trovare . . . ?
Dovay pawsso trovahray . . . ?

a catalogue	**the . . . collection**
un catalogo	la collezione . . .
oon kahtahlogo	*lah kolletsyonay . . .*

a guidebook
una guida
oonah gweedah

the . . . exhibit
la mostra di . . .
lah mostrah dee . . .

post cards
delle cartoline
dellay kahrtoleenay

the souvenir shop
il negozio di ricordi
eel negawtsyo dee reekordee

Am I allowed to take photographs?
Posso fare delle foto?
Pawsso fahray dellay fawto?

ITALIAN

HAVING FUN

Daytime Activities

Soccer

Let's go to the football game.
Andiamo alla partita di calcio.
ahndyahmo ahllah pahrteetah dee kahlcho

Where is the stadium?
Dov'è lo stadio?
Dove lo stahdyo?

Who is playing?
Chi gioca?
kee jawkah?

I would like two tickets . . .
Vorrei due biglietti . . .
vorre-ee dooay beelyettee . . .

in the sun	in the shade
al sole	all'ombra
ahl solay	*ahllombrah*

When does it start?
Quando inizia?
kwahndo eeneetsyah?

What is the score?
Qual'è il punteggio?
Kwahle eel poontejjo?

Tennis

Would you like to play tennis?
Vorrebbe/vuoi giocare a tennis?
Vorrebbay/vwawee jokahray ah tennees?

Where are the tennis courts?
Dove sono i campi da tennis?
Dovay sono ee kahmpee da tennees?

What's the charge for the use of the courts per hour/for half an hour?
Quanto si paga per l'uso d'un campo all'ora/per mezz'ora?
kwahnto see pahgah per loozo doon kahmpo ahllorah/per medzorah?

Is it possible to rent rackets?
È possibile affittare delle racchette?
e posseebeelay ahffeettahray dellay rahkkayttay?

I would like to buy a can of tennis balls.
Vorrei comprare un barattolo di palle da tennis.
vorre-ee komprahray oon bahrahtolo dee pahllay da tennees

Let's go to the tennis tournament.
Andiamo al torneo di tennis.
ahndyahmo ahl tornayo dee tennees

I want to watch/play the men's/women's singles/doubles.
Voglio guardare/giocare il singolo/il doppio maschile/femminile.
vawllyo gwahrdahray jokahray eel seengolo/eel doppyo mahskeelay/femmeeneelay

Golf

Where's the nearest golf course?
Dove si trova il campo da golf più vicino?
*dovay see trawvah eel kahmpo da golf
   pyoo veecheeno?*

Is it open to nonmembers?
È aperto ai non iscritti?
e ahperto ah-ee non eeskreettee?

**How much does it cost per hour/day/
round?**
Quanto costa per un'ora/un giorno/una
   partita?
*kwahnto kawstah per oon orah/oon
   jorno/oonah pahrteetah?*

I would like to rent a caddy/golf clubs.
Vorrei impegnare un caddi/un assortimento di bastoni.
vorre-ee eempenyahray oon kahddee/oon ahssorteemaynto dee bahstonee

I would like to buy some golf balls.
Vorrei comprare delle palle da golf.
*vorre-ee komprahray dellay pahllay
   da golf*

**Would you like to play a round with
me?**
Vuole/vuoi giocare una partita con me?
*Vwawlay/vwawee jokahray oonah
   pahrteetah kon may?*

Where's the next tee?
Dov'è il prossimo "tee"?
Dove eel prawsseemo tee?

Horseback riding

Is there a riding stable nearby?
C'è un campo di equitazione qui vicino?
*Che oon kahmpo dee
   ekweetahtsyonay kwee veecheeno?*

I would like to rent a horse.
Vorrei noleggiare un cavallo.
vorre-ee nolejjahray oon kahvahllo

What's the charge per hour?
Qual'è il prezzo per un'ora?
kwahle eel pretso per oon orah?

I would like to take riding lessons.
Vorrei prendere delle lezioni di
   equitazione.
*vorre-ee prendayray dellay letsyonee
   dee ekweetahtsyonay*

I am a beginner/experienced rider.
Sono un fantino dilettante/esperto.
*sono oon fahnteeno deelettahntay/
   esperto*

**Could you give me a gentle horse,
please?**
Mi può dare un cavallo calmo, per
   favore?
*mee pwaw dahray oon kavahllo
   kahlmo, per fahvoray?*

I would like a good jumper.
Vorrei un saltatore.
vorre-ee oon sahltahtoray

Skiing

Would you ilke to go skiing?
Vuole/vuoi andare a sciare?
*vwawlay/vwawee ahndahray a
   shyahray?*

How do we get to the ski slopes?
Come si accede alle piste di sci?
*Komay see ahchayday ahllay peestay
   dee shee?*

ITALIAN

What are the skiing conditions like at . . . ?
Come sono le condizioni per sciare a . . . ?
komay sono le kondeetsyonee per shyahray ah . . . ?

Is it possible to take skiing lessons?
È possibile prendere delle lezioni di sci?
*e posseebeelay prendayray dellay
letsyonee dee shee?*

**Is it possible to rent skiing
equipment?**
È possibile noleggiare una tenuta da sci?
*e posseebeelay nolejjahray oonah
tenootah dah shee?*

These boots are too tight/loose.
Questi scarponi mi stanno troppo stretti/
larghi.
*kwestee skahrponee mee stahnno
trawppo strayttee lahrgee*

Could you help me put on the skis?
Può aiutarmi a mettere gli sci?
*pwaw ahyootahrmee ah metteray lyee
shee?*

**How much are the lift tickets for a
day/two days/a week?**
Qual'è il prezzo dei bigletti per lo skilift
per un giorno/due giorni/una
settimana?
*kwahle eel pretso de-ee beel-yettee
per lo skee leeft per oon jorno/dooay
jornee/oonah setteemahnah?*

**I'm looking for a beginner's/
intermediate/expert trail.**
Cerco una pista per principianti/
di media difficoltà/per sciatori esperti.
*cherko oonah peestah per
preencheepyahntee/dee maydyah
deefeekawltah/per shyahtoree
espertee*

OR: bianca (**beginner's**)/verde (**intermediate**)/rosso (**advanced**)/nera (**expert**)
(*byahnkah/verday/rosso/nayrah*)

Swimming

Would you like to go swimming?
Vuoi andare a nuotare?
vwaw-ee ahndahray ah nwawtahray?

Let's go to the beach/swimming pool.
Andiamo alla spiaggia/in piscina.
*ahndyahmo ahllah spyahjjah/een
peesheenah*

Is it safe for swimming?
Si può nuotare senza pericolo?
*see pwaw nwawtahray sentsah
pereekolo?*

I'd like to rent . . .
Vorrei noleggiare . . .
vorre-ee nolejjahray . . .

a deckchair
una sedia a sdraio
oonah saydyah a zdrahyo

a changing room
una cabina
oonah kahbeenah

a beach umbrella
un ombrellone
oon ombrellonay

Evening Activities

Would you like to go to . . . ?
Vorrebbe/vorresti andare . . . ?
vorraybay/vorrestee ahndahray . . . ?

the movies	the theatre
al cinema	al teatro
ahl cheenaymah	*ahl tay-ahtro*

the opera   the ballet
all'opera   al balletto
ahllawperah   *ahl bahlletto*

a concert
ad un concerto
ahd oon koncherto

Who's in it?
Chi sono gli interpreti?
kee sono lyee eenterpretee?

Who's singing?
Chi canta?
kee kahntah?

Who's dancing?
Chi danza?
kee dahntsah?

What orchestra is playing?
Che orchestra suona?
kay orkestrah swawnah?

At what time does it begin?
A che ora inizia?
ah kay orah eeneetsyah?

I would like to reserve/buy two tickets for . . .
Vorrei prenotare/comprare due biglietti per . . .
vorre-ee praynotahray komprahray dooay beelyettee per . . .

Could you show me a seating plan of the theatre?
Mi può far vedere un diagramma con la disposizione dei posti?
mee pwaw fahr vaydayray oon deeagrahmah kon lah deespozeetsyone de-ee pawstee?

Please give me two orchestra/ mezzanine/box/balcony seats.
Per favore, mi dia due biglietti di platea/ prima galleria/palco/seconda galleria.
per fahvoray, mee deeah dooay beelyettee dee plahtayah/preemah gahllereeah/pahlko/saykondah gahllereeah

Would you like to go to a night club/ discotheque?
Vorebbe/vuoi andare ad un "night"/ una discoteca?
vorrebbay/vwawee ahndahray ahd oon naheet/oonah deeskotaykah?

How much does it cost to get in?
Quanto costa l'entrata?
kwahnto kawstah lentrahtah?

What's the minimum?
Quant'è la consumazione minima?
kwahnte lah konsoomahtsyonay meeneemah?

Would you like a drink?
Vuole/vuoi qualcosa da bere?
vwawlay/vwaw-ee kwahlkawzah dah bayray?

Would you like to dance?
Vuole/vuoi ballare?
vwawlay/vwawee bahllahray?

Getting to Know People

How are you?
Come sta?
komay stah?

Fine, thanks.
Bene, grazie.
benay grahtsyay

My name is . . .
Mi chiamo . . .
mee kyahmo . . .

ITALIAN

This is . . .
Le presento . . .
lay prayzento . . .

my wife/husband
mia moglie/mio marito
meeah molyay/meeo mahreeto

my daughter/son
mia figlia/mio figlio
meeah feelyah/meeo feelyo

my sister/my brother
mia sorella/mio fratello
meeah sorellah/meeo frahtello

a friend of mine
una mia amica/un mio amico
oonah meeah ahmeekah/oon meeo ahmeeko

Glad to meet you.
Molto lieto/lieta.
molto lyeto/lyetah

Where are you from?
Di dov'è lei?
dee dove le-ee?

I'm from . . .
Sono di . . .
sono dee . . .

Are you here on vacation?
È qui in vacanza?
e kwee een vahkahntsah?

No, I'm on a business trip.
No, sono qui in viaggio d'affari.
naw, sono kwee een vyahjjo dahffahree

I'm here for business and pleasure.
Sono in viaggio d'affari e di piacere.
sonó een vyahjjo dahffahree ay dee pyahchayray

Are you on your own?
È qui da solo/sola?
e kwee dah solo/solah

I'm with a friend/friends/my family.
Sono con un amico/a degli amici/la mia famiglia.
sono kon oon ahmeeko/ah delyee ahmeechee/lah meeahfahmeelyah

How long have you been here?
Da quanto tempo è qui?
dah kwahnto tempo e kwee?

I've just arrived today.
Sono arrivato oggi.
sono ahrreevahto awjjee

I arrived yesterday/a few days ago.
Sono arrivato ieri/qualche giorno fa.
sono ahrreevahto eeyeree kwahlkay jorno fah

I've been here a week/two weeks/ a month.
Sono qui da una settimana/due settimane/un mese.
sono kwee dah oonah setteemahnah/dooay setteemahnay/oon mayzay

How do you like it here?
Le piace qui?
lay pyahchay kwee?

I like it very much.
Mi piace molto.
mee pyahchay molto

It's a . . . place.
È un posto . . .
e oon pawsto . . .

beautiful bellissimo *belleesseemo*	**relaxing** rilassante *reelahssahntay*
fun divertente *deevertentay*	**interesting** interessante *eenteressahntay*

I don't like it very much.
Non mi piace molto.
non mee pyahchay molto

It's too . . .
È troppo . . .
e trawppo . . .

crowded affollato *ahffollahto*	**boring** noioso *noyozo*
noisy rumoroso *roomorozo*	**ugly** brutto *brootto*
depressing triste *treestay*	

How long are you going to stay?
Quanto tempo si trattiene?
kwahnto tempo see trahttyaynay?

A few more days / weeks.
Ancora qualche giorno / settimana.
ahnkorah kwahlkay jorno / setteemahnah

I'm leaving tomorrow / soon.
Parto domani / presto.
pahrto domahnee / presto

Are you having a good time?
Si sta divertendo?
see stah deevertendo?

Yes, very much.
Sì, molto.
see, molto

No, not really.
No, non veramente.
naw, non vayrahmayntay

Where are you staying?
Dove soggiorna?
dovay sojjornah?

We're at the . . . Hotel.
Siamo all'albergo . . .
syahmo ahllahlbergo . . .

We're camping.
Stiamo campeggiando.
styahmo kahmpejjahndo

We haven't found a place yet.
Non abbiamo ancora trovato un posto.
non ahbbyahmo ahnkorah trovahto oon pawsto

Do you know of a good hotel / pension?
Conosce lei un buon albergo / una pensione?
conoshay le-ee oon bwawn ahlbergo / oonah pensyonay?

What do you do?	Di cosa si occupa?	*Dee kawzah see awkkoopah?*
I'm an . . .	Sono . . .	*sono . . .*
artist	artista	*ahrteestah*
businessman	commerciante	*kommerchahntay*
doctor	medico	*medeeko*
factory worker	operaio	*operahyo*
lawyer	avvocato	*ahvvokahto*
secretary	segretaria	*segretahreeah*
student	studente	*stoodentay*
teacher	professore	*professoray*
writer	scrittore	*skreettoray*

Where do you live?
Dove abita?
dovay ahbeetah?

I live in . . .
Abito . . .
ahbeeto . . .

the United States		**Great Britain**
negli Stati Uniti		in Gran Bretagna
nelyee stahtee ooneetee		*een grahn bretahnyah*

Canada	**Australia**	**Let me know if you ever go there.**
in Canada	in Australia	Mi faccia sapere se ci va un giorno.
een Kahnahdah	*een owstrahlyah*	*mee fahtchah sahpayray say chee vah oon jorno*

ITALIAN

Here is my address/phone number
Ecco il mio indirizzo/numero di
telefono.
*ekko eel meeo eendeereetso/noomero
dee taylefono*

I'm interested in . . .
M'interesso di . . .
meenteresso dee . . .

anthropology	antropologia	*ahntropolojeeah*
antiques	antichità	*ahnteekeetah*
archaeology	archeologia	*ahrkayawlojeeah*
architecture	architettura	*ahrkeetettoorah*
art	arte	*ahrtay*
botany	botanica	*botahneekah*
chess	scacchi	*skahkkee*
cinema	cinema	*cheenaymah*
coins	numismatica	*noomeezmahteekah*
cooking	cucina	*coocheenah*
dance	danza	*dahntsah*
foreign languages	lingue straniere	*leengway strahnyeray*
gardening	giardinaggio	*jahrdeenahdjo*
geology	geologia	*jayawlojeeah*
history	storia	*stawreeah*
literature	letteratura	*laytayrahtoorah*
medicine	medicina	*maydeecheenah*
music	musica	*moozeekah*
natural history	storia naturale	*stawreeah nahtoorahlay*
painting	pittura	*peettoorah*
philosophy	filosofia	*feelozofeeah*
photography	fotografia	*fotograhfeeah*
sculpture	scultura	*skooltoorah*
science	scienza	*shentsah*
sociology	sociologia	*socholojeeah*
sports	sport	*sport*
theatre	teatro	*tayahtro*

What are your interests?
Lei che interessi ha?
le-ee kay eenteressee ah?

May I sit here?
Posso sedermi qui?
pawsso saydermee kwee?

Yes, if you wish.
Sì, se vuole.
see, say vwawlay

Can I get you a drink?
Posso offrirle qualcosa da bere?
*pawsso offreerlay kwahlkawzah da
bayray?*

Would you like a cigarette?
Vuole una sigaretta?
vwawlay oonah seegahrettah?

No, thank you. I don't smoke.
No, grazie. non fumo.
naw, grahtsyay. non foomo

Could you give me a light?
Ha da accendere?
ah dah ahchenderay?

**Would you like to go out with me this
evening?**
Vuole uscire con me stasera?
*vwawlay oosheeray kon may
stahsayrah?*

ITALIAN

Would you like to go . . . ?
Vuole andare . . . ?
vwawlay ahndahray . . . ?

to dinner	a cena	*ah chaynah*
to a party	a una festa	*ah oonah festah*
to the movies	al cinema	*ahl cheenaymah*
to the discotheque	ad una discoteca	*ahd oonah deeskotekah*
to a concert	ad un concerto	*ahd oon koncherto*
for a drive	a fare una gita in macchina	*ah fahray oonah jeetah een mahkkeena*
for a walk	a fare una passeggiata	*ah fahray oonah pahssejjahtah*

Yes, thank you. That would be nice.
Si, grazie, molto volentieri.
see, grahtsay, molto volentyeree

No, thank you. I'm not free this evening.
No, grazie. Sono occupato a stasera.
naw, grahtsay. sono awkkoopahto ah stahsayrah

What about tomorrow?
E domani?
ay domahnee?

No, I'll be busy.
No, ho un impegno.
naw, aw oon eempaynyo

Where/when shall we meet?
Dove/quando ci troviamo?
dovay/kwahndo chee trovyahmo?

Could you meet me at . . . ?
Può incontrarmi a . . . ?
pwaw eenkontrahrmee ah . . . ?

I'll meet you at your hotel.
La verrò a prendere all'albergo.
lah verraw ah prendayray ahllahlbergo

May I call you?
Posso chiamarla?
pawsso kyahmahrlah?

At what time?
A che ora?
ah kay orah?

What's your number?
Qual'è il suo numero?
kwahle eel soo-o noomayro?

I'd like to go home now.
Vorrei andare a casa adesso.
vorre-ee ahndahray ah kahsah ahdesso

I'm very tired.
Sono molto stanco/a.
sono molto stahnko/a

Thank you for a lovely evening.
Grazie per una serata piacevole.
grahtysay per oonah sayrahtah pyahchayvolay

ITALIAN

Expressions of Admiration or Dislike

What a beautiful view!
Che bel panorama!
kay bel pahnorahmah

What a lovely place/town/city!
Che bel posto/paese! Che bella città!
kay bel pawsto/pahayzay! kay bella cheettah

The sea/countryside is very beautiful.
Il mare/paesaggio è bellissimo.
eel mahray/pahayzahjjo e belleesseemo

I like this country/city/place very much.
Mi piace molto questo paese/città/posto.
*mee **pyah**chay molto **kwes**to pahayzay/cheettah/**paws**to*

I particularly like . . .
Mi piace in particolare . . .
*mee **pyah**chay een pahrteekolahray . . .*

I don't particularly like . . .
Non mi piace/piacciono particolarmente . . .
*non mee **pyah**chay/**pyah**chono pahrteekolahr**mayn**tay . . .*

the architecture	l'architettura	lahrkeetet**toor**ah
the beaches	le spiagge	lay **spyah**jay
the climate	il clima	eel **klee**mah
the food	la cucina	lah coo**chee**nah
the landscape	il paesaggio	eel pahyza**hjj**o
the night life	la vita notturna	lah **vee**tah not**toor**nah
the people	la gente	lah **jen**tay
the restaurants/cafes	i ristoranti/caffè	ee reesto**rahn**tee/kah**ffe**
the shops	i negozi	ee ne**gaw**tsee
the sights	i luoghi d'interesse	ee **lwawg**ee deen**teres**say

EVERYDAY SITUATIONS

Problems

Are you alone?
È sola?
*e **so**lah?*

Am I disturbing you?
La disturbo?
*lah dee**stoor**bo?*

Are you waiting for someone?
Stà aspettando qualcuno?
*stahahspet**tahn**do kwahl**koo**no?*

Leave me alone.
Mi lasci tranquilla.
*mee **lah**shee trahnk**weel**lah*

Yes, I'm waiting for a friend.
Si, sto aspettando un amico.
*see, sto ahspet**tahn**do oon ah**mee**ko*

Go away or I'll call the police.
Se ne vada oppure chiamo la polizia.
*say nay **vah**dah op**poo**ray **kyah**mo lah poleet**see**ah*

The Weather

It's a lovely day, isn't it?
È una bella giornata, non è vero?
*e **oo**nah **bell**ah jor**nah**tah, non e **vay**ro?*

What beautiful/awful weather we're having!
Che bel/cattivo tempo che fa!
*kay bel/kah**tee**vo **tem**po kay fah*

Do you think it's going to rain/snow/be sunny all day?
Pensa che pioverà/nevicherà/farà bello oggi/domani?
***pen**sah kay pyove**rah**/nayveeke**rah**/fah**rah** bello **awjj**ee/do**mah**nee?*

ITALIAN

It's terribly hot today.
Fa tanto caldo oggi.
fah **tahn**to **kahl**do **awj**jee

It's rather cold today.
Fa abbastanza freddo oggi.
fah **ahbbastahn**tsah **frayd**do **awj**jee

It's windy.
C'è molto vento.
che **molto vayn**to

It looks as though it's going to rain.
Sembra che pioverà.
*saymbrah kay pyover***ah**

Should I take an umbrella?
Devo prendere un ombrello?
*day*vo **pren**dayray oon ohm**brel**lo?

I hope the weather will improve.
Spero che migliori il tempo.
spero *kay meelyoree eel* **tempo**

Using the Telephone

Where is the nearest telephone?
Dov'è il telefono più vicino?
*dove eel tay***lefono** *pyoo vee***chee**eno?

May I use your telephone?
Posso usare il suo telefono?
pawsso oozahray eel **sooo**
*tay***lefono?**

Where can I make a long-distance phone call?
Dove posso fare una interurbana?
dovay **pawsso** *fahray oonah*
eenteroorbahnah?

A token, please.
Un gettone, per favore.
oon **jettonay**, *per* **fah**voray

Do you have a telephone directory?
Ha un elenco telefonico?
*ah oon ay***len**ko taylayfo**neeko?**

Do you speak English?
Parla inglese?
pahrlah *eeng***lay**zay?

I want to make a collect call.
Desidero fare una telefonata con pagamento a destino.
*day***zee**dero **fah**ray *oonah*
*taylayfo***nah**tah *kon pahgah***men**to *ah*
*des***tee**no

Hello. I would like Florence . . .
Buongiorno. Desidero il . . . di Firenze
bwawn **jor**no. *day***zee**dero *eel* . . .
*dee feer***en**tsay

Please let me know the cost of the call afterwards.
Mi faccia sapere il costo della telefonata dopo, per piacere.
mee **faht**chah *sah***pay**ray *eel* **kaws**to
*del*lah *taylayfo***nah**tah *daw*po, *per*
*pyah***chay**ray

Hello. This is . . .
Buongiorno. Sono . . .
bwawn **jor**no. *sono* . . .

May I please speak to . . .
Posso parlare con . . .
*pawsso pahr***lah**ray *kon* . . .

Could you give me extension . . .
Mi può dare la linea interna . . .
mee pwaw **dah**ray *lah* **lee**nay-ah
*een***ter**nah . . .

Is this . . . ?
Parlo con . . . ?
*pahr*lo *kon* . . . ?

He/she isn't here at the moment.
Non c'è in questo momento.

Could you tell him/her that I called? My name is . . . My number is . . .
Vuol dirgli/dirle che ho telefonato?
Mi chiamo . . . Il mio numero è . . .
vwawl **deer**lyee/**deer**lay *kay aw*
*taylayfo***nah**to? *mee* **kyah**mo . . . *eel*
meeo **noo**mero *e* . . .

ITALIAN

Would you take a message, please?
Vuol trasmettere un messaggio, per
   favore?
*vwawl trahzmaytteray oon messahjjo,
   per fahvoray?*

**Do you know when he/she will be
   back?**
Sa quando sarà di ritorno?
sah kwahndo sahrah dee reetorno?

I'll call back later.
Chiamerò di nuovo più tardi.
kyahmeraw dee nwawvo pyoo tahrdee

Operator, could you help me, please?
Signore/signorina, mi può aiutare, per
   favore?
*seenyoray/seenyoreenah, mee pwaw
   ahyootahray, per fahvoray?*

I don't speak Italian very well.
Non parlo bene l'italiano.
non pahrlo benay leetahlyahno

I dialed the wrong number.
Ho sbagliato numero.
aw zbahlyahto noomero

**I was cut off. Can you connect me
   again?**
È caduta la linea. Può darmela di
   nuovo?
*e kahdootah lah leenay-ah. pwaw
   dahrmaylah dee nwawvo?*

Who is this?
Chi parla?
kee pahrlah?

Hold the line, please.
Aspetti un momento.

The line is busy.
La linea è occupata.

Hang up. I will call you back.
Chiuda. La richiamo.

What's your number?
Qual'è il suo numero?

What number are you calling?
Che numero chiama?

I think you've got the wrong number.
Penso che abbia sbagliato numero.

How much was the call?
Qual'è il costo della telefonata?
*kwahle eel kawsto dellah
   taylayfonahtah?*

Post Office   (Ufficio Postale)

Where is the nearest post office?
Dov'è l'ufficio postale più vicino?
dove looffeecho postahlay pyoo veecheeno?

What window do I go to for . . . ?
A quale sportello devo rivolgermi per . . . ?
ah kwahlay sportello dayvo reevawljermee per . . . ?

   stamps
   i francobolli
   ee frahnkobollee

   telegrams
   i telegrammi
   ee taylaygrahmee

   money orders
   i vaglia postali
   ee vahlyah postahlee

   poste restante
   il fermo posta
   eel fermo pawstah

   parcels
   i pacchi
   ee pahkkee

Are there any letters for me? Here is my passport.
Ci sono delle lettere per me? Ecco il mio passaporto.
Chee sono delle lettayray per may? ekko eel meeo pahssaporto.

What's the postage for . . . ?
Qual'è l'affrancatura per . . . ?
kwahle lahffrahnkatoorah per . . . ?

   a letter to England
   una lettera per l'Inghilterra
   oonah lettayrah per leengeelterrah

   a post-card to the United States
   una cartolina per gli Stati Uniti
   oonah kahrtoleenah per lyee stahtee ooneetee

I want to send this (by) . . .
Desidero spedire questo . . .
dayzeedero spaydeeray kwesto per . . .

   air mail
   via aerea
   veeah aherayah

   express
   espresso
   ayspraysso

   registered mail
   raccomandata
   rakkommahndahtah

Please give me . . . 100 lire stamps.
Per favore, mi dia . . . francobolli da
  100 lire.
per fahvoray, mee deeah . . . frahnkobollee dah chento leeray

I want to send this package to . . .
Desidero spedire questo pacchetto a . . .
dayzeedero spaydeeray kwesto pahkkaytto ah . . .

What does it contain?
Che cosa contiene?

I want to send a telegram. Could I have a form, please?
Vorrei inviare un telegramma. Posso avere un modulo, per piacere?
vorre-ee eenvyahray oon taylaygrahmmah. pawsso ahveray oon mawdoolo, per pyahchayray?

How much is it per word?
Quanto costa ogni parola?
kwahnto kawstah onyee pahrawlah?

Bank (Banca)

Where's the nearest bank?
Dov'è la banca piu vicina?
dove lah bahnkah pyoo veecheenah?

Where can I cash a traveler's check?
Dove posso cambiare un traveler's check?
dovay pawsso kambyahray oon travelers check?

Do you charge a fee?
L'operazione è gratuita o bisogna pagare?
loperahtsyonay e grahtooeetah o beezonyah pahgahray?

What's the rate of exchange?
A quant'è il cambio?
ah kwahnte eel kahmbyo?

Do you issue money on a credit card?
Posso ritirare soldi su una carta di credito?
pawsso reeteerahray sawldee soo oonah kahrtah dee kraydeeto?

Can you cash a personal check?
Può cambiare un assegno personale?
pwaw kahmbyahray oon ahssenyo personahlay?

I have a letter of credit/bank draft.
Ho una lettera di credito/vaglia bancario.
aw oonah lettayrah dee kraydeeto/vahlyah bahnkahreeo

ITALIAN

**I'm expecting money from . . .
Has it arrived?**
Aspetto del denaro da . . . E arrivato?
*ah**spaytt**o del de**nah**ro da . . . e
ahrree**vah**to?*

I would like to make a deposit.
Vorrei fare un deposito.
*vorre-ee **fah**ray oon day**pawz**eeto*

I would like to open an account.
Vorrei aprire un conto.
*vorre-ee ah**pree**ray oon **kon**to*

**I would like to buy some foreign
currency.**
Vorrei comprare della valuta straniera.
*vorre-ee kom**prah**ray **del**lah vah**loo**tah
strah**nye**rah*

Shopping   (Fare delle compere)

I'm looking for a . . .
Sto cercando . . .
*staw cher**kahn**do . . .*

bakery	una panetteria	*oonah pahnetter**eee**ah*
barber shop	un barbiere	*oon bahr**bye**ray*
bookshop	una libreria	*oonah leebrer**eee**ah*
butcher shop	un mecellaio	*oon mahchel**lah**yo*
delicatessen	una salumeria	*oonah sahloomer**eee**ah*
department store	un grande magazzino	*oon **grahn**day mahgad**zee**no*
drug store	una farmacia	*oonah fahrmah**chee**ah*
fishmonger's	una pescheria	*oonah pesker**eee**ah*
greengrocer's	un negozio di frutta e verdura	*oon ne**gaw**tsyo dee **froo**tah ay ver**doo**rah*
hairdresser	un parrucchiere	*oon pahrook**kye**ray*
hardware store	un negozio di ferra-menta	*oon ne**gaw**tsyo dee ferrah-**mayn**tah*
laundry/dry cleaner	una lavanderia/tintoria	*oonah lahvahnder**eee**ah/teentor**eee**ah*
liquor store	un'enoteca	*oone**no**taykah*
market	un mercato	*oon mer**kah**to*
newsstand	un'edicola	*oonay**dee**kolah*
shoe repair	un calzolio	*oon kahlt**so**lahyo*
shoe store	un negozio di scarpe	*oon ne**gaw**tsyo dee **skahr**pay*
sporting goods store	un negozio di articoli sportivi	*oon ne**gaw**tsyo dee ahrtee-kolee spor**tee**vee*
stationery store	una cartoleria	*oonah kahrtoler**eee**ah*
supermarket	una supermercato	*oon soopermer**kah**to*
tobacconist's	una tabaccheria	*oonah tahbahkker**eee**ah*

Where can I buy . . . ?
Dove posso comprare . . . ?
*dovay **paws**so kom**prah**ray . . . ?*

May I help you?
Posso aiutarla?

What would you like?
Cosa desidera?

I would like . . .
Vorrei . . .
vorre-ee . . .

Can you show me . . . ?
Mi può mostrare . . . ?
mee pwaw mostrahray . . . ?

Do you have . . . ?
Avete . . . ?
ahvaytay . . . ?

I'm just looking, thanks.
Do soltanto un'occhiata, grazie.
daw soltahnto oonawkkyahta, grahtsyay

How much is this?
Quanto costa questo?
kwahnto kawstah kwesto?

Could you write that down, please?
Me lo può scrivere, per piacere?
may lo pwaw skreeveray, per pyachayray?

Do you accept travelers checks/ credit cards/dollars/pounds?
Accettate i traveler's checks/carte di credito/dollari/sterline?
ahchettahtay ee travelers checks/ kahrtay dee kraydeeto/dollahree/ sterleenay?

I think there's an error on this bill.
Mi sembra che ci sia un errore nel conto.
mee sembrah kay chee seeah oon erroray nel konto

Could you ship it to this address?
Potete spedirlo a questindirizzo?
potaytay spaydeerlo ah kwesteendeereetso?

Bookstore/Newsstand/Stationer (Libreria/Edicola/Cartoleria)

I'd like to buy . . .
Vorrei comprare . . .
vorre-ee komprahray . . .

an address book	un'agenda per gli indirizzi	*oonahjendah per lyee eendeereetsee*
an appointment book	un agenda	*oon ahjendah*
an Italian-English dictionary	un dizionario italiano-inglese	*oon deetsyonahryo eetahlyahno/eenglayzay*
some envelopes	delle buste	*dellay boostay*
an eraser	una gomma	*oonah gommah*
an Italian grammar	una grammatica italiana	*oonah grahmmahteekah eetahlyahnah*
a guidebook	una guida	*oonah gweedah*
a map of the town	una pianta della città	*oonah pyahntah dellah cheetah*
a road map	una carta stradale	*oonah kahrtah strahdahlay*
an American/English newspaper	un giornale americano/inglese	*oon jornahlay ahmayreekahno/eenglayzay*
a notebook	un quaderno	*oon kwahderno*
a pen (ballpoint)	una biro	*oonah beero*
a pen (fountain)	una penna	*oonah paynnah*
a pencil	una matita	*oonah mahteetah*
some post cards	delle cartoline	*dellay kahrtoleenay*
some Scotch tape	del nastro adesivo	*del nahstro ahdayzeevo*
some writing paper	della carta da lettere	*dellah kahrtah dah lettayray*

ITALIAN

Clothing Store (Abbigliamento)

Could you show me a . . . like the one in the window?
Mi può mostrare . . . come quello in vetrina?
mee pwaw mostrahray . . . komay kwello een vaytreenah?

Could you show me something . . . ?
Può farmi vedere qualcosa . . . ?
pwaw fahrmee vaydayray kwahlkawzah . . . ?

bigger/smaller
più grande/più piccolo
pyoo grahnday/pyoo peekolo

lighter/darker
più chiaro/più scuro
pyoo kyahro/pyoo skooro

of a different color
di un colore diverso
dee oon koloray deeverso

less expensive
meno cara
mayno kahrah

of better quality
di una qualità migliore
dee oonah kwahleetah meelyoray

I take size . . .
La mia taglia è . . .
lah meeah tahlyah e . . .

I'm not sure what my size is.
Non sono sicuro della mia taglia.
non sono seekooro dellah meeah tahlyah

May I try it on?
Posso provarlo?
pawsso provahrlo?

I doesn't fit.
Non va bene.
non vah benay

It's too . . .
È troppo . . .
e trawppo . . .

tight/loose   **short/long**
stretto/largo   corto/lungo
straytto/lahrgo   *korto/loongo*

Can you show me anything else?
Può farmi vedere qualcos'altro?
pwaw fahrmee vaydayray kwahlkawzahltro?

Very well; I'll take it.
Va bene; lo prendo.
vah benay; lo prendo

No, it's not really what I was looking for.
No; non è proprio ciò che volevo.
naw; non e prawpreeo chaw kay volayvo

No, it's too expensive. I'll give you . . . for it.
No; è troppo caro. Le darò . . .
naw; e trawppo kahro lay dahraw . . .

Articles of Clothing (Vestiti)

I'd like a/an/some . . .
Vorrei . . .
vorre-ee . . .

bath robe	un accappatoio	*oon ahkkahppahtoyo*
bathing suit	un costume da bagno	*oon kostoomay dah bahnyo*
blouse	una blusa	*oonah bloozah*
boots	degli stivali	*delyee steevahlee*

ITALIAN

bra	un reggiseno	*oon rayjeesayno*
cardigan	una giacca di lana	*oonah jahkkah dee lahnah*
coat	un cappotto	*oon kahppawtto*
dress	un vestito	*oon vesteeto*
evening dress	un abito da sera	*oon ahbeeto da sayrah*
girdle	un busto	*oon boosto*
gloves	dei guanti	*de-ee gwahntee*
hat	un cappello	*oon kahppello*
jacket	una giacca	*oonah jahkkah*
nightgown	una camicia da notte	*oonah kahmeechah dah nawt-tay*
pants	dei pantaloni	*de-ee pahntahlonee*
panty-hose	dei collant	*de-ee kollahnt*
pullover	un maglione	*oon mahlyonay*
pajamas	dei pigiama	*de-ee peejahmah*
raincoat	un impermeabile	*oon eempermayahbeelay*
sandals	dei sandali	*de-ee sahndahlee*
scarf	una sciarpa	*oonah shahrpah*
	un foulard	*oon foolahr*
shirt	una camicia	*oonah kahmeechah*
long sleeves	maniche lunghe	*mahnee loongay*
short sleeves	maniche corte	*mahneekay kortay*
shoes	delle scarpe	*dellay skahrpay*
shorts	degli short	*delyee short*
skirt	una gonna	*oonah gawnnah*
slip	una sottoveste	*oonah sottovestay*
slippers	delle pantofole	*dellay pahntawfawlay*
socks	dei calzini	*de-ee kahltseenee*
stockings	delle calze	*dellay kahltsay*
suit	un completo	*oon komplayto*
sweater	un golf	*oon golf*
T-shirt	una maglietta	*oona mahlyettah*
tennis shoes	delle scarpe da tennis	*dellay skahrpay dah tennees*
tie	una cravatta	*oonah krahvahtah*
tuxedo	uno smoking	*oono zmoking*
underwear (men's)	delle mutande da uomo	*dellay mootahnday dah wawmo*
underwear (women's)	delle mutandine da donna	*dellay mootahndeenay dah dawnah*
belt	la cintura	*lah cheentoorah*
buttons	i bottoni	*ee bottonee*
pocket	la tasca	*lah tahskah*
shoe laces	i lacci da scarpe	*ee lahchee da skahrpay*
zipper	la cerniera lampo	*lah chernyerah lahmpo*

Colors

beige	beige	*bezh*
black	nero	*nayro*
blue	blu	*bloo*
brown	marrone	*mahrronay*

ITALIAN

gold	oro	*awro*
green	verde	*verday*
gray	grigio	*greejo*
off-white	crema	*kremah*
orange	arancio	*ahrahncho*
pink	rosa	*rawzah*
purple	viola	*vyawlah*
red	rosso	*rosso*
silver	argento	*ahrjento*
turquoise	turchese	*toorkayzay*
white	bianco	*byahnko*
yellow	giallo	*jahllo*

Fabrics

acrylic	acrilico	*ahkreeleeko*
corduroy	il velluto a coste	*eel vellooto ah kawstay*
cotton	il cotone	*eel kotonay*
felt	il feltro	*eel feltro*
flannel	la flanella	*lah flahnellah*
lace	il pizzo	*eel peetso*
leather	la pelle	*lah pellay*
linen	il lino	*eel leeno*
rayon	il rayon	*eel rahyon*
satin	il raso	*eel rahzo*
silk	la seta	*lah saytah*
suede	la renna	*lah rennah*
synthetic	sintetico	*seenteteeko*
velvet	il velluto	*eel vellooto*
wool	la lana	*lah lahnah*

Jewelry (Gioielleria)

bracelet	un braccialetto	*oon brahchahlaytto*
necklace	una collana	*oonah kollahnah*
ring	un anello	*oon ahnello*
wristwatch	un orologio da polso	*oon orolawjo dah polso*
diamond	il diamante	*eel deeahmahntay*
gold	l'oro	*lawro*
platinum	il platino	*eel plahteeno*
silver	l'argento	*lahrjento*
stainless steel	l'acciaio inossidabile	*lahchahyo eenosseedahbeelay*
plated	placcato	*plahkkahto*

Buying Food for Picnics and Snacks

I'd like some . . .
Vorrei . . .
vorre-ee . . .

apples	delle mele	***del**lay **may**lay*
apple juice	del succo di mela	*del **sook**ko dee **may**lah*
bananas	delle banane	***del**lay bahn**ah**nay*
bread	del pane	*del **pah**nay*
butter	del burro	*del **boor**ro*
cake	un dolce	*oon **dol**chay*
candy	delle caramelle	***del**lay kahrah**mel**lay*
carrots	delle carote	***del**lay kah**raw**ttay*
cereal	dei cereali	*de-ee chera**yah**lee*
cheese	del formaggio	*del for**mah**jo*
chocolate	del cioccolato	*del chokko**lah**to*
coffee	del caffè	*del kah**ffe***
cold cuts	degli affettati	***del**yee ahffet**tah**tee*
cookies	dei biscotti	*de-ee bes**kaw**tee*
crackers	delle gallettine	***del**lay gahllet**tee**nay*
cucumbers	dei cetrioli	*de-ee chetree**aw**lee*
eggs	delle uova	***del**lay **waw**vah*
frankfurters	dei Würstel	*de-ee **vewr**stel*
grapefruits	dei pompelmi	*de-ee pom**pel**mee*
grapefruit juice	del succo di pompelmo	*del **sook**ko dee pom**pel**mo*
ham	del prosciutto	*del pro**shoot**to*
ice cream	del gelato	*del je**lah**to*
lemons	dei limoni	*de-ee lee**moh**nee*
lettuce	della lattuga	***del**lah lahtt**oo**gah*
melon	dei meloni	*de-ee me**lon**ee*
milk	del latte	*del **laht**tay*
mustard	della senape	***del**la **se**nahpay*
oil	l'olio	***lawl**yo*
oranges	delle arance	***del**lay ah**rahn**chay*
orange juice	del succo di arancia	*del **sook**ko dee ah**rahn**chah*
peaches	delle pesche	***del**lay **pes**kay*
pears	delle pere	***del**lay **pay**ray*
pepper	del pepe	*del **pay**pay*
peppers	dei peperoni	*de-ee paypay**ro**nee*
pickles	dei sottaceti	*de-ee sotta**chay**tee*
plums	delle prugne	***del**lay **proon**yay*
potato chips	delle patatine fritte	***del**lay pahtah**teen**ay **freet**tay*
potatoes	delle patate	***del**lay pah**tah**tay*
raspberries	dei lamponi	*de-ee lahm**pon**ee*
rolls	dei panini	*de-ee pah**nee**nee*
salad	dell'insalata	***del**leensah**lah**tah*
salami	del salame	*del sah**lah**may*
salt	del sale	*del **sah**lay*

ITALIAN

sandwiches	dei sandwich	de-ee **sandwich**
sausages	delle salsicce	**del**lay sahl**see**chay
soft drinks	delle bibite	**del**lay bee**bee**tay
spaghetti	degli spaghetti	**del**yee spah**get**tee
strawberries	delle fragole	**del**lay **frah**golay
sugar	dello zucchero	**del**lo **dzook**kero
tea	del tè	del te
tomatoes	dei pomodori	de-ee pomo**daw**ree
yoghurt	dello yoghurt	**del**lo **yaw**goort

a box of	una scatola di	**oo**nah **skah**tolah dee
a can of	una scatola di	**oo**nah **skah**tolah dee
a jar of	un vaso di	oon **vah**zo dee
a half kilo of	mezzo chilo di	**med**zo **kee**lo dee
a kilo of	un chilo di	oon **kee**lo dee
a packet of	un sacchetto di	oon sah**ket**to dee
a slice of	una fetta di	**oo**nah **fay**tah dee
a bottle opener	un apribottiglia	oon ahpreebot**teel**yah
a corkscrew	un cavatappi	oon kahvah**tahp**pee
paper napkins	dei tovaglioli di carta	de-ee tovahl**yaw**lee dee **kahr**tah
plastic utensils	delle posate di plastica	**del**lay po**zah**tay dee **plah**steekah
a tin (can) opener	un apriscatola	oon ahpree**skah**tolah

I'll have a little more. That's too much.
Ne prendo ancora un po. È troppo.
nay **pren**do ahn**ko**rah oon paw.
e **trawp**po

Could I have a bag, please?
Posso avere un sacchetto, per favore?
pawsso a**vay**ray oon sahk**ket**to, per
fah**vo**ray?

Pharmacy (Farmacia)

Can you make up this prescription?
Può prepararmi questa ricetta?
pwaw praypah**rahr**mee **kwes**tah
ree**chayt**tah?

How long will it take?
Quanto tempo ci vorrà?
kwahnto tempo chee vor**rah?**

I'll come back in a little while.
Tornerò più tarde.
torne**raw** pyoo **tahr**dee

Could you please write down the instructions in English?
Può scrivere le istruzioni in inglese, per piacere?
pwaw **skree**veray lay eestroot**syo**nee
een een**glay**zay, per pya**chay**ray?

Can you give me something for . . . ?
Mi può dare qualche cosa per . . . ?
mee pwaw **dah**ray **kwahl**kay **kaw**zah per . . . ?

a cold	il raffreddore	eel rahffrayd**do**ray
constipation	la stitichezza	lah steetee**ket**sah
a cough	la tosse	lah **tos**say
a cut	un taglio	oon **tahl**yo
diarrhea	la diarrea	lah deeahr**ray**ah

hay fever	la febbre del fieno	*lah **febbray** del **fyeno***
a headache	il malditesta	*eel mahldee**testah***
indigestion	un'indigestione	*oon eendeejes**tyonay***
an insect bite/sting	una puntura d'insetto	***oonah** poon**toorah** deen**setto***
nausea	la nausea	*lah **now**zayah*
a sore throat	il mal di gola	*eel mahl dee **golah***
a sunburn	una scottatura solare	***oonah** skawttah**toorah** so**lahray***
travel sickness	il mal di macchina/mare	*eel mahl dee **mahk**keenah/ **mahray***
an upset stomach	il mal di stomaco	*eel mahl dee **stawmako***

I'd like a/an/some . . .
Vorrei . . .
vorre-ee . . .

aspirin	dell'aspirina	*delahspee**reenah***
bandage	una benda	***oonah** **bendah***
band-aids	dei cerotti	*de-ee che**rawttee***
cough syrup	dello sciroppo ⎫ per la	***dello** shee**rawppo*** ⎫ per lah
cough drops	delle pastiglie ⎭ tosse	***dellay** pah**steelyay*** ⎭ **tos**say
contraceptives	degli anticoncezionali	*de**lyee** ahnteekonchetsyo**nah**lee*
eye drops	delle gocce per gli occhi	*de**llay** **got**chay per lyee **awk**kee*
insect repellent	una crema insetticida	***oonah** **kraymah** eensettee**chee**dah*
laxative	un lassativo	*oon lahssah**teevo***
sleeping pills	dei sonniferi	*de-ee son**nee**feree*
sanitary napkins	degli assorbenti igienici	*de**lyee** ahssor**bentee** eejayneechee*
tampons	dei tampax	*de-ee **tahm**pahx*

Toilet Articles

I'd like to buy a/an/some . . .
Vorrei comprare . . .
*vorre-ee kom**prah**ray . . .*

after shave lotion	una lozione dopobarba	***oonah** lot**syonay** dawpo**bahr**bah*
cream	una crema	***oonah** **kremah***
cleansing cream	una crema detergente	***oonah** **kremah** dayter**jentay***
hand cream	una crema per le mani	***oonah** **kremah** per lay **mahnee***
moisturizing cream	una crema idratante	***oonah** **kremah** eedraht**ahntay***
deodorant	un deodorante	*oon dayodo**rahntay***
emery board	una limetta per unghie	***oonah** lee**mettah** per lay **oon**gyay*
nail file	una lima da unghie	***oonah** **leemah** dah **oon**gyay*
razor	un rasoio	*oon rah**zoyo***

ITALIAN

razor blades	delle lame di rasoio	*dellay lahmay dee rahzoyo*
shampoo	dello shampoo	*dello shahmpoo*
shaving cream	una crema da barba	*oonah kremah dah bahrbah*
soap	del sapone	*del saponay*
sun-tan oil/cream	un olio/crema solare	*oon awlyo/kremah solahray*
talcum powder	del borotalco	*del borotahlko*
tissues	dei fazzolettini di carta	*de-ee fahdzoletteenee dee kahrtah*
toilet paper	della carta igienica	*della kartah eejayneekah*
toothbrush	uno spazzolino da denti	*oono spahtsoleeno dah dentee*
toothpaste	un dentifricio	*oon denteefreecho*
tweezers	delle pinzette	*dellay peentsettay*

Note: For makeup and perfume, go to a *Profumeria*.

Photography

I'd like a good/inexpensive camera, please.
Vorrei una macchina fotografica/di buona qualità/economica
*vorre-ee oonah **mahk**keenah foto**grah**feekah/dee **bwaw**nah kwah**lee**tah/aykon**aw**meekah*

I'd like some . . . film for this camera.
Vorrei una pellicola . . . per questa macchina
*vorre-ee oonah pel**lee**kolah . . . per **kwes**tah **mahk**keenah*

black and white	**color**
bianco e nero	a colori
byahnko ay nayro	*ah koloree*

color slide
diapositive a colori
deeahpozeeteevay ah koloree

I need . . . for this camera.
Ho bisogno di . . . per questa macchina.
*aw beezonyo dee . . . per **kwes**tah **mahk**keenah*

batteries	**a lens**
delle batterie	un obiettivo
dellay bahttereeay	*oon obyetteevo*

flash cubes
dei cubi per il flash
*de-ee **koo**bee per eel flahsh*

How much do you charge for processing?
Quanto costa lo sviluppo?
kwahnto kawstah lo zveelooppo?

I'd like . . . prints/slides of each negative . . .
Vorrei . . . stampe/diapositive per ogni negativa . . .
vorre-ee . . . stahmpay/deeahpozeeteevay per ohnyee naygahteevah . . .

with a matt finish
su carta opaca
soo kahrtah opahkah

with a glossy finish
su carta lucida
soo kahrtah loocheedah

I would like an enlargement of this, please.
Vorrei un ingrandimento di questo, per favore.
vorre-ee oon eengrahndeemaynto dee kwesto, per fahvoray

When will it be ready?
Quando sarà pronto?
kwahndo sahrah pronto?

ITALIAN

Tobacco Shop (Tabaccaio)

I'd like a pack/carton of cigarettes, please.
Vorrei un pacchetto/una stecca di sigarette, per favore.
*vorre-ee oon pahk**ket**to/**oo**nah stay**kk**ah dee seegah**ret**tay, per fah**vo**ray*

Do you have . . . ?
Avete . . . ?
*avay**tay** . . . ?*

I'd like . . .
Vorrei . . .
vorre-ee . . .

pipe tobacco
del tabacco da pipa
*del tah**bahk**ko dah **pee**pah*

a cigarette lighter
un accendino
*oon ahchen**dee**no*

a pipe
una pipa
*oonah **pee**pah*

lighter fluid
della benzina per accendino
***del**lah bend**zee**nah per ahchen**dee**no*

matches
dei fiammiferi
*de-ee fyahm**mee**feree*

Laundry/Dry Cleaner (Lavanderia/Tintoria)

Where is the nearest laundry/dry cleaner?
Dov'è la lavanderia/tintoria più vicina?
*dove lah lahvahnde**ree**ah/teento**ree**ah pyoo vee**chee**nah?*

I'd like to have these clothes washed and ironed.
Vorrei far lavare e stirare questi abiti.
*vorre-ee fahr lah**vah**ray ay stee**rah**ray kwestee ah**bee**tee*

Please have this dry cleaned.
Per favore, mi faccia pulire questo a secco.
*per fah**vo**ray, mee **fah**tchah poo**lee**ray kwesto ah **sayk**ko*

Can you remove this stain?
Può togliere questa macchia?
*pwaw **tawl**yeray kwestah **mahk**kyah?*

Can you mend this?
Mi può rammendare questo?
*mee pwaw rahmmen**dah**ray **kwes**to?*

When will it be ready?
Quando sarà pronto?
*kwando sah**rah** **pron**to?*

I need it . . .
Mi occorre . . .
*mee ok**kor**ray . . .*

this afternoon
oggi pomeriggio
*aw**j**jee pomeree**jjo***

this evening
stasera
*sta**say**rah*

tomorrow
domani
*do**mah**nee*

Repairs

Can you fix this?
Mi può riparare questo?
*mee pwaw reepah**rah**ray **kwes**to?*

How long will it take?
Quanto tempo ci vorrà?
***kwahn**to **tem**po chee vor**rah**?*

ITALIAN

How much will it cost?	When will it be ready?
Quanto costerà?	Quando sarà pronto?
kwahnto kawsterah?	*kwahndo sahrah pronto?*

HEALTH

At the Doctor

I don't feel well.
Non mi sento bene.
non mee sento benay

Where can I find a doctor who speaks English?
Dove posso trovare un medico che parli inglese?
dovay pawsso trovahray oon medeeko kay pahrlee eenglayzay?

Could you call a doctor for me?
Può chiamarmi un medico?
pwaw kyamahrmee oon medeeko?

Is there a doctor here?
C'è qui un medico?
che kwee oon medeeko?

I have (a) . . .
Ho . . .
aw . . .

Must I make an appointment?
Devo prendere un appuntamento?
dayvo prendayray oon ahppoontahmaynto?

I must see a doctor right away.
Devo vedere un medico subito.
dayvo vaydayray oon medeeko soobeeto

I feel ill.
Mi sento male.
mee sento mahlay

I've got a pain here.
Ho un dolore qui.
aw oon doloray kwee

backache	il mal di schiena	*eel mahl dee skyenah*
constipation	la stitichezza	*lah steeteeketsah*
cough	la tosse	*lah tossay*
cramps	i crampi	*ee krahmpee*
diarrhea	la diarrea	*lah deeahrayah*
fever	la febbre	*lah febbray*
hemorrhoids	le emorroidi	*lay aymorraweedee*
headache	il mal di testa	*eel mahl dee testah*
insect bite	una puntura d'insetto	*oonah poontoorah deensetto*
lump	un bernoccolo	*oon bernawkkolo*
nausea	la nausea	*lah nowzayah*
rash	un'eruzione cutanea	*oon ayrootsyonay kootahnayah*
swelling	un gonfiore	*oon gonfyoray*
wound	una ferita	*oonah fayreetah*

ITALIAN

I have difficulty breathing.
Ho difficoltà di respirazione.
*aw deefeekoltah dee
rayspeerahtsyonay*

I feel dizzy/faint.
Mi sento stordito/debole.
*mee **sento** stor**dee**to **day**bolay*

I've been vomiting.
Ho vomitato.
aw vomeetahto

I can't eat/sleep.
Non riesco a mangiare/dormire.
*non ree-**esko** ah mahn**jjah**ray
dor**mee**ray*

I've cut/burned myself.
Mi sono tagliato/bruciato.
*mee **so**no tahl**yah**to/broo**chah**to*

**I think I have sprained/broken my
wrist/ankle.**
Penso di essermi rotto/slogato il polso/
la caviglia.
***pen**so dee es**sayr**mee **rot**to/z**lo**gahto
eel **pol**so/lahkah**vee**lyah*

It hurts when I move . . .
Mi fa male quando muovo . . .
*mee fah **mah**lay **kwahn**do **mwaw**vo . . .*

I am allergic to penicillin/iodine
Sono allergico alla penicillina/allo iodio.
***so**no ahller**jee**ko **ahl**lah
payneechee**lee**nah/**ahl**lo **yaw**dyo*

Doctor to Patient

Where does it hurt?
Dove le fa male?

How long have you had this trouble?
Da quanto tempo ha questo disturbo?

Please undress (to the waist).
Si spogli (fino alla vita).

Does that hurt?
Le fa male questo?

**I'll need a urine specimen/blood
sample.**
Avrò bisogno di un campione dell'urina/
del sangue.

Are you taking any medication?
Prende delle medicine attualmente?

I will prescribe some pills.
Le prescriverò delle compresse.

You have . . .
Lei ha . . .

**Take these . . . times a day before/
after each meal every morning/
evening.**
Prenda queste . . . volte al giorno prima/
dopo i pasti al mattino/alla sera.

**You must rest/stay in bed
for . . . days.**
Deve riposarsi/restare a letto
per . . . giorni.

Are you allergic to . . . ?
È allergico a . . . ?

It's nothing serious.
Non è niente di grave.

You must go to the hospital.
Deve andare all'ospedale.

an abcess	un ascesso
appendicitis	l'appendicite
a bad cold	un brutto raffreddore
food poisoning	un avvelenamento da cibi

ITALIAN

a hernia	l'ernia
an infection	un'infezione
influenza	l'influenza
a sprain	uno strappo muscolare
tonsilitis	la tonsillite
an ulcer	l'ulcera

At the Dentist

Can you recommend a good dentist?
Può consigliarmi un buon dentista?
pwaw konseelyahrmee oon bwawn denteestah?

I would like to see Dr. . . . as soon as possible.
Vorrei vedere il dottor . . . al più presto possibile.
vorre-ee vaydayray eel dottor . . . ahl pyoo presto posseebeelay

I have a bad toothache.
Mi fa molto male un dente.
mee fah molto mahlay oon dentay

My tooth has broken.
Mi si è rotto un dente.
mee see e rotto oon dentay

My gums are sore/bleeding.
Mi dolgono/sanguinano le gengive.
mee dawlgono/sahngweenahno lay jenjeevay

I have an abscess.
Ho un ascesso.
aw oon ahshesso

I've lost/broken a filling.
Mi si è aperta un'otturazione.
mee see e ahpertah oon ottoorahtsyonay

Can you give me temporary treatment?
Può curarlo provvisoriamente?
pwaw koorahrlo provveezoryahmayntay?

Please don't extract it.
Non lo estragga, per favore.
non lo estrahggah, per fahvoray

Please give me a local anaesthesia.
Per favore, mi faccia un'anestesia locale.
per fahvorah, mee fahtchah oonahnaystayzeeah lokahlay

Dentist to Patient

I want to give you an X-ray.
Desidero farle una radiografia.

I will fill the tooth.
Le otturerò il dente.

This tooth must come out.
Questo dente dev'essere estratto.

Optician

I have broken my glasses.
Ho rotto gli occhiali.
aw rotto lyee ahkkyahlee

Can you repair them?
Me li può riparare?
may lee pwaw reepahrahray?

I have lost a contact lens.
Ho perso una lente a contatto.
aw perso oonah lentay ah kontahtto

Could you make me another one?
Me ne può fare un'altra?
may nay pwaw fahray oonahltrah?

When will they/it be ready?
Quando saranno pronte/quando sara pronta?
kwahndo sahrahnno prontay/kwahndo sahrah prontah?

I need soaking/wetting solution for hard/soft contact lenses.
Ho bisogno della soluzione conservante/umettante per lenti a contatto rigide/morbide.
aw beezonyo dellah solootsyonay konservahntay/oomettahntay per lentee a kontahtto reejeeday/morbeeday

My contact lenses are bothering me. Would you have a look at them?
Le mie lenti a contatto mi danno fastidio. Me le può controllare?
lay meeay lentee ah kontahtto mee dahnno fahsteedyo. may lay pwaw kontrollahray?

Paying the Doctor/Dentist/Optician

How much do I owe you? Can you send me a bill?
Quanto le devo? Mi può mandare il conto?
kwahnto lay dayvo? mee pwaw mahndahray eel konto?

I have health insurance.
Sono assicurato.
sono ahsseekoorahto

EMERGENCY

Loss or Theft

Excuse me, can you help me?
Mi scusi, mi può aiutare?
mee skoozee, mee pwaw ahyootahray?

Where's the police station?
Dov'è il Commissariato?
dove eel kommeessahryahto?

Where's the American/British/Canadian consulate?
Dov'è il consolato americano/inglese/canadese?
dove eel konsolahto ahmereekahno/eenglayzay/kahnahdayzay?

I've lost my . . . Someone has stolen my . . .
Ho perso . . . Qualcuno mi ha rubato . . .
aw perso . . . kwahlkoono mee ah roobahto . . .

passport	il passaporto	eel pahssaporto
money	i soldi	ee sawldee
traveler's checks	i traveler's check	ee travelers check
credit cards	le carte di credito	lay kahrtay dee kraydeeto

luggage	i bagagli	*ee bahgahlyee*
plane tickets	i biglietti d'aereo	*ee beelyettee daherayo*
handbag	la borsa	*lah borsah*

Where is the lost and found?	**I left something in the train/taxi/bus.**
Dov'è l'ufficio oggetti smarriti?	Ho lasciato qualcosa sul treno/tassì/autobus.
dove loofeecho awjjettee zmahrreetee?	*aw lahshahto kwahlkawzah sool treno/tahssee/owtoboos*

Asking for Help

Help!	Aiuto!	*ahyooto*
Police!	Polizia!	*poleetseeah*
Fire!	Al fuoco!	*ahl fwawko*

TIME/DATES/NUMBERS

Time, Date

What time is it?
Che ora è?
Che ore sono?
kay orah e?
kay oray sono?

It's . . .
Sono le . . .
sono lay . . .

two o'clock	due	*dooay*
ten past three	tre e dieci	*tray ay dyechee*
four fifteen	quattro e un quarto	*kwahttro ay oon kwahrto*
twenty past five	cinque e venti	*cheenkway ay vayntee*
six-thirty	sei e mezzo	*se-ee ay medzo*
quarter to eight	otto meno un quarto	*awtto mayno oon kwahrto*
five to eight	otto meno cinque	*awtto mayno cheenkway*

| It's midnight. | È mezzanotte. | *e medzanawttay* |
| It's one o'clock. | È l'una. | *e loonah* |

sunrise	l'alba	*lahlbah*
morning	mattina	*mahtteenah*
noon	mezzogiorno	*medzojorno*
afternoon	pomeriggio	*pomereejjo*
sunset	tramonto	*trahmonto*
evening	sera	*sayrah*
night	notte	*nawttay*

ITALIAN

It's early/late.
È presto/tardi.
e presto/tahrdee

What's the date today?
Quanti ne abbiamo oggi?
kwahntee nay ahbbyahmo awjjee?

The date is . . .
Ne abbiamo . . .
nay abbyahmo . . .

Days of the Week

Monday	lunedì	*loonaydee*
Tuesday	martedì	*mahrtaydee*
Wednesday	mercoledì	*merkolaydee*
Thursday	giovedì	*jovaydee*
Friday	venerdì	*vaynayrdee*
Saturday	sabato	*sahbahto*
Sunday	domenica	*domeneekah*

Seasons

spring	primavera	*preemahverah*
summer	estate	*aystahtay*
autumn	autunno	*owtoonno*
winter	inverno	*eenverno*

The Months

January	gennaio	*jennahyo*
February	febbraio	*febbrahyo*
March	marzo	*mahrtso*
April	aprile	*ahpreelay*
May	maggio	*mahjjo*
June	giugno	*joonyo*
July	luglio	*loolyo*
August	agosto	*ahgawsto*
September	settembre	*sayttembray*
October	ottobre	*awttobray*
November	novembre	*novembray*
December	dicembre	*deechembray*
this year	quest'anno	*kwestahnno*
last week	la settimana scorsa	*lah sayteemahnah skorsah*

ITALIAN

next month	il mese prossimo	*eel mayzay prawsseemo*
today	oggi	*awjjee*
yesterday	ieri	*eeyeree*
tomorrow	domani	*domahnee*
the day before yesterday	l'altro ieri	*lahltro eeyeree*
the day after tomorrow	dopodomani	*dawpodomahnee*
Christmas	Natale	*nahtahlay*
Easter	Pasqua	*paskwah*

Numbers

0	zero	*dzero*
1	uno	*oono*
2	due	*dooay*
3	tre	*tray*
4	quattro	*kwahttro*
5	cinque	*cheenkway*
6	sei	*se-ee*
7	sette	*settay*
8	otto	*awtto*
9	nove	*nawvay*
10	dieci	*dyechee*
11	undici	*oondeechee*
12	dodici	*dodeechee*
13	tredici	*traydeechee*
14	quattordici	*kwahttordeechee*
15	quindici	*kweendeechee*
16	sedici	*saydeechee*
17	diciasette	*deechahsettay*
18	diciotto	*deechawto*
19	diciannove	*deechahnawvay*
20	venti	*vayntee*
21	ventuno	*vayntoono*
22	ventidue	*vaynteedooay*
23	ventitrè	*vaynteetray*
24	ventiquattro	*vaynteekwahttro*
25	venticinque	*vaynteecheenkway*
26	ventisei	*vaynteese-ee*
27	ventisette	*vaynteesettay*
28	ventotto	*vayntawtto*
29	ventinove	*vaynteenawvay*
30	trenta	*trayntah*
40	quaranta	*kwahrahntah*
50	cinquanta	*cheenkwahntah*
60	sessanta	*sayssahntah*
70	settanta	*sayttahntah*
80	ottanta	*awttahntah*
90	novanta	*novahntah*

100	cento	*chento*
101	centuno	*chentoono*
102	centodue	*chentodooay*
150	centocinquanta	*chentocheenkwahntah*
200	duecento	*dooaychento*
300	trecento	*traychento*
400	quattrocento	*kwahttrochento*
500	cinquecento	*cheenkwaychento*
600	seicento	*se-eechento*
700	settecento	*settaychento*
800	ottocento	*awttochento*
900	novecento	*nawvaychento*
1000	mille	*meellay*
1100	millecento	*meellaychento*
1200	milleduecento	*meellaydooaychento*
2000	duemila	*dooaymeelah*
5000	cinquemila	*cheenkwaymeelah*
10,000	diecimila	*dyecheemeelah*
50,000	cinquantamila	*cheenquahntahmeelah*
100,000	centomila	*chentomeelah*
1,000,000	un milione	*oon meelyonay*
2,000,000,000	due miliardi	*dooaymeelyahrdee*

first	primo	*preemo*
second	secondo	*saykondo*
third	terzo	*tertso*
fourth	quarto	*kwahrto*
fifth	quinto	*kweento*
sixth	sesto	*sesto*
seventh	settimo	*setteemo*
eighth	ottavo	*awttahvo*
ninth	nono	*nawno*
tenth	decimo	*decheemo*
eleventh	undicesimo	*oondeechezeemo*
twelfth	dodicesimo	*dodeechezeemo*
a half	una metà	*oonah maytah*
a quarter	un quarto	*oon kwahrto*
one third	un terzo	*oon tertso*

ITALIAN

ITALIAN

ITALIAN DICTIONARY

Generally, masculine nouns end in *o* and feminine nouns in *a*. Otherwise, the gender will be indicated.

Only the masculine form of adjectives is given. The feminine is formed by changing the *o* ending to *a*.

A

a, an **uno, una, un**
able, to be **potere, essere capace**
about **circa**
above **sopra, al disopra**
abroad **all'estero**
absent **assente**
absolutely **assolutamente**
accept, to **accettare**
accident **incidente** (m.)
accompany, to **accompagnare**
according to **secondo**
accustomed **abituato**
ache **dolore**
across **attraverso**
acquaintance **conoscenza**
action **azione** (f.)
actor **attore**
add, to **aggiungere**
address **indirizzo**
admire, to **ammirare**
admission **entrata**
advertisement **pubblicità**
advice **consiglio**
advise, to **consigliare**
afraid, to be **avere paura**
after **dopo**
afternoon **pomeriggio**
again **di nuovo**
against **contro**
age **età**
agency **agenzia**
ago **fa**
agree, to **essere d'accordo**
agreeable **gradevole, piacevole**
agreed **d'accordo**
ahead **avanti**
air **aria**

air conditioning **aria condizionata**
air force **forza aerea**
air mail **posta aerea**
airplane **aeroplano**
airport **aeroporto**
alarm clock **sveglia**
alike **uguale, simile**
all **tutto**
allow, to **permettere**
all right **va bene**
almost **quasi**
alone **solo**
already **già**
also **anche**
although **benchè**
always **sempre**
ambulance **ambulanza**
America **America**
American **americano**
among **tra, fra**
amount **somma**
amusement **divertimento**
amusement park **luna park**
amusing **divertente**
ancient **antico**
and **e, ed**
angry **arrabbiato**
animal **animale, bestia**
ankle **caviglia**
announce, to **annunciare**
annoy, to **dar noia a**
answer, to **rispondere**
answer **risposta**
antifreeze **anticongelante** (m.)
anxious **ansioso**
any **alcuno**
anyone **chiunque**
anything **qualsiasi cosa**
anyway **in ogni caso**
anywhere **dovunque, ovunque**
apartment **appartamento**
appear, to **apparire**

ITALIAN

appetite **appetito**
appetizer **antipasto**
apple **mela**
appointment **appuntamento**
appreciate **apprezzare**
approach, to **avvicinarsi** (a)
approve, to **approvare**
arch **arco**
arm **braccio** (pl. **le braccia**)
armchair **poltrona**
army **esercito, militare** (m.)
around **intorno a**
arrest, to **arrestare**
arrival **arrivo**
arrive, to **arrivare**
art **arte** (f.)
artist **artista** (m. and f.)
as **come**
ashtray **portacenere** (m.)
ask, to **chiedere, domandare**
asleep, to fall **addormentarsi**
assure **assicurare**
at **a**
at all **affatto**
at once **subito**
attend **assistere**
attention! **attenzione!** (f.)
attractive **attraente**
audience (Papal) **udienza**
aunt **zia**
Austria **Austria**
Austrian **austriaco**
authentic **autentico**
author **autore** (m.)
automatic **automatico**
automobile **automobile** (f.)
autumn **autunno**
avoid, to **evitare**
awaken, to **svegliare**
away, to go **andare via**

B

baby **bambino**
bachelor **scapolo**
back (adv.) **indietro**
back (n.) **schiena**
backpack **zaino**
bad **cattivo**

badly **male, malamente**
baggage **bagaglio**
baggage room **deposito bagagli**
bakery **panificio**
bank **banca** (m.)
bar (drinking) **bar** (m.)
barber **barbiere** (m.)
basket **cesto**
bath **bagno**
bathe, to **fare il bagno**
bathing suit **costume da bagno** (m.)
bathroom **bagno**
bathtub **vasca**
battery **pila**
battle **battaglia**
be, to **essere**
beach **spiaggia**
bear **orso**
beard **barba**
beat, to **battere**
beautiful **bello**
beauty **bellezza**
because **perchè**
become **diventare**
bed **letto**
bedroom **camera da letto**
beef **manzo**
beer **birra**
before **prima**
beggar **mendicante** (m.)
begin, to **cominciare, iniziare**
behind **dietro**
believe, to **credere**
bell **campanello**
belong, to **appartenere**
below **sotto, al disotto**
belt **cintura**
beside **accanto**
best **migliore, meglio**
bet, to **scommettere**
better **migliore, meglio**
between **fra, tra**
bicycle **bicicletta**
big **grande**
bill **conto, bolletta**
bird **uccello**
birth **nascita**
birthday **compleanno**
bite, to **mordere**
bitter **amaro**
black **nero**

blanket **coperta**
blond **biondo**
blood **sangue** (m.)
blouse **camicetta**
blue **blu, azzurro**
boarding house **pensione** (f.)
boat **barca**
body **corpo**
boil, to **bollire**
bomb **bomba**
book **libro**
bookstore **libreria**
border **confine** (m.)
boring **noioso**
born, to be **nascere**
borrow, to **prendere a prestito**
both **ambedue, tutti e due**
bother, to **seccare, dar noia a**
bottle **bottiglia**
bottom **fondo**
bowl **scodella**
box **scatola**
boy **ragazzo**
brain **cervello**
brake **freno**
brassiere **reggiseno**
bread **pane** (m.)
break, to **rompere**
breakfast **prima colazione**
bride **sposa**
bridge **ponte** (m.)
brief **breve**
bright **luminoso**
bring, to **portare**
broad **largo**
broken **rotto**
broom **scopa**
brother **fratello**
brother-in-law **cognato**
brown **marrone**
brush **spazzola**
bug **insetto**
build, to **costruire**
building **edificio, palazzo**
bus **autobus, pullman** (m.)
bus stop **fermata dell'autobus**
business **affari**
busy **occupato**
but **ma, però**
butcher shop **macelleria**
butter **burro**

button **bottone** (m.)
buy, to **comprare**
by **per**
by chance **per caso**
by means of **per mezzo di**

C

cabbage **cavolo**
cake **dolce** (m.), torta
calendar **calendario**
call, to **chiamare**
call **chiamata**
calm **calmo**
camera **macchina fotografica**
camping site **campeggio**
cancer **cancro**
cap **berretto**
capable **capace**
captain **capitano**
car **macchina**
card **carta, biglietto**
careful **prudente**
carrot **carota**
carry, to **portare**
cash, to **incassare**
cashier **cassiere** (m.)/**cassiera**
castle **castello**
cat **gatto**
cathedral **cattedrale, duomo**
Catholic **cattolico**
cause **causa**
cave **caverna**
ceiling **soffitto**
celebrate, to **festeggiare**
cellar **cantina**
cemetery **cimitero**
center **centro**
central **centrale**
century **secolo**
certain **certo**
certainly **certamente**
chair **sedia**
change, to **cambiare, modificare**
change (money) **spiccioli**
charming **affascinante**
cheap **a buon mercato**
check, to **controllare**

check **assegno**
checkroom **guardaroba**
cheerful **allegro**
cheese **formaggio**
chest **petto**
chicken **pollo**
child **bambino**
childhood **infanzia**
chocolate **cioccolato**
Christian **cristiano**
Christmas **Natale** (m.)
Christmas tree **albero di Natale**
church **chiesa**
cigar **sigaro**
cigarette **sigaretta**
circus **circo**
city **città**
city hall **municipio**
civilization **civiltà**
class **classe** (f.)
clean **pulito**
clean, to **pulire**
clear **chiaro**
clever **furbo, intelligente**
cliff **precipizio**
climate **clima** (m.)
climb **salire**
clock **orologio**
close **vicino**
close, to **chiudere**
closed **chiuso**
closet **armadio**
cloth **tessuto, stoffa**
clothes **vestiti**
cloud **nuvola**
cloudy **nuvoloso**
coal **carbone** (m.)
coast **costa, costiera**
coat **giacca, soprabito, cappotto**
coffee **caffè** (m.)
cold (adj.) **freddo**
cold (illness) **raffreddore** (m.)
collapse, to **crollare**
collar **colletto**
collection **raccolta**
color **colore** (m.)
comb **pettine** (m.)
come, to **venire**
to come in **entrare**
comfort **conforto**
comfortable **confortevole**

to make oneself . . . **accomodarsi**
commerce **commercio**
Communist **comunista** (m. and f.)
company **compagnia, società**
complain **lamentarsi**
completely **completamente**
computer **computer** (m.)
concert **concerto**
concierge **portinaio**
condition **condizione** (f.)
conductor **conduttore** (m.)
congratulate **congratulare, augurare**
connection (train, etc.) **coincidenza**
consist of, to **consistere in**
contract **contratto**
contrary, on the **al contrario**
conversation **conversazione** (f.)
convince, to **convincere**
cook, to **cucinare**
cook **cuoco**
cooked **cotto**
cool **fresco**
copy **copia**
corner **angolo**
correct **corretto**
cost, to **costare**
cotton **cotone** (m.)
cough **tosse** (f.)
count **contare**
country **paese** (m.)
countryside **campagna**
couple **coppia**
courage **coraggio**
course **corso**
of course **beninteso, s'intende**
courtesy **cortesia**
cousin **cugino**
cover, to **coprire**
cow **vacca, mucca**
crazy **pazzo, matto**
cream **crema, panna**
credit **credito**
criminal **criminale** (m.)
cross, to **attraversare**
crossroads **incrocio**
cry, to **piangere**
cup **tazza**
curtain **tenda**
custom **costume** (m.), **usanza**
customs **dogana**
cut, to **tagliare**

D

daily **quotidiano**
damage **danno**
damp **umido**
dance, to **ballare**
danger **pericolo**
dangerous **pericoloso**
dark **oscuro**
date **data, appuntamento**
daughter **figlia**
dawn **alba**
day **giorno, giornata**
dead **morto**
dear **caro**
decide, to **decidere**
decision **decisione** (f.)
declare **dichiarare**
deep **profond**
degree **grado**
delay **ritardo, rinvio**
delicious **squisito**
delighted **lieto**
deliver, to **consegnare**
dentist **dentista** (m. and f.)
dentures **dentiera**
depart, to **partire**
departure **partenza**
deposit **deposito**
describe **descrivere**
description **descrizione** (f.)
desire, to **desiderare**
desk **scrittoio**
dessert **dolce** (m.)
diamond **diamante** (m.)
dictionary **dizionario**
die, to **morire**
difference **differenza**
different **diverso**
difficult **difficile**
dine, to **cenare**
dining room **sala da pranzo**
dinner **cena**
direction **direzione** (f.)
directly **direttamente**
dirty **sporco**
disappear, to **sparire**
disappointed **deluso**

discount **sconto**
discover **scoprire**
disgusting **schifoso**
dish **piatto**
distance **distanza**
distant **distante**
disturb, to **disturbare**
dive, to **tuffare**
divide, to **dividere**
divorced **divorziato**
dizzy **stordito**
do, to **fare**
doctor **medico**
dog **cane** (m.)
dollar **dollaro**
donkey **asino**
door **porta**
double **doppio**
doubt **dubito**
down **giù**
draft **corrente d'aria** (f.)
dream, to **sognare**
dream **sogno**
dress **vestito**
dress, to **vestirsi**
drink, to **bere**
drive, to **guidare**
driver **autista** (m. and f.)
driver's license **patente** (f.)
drunk **ubriaco**
dry **secco**
during **durante**

E

each **ogni**
ear **orecchio**
early **presto**
earn, to **guadagnare**
earth **terra**
east **est**
Easter **Pasqua**
easy **facile**
eat, to **mangiare**
egg **uovo**
either . . . or **o . . . o**
electric **elettrico**
electricity **elettricità**
elevator **ascensore** (m.)

ITALIAN

embark, to **imbarcarsi**
embassy **ambasciata**
embrace, to **abbracciare**
embroidery **ricamo**
emergency **emergenza**
employee **impiegato**
employer **datore di lavoro** (m.)
empty **vuoto**
end **fine** (f.) **termine** (m.)
to end **finire, terminare**
England **Inghilterra**
English **inglese**
enough **abbastanza**
enter **entrare**
enthusiastic **entusiasta**
entire **intero**
entrance **entrata**
envelope **busta**
equal **uguale**
error **errore** (m.) **sbaglio**
escape, to **scappare**
especially **soprattutto, specialmente**
eternal **eterno**
even **pari, regolare**
evening **sera, serata**
event **avvenimento**
ever **mai, sempre**
every **ogni**
everybody **ognuno**
everything **tutto**
everywhere **dappertutto**
exact **esatto**
exaggerate, to **esagerare**
examine, to **esaminare**
example **esempio**
excellent **eccellente, ottimo**
except **eccetto, salvo**
exchange (currency) **cambio**
exchange, to **scambiare**
excuse me **scusi**
exist, to **esistere**
exit **uscita**
expensive **caro**
experience **esperienza**
explain, to **spiegare**
explanation **spiegazione** (f.)
export, to **sportare**
expression **espressione** (f.)
extinguish **estinguere**
extra **in più**
eye **occhio**

F

fabric **tessuto**
face **viso, faccia**
factory **fabbrica**
faithful **fedele**
fall **caduta**
fall, to **cadere**
family **famiglia**
famous **famoso**
far **lontano**
farm **fattoria**
farmer **contadino**
farther **più avanti**
fashion **moda**
fast **veloce**
fat **grasso**
father **padre**
favorable **favorevole**
fear **paura**
feel, to **sentire**
fence **steccato**
fever **febbre** (f.)
few **pochi**
field **campo**
fight, to **combattere**
fill **riempire**
film **film** (m.), **pellicola**
finally **finalmente**
find, to **trovare**
find out **scoprire**
fine (money) **multa**
finger **dito**
fire **fuoco**
fire department **corpo dei pompieri**
first **prima**
fish **pesce** (m.)
fish, to **pescare**
fishing tackle **arnese da pesca**
flame **fiamma**
flight **volo**
floor (ground) **pavimento**
   (of building) **piano**
flower **fiore** (m.)
fly, to **volare**
fly (insect) **mosca**
fog **nebbia**
follow, to **seguire**

food **cibo**
foot **piede** (m.)
for **per**
forbidden **vietato**
foreign **straniero**
foreigner **straniero**
forest **selva**
forget, to **dimenticare**
forgive, to **perdonare**
fork **forchetta**
forward **avanti**
fountain **fontana**
fox **volpe** (f.)
France **Francia**
French **francese**
free **gratis, libero**
freedom **libertà**
freeze, to **gelare**
frequently **spesso**
fresco **affresco**
fresh **fresco**
fried **fritto**
friend **amico**
friendship **amicizia**
frightened, to be **spaventarsi**
from **da**
front of, in **davanti a**
fruit **frutta**
fry **friggere**
frying pan **padella**
full **pieno**
funeral **pompe funebri**
funny **comico, buffo**
furnish, to **arredare**
furnished **arredato**
furniture **mobilia, mobili**
future **avvenire** (m.), **futuro**

G

gamble **giocare**
game **gioco, partita**
garage **garage** (m.)
garden **giardino**
gasoline **benzina**
gas station **distributore** (m.) **di benzina**
gate **cancello**
gather **raccogliere**
gentleman **signore**

genuine **genuino**
Germany **Germania**
get in (car, etc.) **salire**
get out (car, etc.) **scendere**
get up, to **alzarsi**
girl **ragazza**
give, to **dare**
glad **contento**
glass **bicchiere** (m.), **vetro**
glasses **occhiali**
glove **guanto**
go **andare**
God **Dio**
gold **oro**
good **buono**
goodbye **arrivederci**
good evening **buona sera**
good morning **buon giorno**
good night **buona notte**
government **governo**
granddaughter/son **nipote**
grandfather/mother **nonno/nonna**
grape **uva**
grapefruit **pompelmo**
grateful **grato**
grave **tomba**
gray **grigio**
great **grande**
green **verde**
greeting **saluto**
group **gruppo**
grow, to **crescere**
guess **indovinare**
guest **invitato**
guide **guida** (m.)
guitar **chitarra**
gun **arma**
gymnasium **palestra**
gynecologist **ginecologo**

H

hair **capelli** (m.)
hairdresser **parucchiere** (m.)
half **metà**
hall **corridoio**
hand **mano** (f.)
handbag **borsa**
handkerchief **fazzoletto**
happiness **felicità**

ITALIAN

happy **felice**
hard **duro**
hat **cappello**
hate, to **odiare**
have, to **avere**
have to, to **dovere**
he **lui, egli**
head **testa, capo**
health **salute** (f.)
healthfood store **negozio di produtti macrobiotici**
health resort **stazione climatica**
hear, to **sentire**
heart **cuore** (m.)
heat **calore** (m.)
heatstroke **colpo di sole**
heavy **pesante**
heal **guarire**
heel **tacco**
Hello! **Buon giorno**
help, to **aiutare**
help **aiuto**
her, hers **lei, suo**
here **qui**
here is **ecco**
high **alto**
high school **liceo**
highway **autostrada**
hill **collina**
him, his **lui, suo**
history **storia**
hitchhike, to **fare l'autostop**
hold, to **tenere**
hole **buco**
holiday **festa**
holy **santo**
home **casa**
honest **onesto**
honey **miele** (m.)
honeymoon **luna di miele**
honor **onore** (m.)
hope, to **sperare**
hope **speranza**
horn (car) **clacson** (m.)
horse **cavallo**
hospital **ospedale** (m.)
hospitality **ospitalità**
hot **caldo**
hotel **albergo**
hour **ora**
house **casa**

how **come**
humidity **umidità**
hunger **fame** (f.)
hungry, to be **avere fame**
hurry, to be in a **avere fretta**
husband **marito**
hut **capanna**

I

I **io**
ice cream **gelato**
ice skate, to **pattinare**
idea **idea**
identification **identificazione** (f.)
idiot **idiota** (m.), **cretino**
if **se**
ignorant **ignorante**
ill **malato, ammalato**
imagine, to **immaginare**
immediately **immediatamente**
import, to **importare**
important **importante**
impossible **impossibile**
impression **impressione**
in **in**
including **compreso**
incorrect **scorretto, sbagliato**
indeed **veramente**
inexpensive **a buon mercato**
inform, to **informare**
information **informazione** (f.)
inhabitant **abitante** (m.)
inquiry **domanda**
inside **dentro**
instead **invece**
insure, to **assicurare**
interested **interessato**
interesting **interessante**
interpreter **interprete** (m.)
interrupt, to **interrompere**
introduce (person) **presentare**
introduction **introduzione** (f.)
invite, to **invitare**
invitation **invito**
island **isola**
Italy **Italia**
Italian **Italiano**
itinerary **itinerario**

J

jacket **giacca**
jam **marmellata**
jealous **geloso**
jewelry **gioielli**
Jewish **ebreo**
job **lavoro**
joke **scherzo**
joke, to **scherzare**
joy **gioia**
jump, to **saltare**
just (only) **solo**
  (exactly) **proprio**
just (now) **appena**

K

keep, to **tenere**
key **chiave**
kind (adj.) **gentile**
kind (n.) **specie** (f.)
kindness **gentilezza**
king **re** (m.)
kiss **bacio**
kitchen **cucina**
knife **coltello**
knock, to **bussare**
know, to **sapere**
know, to **conoscere**
  (be acquainted with)
knowledge **sapienza, conoscenza**

L

lady **signora**
lake **lago**
lamb **agnello**
lamp **lampada**
land **terra, paese** (m.)
land, to (plane) **atterrare**
language **lingua**

large **grande**
last, to **durare**
last **ultimo**
late **tardi**
laugh, to **ridere**
laundry **lavanderia**
law **legge** (f.)
lawyer **avvocato**
learn **imparare**
least **minimo**
leather **pelle** (f.)
leave, to (go away) **partire**
  (abandon) **lasciare**
left **sinistra**
leg **gamba**
legal **legale**
lend, to **prestare**
less **meno**
lesson **lezione** (f.)
let, to **permettere**
letter **lettera**
lettuce **lattuga**
liberty **libertà**
library **biblioteca**
license plate **targa**
lie, to **mentire**
lie **bugia**
life **vita**
lifeboat **scialuppa di salvataggio**
lifeguard **bagnino**
lift, to **sollevare**
light (illumination) **luce** (f.)
light (color) **chiaro**
light, to **illuminare**
light (weight) **leggero**
light bulb **lampadina**
lightning **fulmine** (m.)
like, to **piacere, gradire**
line **linea**
linen **lino**
lion **leone** (m.)
lip **labbro** (pl. **le labbra**)
list **lista, elenco**
listen, to **ascoltare**
literature **letteratura**
little **piccolo**
live, to **vivere, abitare**
living room **salotto**
load **carico**
locate, to **situare**
lodging **alloggio**

logical **logico**
long **lungo**
look, to **guardare**
lose, to **perdere**
lost **perso**
loud **forte**
love, to **amare**
lover **amante** (m. and f.)
low **basso**
luck **fortuna**
luggage **bagaglio**
lunch **pranzo**
luxury **lusso**

M

machine **macchina**
magazine **rivista**
magnificent **magnifico**
maid **donna di servizio**
mail **posta**
mailbox **cassetta postale**
make, to **fare**
man **uomo** (pl. **uomini**)
management **direzione** (f.)
manager **direttore**
manner **maniera**
map **carta, pianta**
marble **marmo**
market **mercato**
married **sposato**
marry, to **sposare, sposarsi**
marvel **meraviglia**
marvelous **meraviglioso**
Mass **messa**
material **materiale** (m.), **stoffa**
mattress **materasso**
maybe **forse**
mayor **sindaco**
me **me**
meal **pasto**
mean, to **voler dire, significare**
  meaning **significato**
means **mezzo, mezzi**
meat **carne** (f.)
medicine **medicina**
Mediterranean **mediterraneo**
medieval **medievale**

meet, to **incontrare, trovarsi**
meeting **riunione** (f.)
member **membro**
menu **menù** (m.)
merchandise **merce** (f.)
message **messaggio**
middle **mezzo**
Middle Ages **medio evo**
midnight **mezzanotte** (f.)
mile **miglio** (pl. **le miglia**)
milk **latte** (m.)
million **milione** (m.)
mine **mio**
minister **ministro**
minute **minuto**
mirror **specchio**
miss, to **mancare**
Miss **signorina**
mistake **sbaglio, errore**
misunderstanding **equivoco,
  malinteso**
mix, to **mescolare**
model **modello**
modern **moderno**
modest **modesto**
moment **momento**
monastery **monastero**
money **soldi, denaro**
monkey **scimmia**
month **mese** (m.)
monthly **mensilmente**
monument **monumento**
moon **luna**
more **più**
morning **mattina**
most **la maggior parte** (f.)
mostly **per lo più**
mother **madre**
mother-in-law **suocera**
motor **motore** (m.)
motorcycle **motocicletta**
mountain **montagna**
mountain climbing **alpinismo**
mouse **topo**
mouth **bocca**
movement **movimento**
movies **cinema** (m.)
much **molto**
mud **fango**
murder, to **uccidere**
museum **museo**

music **musica**
musician **musicista** (m. and f.)
must **dovere**
mustache **baffi**
mustard **senape** (f.)
mutton **montone** (m.)
my **mio**
myself **me stesso, mi**

N

name **nome** (m.)
napkin **tovagliolo**
narrow **stretto**
navy **marina**
near **vicino**
necessary **necessario**
neck **collo**
necktie **cravatta**
need, to **avere bisogno**
needle **ago**
neighbor **vicino di casa**
neighborhood **quartiere** (m.)
nephew **nipote**
nervous **nervoso**
never **mai**
new **nuovo**
news **novità, notizie**
newspaper **giornale** (m.)
New Year's Eve **Sera di San Silvestro**
next **prossimo**
nice **simpatico, gradevole**
niece **nipote**
night **notte** (f.)
nightclub **night** (m.)
nightgown **camicia da notte**
no **no**
nobody **nessuno**
noise **rumore** (m.)
noon **mezzogiorno**
north **nord**
nose **naso**
not **non**
notebook **quaderno**
nothing **niente**
notice, to **notare**

nowhere **da nessuna parte**
number **numero**
nut **noce** (f.)

O

oar **remo**
object **oggetto**
occasion **occasione** (f.)
occasionally **ogni tanto**
occupied **occupato**
occur, to **succedere, capitare, accadere**
ocean **oceano**
of **di**
offer **offrire**
office **ufficio**
often **spesso**
oil **olio**
old **vecchio**
on **su**
once **una volta**
one **uno, una**
one-way ticket **biglietto di andata solo**
one-way (street) **senso unico**
only **solo, soltanto**
open, to **aprire**
open **aperto**
opera **opera**
opinion **opinione** (f.)
opportunity **opportunità**
opposite **opposto**
or **o, oppure**
orange **arancia**
order, to **ordinare**
in order to **per**
original **originale**
other **altro**
otherwise **altrimenti**
our **nostro**
ourselves **noi, ci**
out of order **guasto**
outside **fuori**
over **sopra**
owe, to **dovere**
own **proprio**
owner **proprietario**

P

package **pacco**
paid **pagato**
pain **dolore**
painter **pittore** (m.)
painting **quadro, pittura**
pair **coppia**
palace **palazzo**
pants **pantaloni** (m.)
paper **carta**
parent **genitore** (m.)
park **parco**
park, to **parcheggiare**
parking **parcheggio**
part **parte** (f.)
party (political) **partito**
passenger **passeggero**
passport **passaporto**
past **passato**
path **sentiero**
pay, to **pagare**
payment **pagamento**
peace **pace** (f.)
pen **penna, biro** (f.)
pencil **matita**
people **gente** (f.)
perfect **perfetto**
perfume **profumo**
perhaps **forse**
period **periodo**
permit, to **permettere**
person **persona**
photograph **fotografia**
photograph, to **fotografare**
piano **pianoforte** (m.)
pickpocket **borseggiatore**
picture **immagine** (f.)
piece **pezzo** (m.)
pig **maiale, porco**
pigeon **piccione** (m.)
pill **pillola**
pillow **guanciale** (m.)
pin **spillo**
pink **rosa**
pitcher **caraffa**
place **luogo**
plan **piano, progetto**

plant **pianta**
plate **piatto**
platform (train) **binario**
play, to **giocare**
play, to
  (music) **suonare**
play **rappresentazione** (f.)
pleasant **gradevole, piacevole**
please **per piacere**
pleasure **piacere** (m.)
pocket **tasca**
poem **poesia**
point, to **indicare**
point **punta**
police **polizia**
police station **questura**
polite **cortese**
pond **stagno**
poor **povero**
pope **papa** (m.)
popular **popolare**
pork **maiale** (m.)
port **porto**
possible **possibile**
post card **cartolina**
post office **ufficio postale**
pot (cooking) **pentola**
potato **patata**
pound **libro**
powerful **potente**
practice, to **praticare**
pray, to **pregare**
precise **preciso, esatto**
pregnant **incinta**
prepare, to **preparare**
prescription **ricetta**
present **regalo**
press, to **premere**
pretty **grazioso, carino**
price **prezzo**
priest **prete**
prison **prigione** (f.),
  carcere (f.)
probable **probabile**
problem **problema** (m.)
profession **mestiere** (m.),
  professione (f.)
profit **guadagno**
program **programma**
promise, to **promettere**
pronounce, to **pronunciare**

property **proprietà**
Protestant **protestante**
public **pubblico**
publisher **editore**
pull, to **tirare**
purchase, to **comprare**
push, to **spingere**
put, to **mettere**
put on, to **mettersi, indossare**

Q

quality **qualità**
quarter **quarto**
queen **regina**
question **domanda**
quick **rapido, veloce**
quiet **tranquillo**
quite **piuttosto**

R

rabbi **rabbino**
rabbit **coniglio**
race **corsa**
radiator (car) **radiatore** (m.)
radiator (room) **termosifone** (m.)
radio **radio** (f.)
railroad **ferrovia**
railway station **stazione ferroviaria**
rain **pioggia**
raincoat **impermeabile** (m.)
raise, to **alzare**
rape **stupro**
rapid **rapido**
rare **raro**
rare (meat) **al sangue**
rarely **raramente**
rather **alquanto, piuttosto**
raw **crudo**
razor **rasoio**
razor blade **lama di rasoio**
reach **raggiungere**
read, to **leggere**
ready **pronto**
real **vero**
really **veramente, proprio**
reason **ragione**

reasonable **ragionevole**
receipt **ricevuta**
receive, to **ricevere**
recently **recentemente**
recognize **riconoscere**
recommend, to **raccomandare**
red **rosso**
refrigerator **frigorifero**
refuse, to **rifiutare**
regards **saluti**
region **regione** (f.)
regret, to **rimpiangere**
regular **regolare**
religion **religione** (f.)
religious **religioso**
remain, to **rimanere**
remainder **resto**
remember, to **ricordarsi**
remind, to **ricordare**
rent, to **noleggiare, affittare**
repair, to **riparare**
repeat, to **ripetere**
replace, to **sostituire**
report **rapporto, referto**
represent, to **rappresentare**
republic **repubblica**
reserve, to **prenotare**
reservation **prenotazione** (f.)
responsible **responsabile**
rest, to **riposarsi**
restaurant **ristorante** (m.)
retail **al minuto**
return, to **ritornare** (intr.)
  restituire (tr.)
ribbon **nastro**
rice **riso**
rich **ricco**
ride, to (horse) **cavalcare**
right (correct) **giusto, corretto**
right (direction) **destra**
right (noun) **diritto**
ring **anello**
rise, to **alzarsi**
river **fiume** (m.)
road **strada, via**
roast **arrosto**
rob **derubare**
robbery **furto**
rock **pietra, roccia**
roll **panino**
roof **tetto**

ITALIAN

room **camera, stanza**
round **rotondo**
round trip **andata e ritorno**
route **strada**
row **fila**
rug **tappeto**
ruins **rovine** (f.)
run, to **correre**
Russia **Russia**
Russian **russo**

S

sacrifice **sacrificio**
sad **triste**
safe **sicuro**
safe (strongbox) **cassaforte**
sail, to **imbarcarsi**
sailboat **veliero**
sailor **marinaio**
saint **santo**
salad **insalata**
salary **stipendio**
sale **vendita, svendita**
salesperson **commesso**
salt **sale**
salty **salato**
same **uguale, stesso**
satisfied **content**
satisfy **soddisfare**
sauce **salsa**
saucer **piattino**
save, to **salvare**
save, to (money) **risparmiare**
savings bank **cassa di risparmio**
say, to **dire**
science **scienza**
school **scuola**
scissors **forbici** (f.)
scream **grido**
sculptor **scultore**
sea **mare** (m.)
seashore **lido, sponda**
seasickness **mal di mare** (m.)
season **stagione** (f.)
seasoning **condimento**
seat **sedia** (m.)
second **secondo**

secretary **segretario**
see, to **vedere**
seek, to **cercare**
seldom **raramente**
sell, to **vendere**
send, to **mandare, spedire**
separate **separato**
serious **grave**
serve **servire**
service **servizio**
set, to **apparecchiare**
several **parecchi**
shade **ombra**
shadow **ombra**
share, to **condividere**
sharp **piccante, tagliente**
shave **radersi**
she **lei, ella**
sheet (bed) **lenzuolo** (pl. **le lenzuota**)
ship **nave**
shirt **camicia**
shoe **scarpa**
shoelaces **lacci**
shop **negozio**
short **corto**
shorts **shorts** (m.)
shoulder **spalla**
show, to **dimostrare, mostrare, far vedere**
shower **doccia**
shut, to **chiudere**
sick **malato**
side **lato**
sidewalk **marciapiede** (m.)
sights **luoghi interessanti**
sign **cartello**
silence **silenzio**
silk **seta**
silver **argento**
similar **simile**
simple **semplice**
since **siccome, poichè**
sing, to **cantare**
singer **cantante**
single **celibe** (m.), **nubile** (f.)
sir **signore**
sister **sorella**
sister-in-law **cognata**
sit, to **sedersi**
size **taglia**

skin **pelle** (f.)
skirt **gonna**
ski, to **sciare**
skis **sci**
sky **cielo**
skyscraper **grattacielo**
sleep, to **dormire**
to go to sleep **addormentarsi**
sleeping bag **sacco a pelo**
sleeve **manica**
slip, to **scivolare**
slow **lento**
small **piccolo**
smell, to **odorare**
smile, to **sorridere**
smoke, to **fumare**
smooth **liscio**
snake **serpente** (m.)
sneeze, to **starnutire**
snow **neve** (f.)
so **così, allora**
soap **sapone** (m.)
sock **calzino**
sofa **divano**
soft **morbido**
soldier **soldato**
some **alcuni,**
  un po', un po' di
somebody **qualcuno**
something **qualche cosa**
sometimes **qualche volta**
somewhat **alquanto**
somewhere **da qualche parte**
son **figlio**
song **canzone** (f.)
soon **presto, fra poco**
soup **zuppa, minestra**
sour **agro**
south **sud**
souvenir **ricordo**
Spain **Spagna**
Spanish **spagnolo**
speak, to **parlare**
special **speciale**
speed limit **limite** (m.) **di velocità**
spend **spendere**
sponge **spugna**
spoon **cucchiaio**
sport **sport** (m.)
sporting goods **articoli sportivi**
spring **primavera**

stairway **scala**
stamp **francobollo, timbro**
stand up **stare in piedi**
star **stella**
start, to **incominciare, iniziare**
station **stazione** (f.)
statue **statua**
stay, to **restare, rimanere**
stay **permanenza**
steak **bistecca**
steal, to **rubare**
steamer (ship) **vapore** (m.)
stick **stecco, bacchetta**
still (adj.) **calmo, immobile**
  (yet) **ancora**
stocking **calza**
stomach **stomaco**
stone **pietra**
stop, to **fermare, fermarsi**
stop (bus, etc.) **fermata**
storm **temporale** (m.)
story **storia, racconto**
stove **stufa**
straight **diritto, dritto**
strange **strano**
street **strada, via**
streetcar **tram** (m.)
strike, to **battere**
strike (labor) **sciopero**
string **spago**
stroll **passeggiata**
strong **forte**
student **studente** (m.)
  studentessa
study, to **studiare**
stupid **stupido**
style **stile** (m.)
subway **metropolitana**
sudden **improvviso**
sugar **zucchero**
suit **completo**
suitcase **valigia**
summer **estate** (f.)
summit **vertice** (m.)
sun **sole** (m.)
sunburn **scottatura solare**
sunglasses **occhiali da sole**
sunset **tramonto**
supplement **supplemento**
sure **sicuro**
surf **frangente** (m.)

surprise **sorpresa**
supper **cena**
suppose, to **supporre**
sweat, to **sudare**
sweater **golf** (m.)
sweet **dolce**
swim, to **nuotare**
swimming pool **piscina**
Swiss **svizzero**
Switzerland **Svizzera**
synagogue **sinagoga**

T

table **tavola**
tablecloth **tovaglia**
tailor **sarto**
take, to **prendere**
take off, to **decollare** (plane)
  togliere (clothes)
talk, to **parlare**
tall **alto**
tape **nastro**
tape recorder **registratore** (m.)
taste, to **gustare, assaggiare**
taste **gusto**
tax **tassa**
taxi **tassì** (m.)
tea **tè** (m.)
teach, to **insegnare**
teacher **insegnante** (m. and f.),
  maestro
team **squadra**
tear (weeping) **lagrima**
tear, to **strappare**
telegram **telegramma** (m.)
telephone **telefono**
television **televisione** (f.)
tell, to **raccontare, dire**
temperature **temperatura**
temporary **provvisorio**
tent **tenda**
terrible **terribile**
than **che, di**
thank, to **ringraziare**
thanks **grazie**
that **quello, che**
the **il, lo, la**
theatre **teatro**
then **allora**

there **là, lì, ci**
there is **c'è**
there are **ci sono**
thermometer **termometro**
they **loro**
thief **ladro**
thin **sottile, magro**
thing **cosa**
think, to **pensare**
third **terzo**
thirst **sete** (f.)
thirsty, to be **avere sete**
this **questo**
those **quelli, quei**
thousand **mille**
thread **filo**
throat **gola**
through **per, attraverso**
throw, to **lanciare, gettare, buttare**
thunder **tuono**
thus **così**
ticket **biglietto**
ticket (speeding, etc.) **verbale** (m.)
tide **marea**
tie **cravatta**
tight **stretto**
time **ora, tempo**
timetable **orario**
tip (money) **mancia**
tire **gomma**
tired **stanco**
to **a**
tobacco **tabacco**
today **oggi**
together **insieme**
toilet **gabinetto**
tomato **pomodoro**
tomorrow **domani**
tongue **lingua**
tonight **stasera**
too (also) **anche**
too much **troppo**
tooth **dente** (m.)
toothbrush **spazzolino da denti**
toothpaste **dentifricio**
top **cima**
touch, to **toccare**
tough **duro**
tour **giro, escursione**
towel **asciugamano**
tower **torre** (f.)

town **cittadina**
towtruck **autogru** (f.)
toy **giocattolo**
trade **commercio**
trade fair **fiera campionaria**
traffic **traffico**
traffic jam **ingorgo**
traffic light **semáforo**
train **treno**
translate **tradurre**
translation **traduzione** (f.)
travel, to **viaggiare**
travel agency **agenzia di viaggi**
traveler **viaggiatore**
tree **albero**
trip **viaggio**
trouble **problemi** (m.), **guai** (m.)
truck **camion** (m.), **autocarro**
true **vero**
trunk **baule** (m.)
truth **verità**
try, to **provare**
try on, to **provare**
turn off, to **spegnere, chiudere**
turn on, to **accendere, aprire**
typewriter **macchina da scrivere**

U

ugly **brutto**
umbrella **ombrello**
uncle **zio**
unconscious **inconscio**
under **sotto**
understand **capire**
underwear **biancheria intima**
undress, to **spogliarsi**
unfortunately **sfortunatamente**
United States **Stati Uniti**
university **università**
unless **ameno che**
until **fino a**
up **su**
upstairs **di sopra**
urgent **urgente**
us **noi**
use, to **usare**
use **uso**
useful **utile**
usual **normale, solito**

V

vacant **libero**
vacation **vacanza, le ferie**
valid **valido**
valuables **oggetti di valore**
value **valore** (m.)
various **vario**
vegetables **legumi** (m.), **verdura**
vehicle **veicolo**
very **molto**
victory **vittoria**
view **vista**
village **villaggio**
vineyard **vigna**
violin **violino**
visit, to **visitare, far visita a**
voice **voce** (f.)
voltage **voltaggio**
voyage **viaggio**

W

waist **vita**
wait, to **aspettare**
waiter **cameriere**
waitress **cameriera**
waiting room **sala d'attesa**
wake up, to **svegliarsi**
walk, to **camminare**
walk **passeggiata**
wall (building) **muro**
wall (room) **parete** (f.)
wallet **portafoglio**
want, to **volere, desiderare**
war **guerra**
warm **caldo**
warn, to **avvertire**
wash, to **lavare**
wash oneself, to **lavarsi**
wash basin **lavabo**
waste, to **sprecare**
watch, to **guardare**
watch **orologio**
water **acqua**
waterfront **riva**
water sports **sport aquatici**

ITALIAN

wave **onda**
way **modo**
we **noi**
weak **debole**
wear, to **portare**
weather **tempo**
wedding **matrimonio**
week **settimana**
weekend **week-end** (m.)
weigh, to **pesare**
weight **peso**
welcome **benvenuto**
well **bene**
west **ovest**
what **che, cosa, che cosa**
whatever **qualsiasi cosa**
wheat **grano**
wheel **ruota**
when **quando**
where **dove**
whether **se**
which **quale**
while **mentre**
white **bianco**
who **chi**
whole **intero**
whose **di chi**
why **perchè**
wide **largo**
widow **vedova**
widower **vedovo**
wife **moglie**
wilderness **deserto**
win, to **vincere**
wind **vento**
wine list **lista dei vini**
window (house) **finestra**
window (train, etc.) **finestrino**
wine **vino**
wing **ala**
winter **inverno**
wish, to **volere, desiderare**
wish **desiderio**

with **con**
without **senza**
wolf **lupo**
woman **donna**
wonder **meraviglia**
wonderful **meraviglioso**
wood **legno**
wool **lana**
word **parola**
work **lavoro**
world **mondo**
worry **preoccuparsi**
worse **peggio; peggiore**
wrap, to **avvolgere**
wrist **polso**
write, to **scrivere**
writer **scrittore** (m.), **scrittrice** (f.)
wrong **sbagliato, scorretto**

Y

year **anno**
yellow **giallo**
yes, **sì**
yesterday **ieri**
yet **ancora**
you **tu, Lei**
young **giovane**
your **tuo, suo**
you're welcome **prego**

Z

zero **zero**
zipper **cerniera lampo**
zone **zona**
zoo **zoo**

SPANISH

PRONUNCIATION GUIDE

	Phonetic Symbol	Approximate Pronunciation	Spanish Example	Phonetic Transcription	Meaning
Vowels					
a	a	like a in father	casa	*kasa*	house
e	e	as in let	comer	ko*mer*	to eat
i	ee	as in seen	escribir	eskree*beer*	to write
o	o	like o in soldier	con	kon	with
u	oo	as in boot	uno	*oo*no	one
		always silent after q	que	ke	what
		usually silent after g and before e and i	alguien	alg-yen	somebody
Diphthongs					
ia	eeya	like ia in Maria	lavandería	labande*reeya*	laundry
ua	wa	like wa in wander	cuándo	*kwando*	when
io	eeyo	as in Rio	adiós	ad*eeyos*	goodbye
ie	yeh	as in woe	antiguo	an*teeg*wo	antique
ie	we	like ye in yes	siete	*seeye*te	seven
ie	we	as in wet	cuento	*kwen*to	story
ai, ay	ah-y	like y in by	baile	*bah-yle*	dance
au	ow	as in cow	autor	ow*tor*	author
oi, oy	oy	as in joy	oigo	*oygo*	I hear
ei, ey	ay	like ay in paying	veinte	*baynte*	twenty
iu	yoo	like yu in Yule	ciudad	theey*oodad*	city
ui, uy	ooee	as in queen	ruido	*rooee*do	noise
Consonants					
b, d, f, k, l, m, n, p, q, s, t		pronounce as in English			
c	th	before e and i pronounced like *th* in thin	centro	*then*-tro	center

Letter	Sound	Explanation	Example	Pronunciation	Meaning
c	k	before all other letters pronounced like c in cat	casa	**kasa**	home
c	ch	as in church	mucho	**moocho**	much
ch	h	before e and i like an exaggerated h in halt	general	hener**al**	general
g	g	before a, o, ua, ue, ui, or a consonant like g in go	gato	**gato**	cat
g		always silent as in hour	hablar	a**blar**	to talk
h	h	before any vowel pronounced like an exaggerated h	jabón	ha**bon**	soap
j	y	like lli in million	milla	**mee**ya	mile
ll or =	ny	like ni in onion	niño	**nee**nyo	boy
ñ or ñ	r	is trilled after r, l or s or at the beginning of a word	rico	**ree**ko	rich
r	rr		perro	**perro**	dog
rr	b	like b in boy	vivir	bee-**beer**	to live
v	s	like s in sand	explorar	ess-plo-**rar**	to explore
x	gs	before a, e, o like gs in eggs	examen	eg**samen**	exam
x	ks	before i, u like ks in taxi	taxi	**tak**see	taxi
y	y	before a vowel as y in yoyo	mayo	**ma**-yo	May
z	th	before any vowel pronounced as th	zapato	tha**pa**-to	shoe

In Latin America the letters **s**, **z** and **c** before **e** and **i** are pronounced like the **s** in sorry. In Spain there is a distinction between **s**, which is pronounced like the English **s**, and **c** and **z** which are pronounced like **th** in think.

SPANISH GRAMMAR

Nouns and Articles

There are two genders in Spanish, masculine and feminine.

Masculine nouns usually end in *o,* and feminine nouns usually end in *a.*

The plural is formed by adding *s* to nouns that end in a vowel and *es* to nouns that end in a consonant.

Articles agree in gender and number with the noun.

The Definite Article (the) with the Masculine Noun

singular		plural
el niño	the boy	los niños
el tío	the uncle	los tíos

The Definite Article (the) with the Feminine Noun

la señora	the woman	las señoras
la mesa	the table	las mesas

The Indefinite Article (a, an) with the Masculine Noun

un amigo	a friend	unos amigos
un estudiante	a student	unos estundiantes

The Indefinite Article (a, an) with the Feminine Noun

una puerta	a door	unas puertas
una amiga	a friend (fem.)	unas amigas

The preposition *de* (of) is used to show possession.

el anillo de Manuel	Manuel's ring
el principio del año	the beginning of the year
las casas de ellos	their houses
(del is the contraction of de + el)	

Adjectives

The adjective agrees in gender and number with the noun it modifies. The plural of those ending in **o** and **a** is formed by adding **s.** Those adjectives ending in consonants form their plurals by adding **es.**

el perro negro	the black dog	los perros negros
un bolso rojo	a red bag	unos bolsos rojos
la niña bonita	the pretty girl	las niñas bonitas
una habitación pequeña	a small room	unas habitaciones pequeñas

Demonstrative Adjectives

this	este, esta	
	este cuadro	this painting
	esta manzana	this apple
these	estos, estas	
	estos cuadros	these paintings
	estas manzanas	these apples
that	ese, esa, aquel, aquella	
those	esos, esas, aquellos, aquellas	
	ese libro	that book
	esa mesa	that table
	aquel muchacho	that boy
	aquella muchacha	that girl
	esos libros	those books
	esas mesas	those tables
	aquellos muchachos	those boys
	aquellas muchachas	those girls

Neutral demonstrative pronouns:
esto, eso, aquello

Personal Pronouns

	Subject	Indirect object	Direct object
I, me	yo	me	me
you (familiar)	tú	te	te
you (formal)	usted	le	lo, la
he	él	le	lo
she	ella	le	la
it	él, ella	le	lo, la

we	nosotros	nos	nos
you (familiar masc.)	vosotros	os	os
you (familiar fem.)	vosotras	os	os
you (formal)	ustedes	les	los, las
they (masc.)	ellos	les	los
they (fem.)	ellas	les	las

Note that the *tú* (familiar) form is used with children, relatives, young people and good friends. The *usted* form is used with people you don't know very well or wish to remain on rather formal terms with.

The subject pronouns are often omitted. When they are used, it is where there is a need for emphasis. For example, it is more common to say: *Voy a la escuela* (I go to school) than to say *Yo voy a la escuela*. The latter places the emphasis on the subject rather than the action.

Possessive Adjectives

	singular	plural
my	mi	mis
your	tu	tus
his, her, its	su	sus
our	nuestro(a)	nuestros(as)
your	vuestro(a)	vuestros(as)
their	su	sus

Possessive Pronouns

	singular		plural	
	masculine	feminine	masculine	feminine
mine	el mío	la mía	los míos	las mías
yours (familiar)	el tuyo	la tuya	los tuyos	las tuyas
your (polite)	el suyo	la suya	los suyos	las suyas
his, her, its	el suyo	la suya	los suyos	las suyas
our	el nuestro	la nuestra	los nuestros	las nuestras
your (fam. pl.)	el vuestro	la vuestra	los vuestros	las vuestras
their	el suyo	la suya	los suyes	las suyas

Possessive adjectives and pronouns agree with their corresponding nouns in gender and number. They agree with what is being possessed.

Interrogative Pronouns

¿qué?	what
¿quién(es)?	who, whom
¿cuál?	which

Interrogative Adjectives

¿qué?	what
¿cuál?	which
¿cuánto?	how much/many

Relative Pronouns

el que	that which
la que	that which
lo que	that which
que	that

The comparative is formed by placing the word *más* (more) in front of the adjective: *más importante* (more important). The superlative is formed by placing the article before the adjective: *el más importante* (the most important). As in English, the adjectives *bueno* and *malo* (good and bad) have special forms to denote better–best and worse–worst:

bueno:	mejor-el mejor
malo:	peor-el peor

Verbs

The two most important auxiliary verbs are *ser* (to be) and *haber* (to have).

ser (to be)		*haber* (to have)	
yo soy	I am	yo he	I have
tú eres	you are	tú has	you have
usted es			
él, ella es	he, she is	él, ella ha	he, she has
nosotros somos	we are	nosotros hemos	we have
vosotros sois	you are	vosotros habéis	you have
ustedes son	you are	ustedes han	you have
ellos, ellas son	they are	ellos, ellas han	they have

SPANISH

Regular verbs are conjugated in one of three ways, according to their endings:

Present Indicative

infinitive ending in	-ar	-er	-ir
	amar	comer	vivir
	to love	to eat	to live
yo	amo	como	vivo
tú	amas	comes	vives
él	ama	come	vive
nosotros	amamos	comemos	vivimos
vosotros	amáis	coméis	vivís
ellos	aman	comen	viven

Some of the most common verbs are irregular:

ir	hacer	decir	ver	poder	saber
to go	to do	to say	to see	to be able	to know
voy	hago	digo	veo	puedo	sé
vas	haces	dices	ves	puedes	sabes
va	hace	dice	ve	puede	sabe
vamos	hacemos	decimos	vemos	podemos	sabemos
vais	hacéis	decís	veis	podéis	sabéis
van	hacen	dicen	ven	pueden	saben

Negatives

Negatives are formed by placing *no* in front of the verb:

Tengo frío.	I'm cold.	No tengo frío.	I'm not cold.

Questions

Questions are usually formed by merely changing the intonation of the voice. For example:

Tenéis hambre.	You are hungry.
¿Tenéis hambre?	Are you hungry?

Questions can also be formed by placing the subject immediately after the verb or at the end of the sentence:

Mario es alto.	Mario is tall.
¿Es Mario alto?	Is Mario tall?
¿Es alto Mario?	Is Mario tall?

Past Tense

The Past Absolute refers to action at a specific moment in the past time. Regular verbs are conjugated, according to their endings, as follows:

infinitve ending in	-ar	-er	-ir
yo	amé	comí	viví
tú	amaste	comiste	viiste
él, ella	amó	comió	vivió
nosotros	amamos	comimos	vivimos
vosotros	amasteis	comisteis	vivisteis
ellos, ellas	amaron	comieron	vivieron

Other forms of the past tense combine the proper form of the auxiliary verb *haber* with the past participle. The past participle is formed by adding one of two endings to the root of the verb: -ado for ar verbs, and -ido for -er and -ir verbs. The past participle is an adjective and agrees in number and gender with the nouns modified.

amar : he amado	I loved, I have loved
comer : he comido	I ate, I have eaten
vivir : he vivido	I lived, I have lived

Prepositions

to, at	a
before (time)	antes
below, under	debajo
close to	cerca de
with	con
against	contra
of	de
from	de, desde
in, into	en
between, among	entre
toward	hacia
till, until	hasta
for	por, para
in order to,	para
according to	según
without	sin
on, upon	sobre
behind	detrás

A few prepositions contract with the definite article:

a (to)	de (of)
a + el = al	de + el = del

SPANISH

EXPRESSIONS FOR EVERYDAY USE

Basic

Yes.
Sí.
see

No.
No.
no

Please.
Por favor.
por fabor.

Thank you.
Gracias.
gratheeyas

Yes, thank you.
Sí, gracias.
si gratheeyas

No, thank you.
No, gracias.
no gratheeyas

Thank you very much.
Muchas gracias.
moochas gratheeyas

Excuse me.
Perdóneme.
perdoneme

Just a moment.
Un momento.
oon momento

Of course.
Claro.
klaro

How much?
¿Cuánto?
kwanto?

Where is the restroom?
¿Dónde está el servicio?
donde esta el serbeetheeyo?

I don't understand.
No entiendo.
no enteeyendo

What did you say?
¿Perdone usted?
perdone oosted?

What did you say?
¿Dispense usted?
deespense oosted?

That's quite all right.
No se preocupe.
no se preokoope

Greetings

Good morning.
Buenos días.
bwenos deeyas

Good afternoon.
Buenas tardes.
bwenas tardes

Good evening.
Buenas tardes.
bwenas tardes

Good night.
Buenas noches.
bwenas noches

Goodbye.
Adiós.
adeeyos

See you later.
Hasta la vista.
asta la beesta

See you this evening.
Hasta la tarde.
asta la tarde

See you tomorrow.
Hasta mañana.
asta manyana

SPANISH

How are you?
¿Cómo está usted?
¿Cómo estás? (informal)
komo esta oosted?
komo estas?

How are things?
¿Cómo le va todo?
¿Cómo te va todo? (informal)
komo le ba todo?
komo te ba todo?

Everything's fine. That's fine.
Todo me va bien. Está bien.
todo me ba beeyehn esta beeyen

Communication Problems

Do you speak English?
¿Habla inglés?
abla eengles?

**Do you speak French/German/
   Spanish?**
¿Habla francés/alemán/español?
abla franthes/aleman/espanyol?

I don't speak Spanish.
No hablo español.
no ablo espanyol

I speak some French.
Hablo un poco de francés.
ablo oom poko de franthes

I don't understand you.
No le/la entiendo.
no lo/la enteeyendo

Could you speak more slowly?
¿Puede hablar más despacio?
pwede ablar mas despatheeyo?

Could you repeat that, please?
¿Puede repetirlo, por favor?
pwede rrepeteerlo, por fabor?

**Could you write that
down, please?**
¿Puede escribirlo,
por favor?
*pwede eskreebeerlo,
por fabor?*

**Could you translate this for me,
   please?**
¿Me puede traducir esto, por favor?
me pwede tradootheer esto por fabor?

I understand.
Comprendo.
komprendo

Do you understand?
¿Comprende usted?
komprende oosted?

**Just a moment. I'll see if I can find it
   in this book.**
Un momento. Voy a ver si lo encuentro
en este libro.
*oon momento boy a ber see lo
enkwentro en este leebro*

Please show your answer in this book.
Por favor, señale su respuesta en
este libro.
*por fabor senyale soo rrespwesta en
este leebro*

**Is there someone here who speaks
   English?**
¿Hay alguien aquí que hable inglés?
ay algeeyen akee ke able eengles?

What does that mean?
¿Qué significa eso?
ke seegneefeeka eso?

How do you say that in Spanish?
¿Cómo se dice en español?
komo se deethe en espanyol?

**I don't speak/understand Spanish
   very well.**
No hablo/entiendo muy bien el español.
*no ablo/enteeyendo mooee beeyen el
espanyol*

SPANISH

Questions

Where is/are . . . ?
¿Dónde está/están . . . ?
donde esta/estan . . . ?

Where?
¿Dónde?
donde?

What?
¿Qué?
ke?

Why?
¿Por qué?
por ke?

How?
¿Cómo?
komo?

When?
¿Cuándo?
kwando?

How much/many?
¿Cuánto/Cuántos?
kwanto/kwantos?

What time is it?
¿Qué hora es?
ke ora es?

Is there . . . ?
¿Hay . . . ?
ah-y . . . ?

Are there . . . ?
¿Hay . . . ?
ah-y . . . ?

Could you tell me . . . ?
¿Me puede decir . . . ?
me pwede detheer . . . ?

Could you show me . . . ?
¿Me puede mostrar . . . ?
me pwede mostrar . . . ?

Could you tell me how go get to . . . ?
¿Me puede decir como llegar a . . . ?
*me pwede detheer komo eeyegar
  a . . . ?*

It Is/Isn't

It is . . .
Es . . .
es . . .

It isn't . . .
No es . . .
no es . . .

Isn't it . . . ?
¿No es . . . ?
no es . . . ?

There is/are . . .
Hay . . .
ah-y . . .

There isn't/aren't . . .
No hay . . .
no ah-y . . .

. . . isn't it?
¿ . . . verdad?
berdad?

Here it is/they are.
Aquí está/están.
akee estah/estan

Common Adjectives and Adverbs and Their Opposites

beautiful/ugly	bello/feo	*beyo/feo*
before/after	antes/después	*antes/despwes*
better/worse	mejor/peor	*mehor/peor*
big/small	grande/pequeño	*grande/pekenyo*
cheap/expensive	barato/caro	*barato/karo*
clean/dirty	limpio/sucio	*leempeeyo/sootheeyo*
cold/hot	frío/caliente	*freeyo/kaleeyente*
cool/warm	fresco/cálido	*fresko/kaleedo*
deep/shallow	profundo/poco profundo	*profoondo/poko profoondo*
early/late	temprano/tarde	*temprano/tarde*
easy/difficult	fácil/difícil	*fatheel/deefeetheel*
empty/full	vacío/lleno	*batheeyo/eeyeno*
first/last	primero/último	*preemero/oolteemo*
good/bad	bueno/malo	*bweno/malo*
heavy/light	pesado/ligero	*pesado/leehero*
here/there	aquí/allí	*akee/ayee*
high/low	alto/bajo	*alto/baho*
ill/well	enfermo/sano	*enfermo/sano*
inside/outside	dentro/fuera	*dentro/fwera*
long/short	largo/corto	*largo/korto*
more/less	más/menos	*mas/menos*
the most/the least	el más/el menos	*el mas/el menos*
much/little	mucho/poco	*moocho/poko*
narrow/wide	estrecho/ancho	*estrecho/ancho*
near/far	cerca/lejos	*therka/lehos*
now/later	ahora/más tarde	*aora/mas tarde*
often/rarely	frecuentemente/raramente	*frekwentemente/ rraramente*
old/new	viejo/nuevo	*beeyeho/nwebo*
old/young	viejo/joven	*beeyeho/hoben*
open/closed	abierto/cerrado	*abeeyerto/therrado*
pleasant/unpleasant	agradable/desagradable	*agradable/desagradable*
quick/slow	rápido/lento	*rrapeedo/lento*
quiet/noisy	silencioso/ruidoso	*seelentheeyoso/ rrooeedoso*
right/left	derecha/izquierda	*derecha/eethkeeyerda*
right/wrong	correcto/incorrecto	*korrekto/eenkorrekto*
still/not yet	todavía/aún no	*todabeeya/aoon no*
thick/thin	grueso/delgado	*grweso/delgado*
under/over	debajo/sobre	*debaho/sobre*
vacant/occupied	vacío/ocupado	*batheeyo/okoopado*
well/badly	bien/mal	*beeyen/mal*

More Useful Words

also	también	*tambeeyen*
and	y	*ee*
enough	bastante	*bastante*
not	no	*no*
nothing	nada	*nada*
or	o	*o*
perhaps	quizás	*keethas*
soon	pronto	*pronto*
very	muy	*mooee*

To Help You Further in Conversation

according to	según	*segoon*
as you wish	como desee usted	*komo dese-e oosted*
best wishes	mejores votos	*mehores botos*
certainly	ciertamente	*theeyertamente*
entirely	completamente	*kompletamente*
everyone	todos	*todos*
I don't know	no lo sé	*no lo se*
I have forgotten	he olvidado	*e olbeedado*
indeed?	¿de veras?	*de beras?*
in any way	de cualquier manera	*de kwalkeeyer manera*
in what way	¿de qué manera?	*de ke manera?*
it's not important	no es importante	*no es importante*
never mind	no importa	*no importa*
no one	nadie	*nadee-ye*
on the contrary	al contrario	*al kontrareeyo*
precisely	precisamente	*pretheesamente*
same to you	igualmente	*eegwalmente*
sometimes	a veces	*a bethes*
that is to say	quiere decir	*kee-yere detheer*
that's correct	es correcto	*es korrekto*
that's impossible	es imposible	*es eemposeeble*
that's incredible	es increíble	*es eenkre-eeble*
that's all	eso es todo	*eso es todo*
that's too bad	eso es una lástima	*eso es oona lasteema*
that's not right	no está bien	*no esta beeyen*
with pleasure	con placer	*kon plather*
where are we going?	¿adónde vamos?	*adonde bamos?*
that's it	eso es todo	*eso es todo*
what's the matter?	¿qué pasa?	*ke pasa?*

SPANISH

Asking for Something

How far is it?	¿A qué distancia está?	a ke dees**tan**theeya esta?
How long will it take?	¿Cuánto tiempo tomará?	**kwan**to tee-**yem**po toma**ra?**
Could you help me, please?	¿Me puede ayudar, por favor?	me **pwede** ah-yoo**dar,** por fa**bor?**
Could I have . . . ?	¿Me puede dar . . .	me **pwede** dar . . . ?
Could you give me . . . ?	¿Me puede dar . . .	me **pwede** dar . . . ?
Could I have one?	¿Me puede dar uno?	me **pwede** dar **oo**no?
I would like . . .	Me gustaría . . .	me goosta**reey**a . . .
I'm looking for . . .	Busco . . .	**boos**ko . . .
I need . . .	Necesito . . .	nethe**seet**o . . .

ARRIVAL

Passport and Customs

Your passport, please
Su pasaporte, por favor.

Here it is.
Tenga.
tenga

Where will you be staying?
¿Dónde piensa hospedarse?

What is the purpose of your visit?
¿Cuál es el propósito de su visita?

How long will you stay here?
¿Cuánto tiempo se quedará?

I'll be staying . . .
Me quedaré . . .
me kedare . . .

a few days	a fortnight
unos días	dos semanas
oonos deeyas	*dos semanas*

a week	a month
una semana	un mes
oona semana	*un mes*

I'm just passing through.
Sólo estoy de paso.
solo estoee de paso

I'm on my way to . . .
Voy a . . .
boy a . . .

I am visiting relatives/friends.
Voy a visitar a familiares/amigos.
*boy a beeseetar a fameeleeyares/
ameegos*

I'm here on vacation.
Estoy aquí de vacaciones.
estoy akee de bakatheeyones

I'm here on business.
Estoy aquí de negocios.
estoy akee de negotheeyos

I'm here to study.
He venido a estudiar.
e beneedo a estoodeeyar

This is my address.
Esta es mi dirección.
esta es mee deerektheeyon

How much money do you have?
¿Cuánto dinero tiene usted?

Do you have any food or plants?
¿Lleva usted comida o plantas?

SPANISH

Do you have anything to declare?
¿Tiene algo que declarar?

No, nothing. I have only personal belongings.
No, nada. Sólo llevo artículos personales.
no nada, solo eeyebo arteekooloos personales

I have . . .
Tengo . . .
tengo . . .

  cigarettes
  cigarrillos
  theegarreeyos

  liquor   **wine**
  licor   vino
  leekor   *beeno*

  perfume   **some gifts**
  perfume   algunos regalos
  perfoome   *algoonos rregalos*

It's for my personal use.
Es para mi uso personal.
es para mee ooso personal

Open your bag, please.
Abra su bolsa, por favor.

You'll have to pay duty on this.
Tendrá que pagar impuestos por esto.

How much do I have to pay?
¿Cuánto tendré que pagar?
kwanto tendre ke pagar?

I can't afford it.
Es muy caro.
es mooee karo

May I go through?
¿Puedo pasar?
pwedo pasar?

Porter/Luggage

Where can I find a luggage cart?
¿Dónde puedo encontrar un carretón para las maletas?
donde pwedo enkontrar oon karreton para las maletas?

Are you using this trolley?
¿Está usando este carretón?
esta oosando este karreton?

Porter!
¡Portero!
portero!

Please take this luggage . . .
Haga el favor de llevar este equipaje . . .
aga el fabor de eeyebar este ekeepahe . . .

  to the bus/to the train/to the taxi/ to the checkroom
  al autobús/al tren/al taxi/a la consigna
  al owtoboos/al tren/al taksee/a la konseegna

Follow me, please.
Sígame, por favor.
seegame por fabor

How much do I owe you?
¿Cuánto le debo?
kwanto le debo?

Changing Money

Can you change these traveler's checks?
¿Puede cambiar estos cheques de viajero?
pwede kambeeyar estos chekes de beeyahero?

I would like to change dollars/pounds.
Deseo cambiar dólares/libras.
deseo kambeeyar dolares/leebras

What is the exchange rate?
¿A cuánto está el cambio?
a kwanto esta el kambeeyo.

Here is my passport.
Aquí tiene mi pasaporte.
akee tee-yene mee pasaporte

Could you please give me . . .
Me podría dar . . .
me podreeya dar . . .

   Swiss/Belgian/French francs
   francos suizos/belgas/franceses
   frankos sooeethos/begeas/frantheses

   large bills
   billetes grandes
   beeyetehs grandes

   small bills
   billetes pequeños
   beeyetes pekenyos

Could you change this bill?
¿Podría cambiar este billete?
podreeya kambeeyar este beeyete?

GETTING INTO TOWN

Taxi

Where can I find a taxi?
¿Dónde se puede encontrar un taxi?
donde se pwede enkontrar un taksee?

Please call a taxi for me.
Por favor llámeme un taxi.
por fabor eeyameme un taksee

Please take me to . . .
Por favor lléveme a . . .
por fabor eeyebeme a . . .

How much will the fare be?
¿Cuánto costará el viaje?
kwanto kostara el beeyahe?

How far is it?
¿A qué distancia está?
a ke deestantheeya esta?

Turn right/left . . .
Gire a la derecha/izquierda . . .
heere a la derecha/eethkeeyerda . . .

   at the next corner
   en la próxima esquina
   en la prokseema eskeena

   at the stoplight
   en el semáforo
   en el semaforo

Go straight ahead.
Siga derecho.
seega derecho

Why are you taking me this way?
¿Por qué me lleva por esta parte?
por ke me eeyeba por esta parte?

Please don't drive so fast.
Por favor no conduzca tan rápido.
por fabor no kondoothka tan rapeedo

Let me out, please.
Por favor déjeme salir.
por fabor deheme saleer

Turn the meter on.
Ponga a funcionar el taxí-metro.
ponga a foonthee-yonar el taksee-metro

I'm rather in a hurry.
Tengo bastante prisa.
tengo bastante preesa

Stop here, please.
Pare aquí, por favor.
pare akee por fabor

Could you wait for me here?
¿Me podría esperar aquí?
me podreeya esperar akee?

How much do I owe you?
¿Cuánto le debo?
kwanto le debo?

Bus/Train

Where can I get a bus/train to . . . ?
¿Dónde puedo coger un autobús/
tren para . . . ?
*donde pwedo koher oon owtoboos/
tren para . . . ?*

Which bus/train do I take for . . . ?
¿Que autobús/tren cojo para . . . ?
ke owtoboos/tren koho para . . . ?

When is the next bus/train for . . . ?
¿Cuándo sale el próximo autobús/
tren para . . . ?
*kwanto sale el prokseemo owtoboos/
tren para . . . ?*

Do I have to change buses/trains?
¿Tengo que cambiar de autobús/tren?
*tengo ke kambeeyar de owtoboos/
tren?*

Where do I buy the ticket?
¿Dónde se compra el boleto?
donde se kompra el boleto?

**Could you tell me when we
reach . . . ?**
¿Me podría avisar cuando lleguemos
a . . . ?
*me podreeya abeesar kwando
eeyegemos a . . . ?*

Please let me off.
Por favor, déjeme salir.
por fabor, deheme saleer

Car Rental

I have a reservation for a car.
He reservado un coche.
e reserbado oon koche

I'd like to rent a small/large car.
Me gustaría alquilar un coche pequeño/
grande.
*me goostareeya alkeelar oon koche
pekenyo/grande*

   with an automatic gearshift
   con cambio automático
   kon kambeeyo owtomateeko

I need it for . . .
Lo necesito por . . .
lo netheseeto por . . .

   a day/two days
   un día/dos días
   oon deeya/dos deeyas

   a week/two weeks
   una semana/dos semanas
   oona semana/dos semanas

How much is it per . . . ?
¿Cuál es la tarifa por . . . ?
kwal es la tareefa por . . . ?

hour	**week**
hora	semana
ora	*semana*
day	**kilometer**
día	kilómetro?
deeya	*keelometro*

Is gas included?
¿Está incluida la gasolina?
esta eenklooeeda la gasoleena?

Is insurance included?
¿Está incluido el seguro?
esta eenklooeedo el segooro?

I would like comprehensive insurance.
Me gustaría un seguro completo.
me goostareeya oon segooro kompleto

Do I have unlimited mileage?
¿Tendría kilometraje ilimitado?
tendreeya keelometrahe eeleemeetado?

Can I pay by credit card?
¿Podría pagar con una tarjeta de crédito?
podreeya pagar kon oona tarheta de kredeeto?

Here is my driver's license.
Aquí tiene mi carnet de conducir.
akee tee-yene mee karnet de kondootheer

What's the deposit?
¿Cuánto es el depósito?
kwanto es el deposeeto?

May I look at the car first, please?
¿Podría ver el coche antes, por favor?
podreeya ber el koche antes, por fabor?

I'm not familiar with this type of car. Please show me . . .
No conozco este tipo de coche. Por favor enséñeme . . .
no konothko este teepo de koche. por fabor ensenyeme . . .

the headlights
los faros delanteros
los faros delanteros

the indicators
los indicadores de dirección
los eendeekadores de deerektheeyon

the ignition
el encendido
el enthendeedo

the hood release
como se abre la cubierta del motor
komo se abre la koobeeyerta del motor

the gas cap
el tapón de la gasolina
el tapon de la gasoleena

Must I return it to this office?
¿Debo devolverlo a esta oficina?
debo debolberlo a esta ofeetheena?

Have you got a branch in . . . ?
¿Tienen ustedes una sucursal en . . . ?
tee-yenen oostedes oona sookoorsal en . . . ?

What kind of gas should I use? unleaded/regular
¿Qué clase de gasolina debo usar? super/normal
ke klase de gasoleena debo oosar? sooper/normal

What do I do if I have car trouble?
¿Qué debo hacer en caso de problemas con el motor?
ke debo ather en kaso de problemas kon el motor?

ACCOMMODATIONS

I'm looking for . . .
Busco . . .
boosko . . .

   a good hotel
   un buen hotel
   oon bwenotel

   an inexpensive hotel
   un hotel barato
   oon otel barato

   a pension
   una pensión
   oona penseeyon

   a youth hostel
   un albergue juvenil
   oon ahlberge hoobeneel

Hotel/Pension

I have a reservation.
Tengo una reservación
tengo oona reserbatheeyon

My name is . . .
Me llamo . . .
me-eeyamo . . .

Do you have a room for tonight?
¿Tiene una habitación para esta noche?
tee-yene oona abeetatheeyon para esta noche?

I would like . . .
Quisera . . .
keesee-yera. . .

   a single/double room
   una habitación individual/doble
   oona abeetatheeyon eendeebeedwal/doble

   a room with twin beds
   una habitación con dos camas
   oona abeetatheeyon kon dos kamas

   a room with a double bed
   una habitación con una cama de matrimonio
   oona abeetatheeyon con oona kama de matreemoneeyo

I want a room with . . .
Quisiera una habitación con . . .
kee see-yera oona abeetatheeyon kon . . .

a bath/shower	**running water**
baño/ducha	agua corriente
banyo/doocha	*agwa korree-yente*

   hot water
   agua caliente
   agwa kalee-yente

   a balcony
   terraza
   terratha

   a view of the sea
   vista al mar
   beesta al mar

How much is the room per day? per week?
¿Cuánto cuesta la habitación por día? por semana?
kwanto kwesta la abeetatheeyon por deeya? por semana?

That's too expensive. Do you have anything cheaper?
Eso es demasiado caro. ¿Tiene algo más barato?
eso es demaseeyado karo. tee-yene algo mas barato?

How much is the room . . . ?
¿Cuánto cuesta la habitación . . .
kwanto kwesta la abeetatheeyon . . .

without meals
sin las comidas
seen las komeedas

with breakfast only
con el desayuno solamente
kon el desaeeyoono solamente

with half board
con media pensión
kon medeeya penseeyon

with full board
con pensión completa
kon penseeyon kompleta

Is there a reduction for children/a longer stay?
¿Hay un descuento para los niños?
¿Hay un descuento por quedarse más tiempo?
ah-y oon deskwento para los neenyos?
ah-y oon deskwento por kedarse mas tee-yempo?

May I see the room?
¿Puedo ver la habitación?
Pwedo ber la abeetatheeyon?

Yes, this room will do.
Sí, esta habitación me gusta.
see esta abeetatheeyon me goosta

No, this room won't do.
No, no me gusta.
no, no me goosta

Do you have any bigger/better rooms?
¿Tiene usted alguna habitación más grande/mejor?
tee-yene oosted algoona abeetatheeyon mas grande/mehor?

This is the only room vacant right now.
Esta es la única habitación disponible.

We'll have another room tomorrow.
Tendremos otra habitación mañana.

How long will you be staying?
¿Cuánto tiempo se quedará?

I will be staying . . .
Me quedaré . . .
me kedare . . .

tonight only
solo esta noche
solo esta noche

a week
una semana
oona semana

two or three days
dos o tres días
dos o tres deeyas

I haven't decided yet.
Aún no lo he decidido.
ahoon no lo e detheedeedo

Here is my passport.
Aquí tiene mi pasaporte.
akee tee-yene mee pasaporte

When may I have it back?
¿Cuándo me lo devolverán?
kwando me lo debolberan?

May I go to the room now?
¿Puedo ir a la habitación ahora?
pwedo eer a la abeetatheeyon ahora?

May I have the key?
¿Me puede dar la llave?
meh pwede dar lah eeyabe?

Shall I take the key with me when I go out or leave it with you?
¿Puedo llevarme la llave al salir o debo dejarla con usted?
pwedo eeyebarme la eeyabe al sahleer o debo deharla kon oosted?

At what time do you lock the front door at night?
¿A qué hora cierra usted el portal?
a ke ora theeyerra oosted el portal?

How do I get in if I come later?
¿Cómo puedo entrar si llego mas tarde?
komo pwedo entrar see eeyego mas tarde?

When is check-out time?
¿A qué hora debo dejar la habitación?
a ke ora debo dehar la abeetatheeyon?

Could I please have . . .
Por favor, me podría dar . . .
por fabor me podreeya dar . . .

another pillow	otra almohada	*otra almoada*
an extra blanket	otra manta	*otra manta*
some towels	unas toallas	*oonas toaeeyas*
some soap	una pastilla de jabón	*oona pasteeya de habon*
a glass	un vaso	*oon baso*
toilet paper	papel higiénico	*papel eeheeyeneeko*
more hangers	más perchas	*mas perchas*
writing paper	papel de escribir	*papel de eskreebeer*
a bottle of mineral water	una botella de agua mineral	*oona boteheeya de agwa meeneral*
an ashtray	un cenicero	*oon theneethero*
a light bulb	una bombilla	*oona bombeeya*

The . . . doesn't work.
. . . no funciona.
. . . no foontheeyona

air conditioning	el aire acondicionado	*el ah-yere akondeetheeyonado*
heating	la calefacción	*la kalefaktheeyon*
hot water	el agua caliente	*el agwa kaleeyente*
light	la luz	*la looth*
lock	la cerradura	*la therradoora*
radio	la radio	*la rradeeyo*
shower	la ducha	*la doocha*
tap	el grifo	*el greefo*
toilet	el water (retrete)	*el bater (rretrete)*

Can the heat/air conditioning be turned up/down?
¿Puede subir/bajar la calefacción/el aire acondicionado?
pwede soobeer/bahar la kalefaktheeyon/ el ah-yere akondeetheeyonado?

The mattress is too soft. May I have a firmer one?
El colchón es muy blando. ¿Me puede dar uno más duro?
el kolchon es mooee blando me pwede dar oono mas dooro?

Could you wake me up tomorrow morning at . . . ?
Me puede despertar mañana a las . . . ?
me pwede despertar manyana a las . . . ?

May we have breakfast in our room?
¿Podemos desayunar en la habitación?
podemos desaeeyoonar en la ahbeetatheeyon?

Until what time do you serve breakfast?
¿Hasta qué hora se sirve el desayuno?
asta ke ora se seerbe el desaeeyoono?

What time is lunch/dinner?
¿A qué hora es el almuerzo/la cena?
a ke ora es el almwertho/la thena?

Could you please have the linen changed today?
¿Por favor, podría cambiar la ropa de cama, hoy?
por fabor, podreeya kambeeyar la rropa de kama oy?

Are there any letters for me?
¿Hay carta para mí?
*ah-y **kar**ta **para** mee?*

I would like to call this number . . .
Quisiera hacer una llamada (telefónica) a
    este número . . .
*kee**see-ye**ra ather **oo**na eeya**ma**da
    (telefo**nee**ka) a **e**ste **noo**mero . . .*

Checking Out

We'll be leaving tomorrow.
Nos vamos mañana.
*nos **ba**mos man**ya**na*

May I have the bill, please?
¿Me puede dar la cuenta, por favor?
*me **pwe**de dar la **kwen**ta, por fa**bor**?*

Could you give me a receipt, please.
¿Me puede dar un recibo, por favor.
*me **pwe**de dar un rre**thee**bo, por
    fa**bor**?*

Could you explain this item?
¿Me puede explicar a qué se refiere
    esto?
*me **pwe**de essplee**kar** a ke se
    re**fee-ye**re **e**sto?*

Thank you for a most enjoyable stay.
Gracias por una estancia muy
    agradable.
*gra**thee**yas por **oo**na estan**thee**ya
    mooee agra**da**ble*

**I hope we'll be able to return some
    day.**
Espero poder volver algún día.
*es**pe**ro po**der** bol**ber** al**goon** **dee**ya*

Youth Hostel

**Do you have dormitory
    accommodations?**
¿Tiene usted alojamiento en
    dormitorios?
*tee-**ye**ne **oo**sted aloha **mee-yen**to en
    dormeeto**ree**yos?*

Is there a curfew?
¿Hay que regresar a una hora
    determinada?
*ah-y ke regre**sar** a **oo**na **o**ra
    determee**na**da?*

Do I have to do chores?
¿Tendría que contribuir en las labores?
*ten**dree**ya ke kontreeboo**eer** en las
    labores?*

**Is there a limit on the number of days
    we can stay?**
¿Por cuánto tiempo nos podemos
    quedar?
*por **kwan**to tee-**yem**po nos po**de**mos
    ke**dar**?*

Camping

Is there a camp site nearby?
¿Hay algún camping cerca de aquí?
*ah-y al**goon** **kam**peeng **ther**ka de
    a**kee**?*

May we camp here?
¿Podemos acampar aquí?
*po**de**mos akam**par** a**kee**?*

What's the charge?
¿Cuánto cuesta?
kwanto kwesta?

Are there . . . ?
¿Hay . . . ?
ah-y . . . ?

baths	toilets
baños	retretes
banyos	*rretretes*

showers
duchas
doochas

Are there cooking/washing facilities?
¿Hay posibilidad de cocinar/lavar?
ah-y poseebeeleedad de kotheenar/labar?

Is it possible to rent a tent/bungalow?
¿Es posible alquilar una tienda/bungalow?
es poseeble alkeelar oona teeyenda boongalob?

May we light a fire?
¿Podemos encender una hoguera?
podemos enthender oona ogera?

Where can we find . . . ?
Dónde podemos encontrar . . . ?
donde podemos enkontrar . . . ?

a camping equipment store
una tienda de artículos de camping
oona teeyenda de arteekoolos de kampeeng

a laundry	shops
una lavandería	tiendas
oona labandereeya	*teeyendas*

a restaurant	telephones
un restaurante	teléfonos
oon rrestowrante	*telefonos*

electric hook-ups
circuitos eléctricos
theerkooeetos elektreekos

Signs

NO CAMPING	PROHIBIDO ACAMPAR
NO TRAILERS	PROHIBIDO ACAMPAR CON CARAVANA
NO TRESPASSING	PROHIBIDA LA ENTRADA
PRIVATE PROPERTY	PROPIEDAD PRIVADA
NO FIRES	PROHIBIDO ENCENDER FUEGO

TRAVELING

Signs

ARRIVALS	LLEGADAS	*eeyegadas*
DEPARTURES	SALIDAS	*saleedas*
ENTRANCE	ENTRADA	*entrada*
EXIT	SALIDA	*saleeda*
TICKETS	BOLETOS	*boletos*
INFORMATION	INFORMACION	*eenformatheeyon*

BAGGAGE	CONSIGNA	*konseegna*
CHANGE	CAMBIO	*kambeeyo*
TO THE PLATFORMS	A LOS ANDENES	*a los andenes*
CUSTOMS	ADUANA	*adwana*
NO SMOKING	PROHIBIDO FUMAR	*proybeedo foomar*
WAITING ROOM	SALA DE ESPERA	*sala de espera*
TOILETS	RETRETES	*rretretes*

Traveling by Air

Is there a bus/train to/from the airport?
¿Hay un autobús/tren al/del aeropuerto?
ah-y oon owtoboos/tren al/del aeropwerto?

Where?
When?
¿Dónde?
¿Cuándo?
donde?
kwando?

Is there a flight to . . . ?
¿Hay un vuelo a . . . ?
ah-y oon bwelo a . . . ?

At what time?
¿A qué hora?
a ke ora?

Is there an earlier/later one?
¿Hay uno más temprano/más tarde?
ah-y oono mas temprano/mas tarde?

When is check-in time?
¿A qué hora debo registrarme?
a ke ora debo rreheestrarme?

When does it arrive?
¿A qué hora llega?
a ke ora eeyega?

How much is the fare to . . . ?
¿Cuánto cuesta el boleto a . . . ?
kwanto kwesta el boleto a . . . ?

What's the flight number?
¿Cuál es el número del vuelo?
kwal es el noomero del bwelo?

I'd like to book a seat on the next flight . . .
Quisiera reservar un asiento en el proximo vuelo . . .
keesee-yera rreserbar oon asee-yento en el prokseemo bwelo . . .

one way	**round trip**
ida	ida y vuelta
eeda	*eeda ee bwelta*

I'd like a seat . . .
Quisiera un asiento . . .
keesee-yera oon aseeyento . . .

> **on the aisle**
> al lado del pasillo
> *al lado del paseeyo*

> **by the window**
> al lado de la ventana
> *al lado de la bentana*

> **in the front**
> en la parte delantera
> *en la parte delantera*

> **in the back**
> en la parte trasera
> *en la parte trasera*

> **in the non-smoking section**
> en la sección de no fumadores
> *en la sektheeyon de no foomadores*

> **in the smoking section**
> en la sección de fumadores
> *en la sektheeyon de foomadores*

Is it a non-stop flight?
¿Es un vuelo directo?
es oon bwelo deerekto?

SPANISH

Will it be necessary to change planes?
¿Será necesario cambiar de avión?
sera nethesareeyo kambeeyar de abeeyon?

How much is charged for excess weight?
¿Cuánto hay que pagar por sobrecarga?
kwanto ah-y ke pagar por sobrekarga?

How many bags am I allowed?
¿Cuántas bolsas me permiten?
kwantas bolsas me permeeten?

How long is the flight delayed?
¿Cuánto tiempo de retraso lleva el vuelo?
kwanto tee-yempo de rretraso ee-yeba el bwelo?

Traveling by Train

When is the next train to . . . ?
¿Cuándo sale el próximo tren para . . . ?
kwanto sale el prokseemo tren para . . . ?

I would like to buy/reserve a one way/round trip ticket to . . . in
Quisiera comprar/reservar un boleto de ida/ida y vuelta para . . .
keesee-yera komprar/rreserbar oon bolehto de eeda/eeda ee bwelta para . . .

    first/second class
    de primera/segunda clase
    de preemera/segoonda klase

What is the fare to . . . ?
¿Cuánto cuesta un boleto para . . . ?
kwanto kwesta oon boleto para . . . ?

How much is it for a child of . . . years?
¿Cuánto cuesta para un niño de . . . años?
kwanto kwesta para oon neenyo de . . . anyos?

What time does the train leave?
¿A qué hora sale el tren?
a ke ora sale el tren?

When does it arrive?
¿A qué hora llega?
a ke ora eeyega?

At what platform?
¿A qué andén llega?
a ke anden eeyega?

Do I have to change trains? Where?
¿Tendré que hacer transborde de tren? ¿Dónde?
tendre ke ather transborde de tren? donde?

When will there be a connection to . . . ?
¿Cuándo habrá una conexión para . . . ?
kwando abra oona konektheeyon para . . . ?

Is there a sleeping car?
¿Hay coche cama?
ah-y koche kama?

Are there couchettes?
¿Hay literas?
ah-y leeteras?

Is this train going to . . . ?
¿Va a . . . este tren?
ba a . . . este tren?

Which car for . . . ?
¿Qué vagón para . . . ?
ke bagon para . . . ?

Could you tell me where car number . . . is?
¿Me podría decir dónde está el vagón número . . . ?
me podreeya detheer donde esta el bagon noomero . . . ?

I have a reservation.
Tengo una reservación.
tengo oona rreserbatheeyon

Where is my couchette?
¿Dónde está mi litera?
donde esta mee leetera?

Is this seat taken?
¿Está ocupado este asiento?
esta okoopado este aseeyento?

Excuse me. I think this is my seat.
Perdón. Creo que este es mi asiento.
perdon. kreo ke este es mee aseeyento

May I get by?
¿Me deja pasar?
me deha pasar?

Where is the dining car?
¿Dónde está el coche restaurante?
donde esta el koche rrestowrante?

May I open/close the window/the curtains?
¿Puedo abrir/cerrar la ventana/las cortinas?
pwedo abreer/therrar la bentana/las korteenas?

Can the heating be turned down/off/ higher?
¿Se puede bajar/apagar/subir la calefacción?
se pwede bahar/apagar/soobeer la kalefaktheeyon?

Could you refrain from smoking, please.
¿Le importaría a usted no fumar?
le eemportareeya a oosted no foomar?

This is a non-smoking compartment.
Este es un compartimiento de no fumadores.
este es oon komparteemeeyento de no foomadores

What station is this?
¿Qué estación es esta?
ke estatheeyon es esta?

Is this where I change for a train to . . . ?
¿Es aquí donde se hace transbordo para . . . ?
es akee donde se athe transbordo para . . . ?

Traveling by Boat

Is there a boat to . . . ?
¿Hay un barco para . . . ?
ah-y oon barko para . . . ?

When does the next boat leave?
¿A qué hora sale el próximo barco?
a ke ora sale el prokseemo barko?

I would like to buy a first/second class round trip/one way ticket.
Quisiera comprar un boleto de ida y vuelta/ida en primera/segunda clase.
keesee-yera komprar oon boleto de eeda ee bwelta/eeda en preemera/ segoonda klase

When does it arrive?
¿A qué hora llega?
a ke ora eeyega?

When does it return?
¿A qué hora regresa?
a ke ora rregresa?

When should I be on board?
¿A qué hora debo subir a bordo?
a ke ora debo soobeer a bordo?

Where can I find pills for seasickness?
¿Dónde puedo encontrar píldoras para el mareo?
donde pwedo enkontrar peeldoras para el mareo?

SPANISH

Traveling by Bus/Streetcar/Subway

Where is the bus station?
¿Dónde está la estación de autobuses?
*donde esta la estatheeyon de
owtobooses?*

**Where is the nearest bus stop/
subway station/streetcar stop?**
Dónde está la parada de autobús/
estación de metro/parada de tranvía
más cercana?
*owtoboos/estatheeyon de metro
parada de trambeeya mas therkana?*

Where can I get a bus/train to . . . ?
¿Dónde puedo coger el autobús/tren
a . . . ?
*donde pwedo koher el owtoboos/tren
a . . . ?*

How long does it take?
¿Cuánto se tarda en llegar?
kwanto se tarda en eeyegar?

Does this bus/train go to . . . ?
¿Va a . . . este autobús/tren . . . ?
ba a . . . este owtoboos/tren?

Which line do I take for . . . ?
¿Qué línea cojo para . . . ?
ke leenea koho para . . . ?

Where do I buy a ticket?
¿Dónde se compra el boleto?
donde se kompra el boleto?

What is the fare to . . . ?
¿Cuánto cuesta ir a . . . ?
kwanto kwesta eer a . . . ?

Do I get off here for . . . ?
¿Me quedo aquí para . . . ?
me kedo akee para . . . ?

**Could you tell me when we
reach . . . ?**
¿Me podría avisar cuándo lleguemos
a . . . ?
*me podreeya abeesar kwando
eeyegemos a . . . ?*

Let me off, please.
Déjeme salir, por favor.
deheme saleer por fabor

Traveling by Car

**Where can I find a gas station/
garage?**
¿Dónde puedo encontrar una
gasolinera/garaje?
*donde pwedo enkontrar oona
gasoleenera/garahe?*

Please . . .
Por favor . . .
por fabor . . .

How much is gas per liter?
¿Cuánto cuesta la gasolina por litro?
*kwanto kwesta la gasoleena por
leetro?*

fill her up	llénelo	*eeyenelo*
give me . . . litres	déme . . . litros	*deme . . . leetros*
of standard/premium	de la normal/de la super	*de la normal/de la sooper*
give me a liter of oil.	déme un litro de aceite.	*deme oon leetro de athayte*

check the oil/water	compruebe el aceite/el agua	**komprwebe el athayte/el agwa**
battery/tires/	la batería/las ruedas	**la batereeya/ las rwedas**
brake fluid	el líquido de frenos	**eel leekeedo de frenos**
clean the windshield	limpie el parabrisas	**leempeeye el parabreesas**
adjust the brakes	ajuste los frenos	**ahooste los frenos**

In Case of a Breakdown

Excuse me. My car has broken down.
¿Perdóne. Mi coche se ha estropeado.
perdone mee koche se a estropeado

May I use your phone?
¿Puedo usar su teléfono?
pwedo oosar soo telefono?

I've had a breakdown at . . . Can you send a mechanic/tow truck?
Tengo un coche estropeado en . . . ¿Puede usted mandar un mecánico/una grúa?
tengo oon koche estropeado en . . . pwede oosted mandar oon mekaneeko/oona grooa?

How long will you be?
¿Cuánto tardarán?
kwanto tardaran?

Thank you for stopping.
Gracias por parar.
gratheeyas por parar

Could you help me?
¿Me podría ayudar?
me podreeya ahyoodar?

There's something wrong with the . . .
No funciona . . .
no foontheeyona . . .

I have a flat tire.
Se me ha pinchado una rueda.
se me a peenchado oona rrweda

The battery is dead.
Se me descargó la batería.
se me deskargo la batereeya

Do you have a jack/jumper cables?
Tiene un gato/un cable para recargar la batería?
tee-yene oon gato/oon kable para rrekargar la batereeya?

I've run out of gas.
Se me ha acabado la gasolina.
se me a akabado la gasoleena

Could you please notify the next garage?
¿Puede avisar el próximo garaje?
pwede abeesar el prokseemo garahe?

Could you have a look at my car?
¿Me puede revisar el coche?
me pwede rrebeesahr el koche?

accelerator	el acelerador	*el athelerador*
brakes	los frenos	*los frenos*
carburetor	el carburador	*el karboorador*
clutch	el embrague	*el embrage*
engine	el motor	*el motor*
fan	la ventilación	*la benteelatheeyon*
gears	la caja de cambios	*la kaha de kambeeyos*

SPANISH

hand brake	el freno de mano	el *freno* de *mano*
headlights	los faros delanteros	los *faros delanteros*
horn	la bocina	la *botheena*
ignition	el encendido	el *enthendeedo*
spark plugs	las bujías	las *booheeyas*
turn signals	el indicador de dirección	el *een-dee-kador* de *deerektheeyon*

I don't know what's wrong with it.
No sé lo que pasa.
no se lo ke **pasa**

A light on the dashboard went on.
Se ha encendido una luz en el panel.
*se a enthen***deedo** *oona looth en el panel*

Will spare parts be needed? Do you have them?
¿Se necesitarán partes de recambio?
se netheseetaran partes de rrekambeeyo?

How long will it take to repair?
¿Cuánto tiempo tardará en repararlo?
kwanto *tee-yempo tardara en repararlo?*

How much will it cost?
¿Cuánto costará?
kwanto *kostara?*

When will the car be ready?
¿Para cuándo estará listo el coche?
para **kwando** *estara* **leesto** *el* **koche?**

Where's the nearest garage that can fix it?
¿Cuál es el garaje más epcercano que puede arreglarlo?
kwal es el garahe mas therkano ke **pwede** *arreglarlo?*

Is the car repaired?
¿Ya está todo arreglado?
eeya esta todo arreglado?

How much do I owe you?
¿Cuánto le debo?
kwanto *le* **debo?**

Could you give me an itemized bill, please?
¿Me podría dar una factura que especifique el trabajo realizado, por favor?
me podreeya dar oona faktoora ke espetheefeeke el trabaho rrealeethado, por fabor?

Trouble with the Police

I don't speak Spanish very well.
No hablo muy bien el español.
no ablo mooee beeyen el espanyol

Do you speak English?
¿Habla usted inglés?
abla oosted eengles?

I'm sorry, I don't understand.
Lo siento, no entiendo.
lo seeyento no enteeyendo

Here's my driver's license.
Aquí tiene mi carnet de conducir.
akee tee-yene mee karnet de kondootheer

Was I driving too fast?
¿Conducía muy rápido?
kondootheeya mooee rrapeedo?

What did I do wrong?
¿Cuál ha sido mi falta?
kwal a seedo mee falta?

Must I pay a fine?
¿Tengo que pagar una multa?
tengo ke pagar oona moolta?

How much is it?
¿Cuánto es?
kwanto *es?*

Traveling by Bicycle/Moped

Where can I rent a bicycle/moped?
¿Dónde puedo alquilar una bicicleta/
motocicleta?
*donde pwedo alkeelar oona
beetheekleta/mototheekleta?*

I'd like to rent a moped.
Quisiera alquilar una motocicleta.
*keesee-yera alkeelar oona
mototheekleta*

How much is it per hour/day?
¿Cuánto cuesta por hora/día?
kwanto kwesta por ora/deeya?

At what time must I return it?
¿A qué hora debo devolverla?
a ke ora debo debolberla?

This bicycle is too big/small.
Esta bicicleta es demasiado grande/
pequeña.
*esta beetheekleta es demaseeyado
grande/pekenya*

This tire needs air.
Esta rueda necesita aire.
esta rrweda netheseeta iyere

The motor keeps stalling.
El motor se sigue atascando.
el motor se seege ataskando

**Something's wrong with the brake/
headlight.**
No funciona el freno/el faro delantero.
*no foontheeyona el freno/el faro
delantero*

Hitchhiking

Could you please give me a lift to . . .
Me podría llevar a . . .
me podreeya eeyebar a . . .

I'm only going as far as . . .
Sólo voy hasta . . .

I can take you as far as . . .
Le/la puedo llevar hasta . . .

Asking the Way

Excuse me. Could you tell me . . . ?
Con permiso. ¿Me podría decir . . . ?
kom permeeso me podreeya detheer . . . ?

how to get to . . .
cómo llegar a . . .
komo eeyegar a . . .

how far is it to . . .
a que distancia está . . .
a ke deestantheeya esta . . .

am I on the right road for . . .
es esta la carretera de . . .
es esta la karretera de . . .

which road do I take for . . .
qué carretera debo tomar para . . .
ke karretera debo tomar para . . .

what is the name of this town
cómo se llama esta ciudad
komo se eeyama esta theeyoodad

Could you direct me to . . . ?
¿Me podría indicar la carretera
para . . . ?
*me podreeya eendeekarla karretera
para . . . ?*

SPANISH

Could you show me where we are on this map?
¿Me podría enseñar dónde estamos en este plano (mapa)?
me podreeya ensenyar donde estamos en este plano (mapa)?

It's not far from here. No está lejos de aquí.	**at the next intersection.** en el próximo cruce
It's a fair distance from here. Está a una distancia razonable de aquí.	**at the next corner.** en la próxima esquina
Go straight ahead. Siga derecho.	**at the traffic circle.** en la circunvalación
Turn left/right . . . Doble a la izquierda/derecha . . .	**follow the signs for . . .** siga los letreros para . . .
at the first/second traffic light. en el primer/segundo semáforo	

Highway Signs

EXIT	SALIDA
ENTRANCE	ENTRADA
ONE WAY	DIRECCION UNICA
NO ENTRY	PROHIBIDO EL PASO
NO PARKING	ESTACIONAMIENTO PROHIBIDO
DETOUR	DESVIACIÓN
DANGER	PELIGRO
MERGING TRAFFIC	CONFLUENCIA DE TRÁFICO
HIGHWAY	AUTOPISTA
SPEED LIMIT	LÍMITE DE VELOCIDAD

TYPES OF EATING ESTABLISHMENTS IN SPAIN

Restaurante: Restaurant. The most sophisticated and expensive type of eating establishment; the dishes tend to be less regionally oriented.

Casa de comidas: A small restaurant that serves simple meals at very reasonable rates; many dishes are local specialties.

Bodega: It usually designates a cellar where wines and appetizers are served.

Taberna, Tasca: An establishment usually in a rural setting that serves wine and simple food.

SPANISH

Cafetería, Café Bar: A "cafe" that serves coffee, tea, alcoholic and non-alcoholic beverages, ready-made sandwiches, rolls, and occasionally hamburgers or grilled sandwiches.

Bar: A snack bar.

Heladería: Ice cream parlor.

Bon appetit!	¡Que Aproveche!	*ke aprobeche*
Cheers!	¡Salud!	*salood*

EATING OUT

Can you suggest a good restaurant . . . ?
¿Me podría recomendar un buen restaurante . . . ?
me podreeya rrekomendar oon bwen rrestowrante . . . ?

for breakfast/lunch/dinner
para desayunar/almorzar/cenar
para desayoonar/almorthar/thenar

We're looking for an inexpensive restaurant. Do you know of one?
Buscamos un restaurante que no sea muy caro. ¿Conoce usted alguno?
booskamos oon rrestowrante ke no sea mooee karo. konothe oosted algoono?

I'd like to make a reservation for two/four at 8:00 this evening.
Quisiera reservar una mesa para dos/cuatro para las 8:00 (ocho) de la noche.
keesee-yera rreserbar oona mesa para dos/kwatro para las ocho de la noche

Good evening. We have a reservation. The name is . . .
Buenas tardes. Hemos reservado una mesa. Está a nombre de . . .
bwenahs tardehs. emos rreserbado oona mesa. esta a nombre de . . .

Do you have a table for three?
¿Tiene usted una mesa para tres?
tee-yene oosted oona mesa para tres?

Could we have a table . . . ?
¿Nos podría dar una mesa . . . ?
nos podreeya dar oona mesa . . . ?

outside/inside afuera/adentro *afwera/adentro*	**on the terrace** en la terraza *en la terratha*
with more privacy en un sitio más privado *en oon seeteeyo mas preebado*	**by the window** cerca de la ventana *therka de la bentana*

May I please see the menu/wine list?
¿Por favor, me podría enseñar el menú/la lista de vinos?
por fabor me podreeya ensenyar el menoo/la leesta de beenos?

Could you please bring me some/a/an . . .
¿Me podría traer . . .
me podreeya traer . . .

ashtray	un cenicero	*oon theneethero*
fork	un tenedor	*oon tenedor*
knife	un cuchillo	*oon koocheeyo*
spoon	una cuchara	*oona koochara*
napkin	una servilleta	*oona serbeeyeta*
plate	un plato	*oon plato*
glass	un vaso	*oon baso*
glass of water	un vaso de agua	*oon baso de agwa*
bottle of mineral	una botella de agua	*oona boteheeya de agwa*
water/wine	mineral/vino?	*meeneral/beeno*
bread/butter	el pan/la mantequilla	*el pan/la mantekeeya*
salt	la sal	*la sal*
pepper	la pimienta	*la peemee-yenta*
oil	el aceite	*el athayte*
vinegar	el vinagre	*el beenagre*
mustard	la mostaza	*la mostatha*

What's the specialty of the house?
¿Cuál es la especialidad de la casa?
kwal es la espetheeyaleedad de la kasa?

What do you recommend?
¿Qué recomienda usted?
ke rrekomee-yenda oosted?

I'd like something light.
Quisiera algo ligero.
keesee-yera algo leehero?

Can you tell me what this is?
¿Me podría decir que es esto?
me podreeya detheer ke es esto?

I'll have . . .
Tomaré . . .
tomare. . .

The lady/gentleman will have . . .
La señora/el caballero tomará . . .
la senyora/el kabaeeyero tomara . . .

It's very good.
Está muy bueno.
esta mooee bweno

I didn't order this. I asked for . . .
No pedí esto. Pedí . . .
no pedee esto pedee . . .

This is . . .
Esto está . . .
esto esta . . .

overcooked	undercooked
muy hecho	poco hecho
mooee echo	*poko echo*

May I have something else?
¿Podría tomar otra cosa?
podreeya tomar otra kosa?

Check, please.
La cuenta, por favor.
la kwenta, por fabor

I think there's a mistake on the bill.
Creo que hay un error en la cuenta.
kreo ke ay oon error en la kwenta

Is service included?
¿Está incluido el servicio?
esta eenklooeedo el serbeetheeyo?

Do you take credit cards/traveler's checks?
¿Aceptan tarjetas de crédito/ cheques de viajero?
atheptan tarhetahs de kredeeto/ chekes de beeyahero?

We enjoyed the meal very much.
Nos gustó mucho la comida.
nos goosto moocho la komeeda

Breakfast (Desayuno)

Good morning. I'd like . . .
Buenos días. Quisiera . . .
bwenos deeyas. keesee-yera . . .

some coffee	un café	*oon kafe*
some coffee with milk	un café con leche	*con kafe kon leche*
some hot tea	un té	*oon té*
with milk/lemon	con leche/límón	*kon lecheh/leemon*
grapefruit/orange juice	un zumo de pomelo/ naranja	*oon thoomo de pomelo/ naranha*
bacon and eggs	huevos con tocino	*webos kon totheeno*
ham and eggs	huevos con jamón	*webos kon hamon*
a boiled egg	un huevo hervido	*oon webo erbeedo*
a soft/hard boiled egg	un huevo duro/pasado por agua	*oon webo dooro/pasado por agwa*
fried eggs	huevos fritos	*webos freetos*
scrambled eggs	huevos revueltos	*webos rrebweltos*
an omelette	una tortilla	*oona torteeya*
bread/rolls	pan/panecillos	*pan /panetheeyos*
butter	mantequilla	*mantekeeya*
jam	mermelada	*marmelada*
sugar	azúcar	*athookar*
yoghurt	yogourt	*yogoort*
honey	miel	*mee-yel*
fruit	fruta	*froota*

Tapas	**Appetizers**	*tapas*
aceitunas rellenas	**stuffed olives**	*athaytoonas rre-ee-yenas*
aguacate	**avocado**	*agwakate*
alcachofas	**artichoke**	*alkachofas*
almejas (a la marinera)	**clams in spicy sauce**	*almehas a la mareenera*
anchoas	**anchovies**	*anchoas*
anguila ahumada	**smoked eel**	*angeela a-oomada*
arenque ahumado	**smoked herring**	*ahrehnke a-oomado*
atún	**tuna**	*atoon*
calamares (a la romana)	**squid (fried in butter)**	*kalamares (a la rromana)*
callos	**tripe**	*kaeeyos*
caracoles	**snails**	*karakoles*
carne de cangrejo	**crabmeat**	*karne de kangreho*
champiñones	**mushrooms**	*champeenyones*
cigalas	**crayfish**	*theegalas*
entremeses variados	**assorted appetizers**	*entremeses baree-yados*
espárragos, puntas de	**asparagus tips**	*esparragos, poontas de*

SPANISH

fiambres	cold cuts	*feeyambres*
gambas	prawns	*gambas*
jamón serrano	cured ham	*hamon serrano*
langosta	lobster	*langosta*
langostinos	prawns	*langosteenos*
mejillones	mussels	*meheeyones*
melón	melon	*melon*
moluscos	mussels	*molooskos*
ostras	oysters	*ostras*
pepino	cucumber	*pepeeno*
quisquillas	shrimp	*keeskeeyas*
salchichón	salami	*salcheechon*
salmón ahumado	smoked salmon	*salmon aoomado*
sardinas	sardines	*sardeenas*

Angulas
(angoolas)

baby eels fried with oil, chili and garlic

Chanquetes
(chahnketes)

tiny fish, similar to whitebait

Chorizo al diablo
(choreetho al deeyablo)

spicy red sausage flambeed in alcohol

Ensaladilla
(ensaladeeya)

Russian salad

Huevos rellenos a la española
*(webos rre-eeyenos a la
espanyola)*

devilled eggs

Pan con tomate y jamón
(pan kon tomate ee hamon)

toast with cured ham, oil and tomato

Sopas
(sopas)

Soups

Caldeirada
(kaldayrada)

a thick fish soup

Consomé al Jerez
(konsome al hereth)

chicken consomme with sherry

**Escudilla barrejada
de Cataluña**
*(eskoodeeya barrehada de
kataloonya)*

vegetable soup with rice and *fideos,* (very thin
spaghetti)

Gazpacho
(gathpacho)

cold soup with the following chopped vegetables: tomatoes, onions, sweet peppers and cu-
cumbers, mixed with oil, breadcrumbs and garlic

Potaje de habas secas
(potahe de abas sekas)

dried bean soup with bacon

Potaje madrileño *(potahe madreelenyo)*	a thick soup made with dried cod, chick peas, and spinach, flavored with chili and saffron
Pote gallego *(pote gaee-yego)*	a broth resulting from a concoction of white beans, pork, sausage, potatoes and cabbage; these ingredients are removed and served later
Purrusalda *(poorroosaldah)*	a salt-cod soup with leeks, garlic and potatoes
Sopa de ajo *(sopa de aho)*	garlic soup, with one egg, and other variable ingredients
Sopa de cuarto de hora *(sopa de kwarto de ora)*	a soup consisting of shellfish, white fish, rice, hardboiled eggs and bacon
Sopa de primavera *(sopa de preemabera)*	soup made with fresh spring vegetables
Sopa de rape *(sopa de rrape)*	a spicy soup of angler fish made with ground hazelnuts and peanuts with tomatoes, onions and breadcrumbs.
Sopa leonesa *(sopa leonesa)*	a wheatmeal, beef gravy, milk and egg yolk soup, flavored with lemon and cinnamon, poured over fried bread

Huevos
(webos)

Eggs

-a la flamenca *(a la flamenka)*	baked on a bed of sausage, ham, peas, and beans, topped with red pepper
al Jerez *(al hereth)*	baked with kidneys in a sherry sauce
-al plato *(al plato)*	on fried sausage and tomato, au gratin
-con arroz *(kon arroth)*	devilled eggs flavored with brandy and served with rice

Tortilla
(torteeya)

Omelette

-alcarreña *(alkarrenya)*	with sausage, ham and asparagus
-campesina *(kampeseena)*	with tomatoes, mushrooms and red peppers
-española *(espanyola)*	usually with potato
-riojana *(rreeyohana)*	with sausage, ham and red peppers

SPANISH

Arroz
(arroth)

Rice

-a banda *(a banda)*	boiled saffron rice served with shellfish and angler fish
-a la marinera *(a la mareenera)*	rice boiled with seafood and garnished with asparagus and sweet peppers
-catalana *(katalana)*	with chicken, snails, beans, peas and artichokes
-de mariscos *(de mareeskos)*	with shellfish, angler fish, squid and tomatoes
Paella *(paeya)*	saffron rice, stock, meat, shellfish, and vegetables, cooked and often served in a heavy iron pan with handles, called a paella

Pescado y mariscos	**Fish and Seafood**	*pethkado ee mareeskos*
almejas	**clams**	*almehas*
anchoas	**anchovies**	*anchoas*
anguilas	**eel**	*angeelas*
arenques	**herring**	*arenkes*
atún	**tuna**	*atoon*
bacalao	**cod**	*bakalao*
besugo	**sea bream**	*besoogo*
bonito	**tuna**	*boneeto*
caballa	**mackerel**	*kabaeeya*
calamares	**squid**	*kalamares*
cangrejo	**crab**	*kangreho*
chipirones	**baby squid**	*cheepeerones*
cigalas	**crayfish**	*theegalas*
congrio	**conger eel**	*kongreeyo*
langosta	**lobster**	*langosta*
langostinos	**prawns**	*langosteenos*
lenguado	**sole**	*lengwado*
mero	**seabass**	*mero*
moluscos	**mussels**	*molooskos*
mujol	**mullet**	*moohol*
ostras	**oysters**	*ostras*
perca	**perch**	*perka*
pez espada	**swordfish**	*peth espada*
pulpo	**octopus**	*poolpo*
quisquillas	**shrimp**	*keeskeeyas*
salmón	**salmon**	*salmon*
salmonetes	**red mullet**	*salmonete*
sardinas	**sardines**	*sardeenas*
trucha	**trout**	*troocha*
venera	**scallops**	*benera*

Bacalao al pil-pil
(bakalao al peel-peel)
salt cod with chilli peppers

Calamares en su tinta
(kalamares en soo teenta)
fried squid in a sauce made from their ink, with onions

Centollos
(thento-eeyos)
minced spider crabs in a tomato, sherry and brandy sauce, served in their shells with melted butter.

Langosta a la barcelonesa
(langosta a la barthelonesa)
sauteed lobster with chicken, tomatoes and almonds

Lenguado a la andaluza
(lengwado a la andahlootza)
a roll of sole with stuffing, served with rice, eggplant, tomatoes and red peppers

Marmitako
(maarmeetako)
tuna fish stew from the Basque country

Pastel de pescado
(pastel de peskado)
a pie containing mashed potatoes, cod, tomatoes and almonds

Salmon con ternera
(salmon kon ternera)
salmon and steak, baked together

Zarzuela
(tharthwela)
spicy seafood stew, with a dash of wine and brandy

Carnes / Meat / karnes

Carnes	Meat	karnes
bistec	**beef steak**	*beestek*
cabrito	**kid goat**	*kabreeto*
carne de buey	**beef**	*karne de bway*
carne de cerdo	**pork**	*karne de therdo*
carne de cordero	**lamb**	*karne de kordero*
carne de ternera	**veal**	*karne de ternera*
carne picada	**minced meat**	*karne peekada*
carnero	**mutton**	*karnero*
hígado	**liver**	*heegado*
lechón	**suckling pig**	*lechon*
morcilla	**blood sausage**	*mortheeya*
rabo de buey	**oxtail**	*rrabo de bway*
riñones	**kidneys**	*rreenyones*
salchichas	**sausages**	*salcheehas*
sesos	**brains**	*sesos*
solomillo	**pork steak**	*solomeeyo*
tocino	**bacon**	*totheeno*
jamón	**ham**	*hamon*

Albóndigas
(albondeegas)
meat balls

Cachelada
(kachelada)
boiled sausage and potatoes

Callos a la andaluza (*kayos a la andalootha*)	tripe stew with ham, calf's feet, vegetables, herbs, and garlic; ingredients variable
Cocido madrileño (*kotheedo madreelenyo*)	a thick stew of beef, ham, chicken, bacon, sausages, pig's foot and vegetables
Cordero al ajillo pastor (*kordero al aheeyo pastor*)	suckling lamb simmered in white wine and herbs and served with fried potatoes
Criadillas fritas (*kreeyadeeyas freetas*)	fried bull's testicles
Croquetas a la española (*kroketas a la espanyola*)	ham and pork croquettes
Chuletas a la parrilla con ali-oli (*chooletas a la parreeya kon alee-olee*)	grilled lamb chops served with garlic mayonnaise
Churrasco (*choorrasko*)	charcoal-grilled steak
Fabada asturiana (*fabada astooree-yana*)	white bean dish with sausages
Lacon con grelos (*lakon kon grelos*)	boiled pork shoulder with turnips
Olla podrida (*oya podreeda*)	see cocido
Pierna de cordero (*peeyerna de kordero*)	leg of lamb cooked with carrots, wine, herbs, garlic, and its own juices
Riñones al Jerez (*rreenyones al hereth*)	kidneys cooked in sherry
Solomillo mechado (*solomeeyo mechado*)	sirloin steak, wrapped in bacon and served with fried artichoke hearts and potatoes
Ternera borracha (*ternera borracha*)	veal topped with a mixture of ham, parsley and a clove, simmered in white wine and cinnamon
Ternera en adobo (*ternerah en adobo*)	veal marinated in wine and cinnamon

Aves y carne de caza	**Poultry and Game**	*aves ee karne de katha*
codorniz	**quail**	*kodorneeth*
conejo	**rabbit**	*koneho*
faisán	**pheasant**	*fah-ysan*
ganso	**goose**	*ganso*
liebre	**hare**	*leeyebre*
pato	**duck**	*pato*
pavo	**turkey**	*pabo*

SPANISH

perdiz	**partridge**	*perdeeth*
pichón	**pigeon**	*peechon*
pollo	**chicken**	*poyo*
venado	**venison**	*benado*

Capón relleno a la catalana
(kapon rrayeno a la katalana)
stuffed roast capon

Gallina en pepitoria
(gayeena en pepeetoreeya)
chicken cooked with wine, almonds, garlic and herbs

Gallina rellena
(gayeena rrayena)
ground chicken, veal and ham stewed with vegetables and served in the chicken skin

Jabalí estofado
(habalee estofado)
stewed wild boar with onions, spices and herbs

Liebre estofada con judías
(leeyebre estofada kon hoodeeyas)
a stew of hare and string beans with a sharp sauce of vinegar and chilli peppers

Pato a la sevillana
(pato a la sebee-yana)
duck cooked with onions, tomatoes, garlic and herbs

Perdices con sardinas
(perdeethes con sardeenas)
partridge cooked with tomatoes and a sardine, which is removed before serving

Pichones con espárragos
(peechones con esparragos)
stuffed pigeons, served cold

Pierna de cordero
(peeyerna de kordero)
leg of lamb cooked with carrots, wine, herbs, garlic and its own juices

Pollo a la chilindron
(poeeyo a la cheeleendron)
chicken cooked in tomato sauce with red peppers

Pollo asado
(poeeyo asado)
roast chicken

Pollo a la brasa
(poeeyo a la brasa)
grilled chicken

Puchero de gallina
(poochero de ga-yeena)
stuffed boiled chicken with a sauce made from its liver

Ways of Preparing Meat, Poultry, Game, and Fish

baked	al horno	*al orno*
braised	estofado	*estofado*
braised in casserole	en salsa	*en salsa*
cured	en salazón	*en salathon*
deep fried	a la romana	*a la rromana*
fried	frito	*freeto*
grilled	a la parrilla	*a la parreeya*

SPANISH

marinated	en escabeche	*en eskabeche*
poached	hervido	*erbeedo*
pot roasted	en su jugo	*en soo hoogo*
roast	al horno	*al orno*
sauteed	salteado	*salteado*
smoked	ahumado	*aoomado*
steamed	cocido al vapor	*kotheedo al bapor*
stewed	estofado	*estofado*
rare	poco hecho	*poko echo*
medium	regular	*rregoolar*
well-done	bien hecho	*beeyen echo*

Legumbres / **Vegetables** / *legoombres*

alcachofas	**artichoke**	*alkachofas*
apio	**celery**	*apeeyo*
berenjena	**eggplant**	*berenhena*
calabacín	**zucchini**	*kalabatheen*
cebolla	**onion**	*theboya*
champiñones	**mushrooms**	*champeenyones*
coles de bruselas	**brussels sprouts**	*koles de brooselas*
coliflor	**cauliflower**	*koleeflor*
escarola	**chicory**	*eskarola*
espárragos	**asparagus**	*esparragos*
espinacas	**spinach**	*espeenakas*
garbanzos	**chick-peas**	*garbanthos*
guisantes	**peas**	*geesantes*
habas	**broad beans**	*abas*
judías blancas	**navy beans**	*hoodeeyas blankas*
judías verdes	**green beans**	*hoodeeyas berdes*
lechuga	**lettuce**	*lechooga*
lentejas	**lentils**	*lentehas*
lombarda	**red cabbage**	*lombarda*
maíz	**corn**	*mah-yeeth*
patatas	**potatoes**	*patatas*
pepino	**cucumber**	*pepeeno*
pimientos morrones	**sweet red peppers**	*peemee-yentos morrones*
puerros	**leeks**	*pwehrros*
rábanos	**radishes**	*rrabanos*
repollo	**cabbage**	*rrepoyo*
tomates	**tomatoes**	*tomates*
trufas	**truffles**	*troofas*
zanahorias	**carrots**	*thanahoree-yas*

Escalibada catalana	eggplants, tomatoes, and sweet peppers, grilled
(eskaleebada katalana)	and seasoned with garlic, parsley, and olive oil
Esparragos al estilo de Malaga	breaded asparagus baked with eggs on top
(esparragos al esteelo de malaga)	
Garbanzos salteados	chick pea stew
(garbanthos salteados)	
Judías encarnadas a la madrileña	red beans, simmered with sausage, bacon, onion, and garlic
(hoodeeyas enkarnadas a la madreelenya)	
Menestra de acelgas	mixed vegetable stew
(menestra de athelgas)	
Patatas a la riojana	sliced potatoes, tomatoes, onions, sausage, and
(patatas a la rreeyohana)	sweet peppers baked with stock in layers
Pisto	stewed red peppers, zucchini, and tomatoes
(peesto)	
Ensalada mixta	lettuce, onions, and tomatoes, dressed with olive
(ensalada meessta)	oil, vinegar, and salt

Frutas	**Fruit**	*frootas*
albaricoques	**apricots**	*albareekokes*
almendras	**almonds**	*almendras*
avellanas	**hazelnuts**	*abayanas*
castañas	**chestnuts**	*kastanyas*
cerezas	**cherries**	*therethas*
ciruelas	**plums, prunes**	*theerwelas*
coco	**coconut**	*koko*
dátiles	**dates**	*dateeles*
frambuesas	**raspberries**	*frahmbwesas*
fresas	**strawberries**	*fresas*
granadas	**pomegranates**	*granadas*
grosellas	**red currants**	*groseyas*
higos	**figs**	*eegos*
lima	**lime**	*leema*
limón	**lemon**	*leemon*
mandarina	**tangerine**	*mandareena*
manzana	**apple**	*manzana*
melocotón	**peach**	*melokoton*
melón	**melon**	*melon*
naranja	**orange**	*naranha*
nueces	**walnuts**	*nwethes*
pasas	**raisins**	*pasas*

pera	**pear**	*pera*
piña	**pineapple**	*peenya*
plátano	**banana**	*platano*
pomelo	**grapefruit**	*pomelo*
sandía	**watermelon**	*sandeeya*
uvas	**grapes**	*oobas*

Postres

Desserts

Arroz con leche
(arroth kon leche)

rice cooked in milk and flavored with cinnamon and lemon

Brazo de gitano
(bratho de heetano)

a spongy roll filled with jam or cream

Churros
(choorros)

long sugared doughnuts

Flan de caramelo
(flan de karamelo)

caramel custard

Helado
(elado)

ice cream

Manzanas asadas asturianas
(manthanas asadas astooree-yanahs)

apples baked in white wine with an aniseed-flavored topping

Natillas
(nateeyas)

lemon and cinnamon flavored custard

Polvorones
(polborones)

shortbread cookies with almond, anise, and cinnamon flavor

Rosquillas
(rroskeeyas)

anise flavored doughnuts

Tocino de cielo
(totheeno de theeyelo)

very thick caramel custard

Torrijas
(torreehas)

small honey cakes made from milk-soaked bread

Turrón de Jijona
(toorron de heehona)

nougat with honey, nuts, and cinnamon

DRINKS

Non-alcoholic Drinks

Cold Beverages

I'd like a . . .
Quiero . . .
*keeye*ro . . .

glass of	**bottle of**	
un vaso de	una botella de	
oon baso de	*oona botaya de*	

(mineral) water	agua (mineral)	*agwa (meeneral)*
carbonated	con gas	*kon gas*
regular	sin gas	*seen gas*
apricot juice	un zumo de albaricoque	*oon thoomo de albareekoke*
grapefruit juice	un zumo de pomelo	*oon thoomo de pomelo*
lemonade	una limonada	*oona leemonada*
orangeade	una naranjada	*oona naranhada*
fresh-squeezed orange/	un zumo de naranja/	*oon thoomo de narana/*
lemon juice	limón natural	*leemon natoorae*
peach juice	un zumo de melocotón	*oon thoomo de melokoton*
pear juice	un zumo de pera	*oon thoomo de pera*
tomato juice	un zumo de tomate	*oon thoomo de tomate*
milkshake with fresh fruit	un batido de frutas	*oon bateedo de frootas*
iced tea	un té con hielo	*oon te con ee-yelo*
iced coffee	un café con hielo	*con kafe con ee-yelo*

Hot Beverages

un expresso	un café solo	*oon kafe solo*
very strong expresso	un café solo doble	*oon kafe solo doble*
somewhat less	un café solo, no muy	*con kafe solo, no mooee*
concentrated expresso	cargado	*kargado*
expresso with a drop	un cortado	*oon kortado*
of milk		
coffee with hot milk	un café con leche	*oon kafe con leche*
steamed milk with a	un café con leche corto	*oon kafeh kon leche korto*
small amount of coffee	de café	*deh kafe*
decaffeinated coffee	un descafeinado	*oon deskafaynado*
hot chocolate	un chocolate	*oon chokolate*
hot tea	un té	*oon te*
with milk/lemon	con leche/limón	*kon leche/leemon*

Alcoholic Drinks

The following alcoholic beverages have the same names in Spanish:

bourbon
brandy
gin fizz
gin & tonic
scotch
vermouth
vodka
whiskey
whiskey and soda

Others:

aperitif	un aperitivo	*oon apereeteebo*
beer	una cerveza	*oona therbetha*
light/dark	clara/negra	*klara/negra*
bottle/draft	embotellada/de barril	*emboteyada/de barreel*
cordial	un licor	*oon leekor*
port	un oporto	*oon oporto*
rum	ron	*rron*
gin	ginebra	*heenebra*
sherry	jerez	*hereth*
cognac	coñac	*konyak*
straight	solo	*solo*
on the rocks	con hielo	*kon ee-yelo*
with soda water	con soda	*kon soda*

Wine

Which wine do you recommend?
¿Qué vino me recomienda?
ke beeno me rrekomee-yenda?

Which wine goes with this dish?
¿Qué vino va bien con este plato?
kel beeno ba beeyen kon este plato?

I'd like a . . . wine
Quisiera un vino . . .
keesee-yera oon beeno . . .

dry	seco	*seko*
sweet	dulce	*doolthe*
sparkling	achampañado	*achampanyado*
red	tinto	*teento*
rose	rosado	*rrosado*
white	blanco	*blanko*

Please bring a . . . of . . .
Por favor, tráigame . . . de . . .
por fabor, traygame . . . de . . .

bottle	una botella	*oona boteya*
carafe	una jarra	*oona harra*
half-bottle	media botella	*medeeya boteya*
liter	un litro	*oon leetro*
half liter	medio liro	*medeeyo leetro*
quarter liter	un cuarto de litro	*oon kwarto de leetro*
glass	un vaso	*oon baso*

I'd like to try some of the local wine.
Me gustaría probar el vino de la casa.
me goostareeya probar el beeno de la kasa

Some Favorite Aperitifs

Coñac
(konyak)
a smooth brandy that becomes an aperitif when served on the rocks

Jerez
(hereth)
a generic term for sherry. On the labels of the best sherries appears the word solera, meaning that some of the contents come from a wine made in the 18th or 19th century. Some sherries are fortified with brandy and alcohol.

Amontillado
(amonteeyado)
a moderately dry sherry with a nutty flavor, with a dark golden color

Fino
(feeno)
a pale, dry, crisp sherry, with a straw color

Manzanilla
(mantsaneeya)
the driest, palest, and lowest in alcoholic content of the sherries mentioned here

Seco
(Seko)
a semi-sweet, bone-dry *oloroso sherry,* full-bodied and golden in color

Vermut
(bermoot)
vermouth, drunk with soda water or on the rocks

After-dinner Drinks

Aguardiente
(agwardeeyente)
literally "fire water," refers to a group of coarse, brandy-like spirit drinks made from grape skins and stalks

Anís
(anees)
a sweet, white, aniseed-based liqueur; a particularly good one is Anís de Chinchón

Aromas de Montserrat
(aromas de monserrat)
an aromatic liqueur made from herbs and spices

Calisay
(kaleesy)
a slightly syrupy quinine liqueur

SPANISH

Cardenal Mendoza
(kardenal mendotha)

a sweet, not so dry brandy made from grapes; widely respected

Carlos I
(karlos preemero)

named after Spain's greatest emperor, one of the finest "eaux de vie"; very expensive

Creme
(kreme)

a dessert sherry, sweet, very full bodied, with a deep golden brown color

Fundador
(foondador)

another famous Spanish *coñac,* it is smoothly mellow, with a full bouquet, sweeter and earthier than most brandies

Gran Duque D'Alba
(gran dooke d'alba)

a sweet brandy with a vanilla-chocolate flavor

Oloroso
(oloroso)

a gently sweet sherry, full bodied, with a rich, golden color

Ponche
(ponche)

a brandy-based liqueur with a flavor of sherry

Viña 25
(beenya bayntee-theenko)

a dessert sherry, very sweet, rich and mellow

SIGHTSEEING

Where is the tourist office?
¿Dónde está la oficina de turismo?
donde esta la ofeetheena de tooreesmo?

We would like to see the main points of interest.
Deseamos ver los lugares de mayor interés.
deseamos ber los looga res de mayor eenteres

We will be here for ...
Nos quedaremos aquí por ...
nos kedaremos akee por ...

a few hours	**a day**
unas horas	un día
oonas oras	*oon deeya*

a few days
unos cuantos días
oonos kwantos deeyas

a week
una semana
oona semana

Is there a sightseeing tour?
¿Hay alguna gira turística?
ah-y algoona heera tooreesteeka?

Where does it go?
¿Adónde va?
adonde ba?

How long is it?
¿Cuánto dura?
kwanto doora?

How much is it?
¿Cuánto cuesta?
kwanto kwesta?

When/where will the bus pick us up?
¿Cuándo/dónde nos recogerá el autobús?
kwando/donde nos rrekohera el owtoboos?

Does the guide speak English?
¿Habla inglés el guía?
abla eengles el geeya?

We would like to see ...
Quisiéramos ver ...
keesee-yeramos ber ...

Could you direct me to the . . . ?
¿Me podría indicar dónde está . . . ?
me podreeya eendeekar donde esta . . . ?

art gallery	la galería de arte	*la galereeya de arte*
castle	el castillo	*el kasteeyo*
catacombs	las catacumbas	*las katakoombas*
cathedral	la catedral	*la katedral*
cemetery	el cementerio	*el thementereeyo*
church	la iglesia	*la eegleseeya*
city center	el centro de la ciudad	*el thentro de la theeyoodad*
fortress	la fortaleza	*la fortaletha*
fountain	la fuente	*la fwente*
gardens	los jardines	*los hardeenes*
harbor	el puerto	*el pwerto*
lake	el lago	*el lago*
monastery	el monasterio	*el monastereeyo*
museum	el museo	*el mooseo*
old city	la parte vieja de la ciudad	*la parte beeyeha de la theeyoodad*
opera house	el teatro de la ópera	*el teatro de la opera*
palace	el palacio	*el palatheeyo*
planetarium	el planetario	*el planetareeyo*
ruins	las ruinas	*las rooeenas*
sanctuary	el santuario	*el santooareeyo*
shops	las tiendas	*las teeyendas*
statue	la estatua	*la estatwa*
tomb	la tumba	*la toomba*
university	la universidad	*la ooneeberseedad*
zoo	el parque zoológico	*el parke thooloheeko*

When is the . . . open?
¿Cuándo está abierto/a/el/la . . . ?
kwando esta abeeyerto/a el/la . . . ?

At what time does it close?
¿A qué hora cierra?
a ke ora theeyerra?

How much is the admission?
¿Cuánto cuesta la entrada?
kwanto kwesta la entrada?

The admission is free.
La entrada es gratis.
la entrada es gratees

Is there a reduction for children/students/senior citizens?
¿Hay rebaja para niños/estudiantes/ancianos?
ah-y rrebaha para neenyos estoodeeyantes/antheeyanos?

Where does one buy tickets?
¿Dónde se compra los boletos?
donde se kompra los boletos?

Where can I find . . . ?
¿Dónde puedo encontrar . . . ?
donde pwedo enkontrar . . . ?

a catalogue
un catálogo
oon katalogo

a guidebook
una guía
oona geeya

the . . . exhibit
la exhibición de . . .
la ekseebeetheeyon de . . .

the . . . collection
la colección . . .
la kolektheeyon . . .

post cards
tarjetas postales
tarhetas postales

the souvenir shop
la tienda de recuerdos
la teeyenda de rrekwerdos

Am I allowed to take photographs?
¿Se puede sacar fotos?
se pwede sakar fotos?

HAVING FUN

Daytime Activities

Soccer

Let's go to the football game.
Vamos al partido de fútbol.
bamos al parteedo de footbol

Where is the stadium?
¿Dónde está el estadio?
donde esta el estadeeyo?

Who is playing?
¿Quién juega?
keeyen hwega?

I would like two tickets . . .
Quisiera dos entradas . . .
keesee-yera dos entradas . . .

in the sun	**in the shade**
al sol	a la sombra
al sol	*a la sombra*

When does it start?
¿Cuándo empieza?
kwando empeeyetha?

What is the score?
¿Cuál es la puntuación?
kwal es la poontwatheeyon?

Tennis

Would you like to play tennis?
¿Desea usted jugar al tenis?
desea oosted hoogar al tenees?

Where are the tennis courts?
¿Dónde están las pistas de tenis?
donde estan las peestas de tenees?

What's the charge for the use of the courts per hour/for ½ hour?
¿Cuánto cuesta el uso de una pista por cada hora/por cada media hora?
kwanto kwesta el ooso de oona peesta por kada ora/por kada medeeya ora?

Is it possible to rent rackets?
¿Se puede alquilar raquetas?
se pwede alkeelar rraketas?

I would like to buy a can of tennis balls.
Me gustaría comprar un bote de pelotas de tenis.
me goostareeya komprar oon bote de pelotas de tenees

Let's go to the tennis tournament.
Vamos al torneo de tenis.
bamos al torneo de tenis

I want to watch/play the men's/women's singles/doubles.
Quiero ver/jugar los individuales/los dobles masculinos/femeninos.
keeyero ber/hoogar los eendeebeedwales/los dobles maskooleenos/femeneenos

Golf

Where's the nearest golf course?
¿Dónde está el campo de golf más cercano?
donde esta el kampo de golf mas therkano?

Is it open to non-members?
¿Está abierto a los no socios?
esta abeeyerto a los no sotheeyos?

How much does it cost per hour/ day/round?
¿Cuánto cuesta por hora/día/partida?
kwanto kwesta por ora/deeya/ parteeda?

I would like to rent a caddy/golf clubs.
Quisiera contratar un "caddie"/alquilar unos palos de golf.
keesee-yera kontratar oon kadee/ alkeelar oonos palos de golf

I would like to buy some golf balls.
Quisiera comprar unas pelotas de golf.
keesee-yera komprar oonas pelotas de golf

Would you like to play a round with me?
¿Quiere usted jugar una partida conmigo?
keeyere oosted hoogar oona parteeda konmeego?

Where's the next tee?
¿Dónde está el próximo "tee"?
donde estah el prokseemo tee?

Horseback Riding

Is there a riding stable nearby?
¿Hay un picadero cerca?
ah-y oon peekadero therka?

I would like to rent a horse.
Quiero alquilar un caballo.
keeyero alkeelar oon kabayo

What's the charge per hour?
¿Cuánto cuesta por hora?
kwanto kwehsta por ora?

I would like to take riding lessons.
Quisiera tomar clases de equitación.
keesee-yera tomar klases de ekeetatheeyon

I am a beginner/experienced rider.
Soy un jinete principiante/avanzado.
soy oon heenete preentheepyante abanthado

Could you give me a gentle horse please?
¿Me podría dar un caballo tranquilo, por favor?
me podreeya dar oon kabayo trankeelo, por fabor?

I would like a good jumper.
Quisiera un buen saltador.
keesee-yera oon bwen saltahdor

Skiing

Would you like to go skiing?
¿Le gustaría ir a esquiar?
le goostareeya eer a eskeeyar

How do we get to the ski slopes?
¿Cómo se llega a la pista de esquí?
komo se eeyega a la peesta de eskee

What are the skiing conditions like at . . . ?
¿Cómo son las condiciones de esquí en . . . ?
komo son las kondeetheeyones de eskee en . . . ?

Is it possible to take skiing lessons?
¿Es posible tomar lecciones de esquí?
es poseeble tomar lektheeyones de eskee?

Is it possible to rent skiing equipment?
¿Es posible alquilar un equipo de esquiar?
es poseeble alkeelar oon ekeepo de eskeeyar?

These boots are too tight/loose.
Estas botas están muy apretadas/sueltas.
estas botas estan mooee apretadas/sweltas

Could you help me put on the skis?
¿Me puede ayudar a ponerme los esquís?
me pwede ahyoodar a ponerme los eskees?

How much are the lift tickets for a day/two days/a week?
¿Cuánto cuesta un boleto para el telesilla por un día/dos días/una semana?
kwanto kwesta oon boleto para el teleseeya por oon deeya/dos deeyas/oona semana?

I'm looking for a beginner's/intermediate/expert trail.
Busco una pista para principiantes/intermedios/avanzados.
boosko oona peesta para preentheepeeyantes/eentermedeeyos/abantha dos

Swimming

Would you like to go swimming?
¿Le/te gustaría ir a nadar?
le/te goostareeya eer a nadar?

Let's go to the beach/swimming pool.
Vamos a la playa/piscina.
bamos a la playa/peestheena

Is it safe for swimming?
¿Se puede nadar sin peligro?
se pwede nadar seen peleegro?

I'd like to rent . . .
Quisiera alquilar . . .
keesee-yera alkeelar . . .

a deckchair
una silla de lona
oona seeya de lona

a changing room
una cabina
oona kabeena

a beach umbrella
una sombrilla
oona sombreeya

Evening Activities

Would you like to go to . . . ?
¿Le/te gustaría ir . . . ?
leh/te goostareeya eer . . . ?

the movies	the ballet
al cine	al ballet
al theene	*al balet*

the theatre	a concert
al teatro	a un concierto
al teatro	*a oon kontheeyerto*

the opera
a la ópera
a la opera

Who's in it?
¿Quién actúa?
keeyen aktooa?

Who's singing?
¿Quién canta?
keeyen kanta?

Who's dancing?
¿Quién baila?
keeyen bah-ya?

What orchestra is playing?
¿Qué orquesta toca?
ke orkesta toka?

At what time does it begin?
¿A qué hora empieza?
a ke ora empeeyetha?

I would like to reserve/buy two tickets for . . .
Quisiera reservar/comprar dos entradas para . . .
keesee-yera rreserbar/komprar dos entradas para . . .

Could you show me a seating plan of the theatre?
¿Me podría enseñar un plano del teatro?
me podreeya ensenyar oon plano del teatro?

Please give me two orchestra/ mezzanine/box balcony seats.
Por favor, me da dos entradas de platea (butacas)/anfiteatro/palco/galería.
por fabor me da dos entradas de platea (bootakas)/anfeeteatro/ palko/galereeya

Would you like to go to a night club/ discotheque?
¿Quiere/quieres ir a un "nightclub"/ una discoteca?
keeyere/keeyeres eer a oon "nightclub"/oona deeskoteka?

How much does it cost to get in?
¿Cuánto cuesta la entrada?
kwanto kwesta la entrada?

What's the minimum?
¿Cuánto es la consumición mínima?
kwanto es la konsoomee theeyon meeneema?

Would you like to have a drink?
¿Desea algo de beber?
desea algo de beber?

Would you like to dance?
¿Quiere/quieres bailar?
keeyere/keeyeres bah-ylar?

Getting to Know People

How are you?
¿Cómo está usted/estás?
komo esta oosted/estas?

Fine, thanks.
Muy bien gracias.
mooee beeyen gratheeyas

My name is . . .
Me llamo . . .
me eeyamo . . .

This is . . .
Le presento a . . .
le presento a . . .

my wife/husband
mi esposa/esposo
mee esposa/esposo

my daughter/son
mi hija/hijo
mee eeha/eeho

my sister/my brother
mi hermana/hermano
mee ermana/ermano

a friend of mine
una amiga/un amigo
oona ameega/oon ameego

Glad to meet you.
Tengo mucho gusto en conocerlo/la.
tengo moocho goosto en konotherlo/la

Where are you from?
¿De dónde es usted?
de donde es oosted?

I'm from . . .
Soy de . . .
soy de . . .

Are you here on vacation?
¿Está aquí de vacaciones?
esta akee de bakatheeyones?

No, I'm on a business trip.
No, estoy en un viaje de negocios.
no, estoy en oon beeyahe de negotheeyos

I'm here for business and pleasure.
Estoy aquí de negocios y de vacaciones.
estoy akee de negotheeyos ee de bakatheeyones

Are you on your own?
¿Estás sólo/sóla?
estas solo/sola?

I'm with a friend/friends/my family.
Estoy con un amigo/amigos/mi familia.
estoy kon mee ameego/ameegos/ mee fameeleeya

How long have you been here?
¿Cuánto tiempo hace que estás aquí?
kwanto teeyempo athe ke estas akee?

I've just arrived today.
Acabo de llegar hoy.
akabo de eeyegar oy

I arrived yesterday/a few days ago.
Llegué ayer/hace unos días.
eeyege ah-yer/athe oonos deeyas

I've been here a week/two weeks/ a month.
Hace una semana/dos semanas/ un mes que estoy aquí.
athe oona semana/dos semanas/ oon mes ke estoy akee

How do you like it here?
¿Qué tal le gusta esto?
ke tal le goosta esto?

I like it very much.
Me gusta mucho.
me goosta moocho

It's a wonderful place.
Es un lugar maravilloso.
es oon loogar marhbeeyo-so

beautiful	**relaxing**
precioso	relajante
pretheeyoso	*rrelahante*
fun	**interesting**
divertido	interesante
deeberteedo	*eenteresante*

I don't like it very much.
No me gusta mucho.
no me goosta moocho

It's . . .
Es . . .
es . . .

too crowded
muy congestionado
mooee konhesteeyonado

noisy	**ugly**
ruidoso	feo
rrooeedoso	*feo*
boring	**depressing**
aburrido	deprimente
aboorreedo	*depreemente*

How long are you going to stay?
¿Cuánto tiempo se va a quedar?
kwanto teeyempo se ba a kedahr?

A few more days/weeks.
Unos cuántos días/semanas más.
oonos kwantos deeyas/semanas mas

I'm leaving tomorrow/soon.
Me marcho mañana/pronto.
me marcho manyana/pronto

Are you having a good time?
¿Se está divirtiendo?
se esta deebeerteeyendo?

Yes, very much.
Sí, mucho.
see, moocho

No, not really.
No, no realmente.
no, no rrealmente

Where are you staying?
¿Dónde se está quedando?
donde se esta kedando?

I'm an ...
Soy ...
Soy ...

We're at the ... hotel.
Estamos en el hotel ...
estamos en el otel ...

We're camping.
Estamos de camping.
estamos de kampeeng

We haven't found a place yet.
No hemos encontrado un lugar todavía.
*no emos enkontrado oon loogar
   todabeeya*

**Do you know of a good hotel/
   pension?**
¿Sabe usted de un buen hotel/una
   buena pensión?
*sabe oosted de oon bwen otel/oona
   bwena penseeyon?*

What do you do?
¿Cuál es su profesión?
kwal es soo profeseeyon?

artist	artista	*arteesta*
businessman	comerciante	*komertheeyante*
doctor	médico	*medeeko*
factory worker	obrero	*obrero*
lawyer	abogado	*abogado*
secretary	secretaria	*sekretareea*
student	estudiante	*estoodeeyante*
teacher	profesor	*profesor*
writer	escritor	*eskreetor*

Where do you live?
¿Dónde vive?
donde beebe?

I live in ...
Vivo en ...
beebo en ...

the United States		**Great Britain**
los Estados Unidos		Gran Bretaña
los ehstados ooneedos		*gran bretanya*
Canada		**Australia**
Canadá		Australia
kanada		*aoostraleea*

Let me know if you ever go there.
Llámeme si pasa por allí algún día.
eeyameme see pasa por ayee algoon deeya

Here is my address/phone number.
Aquí tiene mi dirección/número de teléfono.
akee teeyene mee deerektheeyon/ noomero de telefono

What are your interests?
¿Cuáles son sus intereses?
kwales son soos eentereses?

I'm interested in . . .
Me interesa . . .
me eenteresa . . .

anthropology	la antropología	la antropoloheeya
antiques	las antigüedades	las anteegwedades
archaeology	la arqueología	la arkeoloheeya
architecture	la arquitectura	la arkeetektoora
art	el arte	el arte
botany	la botánica	la botaneeka
chess	el ajedrez	el ahedreth
cinema	el cine	el theene
coins	la numismática	la noomeesmateeka
cooking	la cocina	la kotheena
dance	el baile	el bahyle
foreign language	las lenguas extranjeras	las lengwas esstranheras
gardening	la jardinería	la hardeenereeya
geology	la geología	la heoloheeya
history	la historia	la eestoreea
literature	la literatura	la leeteratoora
medicine	la medicina	la medeetheena
music	la música	la mooseeka
natural history	la historia natural	la eestoreea natooral
painting	la pintura	la peentoora
philosophy	la filosofía	la feelosofeeya
photography	la fotografía	la fotografeeya
sculpture	la escultura	la eskooltoora
science	la ciencia	la theeyentheeya
sociology	la sociología	la sotheeyoloheeya
sports	los deportes	los deportes
theatre	el teatro	el teatro

May I sit here?
¿Puedo sentarme aquí?
pwedo sentarme akee?

Yes, if you wish.
Sí, si lo desea.
see, see lo desea

Can I get you a drink?
¿Le puedo ofrecer algo de beber?
le pwedo ofrether algo de beber?

Would you like a cigarette?
¿Quiere un cigarrillo?
keeyere oon theegarreeyo?

No, thank you. I don't smoke.
No, gracias. No fumo.
no gratheeyas. no foomo

Could you give me a light?
¿Me podría dar fuego?
me podreeya dar fwego?

Would you like to go out with me this evening?
¿Le gustaría salir conmigo esta noche?
le goostareeya saleer konmeego esta noche?

Would you like to go to . . . ?
¿Le gustaría salir a . . . ?
le goostareeya saleer a . . . ?

> **to a party**
> una fiesta
> *oona feeyesta*
>
> **dinner**
> cenar
> *thenar*

> **to the movies**
> el cine
> *el theene*

> **to a discotheque**
> una discoteca
> *oona deeskoteka*

> **to a concert**
> un concierto
> *oon kontheeyerto*

> **for a drive**
> dar un paseo en coche
> *dar oon paseo en koche*

> **for a walk**
> dar un paseo
> *dar oon paseo*

Yes, thank you. I would like that.
Sí, gracias. Me gustaría.
see, gratheeyas. me goostareeya

No, thank you. I'm not free this evening.
No, gracias. No estoy libre esta noche.
no, gratheeyas. no estoy leebre esta noche

What about tomorrow?
¿Qué le parece mañana?
ke le parethe manyana?

No, I'll be busy.
No, mañana estaré ocupado/a.
no, manyana estare okoopado/a.

Where/when shall we meet?
¿Dónde/cuándo nos encontramos?
donde/kwando nos enkontramos?

Could you meet me at . . . ?
¿Me podría encontrar en . . . ?
me podreeya enkontrar en . . . ?

I'll meet you at your hotel.
Lo/la encontraré en su hotel.
lo/la enkontrare en soo otel

May I call you?
¿Puedo llamarlo/la?
pwedo eeyamarlo/la?

At what time?
¿A qué hora?
a ke ora?

What's your number?
¿Cuál es su número?
kwal es soo noomero?

I'd like to go home now.
Quisiera ir a casa ahora.
keesee-yera eer a kasa ahora

I'm very tired.
Estoy muy cansado/a.
estoy mooee kansado/a

Thank you for a lovely evening.
Gracias por una tarde/noche tan agradable.
gratheeyas por oona tarde/noche tan agradable

Expressions of Admiration or Dislike

What a beautiful view!
¡Qué vista más bonita!
ke beesta mas boneeta

What a lovely place/town/city!
¡Qué lugar/pueblo/ciudad más bonito(a)!
ke loogar/pweblo/theeyoodad mas boneeto(a)

SPANISH

The sea/countryside is very
beautiful.
El mar/paisaje es muy hermoso.
el mar/pah-ysahe es mooee ermoso

I particularly like . . .
Me gusta en particular . . .
me goosta en parteekoolar . . .

I don't particularly like . . .
No me gusta en particular . . .
no me goosta en parteekoolar . . .

I like this country/city/place very
much.
Me gusta mucho este país/esta ciudad/
este lugar.
*me goosta moocho este pah-yees/
esta theeyoodad/este loogar*

the architecture	la arquitectura	*la arkeetektoora*
the beaches	las playas	*las plaeeyas*
the climate	el clima	*el kleema*
the food	la comida	*la kahmeeda*
the landscape	el paisaje	*el pysahe*
the night life	la vida nocturna	*la beeda noktoorna*
the people	la gente	*la hente*
the restaurants/cafes	los restaurantes/ cafeterías	*los rrestowrantes/ kafetereeyas*
the shops	las tiendas	*las teeyendas*
the sights	los lugares de interés	*los loogares de eenteres*

EVERYDAY SITUATIONS

Problems

Are you alone?
¿Está sólo(a)?
esta solo(a)?

Are you waiting for someone?
¿Espera a alguien?
espera a algeeyen?

Yes, I'm waiting for a friend.
Sí, espero a un amigo.
see, espero a oon ameego

Am I disturbing you?
Lo/la estoy molestando?
lo/la estoy molestando?

Leave me alone.
Déjeme en paz.
deheme en path

Go away or I'll call the police.
Márchese o llamaré a la policía.
*marchese o eeyamare a la
poleetheeya*

The Weather

It's a lovely day, isn't it?
Es un día muy bonito, ¿verdad?
es oon deeya mooee boneeto, berdad?

What beautiful/awful weather we're
having!
¡Qué buen/mal tiempo tenemos!
ke bwen/mal teeyempo tenemos

Do you think it's going to rain/snow/be sunny all day?
¿Cree usted que va a llover/nevar/hacer sol todo el día?
kree oosted ke ba a eeyober/nebar/ather sol todo el deeya?

It's terribly hot today.
Hace mucho calor hoy.
athe moocho kalor oy

It's rather cold today.
Hace bastante frío hoy.
athe bastante freeyo oy

It's windy.
Hace viento.
athe beeyento

It looks as though it's going to rain.
Parece que va a llover.
parethe ke ba a eeyober

Should I take an umbrella?
¿Debo llevar un paraguas?
debo eeyebar oon paragwas?

I hope the weather will improve.
Espero que se mejore el tiempo.
espero ke se mehore el teeyempo

Telephoning

May I use your telephone?
¿Puedo usar su teléfono?
pwedo oosar soo telefono?

Where can I make a long-distance phone call?
¿Dónde puedo hacer una llamada interurbana?
donde pwedo ather oona eeyamada eenteroorbana?

A token, please.
Una ficha, por favor.
oona feecha, por fabor

Do you have a telephone directory?
¿Tiene usted una guía de teléfonos?
teeyene oosted oona geeya de telefonos?

Do you speak English?
¿Habla usted inglés?
abla oosted eengles?

I want to make a collect call.
Quiero que sea a cobro revertido.
keeyero ke sea a kobro rreberteedo

Hello. I would like La Coruña ——
Oiga. Quiero hablar con el ——
de La Coruña
*oyga. keeyero ablar kon el ——
de la koroonya*

Please let me know the cost of the call afterwards.
Dígame el importe de la llamada después, por favor.
deegame el eemporte de la eeyamada despwes, por fabor

Hello. This is . . .
Hola. Soy . . .
ola. soy . . .

May I please speak to . . .
Quiero hablar con . . .
keeyero ablar kon . . .

Could you give me extension . . . ?
¿Me puede dar la extensión . . . ?
me pwede dar la esstenseeyon . . . ?

Is this . . . ?
¿Es . . . ?
es . . . ?

He/she isn't here at the moment.
El/ella no está en este momento.
el/eya no esta en este momento

Could you tell him/her that I called? My name is . . . My number is . . .
Dígale a él/ella que he llamado. Mi nombre es . . . Mi número de teléfono es . . .
deegale a el/eya ke e eeyamado. mee nombre es . . . mee noomero de telefono es . . .

Would you take a message, please.
¿Por favor, quiere tomar un recado?
por fabor keeyere tomar oon rrekado

Do you know when he/she will be back?
¿Sabe usted cuando estará él/ella de vuelta?
sabe oosted kwando estara el/eya de bwelta?

I'll call back later.
Llamaré más tarde.
eeyamare mas tarde

Operator, could you help me, please?
Señorita, me podría ayudar, por favor?
senyoreeta me podreeya ahyoodar por fabor?

I don't speak Spanish very well.
No hablo español muy bien.
no ablo espanyol mooee beeyen

I dialed the wrong number.
He marcado un número equivocado.
e markado oon noomero ekeebokado

I was cut off.
Me han cortado la línea.
me an kortado la leenea

Who is this?
¿Quién habla?
keeyen abla?

Hold the line, please.
Espere un momento, por favor.

The line is busy.
La línea está ocupada.

Hang up. I will call you back.
Quelque. Le volveré a llamar.

What's your number?
¿Cuál es su número?

What number are you calling?
¿A qué número llama usted?

I think you've got the wrong number.
Creo que se ha equivocado de número.

Post Office (Oficina de Correos)

Where is the nearest post office?
¿Dónde está la oficina de correos más cercana?
donde esta la ofeetheena de korreos mas therkanah?

What window do I go to for . . .
¿Aqué ventanilla debo ir para . . .
a ke bentaneeya debo eer para . . .

stamps
comprar sellos
komprar seyos

parcels
los paquetes?
los paketes

telegrams
mandar un telegrama
mandar oon telegrama

money orders
un giro postal
oon heero postal

poste restante
la lista de correos
la leesta de korreos

Are there any letters for me? Here is my passport.
¿Hay correo para mí? Aquí tiene mi pasaporte.
ah-y korreo para mee? akee tee-yene mee pasaporte

What's the postage for . . . ?
¿Cuál es el franqueo para
kwal es el frankeo para

a letter to England
una carta para Inglaterra
oona karta para eenglaterra

a post-card to the United States
una postal para los Estados Unidos?
oona postal para los estados ooneedos

I want to send this (by) . . .
Quiero mandar esto por . . .
keeyero mandar esto por . . .

air mail
correo aéreo
korreo aereo

express
urgente
oorhente

registered mail
correo certificado
korreo therteefeekado

Please give me . . . 10 pesetas stamps.
Quiero . . . sellos de 10 pesetas.
keeyero . . . seyos de deeyeth pesetas

I want to send this package.
Quiero mandar este paquete.
keeyero mandar este pakete

What does it contain?
¿Qué contiene?
ke kontee-yene?

I want to send a telegram. Could I have a form, please?
Quiero mandar un telegrama. ¿Me da un impreso, por favor?
keeyero mandar oon telegrama. me da oon eempreso, por fabor?

How much is it per word?
¿Cuánto cuesta por palabra?
kwanto kwesta por palabra?

Bank (Banco)

Where's the nearest bank?
¿Dónde está el banco más cercano?
donde esta el banko mas therkano?

Where can I cash a traveler's check?
¿Dónde puedo cambiar un cheque de viajero?
donde pwedo kambeeyar oon cheke de beeyahero?

Do you charge a fee?
¿Cobran comisión?
kobran komeeseeyon?

What's the rate of exchange?
¿A cuánto está el cambio?
a kwanto esta el kambeeyo?

Do you issue money on this credit card?
¿Puedo retirar dinero con esta tarjeta de crédito?
pwedo rreteerar deenero kon esta tarheta de kredeeto?

Can you cash a personal check?
¿Puede hacer efectivo un cheque personal?
pwede ather efekteebo oon cheke personal?

I have a letter of credit/bank draft.
Tengo una garantía bancaria.
tengo oona garanteeya bankareeya

I'm expecting money from . . . Has it arrived?
Espero una transferencia de . . . Ha llegado?
espero oona transferentheeya de . . . a eeyegado?

I would like to make a deposit.
Quiero hacer un depósito.
keeyero ather oon deposeeto

I would like to open an account.
Quisiera abrir una cuenta.
keesee-yera abreer oona kwenta

I would like to buy some foreign currency.
Quisiera comprar moneda extranjera.
keesee-yera komprar moneda esstranhera

I would like to change some . . . for some . . .
Quisiera cambiar unos (as) . . . por unos(as) . . .
keesee-yera kambeeyar oonos (as) . . . por oonos(as) . . .

Shopping

I'm looking for a . . .
Busco . . .
boosko . . .

bakery	una pastelería	*oona pastelereeya*
barber shop	una barbería	*oona barbereeya*
bookshop	una librería	*oona leebrereeya*
butcher shop	una carnicería	*oona karneethereeya*
delicatessen	un ultramarinos	*oon ooltramareenos*
department store	unos grandes almacenes	*oonos grandes almathenes*
drug store	una farmacia	*oona farmatheeya*
fishmonger's	una pescadería	*oona peskadereeya*
greengrocer's	una verdulería	*oona berdoolereeya*
hairdresser	una peluquería	*oona pelookereeya*
hardware store	una ferretería	*oona ferretereeya*
laundry/dry cleaner	una lavandería/tintorería	*oona labandereeya/ teentore-reeya*
liquor store	una tienda de licores	*oona teeyenda de leekores*
market	un mercado	*oon merkado*
newsstand	un quiosco de periódicos	*oon keeyosko de pereeyodeekos*
shoe repair	un zapatero	*oon thapatero*
shoe store	una zapatería	*oona thapatereeya*
sporting goods store	una tienda de artículos de deportes	*oona teeyenda de arteekoolos de deportes*
stationery store	una papelería	*oona papelereeya*
supermarket	un supermercado	*oon soopermerkado*
tobacconist's	un estanco	*oon estanko*

Where can I buy . . . ?
¿Dónde puedo comprar . . . ?
donde pwedo komprar . . . ?

May I help you? What would you like?
¿Le puedo ayudar? ¿Qué desea?
le pwedo ah-yoodar? ke desea?

I would have . . . Can you show me . . . ?
Quiero . . . Me puede mostrar . . . ?
keeyero me pwede mostrar . . . ?

Do you have . . . ?
¿Tiene . . . ?
teeyene . . . ?

I'm just looking, thanks.
Sólo estoy mirando, gracias.
solo estoy meerando, gratheeyas

How much is this?
¿Cuánto cuesta esto?
kwanto kwestah esto?

Would you write that down, please?
Me lo puede escribir, por favor?
me lo pwede eskreebeer, por fabor?

Do you accept travelers checks/ credit cards/dollars/pounds?
¿Acepta usted cheques de viajero/ tarjetas de crédito/dolares/libras esterlinas?
athepta oosted chekes de beeyahero/ tarhetas de kredeeto/dolares/leebras esterleenas?

I think there's an error on this bill.	Would you ship it to this address?
Me parece que hay un error en esta cuenta.	¿Podría enviarlo a esta dirección?
me parethe ke ah-y oon error en esta kwenta	*podreeya embeeyarlo a esta deerektheeyon?*

Bookstore/Newsstand/Stationer (Librería/Quiosco/Papelería)

I'd like to buy . . .
Quiero (comprar) . . .
keeyero (komprar) . . .

an address book	una libreta de direcciones	*oona leebreta de deerektheeyones*
an appointment book	una agenda	*oona ahenda*
a Spanish-English dictionary	un diccionario español-inglés	*oon deektheeyonareeyo espanyol-eengles*
some envelopes	unos sobres	*oonos sobres*
an eraser	una goma de borrar	*oona goma de borrar*
a Spanish grammar	un libro de gramática castellana	*oon leebro de gramateeka kasteyana*
a guidebook	una guía	*oona geeya*
a map of the town	un mapa de la ciudad	*oon mapa de la theeyoodad*
a road map	un mapa de carreteras	*oon mapa de karreteras*
an American/English newspaper	un periódico americano/inglés	*oon pereeyodeeko amereekano/eengles*
a notebook	un cuaderno	*oon kwaderno*
a pen (ballpoint)	un bolígrafo	*oon boleegrafo*
a pen (fountain)	una pluma	*oona plooma*
a pencil	un lápiz	*oon lapeeth*
some post cards	unas tarjetas postales	*oonas tarhetas postales*
some Scotch tape	cinta "cel-lo"	*theenta thel-lo*
some writing paper	papel para cartas	*papel para kartas*

Clothing Store (Tienda de ropa)

Could you show me a . . . like the one in the window?
¿Me podría mostrar un/una . . . como el/la del escaparate?
me podreeya mostrar oon/oona . . . komo el/la del eskapara te?

Could you show me something . . .
¿Me podría enseñar algo . . .
me podreeya ensenyar algo

bigger/smaller	lighter/darker
más grande/más pequeño	más claro/más oscuro
mas grande/mas pekenyo	*mas klaro/mas oskooro*

in a different color
de un color diferente
de oon kolor deeferente

less expensive
más barato
mas barato

of better quality
de mejor calidad
de mehor kaleedad

I take size . . .
Mi talla es. . . .
mee taeeya es . . .

I'm not sure what my size is.
No estoy seguro/a de mi talla
no estoy segooro/a de mee taeeya

May I try it on?
¿Me lo podría probar?
me lo podreeya probar?

It doesn't fit.
No me queda bien.
no me keda beeyen

It's too . . .
Es demasiado . . .
es demaseeyado . . .

tight/loose	short/long
apretado/suelto	corto/largo
apretado/swelto	*korto/largo*

Can you show me anything else?
¿Puede enseñarme otra cosa?
pwede ensenyarme otra kosa?

Very well; I'll take it.
Estupendo; me lo llevo.
estoopendo; me lo eeyebo

No, it's not really what I was looking for.
No, no es realmente lo que buscaba.
no, no es rrealmente lo ke booskaba

No, it's too expensive.
No, es muy caro.
no, es mooee karo

I'll give you . . . for it.
Le doy . . .
le doy . . .

Articles of Clothing (Ropa)

bathing suit	un traje de baño	*oon trahe de banyo*
bath robe	un albornoz	*oon albornoth*
blouse	una blusa	*oona bloosa*
boots	unas botas	*oonas botas*
bra	un sostén	*oon sosten*
cardigan	una chaqueta de punto	*oona chaketa de poonto*
coat	un abrigo	*oon abreego*
dress	un vestido	*oon besteedo*
evening dress	un traje de noche	*oon trahe de noche*
girdle	una faja	*oona faha*
gloves	unos guantes	*oonos gwantes*
hat	un sombrero	*oon sombrero*
jacket	una chaqueta	*oona chaketa*
nightgown	un camisón	*oon kameeson*
pants	unos pantalones	*oonos pantalones*
panty-hose	una media pantalón	*oona medeeya pantalon*
pullover	un jersey	*oon hersahy*
pyjamas	una pijama	*oona peeama*
raincoat	un impermeable	*oon eempermeable*
sandals	unas sandalias	*oonas sandaleeyas*

scarf	una bufanda	*oona boofanda*
	un "foulard"	*oon foolar*
shirt	una camisa	*oona kameesa*
long sleeves	de manga larga	de *manga larga*
short sleeves	de manga corta	de *manga korta*
shoes	unos zapatos	*oonos thapatos*
shorts	unos pantalones cortos	*oonos pantalones kortos*
skirt	una falda	*oona falda*
slip	una combinación	*oona kombeenatheeyon*
slippers	unas zapatillas	*oonas thapateeyas*
socks	unos calcetines	*oonos kaltheteenes*
stockings	unas medias	*oonas medeeyas*
suit	un traje	*oon trahe*
sweater	un suéter	*oon sweter*
T-shirt	una camiseta	*oona kameeseta*
tennis shoes	unos zapatos de tenis	*oonos thapatos de tenees*
tie	una corbata	*oona korbata*
tuxedo	un smoking	*oon esmokeen*
underwear (men's)	unos calzoncillos	*oonos kalthontheeyos*
underwear (women's)	ropa interior	*rropa eentereeyor*
belt	un cinturón	*oon theentooron*
buttons	unos botones	*oonos botones*
pocket	un bolsillo	*oon bolseeyo*
shoe laces	unos cordones para zapatos	*oonos kordones para thapatos*
zipper	una cremallera	*oona kremaeeyera*

Colors

beige	beige	*beys*
black	negro	*negro*
blue	azul	*athool*
brown	marrón	*marron*
gold	oro	*oro*
green	verde	*berde*
grey	gris	*grees*
off-white	crema	*krema*
orange	naranja	*naranha*
pink	rosa	*rrosa*
purple	púrpura	*poorpoora*
red	rojo	*rroho*
silver	plata	*plata*
turquoise	turquesa	*toorkesa*
white	blanco	*blanko*
yellow	amarillo	*amareeyo*

SPANISH

Fabrics

acrylic	acrílico	*akreeleeko*
corduroy	pana	*pana*
cotton	algodón	*algodon*
felt	fieltro	*feeyeltro*
flannel	franela	*franela*
lace	encaje	*enkahe*
leather	cuero	*kwero*
linen	hilo	*eelo*
rayon	rayón	*rraheeyon*
satin	seda	*seda*
suede	ante	*ante*
synthetic	sintético	*seenteteeko*
velvet	terciopelo	*tertheeyopelo*
wool	lana	*lana*

Jewelry (Joyas)

bracelet	una pulsera	*oona poolsera*
necklace	un collar	*oon koeeyar*
ring	un anillo	*oon aneeyo*
wristwatch	un reloj de pulsera	*oon rrelo de poolsera*
diamond	diamante	*deeyamante*
gold	oro	*oro*
platinum	platino	*plateeno*
silver	plata	*plata*
stainless steel	acero inoxidable	*athero eenokseedable*
plated	plateado	*plateado*

Buying Food for Picnics and Snacks

I'd like some . . .
Quisiera . . .
keesee-yera . . .

apples	manzanas	*manthanas*
apple juice	zumo de manzana	*thoomo de manthana*
bananas	unos plátanos	*oonos platanos*
bread	pan	*pan*
butter	mantequilla	*mantekeeya*

cake	unos bizcochos	*oonos* beeth*kochos*
candy	unos caramelos	*oonos* kara*melos*
carrots	unas zanahorias	*oonas* thanaoreeyas
cereal	cereal	the*real*
cheese	queso	*ke*so
chocolate	chocolate	choko*late*
coffee	café	*kafe*
cold cuts	unos fiambres	*oonos* feey*ambres*
cookies	unas galletas	*oonas* gaeey*etas*
crackers	unas galletas saladas	*oonas* gaeey*etas* sa*ladas*
cucumbers	unos pepinos	*oonos* pe*peenos*
eggs	huevos	*webos*
flour	harina	a*reena*
frankfurters	unos perritos calientes	*oonos* perre*tos* kal*eeyentes*
grapefruits	unos pomelos	*oonos* po*melos*
ham	jamón	ha*mon*
ice cream	helado	e*lado*
lemons	unos limones	*oonos* lee*mones*
lettuce	lechuga	le*chooga*
melon	melón	me*lon*
milk	leche	*leche*
mustard	mostaza	mos*tatha*
oil	aceite	a*thayte*
oranges	naranjas	na*ranhas*
orange juice	zumo de naranja	*thoomo* de na*ranha*
peaches	unos melocotones	*oonos* melo*kotones*
pears	unas peras	*oonas* *peras*
pepper	pimienta	peem*eeyenta*
peppers	unos pimientos	*oonos* peem*eeyentos*
pickles	unos pepinillos	*oonos* pepe*eeneeyos*
plums	unas ciruelas	*oonahs* theerw*elas*
potato chips	patatas fritas	pa*tatas* *freetas*
potatoes	unas patatas	*oonas* pa*tatas*
raspberries	unas frambuesas	*oonas* framb*wesas*
rolls	unos panecillos	*oonos* panethee*yos*
salad	una ensalada	*oona* en*salada*
salami	salchichón	salchee*chon*
salt	sal	*sal*
sandwiches	unos bocadillos	*oonos* boka*deeyos*
sausages	unas salchichas	*oonas* salchee*chas*
soft drinks	unos refrscos	*oonos* rrefres*kos*
spaghetti	espaguetis	espage*tees*
strawberries	unas fresas	*oonas* *fresas*
sugar	azúcar	a*thookar*
tea	té	*te*
tomatoes	unos tomates	*oonos* to*mates*
yoghurt	yogourt	eeyo*goort*
a box of	una caja de	*oona* **kaha** de
a can of	una lata de	*oona* *lata* de
a jar of	un tarro de	*oon* *tarro* de
a half kilo of	medio kilo de	me*deeyo* **keelo** de

a kilo of	un kilo de	*oon keelo de*
a packet of	un paquete de	*oon pakete de*
a slice of	un trozo de	*oon trotho de*

a bottle opener	un abridor de botellas	*oon abreedor de boteyas*
a corkscrew	un sacacorchos	*oon sakakorchos*
paper napkins	servilletas de papel	*sébeeyetas de papel*
plastic utensils	cubiertos de plástico	*koobeeyertos de plasteeko*
a tin (can) opener	un abrelatas	*oon abrelatas*

I'll have a little more.
Tomaré un poco más.
tomare oon poko mas

That's too much.
Eso es demasiado.
eso es demaseeyado

Could I have a bag?
¿Me podría dar una bolsa?
me podreeya dar oona bolsa?

Pharmacy (Farmacia)

Can you make up this prescription?
¿Puede usted prepararme esta receta?
pwede oosted prepararme esta rretheta?

How long will it take?
¿Cuánto tardará?
kwanto tardara?

I'll come back in a little while.
Volveré dentro de poco.
bolbere dentro de poko

Could you please write down the instructions in English?
¿Me podría escribir las instrucciones en inglés?
me podreeya eskreebeer las eenstrooktheeyones en eengles?

Can you give me something for . . .
¿Me podría dar algo para . . .
me podreeya dar algo para . . .

a cold	el catarro	*el katarro*
constipation	el estreñimiento	*el estrenyee-meeynto*
a cough	la tos	*la tos*
a cut	una herida	*la ereeda*
diarrhea	la diarrea	*la deeyarrea*
hay fever	la fiebre del heno	*la feeyebre del eno*
a headache	dolor de cabeza	*dolor de kabetha*
indigestion	indigestion	*eendeehesteeyon*
an insect bite/sting	una picadura de insecto	*oona peekadoora de eensekto*
nausea	la náusea	*la naoosea*
a sore throat	dolor de garganta	*dolor de garganta*
a sunburn	las quemaduras del sol	*las kemadooras del sol*
travel sickness	el mareo	*el mareo*
an upset stomach	las molestias del estómago?	*las molesteeyas del estomago?*

I'd like a/an/some . . .
Puede darme . . . ?
pwede darme . . . ?

aspirin	unas aspirinas	*oonas aspeereenas*
bandage	una venda	*oona benda*
Band-aids	curitas	*kooreetas*
cough syrup	un jarabe para la tos	*oon harabe para la tos*
cough drops	unas pastillas para la tos	*oonas pasteeyas para la tos*
contraceptives	unos anticonceptivos	*oonos anteekontheepteebos*
eye drops	unas gotas para los ojos	*oonas gotas para los ohos*
insect repellent	un repelente para insectos	*oon rrepelente para eensektos*
laxative	un laxante	*oon laksante*
mouthwash	un elíxir para enjuagarse la boca	*oon eleekseer para enhwagarse la boka*
sleeping pills	un somnífero	*oon somneefero*
sanitary napkins	unas compresas	*oonas kompresas*
tampons	unos tampones	*oonos tampones*

Toilet Articles

after-shave lotion	una loción para después del afeitado	*oona lotheeyon para despwes del afaytado*
cream	una crema	*oona krema*
cleansing cream	limpiadora	*leempeeyadora*
hand cream	para las manos	*para las manos*
moisturizing cream	hidratante	*eedratante*
deodorant	un desodorante	*oon desodorante*
emery board	una lima de papel	*oona leema de papel*
nail file	una lima para uñas	*oona leema para oonyas*
razor	una navaja de afeitar	*oona nabaha de afaytar*
razor blades	unas hojas de afeitar	*oonas ohas de afaytar*
shampoo	champú	*champoo*
shaving cream	crema de afeitar	*krema de afaytar*
soap	jabón	*habon*
sun-tan oil/cream	un aceite/crema solar	*oon athayte/krema solar*
talcum powder	polvos de talco	*polbos de talko*
tissues	unos pañuelos de papel	*oonos panywelos de papel*
toilet paper	papel higiénico	*papel eeheeyeneeko*
toothbrush	un cepillo de dientes	*oon thepeeyo de deeyentes*
toothpaste	pasta de dientes	*pasta de deeyentes*
tweezers	unas pinzas	*oonas peenthas*

Note: for makeup and perfume, go to a *perfumería.*

SPANISH

Photography

I'd like a good/inexpensive camera, please.
Quiero una cámara de buena calidad/
barata.
*keeyero oona kamara de bwena
kaleedad/barata*

I'd like some film for this camera
Quisiera una película para esta cámara
*keesee-yera oona peleekoola para
esta kamara*

black and white	color
en blanco y negro	de color
en blanko ee negro	*de kolor*

color slides
diapositivas de color
deeyaposeeteebas de kolor

I need . . . for this camera.
necesito . . . para esta cámara.
netheseeto . . . para esta kamara

batteries	a lens
baterías	un objetivo
batereeyas	*oon obheteebo*

flash cubes
unos cubitos de flash
oonos koobeetos de flash

How much do you charge for processing?
¿Cuanto cobra por el revelado?
kwanto kobra por el rrebelado?

I'd like . . . prints/slides of each negative . . .
Quiero . . . copias de cada netivo . . .
*keeyero . . . kopeeyas de kada
negateebo . . .*

with a matt finish
con acabado mate
kon akabado mate

with a glossy finish
con acabado de brillo
kon akabado de breeyo

I would like an enlargement of this, please.
Quiero una ampliación de esta, por favor.
*keeyero oona ampleeyatheeyon de
esta, por fabor*

When will it be ready?
¿Para cuándo estará listo?
para kwando estara leesto?

Tobacconist's (Estanco)

I'd like a pack/carton of cigarettes, please.
Déme un paquete/cartón de cigarrillos.
*deme oon pakete/karton
de theegarreeyos*

Do you have . . . ?
¿Tiene usted . . . ?
teeyene oosted . . . ?

I'd like . . .
Quisiera . . .
keeseeyera . . .

pipe tobacco
tabaco de pipa
tabako de peepa

a cigarette lighter
un encendedor
oon enthendedor

lighter fluid
gasolina para el encendedor
gasoleena para el enthendedor

matches	a pipe
cerillas	una pipa
thereeyas	*oona peepa*

Laundry/Dry Cleaner's (Lavandería/Tintorería)

Where is the nearest laundry/dry cleaner's?
¿Dónde está la lavandería tintorería más cercana?
donde esta la labandereeya teentorereeya mas therkana?

**I'd like to have these clothes
    washed and ironed.**
Quiero que me laven y planchen esta
ropa.
*keeyero ke me laben ee planchen
esta rropa*

Please have this dry cleaned.
Por favor, quiero que me limpien esto
en seco.
*por fabor keeyero ke me leempeeyen
esto en seko*

Can you remove this stain?
¿Puede usted quitar esta mancha?
pwede oosted keetar esta mancha?

Can you mend this?
¿Puede usted remendar esto?
pwede oosted rremendar esto?

When will it be ready?
¿Cuándo estará lista?
kwando estara leesta?

I need it . . .
La necesito para . . .
la netheseeto para . . .

this afternoon	**this evening**
esta tarde	esta noche
esta tarde	*esta noche*
tomorrow	
mañana	
manyana	

Repairs

Can you fix this?
¿Me puede arreglar esto?
me pwede arreglar esto?

How long will it take?
¿Cuánto tardará?
kwanto tardara?

How much will it cost?
¿Cuánto costará?
kwanto kostara?

When will it be ready?
¿Cuándo estará listo?
kwando estara leesto?

HEALTH

At the Doctor's

I don't feel well.
No me encuentro bien.
no me enkwentro beeyen

**Where can I find a doctor who
    speaks English?**
¿Dónde puedo encontrar un médico
que hable inglés?
*donde pwedo enkontrar oon medeeko
ke able eengles?*

Could you call a doctor for me?
¿Me puede llamar a un médico?
Me pwede eeyamar a oon medeeko?

Is there a doctor here?
¿Hay un médico aquí?
ah-y oon medeeko akee?

Must I make an appointment?
¿Tendré que hacer una cita?
tendre ke ather oona theeta?

I have (a) . . .
Tengo . . .
tengo . . .

backache	dolor de espalda	*dolor de espalda*
constipation	estreñimiento	*estrenyeemeeyento*
cough	tos	*tos*
cramps	calambres	*kalambres*
diarrhea	diarrea	*deeyarrea*
fever	fiebre	*feeyebre*
hemorrhoids	hemorroides	*emorroydes*
insect bite	una picadura de insecto	*oona peekadoora de eensekto*
lump	un bulto	*oon boolto*
nausea	náuseas	*naooseas*
rash	sarpullido	*sarpooyeedo*
swelling	una hinchazón	*oona eenchathon*
wound	una herida	*oona ereeda*

I have difficulty breathing.
Tengo dificultad en respirar.
tengo deefeekooltad enrrespeerar

I feel dizzy/faint.
Me siento mareado/desmayado.
me seeyento mareado/desmahyado

I've been vomiting.
He tenido vómitos.
e teneedo bomeetos

I can't eat/sleep.
No puedo comer/dormir.
no pwedo komer/dormeer.

I must see a doctor right away.
Necesito ver a un médico rápidamente.
netheseeto ber ah oon medeeko rrapeedamente?

I feel ill.
Me encuentro enfermo.
me enkwentro enfermo

I've got a pain here.
Tengo un dolor aquí.
tengo oon dolor akee

I've cut/burned myself.
Me he cortado/quemado.
me e kortado/kemado

I think I have sprained/broken my wrist/ankle.
Creo que me he torcido/roto la muñeca/el tobillo.
kreo ke me e torcheedo/rroto la moonyeka/el tobeeyo

It hurts when I move . . .
me duele cuando muevo . . .
me dwele kwando mwebo . . .

I'm allergic to penicillin.
Tengo alergia a la penicilina.
tengo alerheeya a la peneetheeleena

Doctor to Patient:

| **Where does it hurt?** | **I will prescribe some pills.** |
| ¿Dónde le duele? | Le recetaré unas píldoras. |

How long have you had this trouble?	**Take these . . . times a day before/**
¿Cuánto tiempo hace que usted tiene	**after each meal every morning/**
este dolor?	**evening.**
	Tome estas . . . veces al día antes/
Please undress (to the waist).	despues de cada comida por la
Desvístase (hasta la cintura) por favor.	mañana/por la noche.

Does that hurt?	**You must rest/stay in bed for . . .**
¿Le duele esto?	**days.**
	Usted necesita descansar/quedarse en
I'll need a urine specimen/blood	cama . . . días.
sample.	
Necesitaré una muestra de su orina/	**It's nothing serious.**
sangre.	No es nada serio.

| **Are you taking any medication?** | **You must go to the hospital.** |
| ¿Está tomando alguna medicina? | Necesita ir al hospital. |

You have . . .
Usted tiene . . .

an abcess	un flemón
appendicitis	apendicitis
a bad cold	un resfriado malo
food poisoning	una intoxicación por comida
a hernia	una hernia
an infection	una infección
influenza	gripe
a sprain	una torcedura
tonsilitis	amigdalitis
an ulcer	una úlcera

At the Dentist's

Can you recommend a good dentist?
¿Puede recomendarme un buen dentista?
pwede rrekomendarme oon bwen denteesta?

I would like to see Dr. . . . as soon as possible.
Quiero ver al doctor . . . lo antes posible.
keeyero ber al doktor . . . lo antes poseeble

I have a bad toothache.	**My tooth has broken.**
Tengo mucho dolor de muelas.	Se me ha roto un diente.
tengo moocho dolor de mwelas	*se me a rroto oon deeyente*

SPANISH

My gums are sore/bleeding.
Mis encías están inflamadas/
 sangrando.
*mee entheeyas estan een flamadas/
 sangrando*

I have an abscess.
Tengo un flemón.
tengo oon flemon

**Can you give me temporary
 treatment?**
¿Me puede dar una cura provisional?
*me pwede dar oona koora
 probeeseeyonal?*

I've lost/broken a filling.
Se me ha caído/roto un empaste.
se me a kah-ydo/rroto oon empaste

Please don't extract it.
No me la saque, por favor.
no me la sake por fabor

Please give me a local anaesthesia.
Déme un anestésico local, por favor.
deme oon anesteteeko lokal por fabor

Dentist to Patient

I want to give you an X-ray.
Quiero sacarle una radiografía.

I will fill the tooth.
Le voy a empastar el diente.

This tooth must come out.
Este diente tiene que ser extarído.

Optician

I have broken my glasses.
Se me han roto las gafas.
se me an rroto las gafas

Can you repair them?
¿Me las puede arreglar?
me las pwede arreglar?

I have lost a contact lens.
He perdido una lentilla.
e perdeedo oona lenteeya

Could you make me another one?
¿Me pueden hacer otra?
me pwede ather otra?

When will it/they be ready?
¿Cuándo estará(n) lista(s)?
kwando estara(n) leesta(s)?

**I need soaking/wetting solution for
 hard/soft contact lenses.**
Necesito una solución conservante/
 humedecedora para lentillas duras/
 blandas.
*netheseeto oona solootheeyon
 conserbante/oomedethedora
 para lenteeyas dooras/blandas*

**My contact lenses are bothering me.
 Would you have a look at them?**
Las lentillas me están molestando.
 ¿Le importaría examinarlas?
*las lenteeyas me estan molestando.
 le eemporta-reeya egzameenarlas?*

Paying the Doctor/Dentist/Optician

How much do I owe you?
¿Cuánto le debo?
kwanto le debo?

Can you send me a bill?
¿Me podría mandar una factura?
me podreeya mandar oona faktoora?

I have health insurance.
Tengo seguro médico.
tengo segooro medeeko

EMERGENCY

Loss or Theft

Excuse me, can you help me?
Perdone ¿Me podría ayudar?
perdone me. podreeya ahyoodar?

Where's the police station?
¿Dónde está la comisaría?
donde esta la komeesaree-ya?

Where's the American/British/ Canadian consulate?
¿Dónde está el consulado americano/ inglés/canadiense?
donde esta el konsoolado amereekano/eengles/ kanadeeyense?

I've lost my . . . Someone has stolen my . . .
He perdido mi . . . Alguien ha robado mi(s) . . .
e perdeedo mee . . . algeeyen a rrobado mee(s) . . .

passport	pasaporte	*pasaporte*
money	dinero	*deenero*
traveler's checks	cheques de viajero	*chekes de beeyahero*
credit cards	tarjetas de crédito	*tarhetas de kredeeto*
luggage	equipaje	*ekeepahe*
plane tickets	boletos de avión	*boletos de abeeyon*
handbag	bolso	*bolso*

I left something in the train/taxi/bus.
Dejé algo en el tren/taxi/autobús.
dehe algo en el tren/taksee/owtoboos

Asking for Help

Help!	¡Socorro!	*Sokorro*
Police!	¡Policía!	*poleetheeya*
Fire!	¡Fuego!	*fwego*

SPANISH

TIME, DATES, NUMBERS

Time/Date

What time is it?
¿Qué hora es?
ke ora es?

It's . . .
Son las . . .
son las . . .

two o'clock	dos	*dos*
ten past three	tres y diez	*tres ee deeyeth*
four fifteen	cuatro y cuarto	*kwatro ee kwarto*
twenty past five	cinco y veinte	*theenko ee baynte*
six-thirty	seis y media	*says ee medeeya*
quarter to eight	ocho menos cuarto	*ocho menos kwarto*
five to eight	ocho menos cinco	*ocho menos theenko*

It's midnight.
Es medianoche.
es medeeyanoche

It's one o'clock.
Es la una.
es la oona

sunrise	amanecer	*amanether*
morning	mañana	*manyana*
noon	mediodía	*medeeyodeeya*
afternoon	tarde	*tarde*
sunset	puesta del sol	*pwesta del sol*
evening	tarde	*tarde*
night	noche	*noche*

It's early/late.
Es temprano/tarde.
es temprano/tarde

What's the date today?
¿Qué fecha es hoy?
ke fecha es oy?

The date is . . .
Hoy es . . .
oy es . . .

Days of the Week

Monday	lunes	*loones*
Tuesday	martes	*martes*
Wednesday	miércoles	*meeyerkoles*
Thursday	jueves	*hwebes*
Friday	viernes	*beeyernes*
Saturday	sábado	*sabado*
Sunday	domingo	*domeengo*

Seasons

spring	primavera	*preemabera*
summer	verano	*berano*
autumn	otoño	*otonyo*
winter	invierno	*eenbeeyerno*

The Months

January	enero	*enero*
February	febrero	*febrero*
March	marzo	*martho*
April	abril	*abreel*
May	mayo	*mahyo*
June	junio	*hooneeyo*
July	julio	*hooleeyo*
August	agosto	*agosto*
September	septiembre	*seteeyembre*
October	octubre	*oktoobre*
November	noviembre	*nobeeyembre*
December	diciembre	*deetheeyembre*

this year	este año	*este anyo*
last week	la semana pasada	*la semana pasada*
next month	el mes próximo	*el mes prokseemo*

today	hoy	*oy*
yesterday	ayer	*ahyer*
tomorrow	mañana	*manyana*
the day before yesterday	anteayer	*anteahyer*
the day after tomorrow	pasado mañana	*pasado manyana*

Christmas	Navidades	*nabeedades*
Easter	Semana Santa	*semana santa*

SPANISH

Numbers

0	cero	*thero*
1	uno	*oono*
2	dos	*dos*
3	tres	*tres*
4	cuatro	*kwatro*
5	cinco	*theenko*
6	seis	*says*
7	siete	*seeyete*
8	ocho	*ocho*
9	nueve	*nwebe*
10	diez	*deeyeth*
11	once	*onthe*
12	doce	*dothe*
13	trece	*trethe*
14	catorce	*katorthe*
15	quince	*keenthe*
16	dieciséis	*deeyetheesays*
17	diecisiete	*deeyetheeseeyete*
18	dieciocho	*deeyetheeyocho*
19	diecinueve	*deeyetheenwebe*
20	veinte	*baynte*
21	veintiuno	*baynteeyoono*
22	veintidós	*baynteedos*
23	veintitrés	*baynteetres*
24	veinticuatro	*baynteekwatro*
25	veinticinco	*baynteetheenko*
26	veintiséis	*baynteesays*
27	veintisiete	*baynteeseeyete*
28	veintiocho	*baynteeyocho*
29	veintinueve	*baynteenwebe*
30	treinta	*traynta*
40	cuarenta	*kwarenta*
50	cincuenta	*theenkwenta*
60	sesenta	*sesenta*
70	setenta	*setenta*
80	ochenta	*ochenta*
90	noventa	*nobenta*
100	cien	*theeyen*
101	ciento uno	*theeyento oono*
102	ciento dos	*theeyento dos*
150	ciento cincuenta	*theeyento theenkwenta*
200	doscientos	*dostheeyentos*
300	trescientos	*trestheeyentos*
400	cuatrocientos	*kwatrotheeyentos*
500	quinientos	*keeneeyentos*
600	seiscientos	*saystheeyentos*
700	setecientos	*setetheeyentos*

800	ochocientos	*ochotheeyentos*
900	novecientos	*nobetheeyentos*
1000	mil	*meel*
1100	mil cien	*meel theeyen*
1200	mil doscientos	*meel dostheeyentos*
2000	dos mil	*dos meel*
5000	cinco mil	***theen**ko meel*
10,000	diez mil	*deeyeth meel*
50,000	cincuenta mil	*theen**kwen**ta meel*
100,000	cien mil	*theeyen meel*
1,000,000	un millón	*oon mee**yon***

first	primero	*pree**mer**o*
second	segundo	*se**goon**do*
third	tercero	*ter**ther**o*
fourth	cuarto	***kwar**to*
fifth	quinto	***keen**to*
sixth	sexto	***sess**to*
seventh	séptimo	***sep**teemo*
eighth	octavo	*ok**tab**o*
ninth	noveno	*no**ben**o*
tenth	décimo	***de**theemo*
eleventh	undécimo	*oon**de**theemo*
twelfth	duodécimo	*dwo**de**theemo*

a half	un medio	*oon **med**eeyo*
a quarter	un cuarto	*oon **kwar**to*
one third	un tercio	*oon **ter**theeyo*

SPANISH DICTIONARY

Generally, masculine nouns end in *o* and feminine nouns in *a*. In other cases, the gender will be indicated.

Only the masculine form of adjectives is shown. The feminine is usually formed by changing the final *o* to *a*.

A

a, an **uno, una, un**
able, to be **poder, ser capaz**
about **acerca de**
above **sobre**
abroad **en el extranjero**
absent **ausente**
absolutely **absolutamente**
accept, to **aceptar**
accident **accidente** (m.)
accompany, to **acompañar**
according, to **según**
accustomed **acostumbrado**
ache **dolor** (m.)
across **al otro lado de, a través**
acquaintance **conocido**
actor **actor**
add, to **sumar**
address **dirección** (f.)
admire, to **admirar**
admission **admisión** (f.)
advertisement **anuncio, aviso**
advice **consejo**
advice, to **aconsejar**
afraid, to be **tener miedo**
after **después de, detrás**
afternoon **tarde**
again **otra vez**
against **contra**
age **edad** (f.)
agency **agencia**
ago **hace**
agree, to **estar de acuerdo**
agreeable **agradable**
agreed **de acuerdo**
ahead **adelante**
air **aire** (m.)
air conditioning **aire acondicionado**
air force **fuerzas armadas**

air mail **correo aéreo**
airplane **aeroplano, avión** (m.)
airport **aeropuerto**
alarm clock **despertador** (m.)
alike **semejante, igual**
all **todo**
allow, to **permitir**
all right **bien**
almost **casi**
alone **solo**
already **ya**
also **también**
although **aunque**
always **siempre**
ambulance **ambulancia**
America **América**
American **americano**
among **entre**
amount **importe** (m.), **suma** (f.)
amusement **diversión** (f.)
amusement park **parque** (m.) **de atracciones**
amusing **divertido**
ancient **antiguo**
and **y**
angry **enojado, enfadado**
animal **animal** (m.)
ankle **tobillo**
announce, to **anunciar**
annoy, to **molestar**
answer, to **contestar**
answer **respuesta**
antifreeze **antigongelante** (m.)
anxious **inquieto, ansioso**
any **alguno**
anyone **alguien**
anything **algo, alguna cosa**
anyway **de todos modos**

anywhere **en alguna parte**
apartment **apartamento**
appear, to **aparecer, salir**
appetite **apetito**
appetizer **aperitivo**
apple **manzana**
appointment **cita**
appreciate **apreciar**
approach, to **acercarse**
approve, to **aprobar**
arm **brazo**
armchair **butaca** (f.), **sillón** (m.)
around **alrededor de**
arrest, to **arrestar**
arrival **llegada**
arrive, to **llegar**
art **arte**
artist **artista**
as **como**
ask, to **preguntar**
asleep, to fall **dormirse, quedarse dormido**
assure **asegurar**
at **en**
at all **nada de**
at once **en seguida**
attack **atacar**
attend **asistir a**
attention! **¡atención!**
attractive **atractivo, atrayente**
aunt **tía**
authentic **auténtico**
author **autor**
automatic **automático**
automobile **automóvil** (m.)
autumn **otoño**
avoid, to **evitar**
awaken, to **despertar**
away **fuera**

B

baby **bebé, niño**
bachelor **soltero**
back (adv.) **detrás**
back (n.) **espalda**
backpack **mochila**
bad **malo**
badly **mal, malamente**

baggage **equipaje** (m.)
bakery **panadería**
band (music) **banda**
bank **banco**
bar (drinking) **bar**
barber **barbero, peluquero**
basket **cesta**
bath **baño**
bathe, to **bañarse**
bathing suit **traje de baño** (m.)
bathroom **cuarto de baño**
bathtub **bañera**
battery **batería**
battle **batalla**
be, to **ser, estar**
beach **playa**
beans **frijol** (m.)
bear **oso**
beard **barba**
beat, to **golpear**
beautiful **bello**
beauty **belleza**
because **porque**
become **hacerse**
bed **cama**
bedroom **dormitorio**
beef **carne de vaca**
beer **cerveza**
before **antes**
begin, to **empezar**
behind **atrás, detrás de**
believe, to **creer**
bell (church) **campana**
bell (door) **timbre**
belong, to **pertenecer**
below **abajo**
belt **cinturón** (m.)
beside **al lado de**
best **mejor**
bet, to **apostar**
better **mejor**
between **entre**
bicycle **bicicleta**
big **grande**
bill **cuenta**
bird **pájaro**
birth **nacimiento**
birthday **cumpleaños** (m.)
bite, to **morder**
bitter **amargo**
black **negro**

blanket **manta**
blond **rubio**
blood **sangre** (f.)
blouse **blusa**
blue **azul**
boarding house **casa de huéspedes**
boat **barca**
boat (small) **bote** (m.)
body **cuerpo**
boil, to **hervir**
bomb **bomba**
book **libro**
born, to be **nacer**
border **límite** (m.), **borde** (m.),
  frontera
boring **aburrido**
borrow, to **pedir prestado**
both **ambos**
bother, to **molestar**
bottle **botella**
bottom **fondo**
bowl **tazón** (m.)
box **caja, cajón**
boy **niño**
brain **cerebro**
brake **freno**
brassiere **sostén** (m.)
bread **pan** (m.)
break, (to) **romper**
breakfast **desayuno**
bride **novia**
bridge **puente**
brief **breve**
bright **claro**
bring, to **llevar, traer**
broad **ancho**
broken **estropeado**
broom **escoba**
brother **hermano**
brother-in-law **cuñado**
brown **marrón**
brush **cepillo**
bug **insecto**
build, to **construir**
building **edificio**
bum **vagabundo**
bus **autobús** (m.)
bus stop **parada de autobuses**
business **oficio, negocio**
busy **ocupado**
but **pero**

butcher shop **carnicero**
butter **mantequilla**
button **botón** (m.)
buy, to **comprar**
by **por**
by means of **por medio de**
by chance **por casualidad**

C

cabbage **repollo**
cake **bizcocho**
calendar **calendario**
call, to **llamar**
call **llamada**
calm **tranquilo**
camera **cámara, máquina**
  fotográfica
canoe **canoa**
cap **gorra**
capable **capaz, competente**
captain **capitán**
car **coche**
card **ficha, tarjeta**
careful **cuidadoso**
carrot **zanahoria**
carry, to **llevar**
cash, to **cambiar**
cashier **cajero**
castle **castillo**
cat **gato**
cathedral **catedral**
catholic **católico**
cause **causa**
cave **caverna, gruta**
ceiling **cielo raso, techo (interior)**
celebrate, to **celebrar**
cellar **sótano**
cemetery **cementerio**
center **centro**
central **central**
century **siglo**
certain **seguro**
certainly **ciertamente**
chair **silla**
champagne **champaña**
change, to **cambiar**
change **cambio**
charming **encantador**

cheap **barato**
check, to **examinar**
checkroom **guardarropa**
cheerful **animado**
cheese **queso**
chest **pecho**
chicken **pollo**
child **niño**
childhood **infancia**
chocolate **chocolate**
Christian **cristiano**
Christmas **Pascuas de Navidad**
Christmas tree **árbol de Navidad**
church **iglesia**
cigar **cigarro**
cigarette **cigarrillo, pitillo**
city **ciudad** (f.)
city hall **ayuntamiento**
civilization **civilización**
class **clase**
clean (adj.) **limpio**
clean, to **limpiar**
clear **claro**
clever **listo**
cliff **risco, peñasco**
climate **clima** (m.)
climb **subida**
climb **escalar, ascender, subir**
clock **reloj** (m.)
close **cercano**
close, to **cerrar**
closed **cerrado**
closet **armario**
cloth **tela**
clothes **ropa**
cloud **nube** (f.)
cloudy **nublado**
club **club** (m.)
coal **carbón** (m.)
coast **costa**
coat **abrigo**
coffee **café** (m.)
cold (adj.) **frío**
cold (n.) **resfriado**
collapse, to **derrumbarse**
collar **cuello**
collection **colección**
color **color**
comb **peine** (m.)
come, to **venir**
to come in **entrar**

comfort **comodidad**
comfortable **cómodo**
to make oneself **ponerse cómodo**
commerce **comercio**
company **compañía, visita**
compartment **compartimiento**
complain **quejarse**
completely **completamente**
computer **computadora**
communism **comunismo**
concert **concierto**
condition **condición** (f.)
conductor **conductor** (m.)
congratulate **felicitar**
connection **empalme, entronque**
   (m.)
consist of, to **consistir en**
contract **contrato**
contrary, on the **al contrario**
conversation **conversación**
convince, to **convencer**
cook **cocinero**
cook, to **cocinar**
cooked **cocinado**
cool **fresco**
copy **copia**
corner **esquina**
correct **correcto**
cost, to **costar**
cotton **algodón**
cough **tos** (f.)
count **contar** (v., n.)
country **país, campo**
couple **par** (m.)
courage **valor** (m.)
course **curso**
of course **claro**
courtesy **cortesía**
cousin **primo**
cover, to **cubrir**
cow **vaca**
crazy **loco, extravagante**
cream **crema**
credit **crédito, mérito**
criminal **criminal**
crook **gancho, gartio**
cross, to **cruzar**
crossroads **encrucijada**
cruise **crucero, excursión**
cry, to **llorar**
cup **taza**

curtain **cortina**
custom **costumbre**
customs **aduana**
cut, to **cortar**

D

daily **diariamente**
damage **daño**
damage, to **hacer daño**
damp **húmedo**
dance, to **bailar**
danger **peligro**
dangerous **peligroso**
dark **oscuro**
date (time) **fecha**
date (rendezvous) **cita**
daughter **hija**
dawn **amanecer**
day **día**
dead **muerto**
dear **querido, caro**
decide, to **decidir**
decision **decisión**
declare **declarar**
deep **profundo**
degree **grado**
delay **demora**
delicious **delicioso**
delighted **encantado**
deliver, to **entregar**
dentist **dentista** (m.)
denture **dentadura**
depart, to **irse**
departure **partida**
deposit **depósito**
deposit, to **depositar**
describe **describir**
description **descripción**
desire, to **desear**
desk **escritorio**
dessert **postre** (m.)
diamond **diamante** (m.)
dictionary **diccionario**
die, to **morir, morirse**
difference **diferencia**
different **diferente**
difficult **difícil**
dine, to **cenar**

dining room **comedor**
dinner **cena**
direction **dirección**
directly **directamente**
dirty **sucio**
disappear, to **desaparecer**
disappointed **desilusionado**
discount **descuento**
discover **descubrir**
disgusting **repugnante,
  desagradable**
dish **plato**
distance **distancia**
distant **distante**
disturb, to **molestar**
divide, to **dividir**
diving (underwater sport) **bucear**
divorced **divorciado**
dizzy **mareado**
do, to **hacer**
doctor **doctor**
dog **perro**
dollar **dólar**
donkey **burro**
door **puerta**
double **doble**
doubt **duda**
down **abajo**
draft **corriente de aire** (f.)
dream, to **soñar**
dream **sueño**
dress, to **vestir**
drink, to **beber**
drive, to **conducir**
driver **conductor**
driver's license **licencia de conducir**
drown, to **ahogarse**
drunk **borracho**
dry **seco**
during **durante**

E

each **cada**
ear **oído**
early **temprano**
earn, to **ganar**
earth **tierra**
east **este**
Easter **Pascua**

easy **fácil**
eat, to **comer**
editor **director, redactor titular,**
egg **huevo**
either . . . or **o . . . o**
electric **eléctrico**
electricity **electricidad** (f.)
elevator **ascensor** (m.)
else **más**
or else **o si no**
embark, to **embarcar**
embassy **embajada**
embrace, to **abrazar**
embroidery **bordado**
emergency **emergencia**
employee **empleado**
employer **patrón**
empty **vacío**
end **fin, final**
to end **terminar**
Englishman **inglés**
enough **suficiente**
enter **entrar**
enthusiastic, to be **entusiasmarse**
entire **entero**
envelope **sobre** (m.)
equal **igual**
error **error** (m.)
escape, to **escapar**
especially **especialmente**
eternal **eterno**
even **liso, par**
evening **tarde, noche** (f.)
event **acontecimiento**
ever **alguna vez**
every **cada**
everybody **todo el mundo**
everything **todo**
everywhere **en todas partes**
exact **exacto**
exaggerate, to **exagerar**
examine, to **examinar**
example **ejemplo**
excellent **excelente**
except **excepto**
exchange **cambio**
exchange, to **cambiar**
excuse, to **perdonar**
exist, to **existir**
exit **salida**
expensive **caro**
experience **experiencia**

explain, to **explicar**
explanation **explicación** (f.)
export, to **exportar**
expression **expresión** (f.)
extinguish **extinguir**
extra **extra, de más**
eye **ojo**
eye doctor **oculista**

F

fabric **tela**
face **cara**
factory **fábrica**
faithful **fiel**
fall **caída**
fall (season) **otoño**
fall, to **caer**
family **familia**
famous **famoso**
far **lejano, lejos**
farm **granja**
farmer **campesino**
farther **más lejos**
fashion **moda**
fast **rápido**
fat **gordo**
father **padre**
favorable **favorable**
fear **temor**
feel, to **sentir**
fence **cerca, cercado, valla**
fever **fiebre**
few **pocos**
field **campo**
fight, to **pelear**
fill **llenar**
film **película**
finally **finalmente**
find, to **encontrar**
find out **averiguar**
fine (money) **multa**
finger **dedo**
finish **acabado**
finish, to **acabar, terminar**
fire **fuego**
fire department **cuerpo de bomberos**
first **primer, primero**
fish, to **pescar**
fish **pez** (m.)

fishing tackle **avíos, aparejos de pesca**
flame **llama**
flight **vuelo**
floor **piso, suelo**
flower **flor**
fly **mosca**
fly, to **volar**
fog **niebla**
follow, to **seguir**
food **comida**
foot **pie**
for **para, por**
forbidden **prohibido**
foreign **extranjero**
foreigner **extranjero**
forest **bosque** (m.)
forget, to **olvidar** (se)
forgive, to **perdonar**
fork **tenedor**
forward **adelante**
fountain **fuente**
fox **zorro**
France **Francia**
free **gratis, libre**
freedom **libertad** (f.)
freeze, to **helar**
frequently **frecuentemente**
fresh **fresco**
fried **frito**
friend **amigo**
friendship **amistad** (f.)
frightened, to be **asustado**
from **de**
front of, in **delante de**
frost **escarcha**
fruit **fruta**
fry **freír**
full **lleno**
funeral **entierro**
funny **gracioso**
furnish, to **amueblar, proporcionar**
furnished **amueblado**
furniture **muebles** (m. pl.)
future **porvenir, futuro**

G

game **juego, partida**
garage **garaje**
garden **jardín** (m.)
gasoline **gasolina**

gather **recoger**
gentleman **caballero**
genuine **genuino**
get up, to **levantarse**
girl **muchacha**
give, to **dar**
glad **contento**
glass **vidrio**
glasses **gafas** (f. pl.)
glove **guante** (m.)
go **ir**
God **Dios**
gold **oro**
good **bueno**
goodbye **adiós**
good evening **buenas tardes**
good morning **buenos días**
government **gobierno**
granddaughter/son **nieta/nieto**
grandfather/mother **abuelo/abuela**
grape **uva**
grapefruit **pomelo**
grateful **agradecido**
grave **tumba**
gray **gris**
great **gran**
green **verde**
greeting **saludo**
group **grupo**
grow, to **crecer**
guess **adivinar**
guest **invitado**
guide **guía** (m.)
guitar **guitarra**
gum **arma**
gymnasium **gimnasio**
gynecologist **ginecólogo**

H

hair **cabello**
half **medio, mitad**
hall **corredor, vestíbulo**
ham **jamón** (m.)
hammer **martillo**
hand **mano** (f.)
handbag **bolsa**
handkerchief **pañuelo**
happiness **felicidad** (f.)
happy **feliz**
hard **duro**

SPANISH

hat **sombrero**
hate, to **odiar**
have, to **tener**
have to, to **tener que**
he **él**
head **cabeza**
health **salud** (f.)
health resort **centro de salud, sanatorio**
hear, to **oír**
heart **corazón** (m.)
heat **calor** (m.)
heating **calefacción** (f.)
heavy **pesado**
heal **sanar**
heel **talón** (m.)
hello, hallo **hola**
help, to **ayudar**
help **ayuda**
her, hers **la, suyo**
here **aquí**
here is **aquí tiene**
high **alto**
high school **escuela secundaria**
highway **autopista**
hike **marchar, caminar, viajar**
hill **colina**
him, his **le, suyo**
history **historia**
hitchhike **viajar por autostop**
hold, to **tener**
hole **agujero**
holiday **fiesta**
holy **sagrado**
home **casa**
honest **honesto**
honey **miel** (f.)
honeymoon **luna de miel**
honor **honor** (m.)
hope, to **esperar**
hope **esperanza**
horn **cuerno, bocina**
horse **caballo**
hospital **hospital** (m.)
hospitality **hospitalidad** (f.)
hot **caliente**
hotel **hotel** (m.)
hour **hora**
house **casa**
how **como**
humidity **humedad** (f.)

hunger **hambre**
hungry, to be **tener hambre**
hunter **cazador**
hunting **caza**
hurry, to be in a **tener prisa**
husband **esposo**
hut **choza, cabaña**

I

I **yo**
ice cream **helado**
ice skate **esquiar**
idea **idea**
identification **identificación** (f.)
idiot **idiota, cretino**
if **si**
ignorant **ignorante**
ill **enfermo**
imagine, to **imaginar**
immediately **inmediatamente**
import, to **importar**
important **importante**
impossible **imposible**
impression **impresión**
in **en**
including **incluso**
incorrect **incorrecto**
indeed **verdaderamente**
inexpensive **barato**
inform, to **informar**
information **información**
inhabitant **habitante** (m.)
inquiry **averiguación** (f.)
inside **adentro, interior**
instead **en lugar de eso**
insurance **seguro**
interested **interesado**
interesting **interesante**
interpreter **intérprete**
interrupt, to **interrumpir**
introduce **presentar**
introduction **introducción** (f.)
invite, to **invitar**
invitation **invitación** (f.)
island **isla**
Italy **Italia**
itinerary **itinerario**

J

jacket **chaqueta**
jam **mermelada**
jealous **celoso**
Jewish, Jew **judío**
jewelry **joyas** (f. pl.)
job **empleo**
joke **chiste**
joke, to **bromear**
joy **alegría**
judge **juez** (m.)
jump, to **saltar**
just (only) **sólo**
just (exactly) **precisamente**
just (now) **ahora mismo**

K

keep, to **tener, quedarse**
key **llave** (f.)
kind (adj.) **amable**
kind (n.) **especie**
kindness **cariño**
king **rey** (m.)
kiss **beso**
kitchen **cocina**
knife **cuchillo**
knock, to **llamar a la puerta,
  tropezar**
know, to **saber**
know, to (be acquainted
  with) **conocer**
knowledge **conocimiento**

L

lady **señora**
lake **lago**
lamb **cordero**
lamp **lámpara**
land **tierra**
language **idioma**
large **grande**
last, to **durar**

last **último**
late **tarde**
laugh, to **reírse**
laundry **lavandería**
law **ley** (f.)
lawyer **abogado**
learn **aprender**
least **menor**
leather **cuero**
leave, to **salir**
left **izquierda**
leg **pierna**
legal **legal**
lend, to **prestar**
less **menos**
lesson **lección**
let, to **permitir**
letter **carta**
lettuce **lechuga**
liberty **libertad**
library **biblioteca**
license plate **chapa de matrícula**
lie, to **mentir**
lie **mentira**
life **vida**
life boat **bote salvavidas**
life guard **salvavidas**
lift, to **levantar**
light, to **encender**
light (weight) **ligero**
light (illumination) **luz** (f.)
light (color) **claro**
light bulb **bombilla**
lightning **relámpago**
like, to **querer, gustar**
line **línea**
linen **ropa blanca**
lion **león**
lip **labio**
list **lista**
listen, to **escuchar**
literature **literatura**
little **pequeño**
live, to **vivir**
living room **sala**
load **carga**
locate, to **situar**
lodging **alojamiento**
logical **lógico**
long **largo**
look, to **mirar**

lose, to **perder**
lost **perdido**
loud **fuerte**
love, to **querer, amar**
lover **amante**
low **bajo**
luck **suerte**
luggage **equipaje**
lunch **almuerzo**
luxury **lujo**

M

machine **máquina**
magazine **revista**
magnificent **magnífico**
maid **criada**
mail **correo**
mail-box **buzón** (m.)
make, to **hacer**
man **hombre**
manager **gerente**
management **gerencia**
manner **manera**
map **mapa** (m.), **plano** (m.)
marble **mármol** (m.)
market **mercado**
married **casado**
marry, to **casarse**
marvel **maravilla**
marvelous **maravilloso**
Mass **misa**
material **tela, material**
mattress **colchón** (m.)
maybe **tal vez**
mayor **alcalde**
me **me**
meal **comida**
mean, to **querer decir, significar**
meaning **significado**
means **medios, dinero**
meat **carne** (f.)
medicine **medicina**
Mediterranean **mediterráneo**
medieval **medieval**
meet, to **encontrar, conocer**
meeting **reunión** (f.)
member **socio**
menu **menú** (m.)
merchandise **mercancía**

message **recado**
middle **centro, medio**
Middle Ages **edad media**
midnight **media noche**
mild **suave**
mile **milla**
milk **leche** (f.)
million **millón**
mine **mío**
minister **ministro**
minute **minuto**
mirror **espejo**
miss, to **perder, echar de menos**
Miss **señorita**
mistake **error**
misunderstanding **equivocación** (f.)
mix, to **mezclar**
model **modelo**
modern **moderno**
modest **modesto**
moment **momento**
monastery **monasterio**
money **dinero**
monkey **mono**
month **mes** (m.)
monthly **mensualmente**
monument **monumento**
moon **luna**
more **más**
morning **mañana**
most **lo máximo**
mostly **en su mayor parte**
mother **madre**
mother-in-law **suegra**
motor **motor** (m.)
motorcycle **motocicleta**
mountain **montaña**
mountain climbing **alpinismo**
mouse **ratón** (m.)
mouth **boca**
movement **movimiento**
much **mucho**
mud **fango**
murder **asesinato**
music **música**
musician **músico**
must **tener que**
mustache **bigote**
mustard **mostaza**
mutton **carnero**
my, myself **mí, mío, yo mismo**

N

name **nombre**
napkin **servilleta**
narrow **estrecho**
nature **naturaleza**
navy **marina**
near **cercano**
necessary **necesario**
neck **cuello**
necktie **corbata**
need, to **necesitar**
needle **aguja**
neighbor **vecino**
neighborhood **vecindad** (f.), **barrio**
nephew **sobrino**
nervous **nervioso**
never **nunca**
new **nuevo**
New Year's Eve **Nochevieja**
news **noticias**
newspaper **periódico**
next **próximo**
nice **simpático, agradable**
niece **sobrina**
night **noche** (f.)
nightclub **cabaret** (m.)
nightgown **camisón** (m.)
no **no**
nobody **nadie**
noise **ruido**
noon **mediodía**
north **norte**
nose **nariz** (f.)
not **no**
notebook **cuaderno**
nothing **nada**
notice, to **darse cuenta de**
nowhere **en ninguna parte**
number **número**
nurse **enfermera**
nut **nuez** (f.)

O

oar **nemo**
object **objeto**
occasion **ocasión**

occasionally **a veces**
occupied **ocupado**
occur, to **suceder**
ocean **océano**
of **de**
offer **oferta**
office **oficina**
often **a menudo**
oil **aceite**
old **viejo**
on **sobre**
once **una vez**
one **uno, una, un**
one way **de una sola dirección**
only **único, solamente**
open **abierto**
open, to **abrir**
opera **ópera**
opinion **opinión** (f.)
opportunity **oportunidad** (f.)
opposite **opuesto**
or **o**
orange **naranja**
order, to **ordenar**
in order to **para**
original **original**
other **otro**
otherwise **de otro modo**
our **nuestro**
ourselves **nosotros mismos**
out of order **fuera de servicio**
outside **fuera**
over **sobre**
owe, to **deber**
own **propio**
owner **propietario**

P

package **paquete** (m.)
paid **pagado**
pain **dolor** (m.)
painter **pintor**
painting **cuadro, pintura**
pair **par** (m.)
palace **palacio**
pants **pantalones**
paper **papel**
parent **padre**
park **parque**

park, to **aparcar**
parking lot **parque (para estacionar automóviles)**
part **parte** (f.)
party **fiesta**
passenger **pasajero**
passport **pasaporte**
past **pasado**
path **sendero**
pay, to **pagar**
payment **pago**
peace **paz** (f.)
pen **bolígrafo, pluma**
pencil **lápiz** (m.)
people **gente**
perfect **perfecto**
perfume **perfume** (m.)
perhaps **quizás**
period **período**
permit, to **permitir**
person **persona**
photograph **fotografía**
photograph, to **sorcar fotos**
piano **piano**
pickpocket **carterista**
picture **cuadro, retrato**
piece **pieza, trozo**
pig **cerdo, puerco**
pigeon **paloma**
pill **píldora**
pillow **almohada**
pin **prendedor**
pink **rosa**
pitcher **jarro**
place **lugar** (m.)
plan **plano, plan**
plant **planta**
plate **plato**
platform **plataforma, andén** (m.)
play, to **jugar**
play, to (music) **tocar**
play **representación** (f.)
pleasant **agradable**
please **agradar**
pleasure **placer**
pocket **bolsillo**
poem **poema**
point **punta**
point, to **señalar**
police **policía**
policeman **agente de policía**

police station **estación de policía, comisaría**
polite **cortés**
pond **charca, estanque** (m.)
poor **pobre**
pope **papa** (m.)
popular **popular**
pork **puerco**
port **puerto**
possible **posible**
postcard **tarjeta postal**
post office **correos**
pot (cooking) **olla**
potato **patata**
pound **libra**
powerful **poderoso**
practice, to **practicar**
pray, to **rezar**
precise **preciso**
pregnant **embarazada**
prepare, to **preparar**
prescription **receta**
present **regalo**
press, to **planchar, apretar**
pretty **bonito**
price **precio**
priest **sacerdote**
prison **prisón** (f.), **cárcel** (f.)
probable **probable**
problem **problema** (m.)
profit **beneficio**
profession **profesión**
program **programa** (m.)
promise, to **prometer**
pronounce, to **pronunciar**
property **propiedad** (f.)
Protestant **protestante**
public **público**
publisher **editor**
pull, to **tirar (de)**
purchase, to **comprar**
push, to **empujar**
put, to **poner**
put on, to **ponerse**

Q

quality **calidad** (f.)
quarter **cuarta parte**
queen **reina**
question **pregunta**

quickly **rápidamente**
quiet **tranquilo**
quite **completamente**

R

rabbi **rabino**
rabbit **conejo**
race (contest) **carrera**
radiator (room or car) **radiador**
radio **la radio**
railroad **ferrocarril** (m.)
railway station **estación de ferrocarriles**
rain **lluvia**
raincoat **impermeable** (m.)
raise, to **levantar**
rape **violación**
rapid **rápido**
rare (meat) **medio cruda**
rare (unusual) **raro**
rarely **raramente**
rather **un poco, más bien**
raw **crudo**
razor **navaja de afeitar**
razor blade **hoja de afeitar**
reach, to **alcanzar**
read, to **leer**
ready **listo**
real **verdadero**
really **verdaderamente**
reason **razón** (f.)
reasonable **razonable**
receipt **recibo**
receive, to **recibir**
recently **recientemente**
recognize, to **reconocer**
recommend, to **recomendar**
record (phonograph) **grabar**
red **rojo**
refrigerator **refrigerador**
refuse, to **rechazar**
regards **recuerdos**
region **región** (f.)
regret, to **sentir**
regular **regular**
religion **religión**
religious **religioso**
remain, to **quedar**
remainder **resto**

remember, to **acordarse**
remind, to **recordar**
rent, to **alquilar**
repair, to **reparar**
repeat, to **repetir**
replace, to **reemplazar**
report **informe** (m.)
represent, to **representar**
republic **república**
reserve, to **reservar**
reservation **reservación**
responsible **responsable**
rest, to **descansar**
restaurant **restaurante** (m.)
retail **al por menor**
return, to **devolver**
return trip **vuelta**
ribbon **cinta**
rice **arroz** (m.)
rich **rico**
ride, to (horse) **montar**
ride, to (travel) **viajar**
right (direction) **derecha**
right (correct) **correcto**
right (noun) **derecho**
rise, to **crecer, levantarse**
river **río**
road **carretera**
roast **asado**
rob **robar**
robbery **robo**
rock **roca**
roll **rollo**
roof **tejado**
room **habitación** (f.)
round **redondo**
round trip **ida y vuelta**
route **ruta**
row **fila**
row, to **navegar a remo, remar**
rowboat **bote de remos**
rug **alfombra**
ruins **ruinas**
run, to **correr**

S

sacrifice **sacrificio**
sad **triste**
safe **seguro**

safe (strongbox) **caja fuerte**
sail **embarcarse**
sailboat **velero, buque de vela**
sailor **marinero**
saint **santo**
salad **ensalada**
salary **salario**
sale **venta**
salesman **vendedor**
salt **sal**
salty **salado**
same **igual, mismo**
satisfy **satisfacer**
satisfied **satisfecho**
sauce **salsa**
saucer **platillo**
save, to **salvar, guardar**
savings bank **banco o caja de ahorros**
say, to **decir**
science **ciencia**
school **escuela**
scissors **tijera** (f.)
scream **grito**
sculptor **escultor**
sea **mar**
seashore **costa**
seasick **mareado**
season **estación** (f.)
seasoning **condimento**
seat **asiento**
second **segundo**
secretary **secretaria**
see, to **ver**
seek, to **buscar**
seldom **raramente**
sell, to **vender**
send, to **mandar**
separate **separado**
serious **grave**
serve **servir**
service **servicio**
set, to **poner, colocar**
several **varios**
shade **sombra**
shadow **sombra**
share, to **compartir**
sharp **afilado, agudo**
shave **afeitar**
she **ella**
sheet (bed) **sábana**

ship **barco**
shirt **camisa**
shoe **zapato**
shoelace **cordón de zapato**
shop **tienda**
short **corto**
shorts **calzocillos**
shoulder **hombro**
show, to **enseñar, mostrar**
shower **ducha**
shut, to **cerrar**
sick **enfermo**
side **lado**
sidewalk **acera**
sight **vista, perspectiva**
sign **cartel** (m.)
silence **silencio**
silk **seda**
silver **plata**
similar **similar**
simple **simple**
since **desde**
sing, to **cantar**
singer **cantante**
single **soltero, solo**
sir **señor**
sister **hermana**
sister-in-law **cuñada**
sit, to **sentarse**
size **tamaño**
ski **esquí** (m.)
skiing **el esquí, deporte de esquiar**
skin **piel** (f.)
skirt **falda**
sky **cielo**
skyscraper **rascacielos** (m.)
sleep, to **dormir**
sleep, to go to **adormecer (se)**
sleeping bag **saco o talego para dormir**
sleeve **manga**
slip, to **deslizar**
slow **lento**
small **pequeño**
smell, to **oler**
smile, to **sonreír**
smoke, to **fumar**
smooth **llano, lisonjero**
snake **serpiente** (f.)
sneeze, to **estornudar**
snow **nieve**

so **así**
soap **jabón**
sock **calcetín** (m.)
sofa **sofá**
soft **suave**
soldier **soldado**
some **algo, algunos**
somebody **alguien**
something **algo**
sometimes **a veces**
somewhat **algo**
somewhere **alguna parte**
son **hijo**
song **canción** (f.)
soon **pronto**
soup **sopa**
sour **agrio, ácido**
south **sur**
souvenir **recuerdo**
Spain **España**
speak, to **hablar**
special **especial**
spend **gastar**
speed limit **límite de velocidad**
sponge **esponja**
spoon **cuchara**
sport **deporte** (m.)
sporting goods **artículos deportivos**
spring **primavera**
stairs **escalera**
stamp **sello**
stand up **ponerse en pie**
star **estrella**
start, to **comenzar**
station **estación** (f.)
statue **estatua**
stay, to **permanecer**
stay **temporada, estancia**
steak **bistec** (m.)
steal, to **robar**
steamer (boat) **vapor, buque de vapor**
stick **palo, vara**
still (yet) **todavía, aún, no obstante**
still (quiet) **quieto**
stocking **media**
stomach **estómago**
stone **piedra**
stop, to **parar**
stop (bus, etc) **parada**
storm **tormenta**

story **relato, cuento**
stove **estufa**
straight **recto, derecho**
strange **estraño**
street **calle**
streetcar **tranvía** (m.)
strike, to **pegar**
string **cuerda**
strong **fuerte**
student **estudiante**
study, to **estudiar**
stupid **estúpido, tonto**
style **estilo**
subway **metro, subterráneo**
sudden **repentino**
sugar **azúcar**
suit **traje** (m.)
suitcase **maleta**
summer **verano**
summit **ápice, cumbre, cima**
sun **sol** (m.)
sunburn **quemadura de sol**
sunset **puesta de sol**
sure **seguro**
surf **oleaje, resaca**
surprise **sorpresa**
supper **cena**
supplement **suplemento**
suppose, to **suponer**
sweat **sudor** (m.)
sweater **jersey** (m.)
sweet **dulce**
swim, to **nadar**
swimming pool **piscina**
Switzerland **Suiza**
synagogue **sinagoga**

T

table **mesa**
tablecloth **mantel** (m.)
tailor **sastre**
take, to **coger**
take off, to **quitarse**
take off, to **despegar**
talk, to **hablar**
tall **alto**
tape **cinta**
tape recorder **magnetófono**
taste **gusto**

SPANISH

taste, to **probar**
tax **impuesto**
taxi **taxi** (m.)
tea **té** (m.)
teach, to **enseñar**
teacher **maestro**
team **equipo**
tear **lágrima**
tear, to **desgarrsar, romper**
telegram **telegrama** (m.)
telephone **teléfono**
television **televisión** (f.)
tell, to **decir**
temperature **temperatura**
temporarily **temporalmente**
tent **tienda, tienda le campaña**
terrible **terrible**
than **que**
thank, to **dar las gracias**
thanks **gracias**
the **el, la**
theatre **teatro**
then **entonces**
there **allí, ahí, allá**
there is/are **hay**
thermometer **termómetro**
they **ellos** (m.), **ellas** (f.)
thief **ladrón**
thin **delgado, flaco**
thing **cosa**
think, to **pensar**
third **tercero**
thirst **sed** (f.)
thirsty, to be **tener sed**
this **esto**
those **ésos**
thousand **mil**
thread **hilo**
throat **garganta**
through **por**
throw, **tirada, tirar**
thunder **trueno**
thus **así**
ticket (for speeding) **multa**
ticket (theatre) **boleto**
tide **marea**
tie **corbata**
tight **apretado**
time **hora, tiempo**
timetable **horario**
tip **propina, punta**

tire **neumático**
tired **cansado**
to **a**
tobacco **tabaco**
today **hoy**
together **juntos**
toilet **retrete, servicio**
tomato **tomate**
tomorrow **mañana**
tongue **lengua**
tonight **esta noche**
too **también, demasiado**
tooth **diente** (m.), **muela**
toothbrush **cepillo de dientes**
toothpaste **pasta para los dientes**
top **cima**
topless **sin parte superior**
touch, to **tocar**
tough **duro**
tour **excursión**
towel **toalla**
tower **torre** (f.)
town **pueblo**
tow car **camión remolcador**
toy **juguete** (m.)
trade **comercio**
trade fair **feria**
traffic **tráfico**
traffic jam **atascamiento o embotellamiento de tráfico**
traffic light **semáforo**
train **tren** (m.)
translate **traducir**
translation **traducción** (f.)
travel **viajar**
travel agency **agencia de viajes**
traveler **viajero**
tree **árbol**
trip **viaje** (m.)
trouble **apuro, dificultad**
truck **camión** (m.)
true **verdadero**
trunk **baúl** (m.)
truth **verdad** (f.)
try, to **probar**
try on, to **probarse**
turkey **pavo**
turn, to **dar vuelta a**
turn off, to **apagar**
turn on, to **encender**
typewriter **máquina de escribir**

U

ugly **feo**
umbrella **paraguas** (m.)
uncle **tío**
unconscious **inconciente**
under **debajo de**
understand **comprender, entender**
underwear **ropa interior**
undress, to **desnudarse**
unfortunately **desafortunadamente**
United States **Estados Unidos**
university **universidad** (f.)
unless **a menos que**
until **hasta**
up **arriba**
upstairs **arriba**
urgent **urgente**
us **nos, nosotros**
use **uso**
use, to **usar**
useful **útil**
usual **usual**

V

vacant **vacante**
vacation **vacaciónes** (f.)
valid **válido**
valuables **objetos de valor**
value **valor** (m.)
various **varios**
vegetables **legumbres, verdura**
vehicle **vehículo**
very **muy**
victory **victoria**
Vienna **Viena**
view **vista**
village **pueblo**
vineyard **viña, viñedo**
visit, to **visitar**
violin **violín** (m.)
voice **voz** (f.)
voltage **voltaje** (m.)
voyage **viaje** (m.)

W

waist **cintura**
wait, to **esperar**
waiter **camarero**
waitress **camarera**
waiting room **sala de espera**
wake up, to **abrir los ojos**
walk, to **caminar**
walk **paseo**
wall **pared, tapia**
wallet **cartera**
want, to **querer**
war **guerra**
warm **cálido**
warn, to **advertir**
wash, to **lavar**
wash basin **lavabo**
wash oneself, to **lavarse**
waste, to **desperdiciar**
watch, to **observar**
watch **reloj** (m.)
water **agua**
waterfront **terreno ribereño o costero**
water sports **deportes acuáticos**
wave **ola**
way **camino, modo**
we **nosotros**
weak **débil**
wealth **riqueza**
wear, to **llevar**
weather **tiempo**
wedding **matrimonio, boda**
week **semana**
weekend **fin de semana** (m.)
weigh, to **pesar**
weight **peso**
welcome **bienvenida**
well **bien**
west **oeste**
West Germany **Alemania Occidental**
what **que, lo que**
whatever **lo que, cuanto**
wheat **trigo**
wheel **rueda**
when **cuando**
where **donde**

SPANISH

whether **si**
which **cuál**
while **mientras**
white **blanco**
who **quién**
whole **todo, entero**
whose **de quién**
why **por qué**
wide **ancho**
widow **viuda**
widower **viudo**
wife **esposa**
wilderness **desierto, selva**
win, to **ganar**
wind **viento**
window **ventana**
windy **ventoso**
wine **vino**
wine list **lista de vinos**
wing **ala**
winter **invierno**
wish **deseo**
wish, to **desear, gustar**
with **con**
without **sin**
woman **mujer**
wonder **maravilla**
wonderful **maravilloso**
wood **madera**
wool **lana**
word **palabra**
work **trabajo**

world **mundo**
worse **peor**
wrap, to **envolver**
wrist **muñeca**
write, to **escribir**
writer **escritor**
wrong **equivocado**

Y

yacht **yate**
year **año**
yellow **amarillo**
yes **sí**
yesterday **ayer**
yet **todavía no**
you **usted, tú**
you're welcome **de nada**
young **joven**
your **su, tu, vuestro**

Z

zero **cero**
zipper **cremallera**
zone **zona**
zoo **zoológico**

Reference

CLOTHING SIZES

For the most part, the countries of Europe all use the same clothing sizes. The sizes of women's stockings and men's socks are international.

For Women

Junior Miss		Regular Dresses		Shoes	
U.S.	Europe	U.S.	Europe	U.S.	Europe
5	34	10	40	5	36
7	36	12	42	5½	36½
9	38	14	44	6½	37½
11	40	16	46	7½	38½
		18	48	8	39
		20	50	8½	39½
				9	40

For Men

Shirts		Slacks		Shoes	
U.S.	Europe	U.S.	Europe	U.S.	Europe
14	36	32	42	5	36
14½	37	34	44	6	37
15	38	36	46	7	38
15½	39	38	48	7½	39
15¾	40	40	50	8	40
16	41			9	41
16½	42			10	42
17	43			10½	43
				11	44
				12	45

This chart should be followed only as a very general outline, as in the same country there are big differences in sizes. If possible, try on all clothing or shoes before making a purchase. You'll be glad you did.

DRY WEIGHTS

1 ounce = 28.3 grams
1 pound = 454 grams
2.2 pounds = 1 kilogram (1000 grams)

100 grams = 3.33 ounces
500 grams = 16.07 ounces
1 kilogram = 2.20 pounds

Metric Conversion

Pounds to Kilograms		Kilograms to Pounds	
1 lb =	0.45 kg	1 kg =	2.20 lb
2 lb =	0.91 kg	2 kg =	4.41 lb
3 lb =	1.36 kg	3 kg =	6.61 lb
4 lb =	1.81 kg	4 kg =	8.82 lb
5 lb =	2.27 kg	5 kg =	11.02 lb
6 lb =	2.72 kg	6 kg =	13.23 lb
7 lb =	3.18 kg	7 kg =	15.43 lb
8 lb =	3.63 kg	8 kg =	17.64 lb
9 lb =	4.08 kg	9 kg =	19.84 lb
10 lb =	4.54 kg	10 kg =	22.05 lb
20 lb =	9.07 kg	20 kg =	44.09 lb
30 lb =	13.61 kg	30 kg =	66.14 lb
40 lb =	18.14 kg	40 kg =	88.18 lb
50 lb =	22.68 kg	50 kg =	110.23 lb
60 lb =	27.22 kg	60 kg =	132.28 lb
70 lb =	31.75 kg	70 kg =	154.32 lb
80 lb =	36.29 kg	80 kg =	176.37 lb
90 lb =	40.82 kg	90 kg =	198.41 lb
100 lb =	45.36 kg	100 kg =	220.46 lb

To convert grams to ounces, multiply by .035.
To convert kilograms to pounds, multiply by 2.2.

LIQUID MEASURES

1 pint = 0.47 liters
1 quart = 0.95 liters
1 gallon (U.S.) = 3.79 liters

1 Imperial gallon (British) =
4.54 liters

Metric Conversion

Quarts to Liters		Liters to Quarts	
1 qt =	0.95 l	1 l =	1.06 qt
2 qt =	1.89 l	2 l =	2.11 qt
3 qt =	2.84 l	3 l =	3.17 qt
4 qt =	3.79 l	4 l =	4.23 qt
5 qt =	4.75 l	5 l =	5.28 qt
10 qt =	9.46 l	10 l =	10.57 qt
20 qt =	18.93 l	20 l =	21.13 qt
50 qt =	47.32 l	50 l =	52.84 qt

To convert liters to quarts, multiply by 1.06; to convert liters to gallons (U.S.), multiply by .26.

LENGTHS

1 inch = 2.54 centimeters
1 foot = 0.3 meters
1 yard = 0.91 meters
1.09 yards = 1 meter

1 mile = 1.61 kilometer
0.62 mile = 1 kilometer

Metric Conversion

Miles to Kilometers		Kilometers to Miles	
1 mi =	1.61 km	1 km =	.62 mi
10 mi =	16.09 km	10 km =	6.21 mi
20 mi =	32.19 km	20 km =	12.43 mi
30 mi =	48.28 km	30 km =	18.64 mi
40 mi =	64.37 km	40 km =	24.86 mi
50 mi =	80.46 km	50 km =	31.07 mi
60 mi =	96.56 km	60 km =	37.28 mi
70 mi =	112.65 km	70 km =	43.50 mi
80 mi =	128.74 km	80 km =	49.71 mi
90 mi =	144.83 km	90 km =	55.93 mi
100 mi =	160.93 km	100 km =	62.14 mi

To convert kilometers to miles, multiply by .6. To convert meters to yards, multiply by 1.1.

TIRE PRESSURE

Pounds per Square Inch	Kilograms per Square Centimeter
10	0.7
15	1.1
20	1.4
22	1.5
24	1.7
26	1.8
28	2.0
30	2.1
40	2.8

TEMPERATURE

To convert Celsius temperature (°C) to Fahrenheit temperature (°F), multiply 9/5 (°C) + 32.

NOTES

NOTES

NOTES

Now, Save Money on All Your Travels!

Join Arthur Frommer's

$25-A-Day Travel Club

Saving money while traveling is never a simple matter, which is why, over 21 years ago, the **$25-A-Day Travel Club** was formed. Actually, the idea came from readers of the Arthur Frommer Publications who felt that such an organization could bring financial benefits, continuing travel information, and a sense of community to economy-minded travelers all over the world.

In keeping with the money-saving concept, the membership fee is low—$14 (U.S. residents) or $16 U.S. (Canadian, Mexican, and foreign residents)—and is immediately exceeded by the value of your benefits which include:

(1) An annual subscription to an 8-page tabloid newspaper *The Wonderful World of Budget Travel* which keeps you up-to-date on fastbreaking developments in low-cost travel in all parts of the world—bringing you the kind of information you'd have to pay over $25 a year to obtain elsewhere. This consumer-conscious publication also provides special services to readers:

Travelers' Directory—a list of members all over the world who are willing to provide hospitality to other members as they pass through their home cities.

Please turn page for additional listings and order form.

Share-a-Trip—requests from members for travel companions who can share costs and help avoid the burdensome single supplement.

Readers Ask ... Readers Reply—travel questions from members to which other members reply with authentic firsthand information.

(2) The latest edition of any TWO of the books listed on the following pages.

(3) A copy of *Arthur Frommer's Guide to New York.*

(4) Your personal membership card which entitles you to purchase through the Club all Arthur Frommer Publications for a third to a half off their regular retail prices during the term of your membership.

So why not join this hardy band of international budgeteers NOW and participate in its exchange of information and hospitality? Simply send $14 (U.S. residents) or $16 U.S. (Canadian, Mexican, and other foreign residents) along with your name and address to: $25-A-Day Travel Club, Inc., 1230 Avenue of the Americas, New York, NY 10020. Remember to specify which *two* of the books in section (2) above you wish to receive in your initial package of members' benefits. Or tear out the order form on the following pages, check off any two books you wish to receive, and send the form to us with your membership fee.

FROMMER/PASMANTIER PUBLISHERS

Date _____

**1230 AVE. OF THE AMERICAS
NEW YORK, NY 10020**

Friends, please send me the books checked below:

$-A-DAY GUIDES (In-depth guides to low-cost tourist accommodations and facilities.)

☐ Europe on $25 a Day	$10.95
☐ Australia on $25 a Day	$9.95
☐ England and Scotland on $25 a Day	$9.95
☐ Greece on $25 a Day	$9.95
☐ Hawaii on $35 a Day	$9.95
☐ Ireland on $25 a Day	$7.95
☐ Israel on $30 & $35 a Day	$9.95
☐ Mexico on $20 a Day	$8.95
☐ New Zealand on $20 & $25 a Day	$9.95
☐ New York on $35 a Day	$8.95
☐ Scandinavia on $25 a Day	$7.95
☐ South America on $25 a Day	$8.95
☐ Spain and Morocco (plus the Canary Is.) on $25 a Day	$8.95
☐ Washington, D.C. on $35 a Day	$8.95

DOLLARWISE GUIDES (Guides to tourist accommodations and facilities from budget to deluxe, with emphasis on the medium-priced.)

☐ Egypt	$9.95	☐ Canada	$10.95
☐ England & Scotland	$7.95	☐ Caribbean (incl. Bermuda & the Bahamas)	$10.95
☐ France	$8.95		
☐ Germany	$9.95	☐ California & Las Vegas	$7.95
☐ Italy	$7.95	☐ Florida	$9.95
☐ Portugal (incl. Madeira & the Azores)	$9.95	☐ New England	$9.95
		☐ Southeast & New Orleans	
☐ Switzerland	$9.95		$9.95

Please turn page for additional listings and order form.